THE POLITICS OF MEMORY LAWS

This open access book explores the political utility and consequences of memory laws with a focus on how militant memory laws frame, underpin and generate international conflicts.

Proceeding from Russia's ongoing aggression against Ukraine, this examination plots how memory laws have preceded, partially led to, and encouraged the outbreak of the war itself via Russian propaganda. It also offers a broader perspective looking at developments in the Baltic States, Belarus, Finland, Germany, Hungary, and Poland, as well as in European (Council of Europe and European Union) law. Bringing together specialists with diverse perspectives, this book provides both analysis and conceptual reflection for scholars assessing the politics of memory laws.

The Politics of Memory Laws

Russia, Ukraine and Beyond

Edited by
Uladzislau Belavusau
Aleksandra Gliszczyńska-Grabias
Maria Mälksoo
and
Angelika Nußberger

•HART•
OXFORD • LONDON • NEW YORK • NEW DELHI • SYDNEY

HART PUBLISHING

Bloomsbury Publishing Plc

Kemp House, Chawley Park, Cumnor Hill, Oxford, OX2 9PH, UK

1385 Broadway, New York, NY 10018, USA

Bloomsbury Publishing Ireland Limited, 29 Earlsfort Terrace, Dublin 2, D02 AY28, Ireland

HART PUBLISHING, the Hart/Stag logo, BLOOMSBURY and the Diana logo are trademarks of Bloomsbury Publishing Plc

First published in Great Britain 2025

A catalogue record for this book is available from the British Library.

A catalogue record for this book is available from the Library of Congress.

ISBN: HB: 978-1-50997-530-3
ePDF: 978-1-50997-532-7
ePub: 978-1-50997-531-0

Typeset by Compuscript Ltd, Shannon

For product safety related questions contact productsafety@bloomsbury.com

To find out more about our authors and books visit www.hartpublishing.co.uk. Here you will find extracts, author information, details of forthcoming events and the option to sign up for our newsletters.

Acknowledgements

IN 2021, a year before Russia's full-scale invasion of Ukraine, the four co-editors of this volume cooperated on an academic article addressing memory laws and policies in Central and Eastern Europe. By that time, it was becoming increasingly evident that Russia was intensifying its use of historical propaganda, reinforced by memory laws, to incite conflict. This shift compelled neighbouring countries to respond with their own legislative measures concerning historical memory. In essence, historical memory – regulated through criminal, administrative, and even constitutional law – was weaponised, particularly following Russia's annexation of Crimea and the occupation of Ukraine's Donbas region in 2014. In response, Ukraine introduced the so-called 'decommunisation laws' in 2015, which at the time were heavily criticised by nearly all leading Western scholars. However, with the benefit of hindsight, these Ukrainian memory laws were, at least in part, far more justified than many of their counterparts in neighbouring countries, given the ontological security they provided to Ukraine in the face of dehumanising Russian propaganda during the military conflict ongoing since 2014.

Yet, it is evident that, even when well-intended – as in the current Ukrainian case – memory laws are rarely a comfortable topic due to their inherent tensions with human rights, particularly freedom of expression and rule-of-law principles. That is why we explored this topic in our foundational (for this study area in comparative constitutional law) volume, *Law and Memory: Towards Legal Governance of History* (edited by Belavusau and Gliszczyńska-Grabias, Cambridge University Press, 2017). In 2021, we broadened our approach and launched the MEMOCRACY project (*memocracy.eu*) – an international research consortium involving four European academic institutions (the Academy for European Human Rights Protection – Cologne University, the Asser Institute – University of Amsterdam, the University of Copenhagen, and the Polish Academy of Sciences) – to examine memory laws in Germany (as Europe's and even the world's paradigmatic study with its Holocaust denial laws), alongside seven Central and Eastern European countries (Estonia, Hungary, Latvia, Lithuania, Poland, Russia, and Ukraine). The term 'memocracy', coined for the purposes of this study, was derived from *memorare* (Latin for 'to remember') and *κράτος* (Ancient Greek for 'rule'), meaning 'rule based on memory'. Whilst neutral in its original conception, the term, when instrumentalised for particular purposes, can signal a shift from democracy towards autocracy.

Our worst concerns regarding this 'rule based on memory' materialised shortly after the start of our project when in February 2022, Russia advanced its full-scale military invasion of Ukraine. Putin's primary justifications for this 'special military operation' were based on vague assertions about NATO expansion and a denial of Ukraine's historical agency, combined with the alleged need to eradicate 'Nazis' from Ukraine's leadership – a patently absurd narrative propagated by Russian state media, blending both imperial and Soviet historical myths about Ukraine. Memory laws played a central role in fostering this rhetoric, as reflected in interviews with Putin and statements from Russian officials.

By now, memory laws have become a pervasive issue and even gained global relevance, from Mexico to China, though with Europe remaining a central hub for their proliferation and often serving as a model for other regions. In this present volume, eight years after our first exploration of the topic, we return to the subject of memory laws, though now in the context of memory wars (specifically the Russo-Ukrainian war) and their impact on not only those two countries, but also the entire East-Central European neighbourhood, Europe more broadly, and the world.

We are deeply grateful to the Volkswagen Foundation for supporting the MEMOCRACY project (2021–24), which enabled the formation of our international research consortium and the employment of several postdoctoral researchers. A selection of these researchers, including Dr Paula Rhein-Fischer, Dr Dovilė Sagatienė, Dr Anna Wójcik, and Dr Andrii Nekoliak, have contributed chapters to this volume. Others, including Prof Grażyna Baranowska, Dr Mirosław Sadowski, Dr Patryk Labuda, and PhD candidates Anastasiia Vorobiova and Simon Mensing, have provided valuable input through study reports and their academic publications. We are also thankful to our home institutions in Copenhagen, Cologne, The Hague, and Warsaw for their administrative support.

Additionally, we would like to express our gratitude to the European University Institute, particularly to Prof Monika Báar, for hosting our workshop in Florence on memory laws in Russia and Ukraine in May 2024, and to Ludwig Maximilian University, particularly to Prof Martin Schulze Wessel, and the Internationales Begegnungszentrum der Wissenschaft for hosting our final MEMOCRACY conference in Munich in September 2024. Special thanks are also due to Siân Lord and Charles Bennett for their excellent assistance during their internships, with a particular note of appreciation to Siân for her language editing and help in the final stages of this book submission.

Finally, we extend our sincerest thanks to Hart-Bloomsbury, our publisher, for their unwavering support throughout this project, and to all our contributing authors. This book, written not only amidst literal 'memory wars' but also during an actual war raging in Ukraine, bears witness to narratives that we believe will one day shape future memory laws and historical policies.

Uladzislau Belavusau
Aleksandra Gliszczyńska-Grabias
Maria Mälksoo
Angelika Nußberger
October 2024

Contents

PART III
NEIGHBOURS ACTIVELY INVOLVED IN THE REGIONAL MEMORY WARS

PART IV
SHAPING EUROPEAN LAW AND POLITICS IN THE CONTEXT OF MEMORY WARS

List of Contributors

Editors

Uladzislau Belavusau is a Senior Researcher in European law at the TMC Asser Institute – University of Amsterdam (the Netherlands), where he led the Dutch teams of the MEMOCRACY (2021–24) and MELA (2016–19) international research consortiums for the study of memory laws. Previously he was Assistant Professor of EU Law and Human Rights at the Vrije Universiteit Amsterdam (2011–15). He is the author of a monograph *Freedom of Speech: Importing European US Constitutional Models in Transitional Democracies* (Routledge, 2013), and co-editor of three books: *Constitutionalism Under Stress: Essays in Honour of Wojciech Sadurski* (Oxford University Press, 2020), *EU Anti-Discrimination Law beyond Gender* (Hart-Bloomsbury, 2018) and *Law and Memory: Towards Legal Governance of History* (Cambridge University Press, 2017).

Aleksandra Gliszczyńska-Grabias is Professor of International Human Rights Law at the Institute of Law Studies of the Polish Academy of Sciences. She is the co-editor of *Law and Memory: Towards Legal Governance of History* (Cambridge University Press, 2017) and *Constitutionalism Under Stress* (Oxford University Press, 2020). She led the Polish team of the international research consortium 'The Challenge of Populist Memory Politics for Europe: Towards Effective Responses to Militant Legislation on the Past' (2021–24) and is currently leading the project 'Rethinking Militant Democracy Doctrine', funded by the Polish National Science Centre (2024–27). Recipient of numerous fellowships, including at the University of Cambridge, Yale University and the European University Institute.

Maria Mälksoo is Professor of International Relations at the Department of Political Science, University of Copenhagen where she led the Baltic chapter of the MEMOCRACY project (2021–24). She holds the European Research Council Consolidator Grant RITUAL DETERRENCE (2022–27) and is an editor of the *Review of International Studies* (CUP). Professor Mälksoo is the author of *The Politics of Becoming European: A Study of Polish and Baltic Post-Cold War Security Imaginaries* (Routledge, 2010), a co-author of *Remembering Katyn* (Polity, 2012), an editor of the *Journal of International Relations and Development* Special Issue 'Uses of "the East" in International Studies: provincializing IR from Central and Eastern Europe' (2022) and the *Handbook on the Politics of Memory* (Edward Elgar Publishing, 2023).

Angelika Nußberger is Professor of Law at the University of Cologne, member of the Venice Commission and international judge at the Constitutional Court of Bosnia Herzegovina. Previously, she was a judge at the European Court of Human Rights (2011–19), the last three years serving as its vice-president. She is the author of *The European Court of Human Rights* (Oxford University Press, 2020) and *Die Menschenrechte: Geschichte, Philosophie, Konflikte* (CH Beck, 2021), a co-author of *Osteuropa zwischen Mauerfall und Ukrainekrieg* (Suhrkamp Verlag, 2022) and a co-editor of *Rechtsphilosophisches Denken im Osten Europas* (Mohr Siebeck, 2015).

Authors

Marina Bán is a Doctor of Law specialising in the intersection of history, law and democracy, formerly a PhD researcher at the Asser Institute for International and European Law in The Hague, and postdoctoral researcher the Centre of Excellence for International Courts (iCourts) at the University of Copenhagen.

Gleb Bogush is a Research Fellow at the Institute for International Peace and Security Law at the University of Cologne.

Dovilė Budrytė is Professor of Political Science and International Studies at Georgia Gwinnett College in the United States and Invited Senior Researcher at Vytautas Kavolis Transdisciplinary Research Institute, Vytautas Magnus University in Lithuania.

Alina Cherviatsova is Marie Skłodowska-Curie Research Fellow and coordinator of the Jean Monnet Module *Academy4UA* at the Faculty of Law and Criminology – Ghent University (Belgium).

Tuomas Forsberg is Professor of International Relations at Tampere University in Finland since 2008. He was Director of the Helsinki Collegium for Advanced Studies (2018–23).

David R Marples is a Distinguished Professor of Russian and East European History at the University of Alberta (Canada).

Andrii Nekoliak is a Postdoctoral Researcher at the TMC Asser Institute – University of Amsterdam (The Hague) within the MEMOCRACY research project.

Ilya Nuzov, JD, LLM, is the Head of the Eastern Europe and Central Asia Desk at the International Federation for Human Rights (FIDH) and a Lecturer on Human Rights and Transitional Justice at Sciences Po, Paris.

Paul Primbs is a PhD candidate in history at the LMU Munich in Germany supported by the Gerda Henkel Foundation.

Paula Rhein-Fischer is a Postdoctoral Researcher at the Academy of European Human Rights Protection of the University of Cologne.

Dovilė Sagatienė is a legal historian specialising in Soviet crimes in the Baltic states and the memory politics thereof, formerly a Postdoctoral Researcher at the University of Copenhagen team of the MEMOCRACY project.

Anna Wójcik is an Assistant Professor at Kozminski University, Warsaw. The chapter was written while she was a Postdoctoral Researcher in the MEMOCRACY research consortium, which was funded by the Volkswagen Stiftung.

Tatiana Zhurzhenko is a Research Affiliate at the Centre for East European and International Studies (ZOiS), Berlin, and a Research Associate within the SOCIOBORD project at the European University Institute (EUI), Florence.

Introduction

Shadows of History: Memory Laws in Europe in the Context of the Russo-Ukrainian War

ULADZISLAU BELAVUSAU, ALEKSANDRA GLISZCZYŃSKA-GRABIAS, MARIA MÄLKSOO, AND ANGELIKA NUẞBERGER

> 'The past is never dead. It's not even past. All of us labor in webs spun long before we were born, webs of heredity and environment, of desire and consequence, of history and eternity'.
>
> William Faulkner, *Requiem for a Nun*[1]

I. MEMORY GOVERNANCE AND WAR: AN ENDURING CHALLENGE FOR INTERNATIONAL POLITICS AND LAW

A. Russia's Agenda of Mnemopolitical Militancy

Russia's invasion of Ukraine in February 2022 opened a novel and devastating phase in the conflict that Russia has waged against Ukraine since 2014. Vladimir Putin's rationale for this full-scaled aggression against Ukraine drew on a rich brew of factually convoluted 'lessons of history', which denied Ukraine's longstanding tradition of statehood. Russia's military assault was preceded, and has subsequently been accompanied, by an intense 'memory war' that has refuted Ukraine's political subjectivity and sovereignty at key historical moments. Throughout the past decade, Russia has engaged in mnemopolitical militancy, having managed to codify its selective historical narratives into 'memory laws', in the form of diverse – including punitive – legal regulations of the historical past (having even anchored them in the Russian Constitution).[2] The Russian framing of the war and its wider repercussions

[1] W Faulkner, *Requiem for a Nun* (Knopf Doubleday Publishing Group, 2011 [1951]) Act 1, Scene 3.

[2] U Belavusau, 'Rule of Law and Constitutionalisation of Memory Politics in Hungary and Russia' in M Belov (ed), *Rule of Law in Flux* (Routledge, 2022) 87–107 (regarding embedding memory politics into the newest version of the Russian constitution more specifically, see 92–94).

across Europe have accentuated the enduring power of the past in contemporary international relations. Competing interpretations of history have not only motivated this war, but paved the way for its development, with contestations over distinct lessons of the twentieth century reflected in legal regulations which continue to inform and mobilise the politics of today.

B. The 'Ukrainian Girl' by Repin: Reassessing Historical Value Judgements

For the cover of this volume, we opted for the painting, Ukrainian Girl (1875) by Ukrainian-born painter Ilya Repin, or Illia Ripyn in Ukrainian transliteration (1844–1930). Recently, controversy was sparked when a Finnish museum reclassified this realist painter's nationality as Ukrainian rather than Russian in response to Russia's invasion of Ukraine in 2022 and protests from the Ukrainian diaspora.[3] Similarly, the New York Metropolitan Museum of Art reattributed the nationalities of Ilya Repin and romantic painter Ivan Aivazovsky (1817–1900, born into an Armenian family in Crimean Feodosia) to Ukrainian. Other institutions, such as the Stedelijk Museum in Amsterdam, which holds one of the world's largest collections of avant-garde artist Kazimir Malevich (1879–1935, who was born in Kyiv into a family with Polish roots), have likewise changed his nationality from Russian to Ukrainian.

The global reclassification of artists, musicians, writers, poets and scientists with Ukrainian roots reveals the extent to which they have become key figures in ongoing memory wars. This mnemonic contestation involves far more than just art or scientific attribution; it encompasses a myriad of symbolic acts, including historiographical debates, changes in geographical nomenclature, transliterations from Cyrillic script, the renaming of cities and streets, reattribution of monuments and songs, and even heated debates over elements of traditional cuisine in the region.[4] These efforts reflect an ongoing struggle over cultural identity and memory which has gained significant momentum since 2022. They underscore the far-reaching impacts of geopolitical conflict on the collective memory and heritage of Ukrainians, Russians and other ethnicities within these multi-national nations. Amongst the turbulent waters of the identity disputations over Repin, the attribution of *Borsch*, and Kyiv versus Kiev, memory laws play a crucial role in converting certain narratives – sometimes with their punitive force – into the powerful waves

[3] T Solomon, 'Finnish Museum Acknowledges Painter Ilya Repin, Long Classified Russian, as Ukrainian' (*ARTnews*, 1 February 2024): https://www.artnews.com/art-news/news/finnish-museum-acknowledges-painter-ilya-repin-long-classified-russian-as-ukrainian-1234694820/.

[4] A von Bremzen, 'How Ukraine's National Dish Became a Symbol of Putin's Invasion' *The Guardian* (*The Guardian*, 22 June 2023): https://www.theguardian.com/news/2023/jun/22/i-no-longer-know-how-to-think-about-borsch. For a theoretically compelling analysis of the wider phenomenon, see, E Gaufman, 'Eating Identity: Theorizing the Everyday Foreign Policy Assemblage' (2021) 1 *Global Studies Quarterly* 1.

of a mnemonic tsunami. These waves, emerging around the epicentre of the conflict between Ukraine and Russia, have naturally swept over neighbouring countries, with echoes of smaller cultural earthquakes reverberating surprisingly far beyond the region.

Amidst these mnemonic controversies, Putin's justification for the invasion of Ukraine is built on a curious mixture of twisted historical references, weaving together the self-assumed mission to 'denazify' another state whilst also engaging in efforts to take its 'decommunisation' to the logical conclusion.[5] Both tropes played on historically charged analogues, yet emptied them of their original meaning, with these seemingly incompatible signifiers used to deny the distinctiveness of Ukrainians and the legitimacy of Ukraine as a sovereign nation-state.[6] The convoluted 'denazification' and 'decommunisation' campaigns thus became a rallying cry for a war of destruction against a neighbouring nation and state.[7] Meanwhile, Putin's 'special military operation' against Ukraine had at least a decade-long prelude in memory politics, underpinned by a number of punitive memory laws and aggressive rhetoric that signalled political intent to prescribe and proscribe particular historical narratives in the former Soviet space, as well as the wider international plane.

C. The Influence of Memory Politics on the European Security Order

This book unfolds the story of memory laws and policies that resurged in the context of the Russo-Ukrainian war, with Russia's aggression marking a critical juncture for the European security order. The context of this war within memory and politics, accompanied by its broader political ramifications in Europe, will shape its distinct imprint on international politics, and influence how these events will be remembered in the future. In light of discussions regarding Ukraine's desired victory and the long-tiptoed-around theme of Russia's defeat becoming more widespread, granular and serious by the day, this volume delves into the mechanics of the conflict and provides insight into the politics and memory operating in the background. Should Ukraine face defeat, there are numerous

[5] As Putin maintained in his statement in the run-up to the invasion, Soviet Ukraine was the creation of the Bolsheviks, and thus, full decommunisation would translate into the eradication of the Ukrainian state: '… why stop halfway? We are ready to show what real decommunizations would mean for Ukraine', en.Kremlin.ru, 'Transcripts: Address by the President of the Russian Federation' (21 February 2022): http://www.en.kremlin.ru/events/president/transcripts/67828; en.Kremlin.ru, 'Events: Address by the President of the Russian Federation' (24 February 2022): http://en.kremlin.ru/events/president/news/67843.

[6] See V Putin, 'On the Historical Unity of Russians and Ukrainians' (12 July 2021): http://en.kremlin.ru/events/president/news/66181.

[7] M Shaw, 'Russia's Genocidal War in Ukraine: Radicalisation and Social Destruction' (2023) 25 *Journal of Genocide Research* 352; D Azarov, D Koval, G Nurdizhanian and V Venher, 'Understanding Russia's Actions in Ukraine as the Crime of Genocide' (2023) 21 *Journal of International Criminal Justice* 233.

scenarios which could emerge within political and intellectual discourse, including territorial concessions, a frozen conflict, expansion of Russian imperial memory politics and propaganda, or even the restructuring of the European security order. In any of these scenarios, more militant memory laws are sure to emerge, for the vision of reconciliation remains unimaginable in the foreseeable future. As stated by Hannah Arendt, for the reconciliation process to start, there must be some kind of common ethical ground connecting the forgiver and the wrong-doer that allows them to come to an understanding; and yet, at the same time, according to Arendt, radical evil cannot be forgiven because it transcends human affairs.[8] Through its 15 substantive chapters, this volume provides a thorough analysis of the complex interplay between legal and political dynamics of memory governance in Russia and Ukraine, with an additional contextualisation of these memory-political undercurrents within neighbouring countries, European institutions and politics generally. This approach is crucial not only for understanding the causes and consequences of the ongoing Russo-Ukrainian war and its implications for the regional and international security order, but also for appreciating the role of memory in international relations, as well as the power stemming from memory politics wielded by legal means.

D. Militant Memory Politics and International Law

Our volume investigates the nexus between Russia's militant memory politics and its increasingly belligerent international stance, which openly defies – or cynically reinterprets – international law and the established rules of co-existence in light of its ongoing aggression against Ukraine. The book does so by engaging manifold legal and political attempts to translate the memories of World War II (WWII) and the Cold War in Eastern Europe into various 'memory laws', ranging from declarative to regulatory and outright punitive. The approach of international memory politics to different interpretations of history in response to the war in Ukraine further highlights the enduring gravity of splintered WWII memories in contemporary Europe, East and West alike.

The book sets out to conceptualise the link between militant memory laws and international conflict in an empirically embedded way. In recent years, there has been a steady flow of monographs and edited volumes on the politics of memory (otherwise framed as politics of the past, or politics of history in the Central and Eastern European (CEE) region).[9] Most pertinent, to our empirical interest,

[8] H Arendt, *The Human Condition*, 2nd edn (The University of Chicago Press, 2018) 241. In relation to these dilemmas see also, T Adorno and R Tiedemann (ed), *Can One Live After Auschwitz? A Philosophical Reader* (Stanford University Press, 2003); P Levi, *I sommersi e i salvati* (Einaudi, 2014).

[9] eg M Kopeček (ed), *Past in the Making: Historical Revisionism in Central Europe after 1989* (Central European University Press, 2007); M Pakier and B Stråth (eds), *A European Memory? Contested Histories and Politics of Remembrance* (Berghahn Books, 2010); U Blacker, A Etkind, and J Fedor (eds), *Memory and Theory in Eastern Europe* (Palgrave Macmillan, 2013); M Bernhard

was an edited volume by Julie Fedor, Jussi Kangaspuro and Tatiana Zhurzhenko (2017),[10] which provided an illuminating discussion on the political instrumentalisation and re-mythologisation of WWII memories in the Russian, Ukrainian, and Belarusian triangle in the wake of the 2014 Russian annexation of Crimea and the war in Ukraine. More recent stimulating additions to scholarship in the field include Georgiy Kasianov's *Memory Crash: Politics of History In and Around Ukraine, 1980s–2010s* (2022),[11] and a volume edited by Elazar Barkan and Ariella Lang entitled *Memory Laws and Historical Justice: The Politics of Criminalizing the Past* (2022).[12] Kasianov focuses on the role and meaning of various actors engaged in using and abusing the Ukrainian past (including state institutions, non-governmental organisations, political parties, historians, and local governments), whilst Barkan and Lang's collection continues the pattern of analysis and mapping of memory laws established several years earlier in the edited volume by Uladzislau Belavusau and Alekandra Gliszczyńska-Grabias entitled *Law and Memory: Towards Legal Governance of History* (2017), which offered the first comparative outlook on memory laws worldwide.[13] Similarly to the seminal work by Belavusau and Gliszczyńska-Grabias, Barkan and Lang's volume focuses on the broad thematic field of legal dimensions of historical justice, with country studies, inter alia, of Israel, former Yugoslavia, Rwanda and the CEE region, including a chapter on Ukraine.

E. The Geographical and Temporal Context of Russia's Mnemopolitical Militancy

The empirical discussion pursued during the course of this volume considerably expands temporal (beyond 2014) and geographical limits through the incorporation of country studies from Belarus, Poland, Hungary, the Baltic

and J Kubik (eds), *Twenty Years After Communism: The Politics of Memory and Commemoration* (Oxford University Press, 2014); M Pakier and J Wawrzyniak (eds), *Memory and Change in Europe: Eastern Perspectives* (Berghahn, 2015); N Koposov, *Memory Laws, Memory Wars: The Politics of the Past in Europe and Russia* (Cambridge University Press, 2017); J Fedor, M Kangaspuro, J Lassila, and T Zhurzhenko (eds), *War and Memory in Russia, Ukraine and Belarus* (Palgrave Macmillan, 2017); G Kasianov, *Memory Crash: The Politics of History in and around Ukraine, 1980s–2010s* (Budapest, Central European University Press, 2022); J McGlynn, *Memory Makers: The Politics of the Past in Putin's Russia* (Bloomsbury, 2023); U Belavusau and A Gliszczyńska-Grabias (eds), *Law and Memory: Towards Legal Governance of History* (Cambridge University Press, 2017).

[10] Fedor, Kangaspuro, Lassila, and Zhurzhenko (n 9).

[11] Kasianov (n 9).

[12] E Barkan and A Lang (eds), *Memory Laws and Historical Justice: The Politics of Criminalizing the Past* (Springer/Palgrave, 2022).

[13] Belavusau and Gliszczyńska-Grabias, *Law and Memory* (n 9). See in particular, the chapter (from 2017) by U Belavusau and A Gliszczyńska-Grabias, 'Memory Laws: Mapping a New Subject in Comparative Law and Justice' (1–26), and a similarly titled introductory chapter (from 2022), 'Mapping Memory Laws' in the Barkan and Lang volume (n 12) (1–21), continuing the formative work set out in *Law and Memory*, along with that of Koposov whose monograph appeared in the same month as Belavusau and Gliszczyńska-Grabias's volume (see Koposov (n 9)).

states, and Germany, and by situating said studies in the context of broader European debates. Likewise, it offers a distinct theoretical focus on the politics and implications of militant memory laws. A systematic exploration of the international aims and ramifications of what we identify as mnemopolitical militancy,[14] via various memory laws, has been an aspect absent from existing literature. Prompted by the current Russo-Ukrainian war, this volume addresses this critical gap in an urgent, yet relevant, context. It does so in a theoretically sustained and transdisciplinary manner, consolidating a comprehensive synergy of legal, historical, and political analysis that transcends the restrictions of conventional disciplinary studies. Our empirical focus on the nexus between militant memory laws and international conflict, along with the theoretical approach of combining ontological security studies with socio-legal studies, provides a comprehensive vision of memory politics in Europe pertinent to the Russo-Ukrainian war. Building on the seminal historical study on memory wars via memory laws offered by Koposov (2017),[15] our volume further explores the international effects of domestic memory laws in the CEE region and contextualises them within international relations and comparative legal studies. Collectively, we previously delved into this approach – namely, exploring memory *laws* in the context of memory *wars* – during the period leading up to Russia's fully-fledged military invasion of Ukraine in 2022.[16] At that time, we anticipated that memory laws in the region were being converted into 'shields and swords' of such memory wars. Accordingly, in the present volume, we utilise key theoretical frameworks to explain the mechanics of this nexus, through concepts introduced and theorised earlier, namely, *militant memocracy* (the governance of historical memory for political ends)[17] and *mnemonic constitutionalism* (the embedding of historical memory within constitutional frameworks to shape collective identity and state legitimacy).[18]

In this introductory chapter, we set the stage for exploring the key question addressed in this volume, namely: 'In what ways, and under what circumstances, do memory laws become militant tools in the service of armed conflict, and how can this be prevented?' We begin (in section II) by tracing the contemporary legal

[14] On 'militant memocracy' as the mobilisation of state power behind its authorised past with a preference to outlaw accounts challenging a state's preferred self-identity, see M Mälksoo, 'Militant Memocracy in International Relations: Mnemonical Status Anxiety and Memory Laws in Eastern Europe' (2021) 47 *Review of International Studies* 489.

[15] Koposov (n 9).

[16] U Belavusau, A Gliszczyńska-Grabias and M Mälksoo, 'Memory Laws and Memory Wars in Poland, Russia and Ukraine' (2021) 69 *Jahrbuch des öffentlichen Rechts* 95.

[17] Mälksoo (n 14) 'Militant Memocracy in International Relations'.

[18] U Belavusau, 'Final Thoughts on Mnemonic Constitutionalism' (*Verfassungsblog*, 15 January 2018): https://verfassungsblog.de/final-thoughts-on-mnemonic-constitutionalism/; U Belavusau and A Gliszczyńska-Grabias, 'Mnemonic Constitutionalism in Central and Eastern Europe' (2020) 5 *European Papers* 1231; U Belavusau, 'Jewish Past, Mnemonic Constitutionalism and the Politics of Citizenship' (*Verfassungsblog*, 28 July 2024): https://verfassungsblog.de/jewish-past-mnemonic-constitutionalism-and-the-politics-of-citizenship/.

governance of history in Europe in the context of Russian aggression in Ukraine, with a special focus on the role of memory-political militancy in the international context. Following this, section III summarises the accounts presented in this volume. Finally, in the conclusion (section IV), we outline some of the more specific research questions posed to our contributors, designed to further explore and unpack the aforementioned overarching question.

II. MNEMONIC CONSTITUTIONALISM AND THE MILITANT POTENTIAL OF MEMORY LAWS

A. Unsettling and Redefining the Discourse

With the Russian invasion of Ukraine on 24 February 2022, the militant potential of memory laws has gained renewed political urgency in Europe. The abuse of the tropes of genocide, Nazism, and of the 'real lessons' of WWII[19] in the context of Russia's war against Ukraine has generated a lively debate across Europe – with some German intellectuals, most notably, Jürgen Habermas, offering history lessons to Europe and Ukraine respectively during their hour of distress and at the juncture of Germany's *Zeitenwende* in their turn.[20] Russia's war on Ukraine[21] has exposed the role of memory laws and policies in the context of existent memory wars involving real victims and ongoing human suffering, along with their capacity to stir up military rhetoric and propaganda. The earliest and most conventional examples of legal regulation on the matter in Germany and continental Europe have been mischaracterised by Putin's Russia, invoking instrumentalised historical parallels and accusing Ukrainians of being Nazi collaborators (whilst also attributing 'Nazi' characteristics to Ukrainian

[19] See V Putin, 'The Real Lessons of the 75th Anniversary of World War II' *The National Interest* (18 June 2020): https://nationalinterest.org/feature/vladimir-putin-real-lessons-75th-anniversary-world-war-ii-162982. See also Kremlin 'Interview to Tucker Carlson' (*YouTube*, 9 February 2024): www.youtube.com/watch?v=hYfByTcY49k, where Putin hijacked the available time by delivering historical lessons about Russo-Ukrainian history for the Western public, advancing the imperialistic interpretations of history as the major reasons for the ongoing Russo-Ukrainian war, or the 'special military operation' as per the headlines of the Russian propaganda.

[20] See J Habermas, 'War and Indignation: The West's Red Line Dilemma' (*Reset Dialogues on Civilizations*, 6 May 2022): https://www.resetdoc.org/story/jurgen-habermas-war-indignation-west-red-line-dilemma/; A Tooze, 'After the Zeitenwende: Jürgen Habermas and Germany's new identity crisis' (*New Statesman*, 12 May 2022): https://www.newstatesman.com/ideas/2022/05/after-the-zeitenwende-jurgen-habermas-and-germanys-new-identity-crisis; T Snyder, 'Germans have been involved in the war, chiefly on the wrong side' (*Frankfurter Allgemeine Zeitung*, 27 June 2022): https://www.faz.net/aktuell/politik/ausland/juergen-habermas-and-ukraine-germans-have-been-involved-in-the-war-18131718.html; M Schulze Wessel, 'Faschismus? Genozid? Vernichtungskrieg?' (*Frankfurter Allgemeine Zeitung*, 25 July 2022): https://zeitgeschichte-online.de/themen/faschismus-genozid-vernichtungskrieg.

[21] S Plokhy, *The Russo-Ukrainian War: The Return of History* (WW Norton & Co, 2023); S Medvedev, *A War Made in Russia* (Polity Press, 2023); A Etkind, *Russia against Modernity* (Polity Press, 2023); G Sasse, *Russia's War Against Ukraine* (Polity Press, 2023).

political and cultural elites as a justification for the current Russian 'special military operation').[22] Putin's rhetoric has been nourished by years of historical propaganda and by a distortion of facts that has accompanied legalisation of the regime's preferred 'state story' in a range of memory laws and policies.[23] In response, Ukraine has introduced militant laws and policies seeking to protect its own ontological security, or its sense of self, especially in the aftermath of the annexation of Crimea and occupation of Donbas in 2014.[24]

B. The Role of Law in Reshaping Identitarian (Un-)Certainties

During the 2000s, academic fields of study beyond the politics of memory, such as law and society, as well as comparative constitutional and criminal law, have been characterised by burgeoning literature addressing controversial 'memory laws' concerning the past.[25] Such legal developments have contributed to identitarian, and often outright nationalistic ways of shaping historical narratives, at least insofar as they have tried to impose or even ban the collective understandings of historical events. The application of these laws has been a challenge for national and international courts, which have had to balance them against freedom of expression. In turn, this has led to a vivid articulation of the role of the legal profession in the politics of memory. Judicial responses have ranged from neutral evaluation of the constitutionality of certain provisions to judicial reasoning dictated by ideological and political pressure, such as the April 2022 ruling by Russian courts ordering the dissolution of 'Memorial' – Russia's oldest and most prominent non-governmental organisation, fearlessly engaged in revealing the crimes of Soviet regime and defending historical truth.[26]

In general, it can be argued that the rise of memory laws in Europe has signalled a broader shift towards a nationalist, anti-European discourse, marked by the fortification of populist movements and a greater interference with academic freedom. Furthermore, recent memory politics in Europe and elsewhere have been largely driven by dramatic accounts of a dark past, populated with unimpeachable heroes fighting for national independence and victims of

[22] Paul Kirby, 'Has Putin's war failed and what does Russia want from Ukraine?' (*BBC News*, 24 February 2023): https://www.bbc.com/news/world-europe-56720589.

[23] U Belavusau, 'Mnemonic Constitutionalism and Rule of Law in Hungary and Russia' (2020) 1 *Interdisciplinary Journal of Populism* 16; M Mälksoo, 'The Postcolonial Moment in Russia's War Against Ukraine' (2023) 25 *Journal of Genocide Research* 471; *cf* JM Dixon, *Dark Pasts: Changing the State's Story in Turkey and Japan* (Cornell University Press, 2018).

[24] Belavusau, Gliszczyńska-Grabias and Mälksoo (n 16).

[25] U Belavusau and A Gliszczyńska-Grabias, 'The Remarkable Rise of 'Law and Historical Memory' in Europe: Theorizing Tendencies and Prospects in Recent Literature' (2020) 47 *Journal of Law and Society* 325.

[26] M Gessen, 'The Russian Memory Project That Became an Enemy of the State' (*The New Yorker*, 6 January 2022): https://www.newyorker.com/news/news-desk/the-russian-memory-project-that-became-an-enemy-of-the-state.

atrocities perpetrated by cruel foreign oppressors. The most problematic aspect has been the extent to which legislators, prosecutors, judges, national institutes of memory, and other relevant actors have not resisted the nationalist impulse, but instead have certified these simplistic narratives as legitimate and obligatory for social reproduction.

C. The Fine Line between Legitimate Mnemonic Constitutionalism and Illegitimate Propaganda

Legal governance of history and memory to legitimise a given socio-political order is neither novel nor an exclusively Russian phenomenon. Such dynamics have been a recurrent part of modern history. Its presence is of a global character, with varying thematic, geopolitical, or ideological settings. One such setting pertains to the sphere of constitutionalism, understood as a coherent system of limitations of governmental powers where the authority and legitimacy of the government is recognised only if such limitations are respected. Placed in this context, *mnemonic constitutionalism* can be defined as a process of embedding certain historical paradigms in the structures and frames of national constitutional law, memory laws, and judicial assessments of attitudes towards the past.[27]

Thus, legal governance of historical memory and the legitimate bounds of collective remembrance do not only entail historical distortions.[28] Hardly any state can avoid a degree of memory governance when it comes to, for instance, teaching history or various commemorative practices. The common elements include references to profoundly important historical events in constitutional preambles, particularly significant in transitional justice[29] and post-colonial contexts;[30] establishing truth

[27] U Belavusau, 'Rule of Law and Constitutionalisation of Memory Politics in Hungary and Russia' in M Belov (ed), *Rule of Law in Flux* (Routledge, 2022) 87–107; Belavusau (n 18); A Gliszczyńska-Grabias, 'The Politics of Constitutional Memory: Mnemonic Constitutionalism, Historical Memory, and Collective Identity in Poland, Germany and Russia' in M Tushnet and D Kochenov (eds), *Research Handbook on the Politics of Constitutional Law* (Edward Elgar, 2023) 592–610.

[28] U Belavusau, 'Memory Laws and Freedom of Speech: Governance of History in European Law' in A Koltay (ed), *Comparative Perspectives on the Fundamental Freedom of Expression* (Wolters Kluwer, 2015) 537–58.

[29] N Hajji, 'Post-Transitional Justice in Spain: Passing the Historic Memory Law' (2014) *Columbia University Journal of Politics and Society* 83; M Vorbaum, 'The Long Shadows of Gwangju: Transitional Criminal Justice in South Korea' (2022) 16 *International Journal of Transitional Justice*, 331.

[30] U Belavusau, 'Adopting a Memory Law on the Dutch Slavery Past?' (TMC Asser Institute Centre for International and European Law, a study prepared for the Advisory Board Dialogue Group on the Slavery Past and the Dutch Ministry of the Interior and Kingdom Relations, 2021) 1–33. See also U Belavusau, 'From Guillotines to Windmills: Memory Laws on Slavery in France and the Netherlands' (2025) 36 *Law and Critique*, forthcoming; S Löytömäki, 'French Memory Laws and the Ambivalence about the Meaning of Colonialism' in B Bevernage and N Wouters (eds), *Palgrave Handbook of State-Sponsored History After 1945* (Palgrave Macmillan, 2018) 87–100.

commissions and national remembrance institutions; citizenship laws that broaden the scope of eligibility for citizenship based on historical criteria; lustration laws[31] and various measures which belong to the legal framework of militant democracy which permits limits on freedom of speech and other fundamental rights in order to protect liberal democracies from their enemies.[32] For example, the German Basic Law states that political parties that seek to undermine or abolish the free democratic order shall be found unconstitutional.[33] Mnemonic constitutionalism has also manifested itself in the form of memory laws adopted in almost all European states, including Holocaust denial bans, guided by the powerful post-WWII call of 'Never again!', as well as the delivery of compensatory justice by granting citizenship to persecuted – Ashkenazi or Sephardic – Jews or their offspring in Austria, Germany, Portugal, Spain and other countries, along with Israel building its constitutionalism, without a formal Basic Law, around citizenship laws, and thus, granting the right of return to the Jewish historical cradle in the Middle East.[34]

Memory laws are not exactly a novel subject in academic literature; as demonstrated in previous studies, memory governance dates back to at least the French Revolution.[35] Punitive memory laws akin to the prohibition of genocide denialism appeared in the 1980s and 1990s and have spread from Germany through continental Europe. Though the German model gradually expanded from Holocaust denial laws per se to a wider prohibition of genocide denialism.[36] During Germany's presidency of the Council of Europe in 2008, such provisions were incorporated in secondary legislation of the European Union (EU) by virtue of the Framework Decision on xenophobic speech.[37]

[31] Lustration is the removal of public officials and judges who are associated with a tainted earlier political regime.

[32] This classical account is provided by K Loewenstein, 'Militant Democracy and Fundamental Rights I–II' (1937) 31 *American Political Science Review* 417–32, 638–58. See also, U Belavusau, 'Hate Speech and Cosntitutional Democracy in Eastern Europe: Transitional and Militant?' (2014) 47 *Israel Law Review* 27.

[33] See Basic Law of the Federal Republic of Germany, Articles 8(2) and 21(2).

[34] Belavusau (n 18) Jewish Past, Mnemonic Constitutionalism and the Politics of Citizenship; I Gutman, 'The Denial of the Holocaust and Its Consequences' in Y Bauer (ed), *Remembering for the Future: Working Papers and Addenda* (Pergamon Press, 1989) 2116–24; A Gliszczyńska-Grabias, 'Israel's Politics of Memory' in J Lubecka and M Zakrzewski (eds), *Politics of Memory* (Ignatianum University Press, 2024) 315–30.

[35] Belavusau (n 28) ('Memory Laws and Freedom of Speech') 537.

[36] *Volksverhetzung*, the German analogue of 'hate speech' terminology, is a criminal offence under section 130 of the Criminal Code (Strafgesetzbuch) in Germany. Similar provisions about the incitement of group hatred have been enshrined in the majority of continental European criminal codes or via special statutes. In Germany, this criminal offence can result in up to five years' imprisonment. For many years, section 130 was interpreted as covering Holocaust denial. Special provisions on Holocaust denial were added in the 1990s followed later by provisions on justifying or glorifying the Nazi government. Similar, self-standing (ie, separate from 'hate speech') provisions on Holocaust denial exist today in various states, from Israel to France.

[37] For a broader analysis, see U Belavusau, 'Memory Laws and Freedom of Speech: Governance of History in European Law' in A Koltay (ed), *Comparative Perspectives on the Fundamental Freedom of Expression* (Wolters Kluwer, 2015) 537–58; L Cajani, 'Legislating History: The European Union and the Denial of International Crimes' in Belavusau and Gliszczyńska-Grabias (n 9) (*Law and Memory*) 129.

D. The Inevitable Outreach of National Memory Policies and its Consequences

Unsurprisingly, one of the most contested issues in the studies of legal governance of history pertains to the conceptualisation and classification of memory laws. For example, Nikolay Koposov defines 'memory laws per se' as laws criminalising certain statements about the past.[38] However, there are also other approaches towards defining legislation of this kind. According to Eric Heinze, laws affecting historical memory do not have to explicitly condemn other competing narratives; they are instruments used by the state in the process of constructing, disseminating, promoting, and ordering public knowledge about the past.[39] In turn, Marta Bucholc finds the specific characteristic that distinguishes memory laws not in the criminal sanctions attached to these laws but in their limitations on the freedom of expression of individuals, including the freedom to tell their personal stories and memories. Such limitations can prevent certain parts of historical narratives from circulating freely within societies, resulting in the deletion of stories told by those perceived by the governing powers to be endangering the official version of the past.[40]

These differences in the perception of memory laws do nothing, however, to alter the nature of the impact they have, and the often far-reaching consequences that they bring about. Such consequences include the risk of historical records being falsified or trivialised to suit the purposes of those in power; the actual perpetrators of crimes being absolved of their guilt; the consolidation of specific paradigms of memory (mainly through Holocaust denial bans); and the introduction of a new element into international relations, potentially aggravating what are already grave tensions between some countries.

Unlike other areas of national legislation, which are intended to have an inward effect only, memory laws will inevitably be linked to those of neighbouring states who share a common history. Contradictions and divergent visions are highly emotionalised and can turn into 'memory wars'.[41] They are most often fought in defence of an idealised vision of the past, with particular states and nations portraying themselves as victims or saviours of others and never as perpetrators of atrocities committed against the others. The Hungarian Constitution adopted in 2010, which marked Viktor Orbán's return to power, serves as an example here, where even the eccentric Preamble acknowledges exclusively the

[38] Koposov (n 9).

[39] E Heinze, 'Epilogue: Beyond "Memory Laws"' in Belavusau and Gliszczyńska-Grabias (n 9) (*Law and Memory*) 413.

[40] M Bucholc, 'Commemorative Lawmaking: Memory Frames of the Democratic Backsliding in Poland after 2015' (2018) 11 *Hague Journal of the Rule of Law* 85.

[41] Koposov (n 9); I Nuzov, 'Freedom of Symbolic Speech in the Context of Memory Wars in Eastern Europe' (2019) 19 *Human Rights Law Review* 231.

positive aspects of Hungarian history, presented in a self-exculpatory manner.[42] Another example is the Belarusian Constitution, amended in a 2022 sham national referendum, which narrates a self-glorifying past by omitting any elements of criticism of the Soviet engagement in WWII and the post-war period in the region.[43] The use of such tools for re-writing history, as prescribed by law, most often go hand-in-hand with populist or even authoritarian tendencies, despite being portrayed as a necessary attempt to secure 'historical truth'.

E. Memory Laws as a Challenge for Democracy

On the surface, even dramatic perspectives of the past embedded through legal governance of history are compatible with democracy, and can be perceived as a necessary step towards building an idealised, indeed Utopian, present and future. For example, the prohibition of Holocaust denialism and the legally imposed commemoration of Nazi victims in continental Europe has for a long time been regarded as part of *militant democracy* – that is, a system of governance bent on preventing future atrocities by curtailing certain fundamental freedoms and reminding future generations of the horrors of the past.[44] However, in portraying the past as exclusively dystopian, the risk of venerating the *present* political regime increases. Likewise, there is the danger of disregarding minorities for the sake of extolling the heroism and victimhood of titular nations fighting foreign oppressors, and of stirring up new international conflicts via such memory wars. Finally, memory laws can at times be a clear normative threat to democracy itself, when historical memory is severely controlled and alternative readings of the past are censored.[45] Some scholars have recently even theorised about the existence of a cluster of 'crimes against history', exploring various ways in which history is censored and historians are silenced or outright killed for political reasons.[46]

[42] G Halmai 'National(ist) Constitutional Identity? Hungary's Road to Abuse Constitutional Pluralism (*EUI Working Paper 2017/08*); M Bán, 'The Legal Governance of Historical Memory and the Rule of Law' (PhD Thesis, University of Amsterdam, 2020): https://dare.uva.nl/search?identifier=34a3626e-1f2e-4272-981c-d8b1ecd5ab2a; A Gliszczyńska-Grabias, G Baranowska, A Wójcik, M Sadowski and A Vorobiova, 'Memory Laws in Poland and Hungary: Report of the Research Consortium "The Challenges of Populist Memory Politics and Militant Memory Laws (MEMOCRACY)"' (Publishing House of ILS Pas, 2023).

[43] U Belavusau, 'Historical Imagery and Mnemonic Constitutionalism in Belarus' (2024) 49 *Review of Central and East European Law* 324–49; U Belavusau, 'The "Year of Historical Memory" and Mnemonic Constitutionalism in Belarus' (*Verfassungsblog*, 8 September 2022): https://verfassungsblog.de/mnemonic-constit-belarus/.

[44] A Sajó (ed), *Militant Democracy* (Eleven International Publishing, 2004); U Belavusau, 'Hate Speech and Constitutional Democracy in Eastern Europe: Transitional and Militant?' (2014) 47 *Israel Law Review* 27, 27–61; M Mälksoo, 'Decommunization in Times of War: Ukraine's Militant Democracy Problem' (*Verfassungsblog: On Matters Constitutional*, 2018) https://verfassungsblog.de/decommunization-in-times-of-war-ukraines-militant-democracy-problem/.

[45] Belavusau (n 18) ('Final Thoughts on Mnemonic Constitutionalism'); Bucholc (n 40).

[46] See, in particular, A De Baets, *Crimes against History* (Routledge, 2018).

F. Memory Laws as a Challenge for the Rule of Law

The subject of memory laws in the context of fundamental rights has come to yield a well-established stream of interdisciplinary research and public discussion,[47] increasingly probing the relationship of these laws to the rule of law.[48] One of the most telling examples of this troubling interdependence was the January 2018 Polish Amendment to the Act on the Institute of National Remembrance[49] which penalised any public statements that falsely attributed responsibility or co-responsibility for the Nazi crimes (including the Holocaust) to Poland or the Polish nation.[50] The fact that this law (which was vehemently protested by representatives from academia and various diplomatic actors) was initiated by a populist Polish government, itself actively engaged in dismantling the rule of law as well as in nationalistic manipulation of history, is telling. Even more telling, however, is the fact that it is precisely a result of the destruction of the rule of law, including the guarantee of judicial independence and the political takeover of the Constitutional Tribunal, that democratic methods which normally allow for the challenge of such laws have not been available in Poland.[51] An additional element in this case was the distorted legislative process that ignored constitutional and Strasbourg human right standards in the area of freedom of expression.[52] The most controversial part of the amendment, which introduced a criminal law sanction, was eventually withdrawn in the June Amendment, after immense international political pressure (legal arguments were irrelevant here). The examples which largely form the axis of this book, and which concern Russia, are even more evocative, with the Russian Federation openly ignoring the rule of law, and amending discourse on historical memory

[47] Belavusau and Gliszczyńska-Grabias (n 9); F Fronza, *Memory and Punishment: Historical Denialism, Free Speech and the Limits of Criminal Law* (Springer and TMC Asser Press, 2018).

[48] See G Baranowska and L Castellanos-Jankiewicz (eds), 'Historical Memory in Post-communist Europe and the Rule of Law' (2020) 5 *European Papers* 95, 95–106 (Special Section – First and Second Part); A Wójcik and P Rhein-Fischer, 'Introduction to the Special Section "Memory Laws and the Rule of Law"' (2023) 19 *European Constitutional Law Review* 591, 591–601; Bán (n 42). See also the findings of the project MEMOCRACY at its website, memocracy.eu, 'MEMOCRACY: The Challenge of Populist Memory Politics for Europe: Towards Effective Responses to Militant Legislation on the Past 2021–2024'.

[49] The Act of 26 January 2018 amending the Act on the Institute of National Remembrance – Commission for Investigating Crimes Against the Polish Nation, the Act on Military Graves and Cemeteries, the Act on Museums and the Act on Corporate Liability for Proscribed Punishable Conduct, Polish Official Journal of Laws 2018 item. 369 [*Ustawa z dnia 26 stycznia 2018 r. o zmianie ustawy o Instytucie Pamięci Narodowej – Komisji Ścigania Zbrodni przeciwko Narodowi Polskiemu, ustawy o grobach i cmentarzach wojennych, ustawy o muzeach oraz ustawy o odpowiedzialności podmiotów zbiorowych za czyny zabronione pod groźbą kary, Dz.U. 2018 poz. 369*].

[50] A Gliszczyńska-Grabias, 'Deployments of Memory with the Tools of Law – the Case of Poland' (2019) 44 *Review of Central and East European Law* 464.

[51] For more insight into the Polish constitutional crisis, see W Sadurski, *Poland's Constitutional Breakdown* (Oxford University Press, 2019).

[52] Gliszczyńska-Grabias, Baranowska, Wójcik, Sadowski and Vorobiova (n 41).

in a completely arbitrary manner, distorting and falsifying recollections in its own constitution, criminal law, and school curriculum.[53]

From a legal viewpoint, therefore, memory laws may constitute an indicator of the status of democracy and the rule of law in a country: the more restrictive memory laws are of freedom of expression and the harsher the sanctions, the clearer they are in dictating a 'historical truth' handy for a ruling political regime.[54]

As far as respect for international law is concerned, memory laws must be viewed in a differentiated way. Whilst nation-preserving memory laws are generally acceptable, mnemopolitical militancy that prepares the ground for revision of existing borders is not. At the same time, memory laws constitute a particularly sensitive issue for minorities; in almost all of the countries observed, the enactment of new memory laws has been accompanied by ethnic tensions.[55] While an open dialogue about past traumas would be helpful for divided societies, the *Zeitgeist* of the last 20 years has clearly been towards cementing black and white visions of history. The driving force behind these developments is Russia's agenda of mnemopolitical militancy. However, policy changes in neighbouring countries and at the level of European institutions are not only reactive, some – such as Hungary – have their own clear policy agenda, while others are going back and forth, trying to find their way. Changes linked to individuals (such as politicians and heads of national memory institutions) can be abrupt, and tend to have a potential for escalation and spill-over effects.

III. THE POLITICAL UTILITY AND CONSEQUENCES OF MEMORY LAWS: A GUIDE TO CHAPTERS

This volume proceeds from, and expands upon, the conclusions arrived at in an earlier edited volume under part of our editorial team's guardianship.[56] *Law and Memory* (2017) assembled the leading authors in the area of legal governance of memory, setting up the most diverse geographic perspective on memory laws from Canada to Israel, Peru to Russia, and the CEE region. Furthermore, the prediction of the editors of this earlier field-defining volume about the rise of

[53] A Vorobiova, 'Education as Indoctrination: Mnemonic Constitutionalism and History Teaching in Russia' (*Verfassungsblog*, April 2023): https://verfassungsblog.de/education-as-indoctrination-mnemonic-constitutionalism-and-history-teaching-in-russia/.

[54] U Belavusau and A Gliszczyńska-Grabias, 'Academic Legacy of Wojciech Sadurski, Rule of Law, and Mnemonic Constitutionalism in Central and Eastern Europe' in U Belavusau and A Gliszczyńska-Grabias (eds), *Constitutionalism under Stress: Essays in Honour of Wojciech Sadurski* (Oxford University Press, 2020) 1–18; L David, *The Past Can't Heal Us: The Dangers of Mandating Memory in the Name of Human Rights* (Cambridge University Press, 2020).

[55] In this regard, see also L Zannier, 'Preventing Crises and Conflicts through Promotion of Integration of Diverse Societies' in *HCNM at 25: Personal Reflections of the High Commissioners* (Office for the High Commissioner on National Minorities, 2018) 42.

[56] Belavusau and Gliszczyńska-Grabias (n 9) (*Law and Memory*).

the topicality of memory laws, specifically in CEE, has unfortunately turned out to be prophetic in the past five years, culminating in the full-scale Russian invasion of Ukraine in 2022. Within this context, we take a step forward in focusing on memory laws specifically through the lens of memory wars, placing Putin's instrumentalisation of memory laws and policies at the centre of our analysis, and zooming in on the Ukrainian country study in the context of bilateral and wider regional memory wars.

This book concentrates on the generative power of militant memory legislation in the context of the ongoing war in Ukraine, along with a variety of WWII-related mnemonical repercussions that have surfaced in Western and Eastern Europe in relation to the current war. Each of the collected chapters contributes to this general focus, proceeding from various disciplines, methods and theoretical frameworks. All contributions comprehensively consider the politics of memory laws in Russia, Ukraine, and beyond from each respective standpoint, intertwined with the multiple conceptual dimensions of legal and political governance of social memory.

The book comprises four Parts, covering: (1) Memory laws in Russia, (2) Memory laws in Ukraine, (3) Memory laws in the neighbouring countries in the context of the Russo-Ukrainian war, and finally, (4) European and international accounts of memory laws in the context of the war. The first Part of the book zooms in on Russia, not only because of its dominant role in militant memory politics in the region but for the rootedness of mnemopolitical militancy in the Russian past. More specifically, this section deals with Russia's militant memory laws and politics, with particular emphasis on their connection to Ukraine and the current conflict. Russia's legislation on historical memory has prominently emerged as a mechanism used for targeted international dissuasion and as a disciplinary device in the still heated contestations over the legitimate remembering and 'rightful' narratives of WWII and the broader Soviet legacy.[57] Whereas other CEE states have called for consideration of the Soviet legacy as being on par with the Nazi regime, Russia's countering of any attempts to critically probe its role during, and after, WWII has been the leitmotif of its recent memory laws and policies (with its notable self-exculpatory framing).[58] Readers are introduced to these issues in a chapter by Andrii Nekoliak and Paul Primbs, who show how, and for what reasons, history became criminalised in Russia, concentrating on the early period of Russian legislation in late-Soviet and early post-Soviet times. Exposure to the background of the phenomena we observe today in the context of Russian memory propaganda is arguably crucial for understanding the legal instruments and narratives in the area of memory that Russia began to use in the aftermath of the 2014 annexation of Crimea and

[57] K Gustafsson and M Mälksoo, 'Memory-Political Deterrence: Shielding Collective Memory and Ontological Security through Dissuasion' (2024) 68 *International Studies Quarterly* 1.

[58] eg Art 354-1 of the Russian Criminal Code (2014); Art 243.4 of the Russian Criminal Code (2020); Art 67.1. of the amended Constitution (2020).

occupation of Donbas. The second chapter in this Part, written by Ilya Nuzov, is devoted to this time period. Nuzov claims that the spike in the adoption of memory laws during this time served to bolster the rhetorical justification for Russia's aggressive foreign policy. The Part closes with the contribution by Gleb Bogush, who focuses on those aspects of the memory policies of Putin's Russia which were instrumental in preparing and implementing Russia's aggression against Ukraine in 2022. Bogush demonstrates how new historical myths have already been built around the war, such as the Russian accusations of 'extermination of the people of Donbas by Ukrainian neo-Nazis'. Thus, this Part presents three successive stages of Russian abuse and manipulation of history, which lead to consequences far beyond the mere impact of specific laws and policies in the realm of memory, namely, military aggression and regional destabilisation.

The next Part is dedicated to Ukrainian memory legislation and policies. Its chronological arrangement mirrors the structure of the initial section devoted to Russia. Thus, the contributors of this section guide readers through the pre-2014 Ukrainian memory laws and policies, the 2015 decommunisation laws (and their topical aspects in relation to monuments and the regulation of historical symbols in Ukraine), and finally, the mnemonic dimension of the 2022 invasion. The first contribution in this Part, by Alina Cherviatsova, sets the stage for understanding the Ukrainian perspective by analysing how Ukraine handled its national history through policies and laws dating from the 1990s until the annexation of Crimea. Cherviatsova reflects on the formative historical experiences of Ukraine, which have translated into laws and policies, including the regulation of historical memory regarding the *Holodomor*, as well as the entangled past with its neighbours, particularly, Russia and Poland. Moving to the next chapter, Tatiana Zhurzhenko offers a comprehensive account on the controversial package of 2015 decommunisation laws, which is perhaps only now, against the backdrop of Russia's 2022 invasion, better understood among Ukraine's western partners as a package of memory laws which ran parallel – and arguably in counteraction – to the annexation of Crimea and the war in Donbas (manufactured by Putin's regime). As noted in the chapter, the imperative of mnemonic security was rightfully identified as the main rationale behind the implementation of Ukraine's decommunisation agenda. At the same time, the package turned out to raise doubts concerning its inconsistency with free speech standards, as well as with competing historical narratives, to a large extent concerning not only Russia but also Poland: the individuals and organisations praised by these memory laws as national heroes were also accused, by the opponents of this legislation, of murdering thousands of Poles and Jews, thus, transcending purely Russian propaganda of that period. Zhurzhenko smoothly navigates through the meanders of these controversies, showing how complex the motives for and consequences of decreeing memory and history through law can be. Finally, the Part offers a chapter by Andrii Nekoliak, who maps and analyses the newest memory laws and policies in Ukraine – subsequent to the Russian invasion in February 2022 – meant to counteract the remnants of Russification and

Sovietisation splinters in the Ukrainian public space, and to translate de-colonial discourses into the socio-legal realm of Ukraine amidst the war.

Given the presence of frequently conflicting mnemonic narratives across bordering regions, the third Part of the volume delves into the respective mnemonical legislation and politics in states neighbouring the central protagonists of this book, which are inadvertently involved in the conflict by virtue of their memory laws, policies, and social perceptions. In doing so, this Part seeks to shed light on regional repercussions stemming from the current Russo-Ukrainian war, including its wider mnemopolitical underpinnings and implications. To begin, the chapter by Aleksandra Gliszczyńska-Grabias introduces the matrix of Polish-Ukrainian and Polish-Russian politics of memory. She maintains that there has been a historic chance for healing Polish-Ukrainian mnemonic wounds. Yet, the process that emerged with the beginning of Russia's aggression against Ukraine and the subsequent, unprecedented scale of aid, support, and care that Poles offered to Ukrainians fleeing the horrors of the war, has been fragile and uncertain.

What becomes evident from this discussion is the fact that Polish-Russian wounds inflicted by the past have deepened to such an extent that recovery has been stifled, with the time frame for healing being presented as potentially indefinite. With this in mind, Gliszczyńska-Grabias proceeds to investigate the interaction between the current state of affairs within international relations and the politics of the past. This reflection encompasses reference to Polish memory laws which have been designed as a direct response to the question of whose truth is the 'rightful truth', the Polish, the Ukrainian or the Russian one?

The next chapter moves to another crucial actor at play on the mnemonic stage, namely, Belarus, the country through which the Russian army managed to infiltrate Ukraine back in 2022, with such actions potentially elevating Belarus's status to that of co-aggressor in the ongoing war. Having shifted the discussion to the role of Belarus, Uladzislau Belavusau's addition to this Part addresses the evolution of Łukašenka's memory politics and the regime's recent adoption of memory laws, in particular, on the 'genocide of the Belarusian people'. A significant development, given the country's previous ability to distance itself from explicit memory wars, unfolded via articulated memory laws (such as those visible in neighbouring Polish, Russian and Ukrainian country studies). To explain how Belarus was able to reach this stage, Belavusau demonstrates why 2020 and 2022 are both crucial to understanding memory legislation and policies in Belarus, whilst also highlighting the fact that such instruments have been populated with Polonophobic, anti-Ukrainian, positive recollections of the Soviet past, and more recently, with Russophile historical interpretations.

Continuing on from Belarus, this Part moves to the contribution by Dovilė Budrytė and her insight into the Baltic states of Estonia, Latvia, and Lithuania, and their respective memory wars with Russia. As noted by Budrytė, mnemonic conflicts with Russia have been closely related to the actual military conflicts initiated by Russia, at a time when major changes in states' identities and discourses were taking place and when existential threats were especially relevant. In particular, she argues that a specific feature of the Baltic attitude towards Ukraine is that it lacks distance and can thus be characterised as 'vicarious identification'. Following this account, the next contribution, the chapter by Marina Bán, examines the transformation of Russia's role in Hungary's memory governance, adding another troubling piece to the puzzle. This new national dimension examines the drastic transformation of the Hungarian memory regime and memory laws, including the language and policy of nationalism, mnemonic security and the defence of national values. For the final part of this Part, Tuomas Forsberg presents the case of Finland, which provides insight beyond the CEE-context of memory-based neighbourly relations, along with Finland's outlook on historical memory as part of its war against the Soviet Union. This country study shows how political decisions, such as NATO membership, can change a long-term pragmatic approach to open questions about history and stir up the evil ghosts of the past.

A recurring theme in all the CEE country studies examined is that of 'colonialism', whether in it be relation to the Soviet period or the fear moving forward regarding Russia's potential new colonial ambitions. An important distinction must be made, though, between de-colonisation and de-communisation, as they are similar but not the same. This discourse contradicts the paradigm of Russia's self-identification as the leading power in the fight against colonialism and imperialism. In the case of Hungary, however, this discourse is turned on its head, with rhetoric instead positioning the EU as the new coloniser. Within the realm of memory politics, terms such as 'colonialism', 'Nazism' and 'Fascism' bear negative connotations, but in diametrically opposed ways. What has become evident is that not many new buzzwords have been invented, with the old ones deemed perfectly suited to mark the new divisions.

The fourth, and final, Part of the volume investigates broader aspects of European memory politics and international relations in the context of Russo-Ukrainian memory wars, and in doing so, analyses responses to the current war in Ukraine. To elaborate, the contributors reflect on how European law and memory politics have not only been shaped by memory laws, but also how they are being reshaped in view of recent military developments. The German case, tackled by Paula Rhein-Fischer, is the most evocative here for the powerful precedent it has set in relation to memory politics and militant democracy through memory laws, which are often consequently replicated in other (particularly CEE) instances of memory governance. Germany in particular has served as an important reference point for Putin's 2022 claim of 'de-Nazification' directed at Ukraine. Discussion within this Part is not limited to the role of state actors; rather, it extends to other prominent stakeholders, including the EU and the Council of Europe, who respectively provide a significant normative and political backdrop to mnemopolitical contestations in the CEE region. These memory-political fora are comprehensively examined by Anna Wójcik, who argues that European supranational organisations have attempted to strengthen a common European remembrance based on the condemnation of imperialism, Nazi and Soviet totalitarianism, historical and border revisionism in response to Putin's Russia's revisionist historical policy, and military aggression in Ukraine from 2014 onwards – though alas with mixed results. This analysis raises questions regarding the position of another important actor relevant to memory disputes examined in this volume, namely, the European Court of Human Rights (ECtHR). This topic is addressed in the subsequent chapter by Dovilė Sagatienė, who contextualises the role of the ECtHR in the governance of historical memory before and after 2022: a discourse which includes insight into pertinent case law on protecting historical narratives, specific challenges related to addressing the Soviet past, and the ECtHR's case law on historical issues emerging from Russia and Ukraine. The concluding chapter, presented by Maria Mälksoo, reflects on the contrast between what has been lost and what has been found, in the mutual attempts to translate the memories of WWII and the Cold War within Western and Eastern Europe in the context of Russia's current war against Ukraine. Mälksoo maintains that a number of mnemonical templates have become re-animated in European politics as a response to Russian aggression – including the reference points of the Holocaust, Nuremberg and appeasement – which are engaged in distinct political work in an effort to answer the question of how best to handle the aggressor during and after the war.

The final Part, the Epilogue: 'The Battle for the Past: War and Memory in the Post-Soviet Space', is written by one of the world's leading scholars of memory politics in Belarus, Russia and Ukraine, David Marples, who provides some original reflections and offers a bird's eye view of memory politics in the post-Soviet space in light of the Russian military invasion in Ukraine.

We trust that each individual part of this book will provide readers with a comprehensive knowledge of the complex, yet interrelated, factors shaping the specific sphere of historical memory. Furthermore, we hope that our contributions will offer, at least, a partial answer to the question of how to protect memory from manipulation. This volume brings together the combined legal and political expertise of a transnational research consortium dedicated to the comparative study of CEE memory laws and memory wars waged in the past decade against the backdrop of the prototype of classic Holocaust denial regulation in Germany.[59] By assembling scholars with a wide array of perspectives on memory politics and memory laws, and by offering numerous accounts from various jurisdictions – including accounts by non-lawyers – we hope that this book serves as a repository of information for the reader wishing to grasp, and make sense of, the complex politics of memory laws in comparative perspective.

[59] Memocracy.eu (n 48). See, in particular, P Rhein-Fischer and S Mesing, *Memory Laws in Germany: How Remembering National Socialism is Governed Through Law* (Torkel Opsahl Academic EPublisher, 2022): https://admin.memocracy.eu/wp-content/uploads/2022/11/221109-OPS-14-1-1.pdf.

We trust that this book will also prove to be a useful guide for anyone trying to better understand the subtexts of the current Russo-Ukrainian war and the climate of aggression that has distinctly informed the diagnosis of, and the reactions to, the war in Europe and beyond. Aside from the usual academic suspects from the fields of politics and international relations, comparative legal studies, history, anthropology, social psychology, security studies, and cultural studies, this books aspires to be of interest to policy-makers, judges, legislators and other stakeholders actively involved in the handling of practical dimensions and consequences of mnemonic governance.

IV. CONCLUSION: UNDERSTANDING THE SURGE OF MILITANT MEMORY LAWS

Especially in times as geopolitically and axiologically volatile and uncertain as the present, with polarised societies and full-scale war in Europe, the law, embedded in its social functions and roles, should be immune to manipulation for political and ideological purposes. However, with reality demonstrating that the opposite is true, the topics covered in this book prove to be of significance.

Contributors to this volume were invited to address the following pertinent questions, within their respective empirical contexts:

(1) What embues memory laws with political potency, and to what extent do they stimulate present-day transgressions based on alleged wrongs from the past?
(2) Is identity-building based on memory laws conducive to aggressive behaviour towards neighbouring states?
(3) Which memory laws cultivate fertile conditions for gross human rights violations, including those resulting from war crimes and crimes against humanity?
(4) What sparks the potential of militant memory laws to frame, underpin and further perpetuate internal and international conflicts?
(5) How should we interpret the capacity of memory laws to generate power in the context of the current Russian aggression against Ukraine?

The pursuit of accurate answers to these questions is not only a fascinating intellectual endeavour, but also an urgent necessity in times where we seem to be drowning in political tensions and incessant 'mis-' and disinformation campaigns that seek to destabilise and muddy the waters of memory laws. This book finds itself emerging at a poignant moment, just before the 80th anniversary of the cessation of WWII, and yet amidst the fiery storms of heated armed conflicts (the origins of which can be traced back to WWII and the post-war struggle with memory). All the more profoundly, we hope that this volume will provide guidance on how to navigate the tumultuous waters of memory laws during the turbulent times of the Russo-Ukrainian war, while also shedding light on the mechanism through which such memory laws can deepen conflicts and cause tensions to explode.

Part I

Memory Laws and Policies in Russia

1

The Politics of Memory and Legislative Discourse on Rehabilitation of Nazism in Russia in the 1990s and 2000s

ANDRII NEKOLIAK AND PAUL PRIMBS

I. INTRODUCTION

THIS CHAPTER EXAMINES legislative aspects of the politics of memory in Russia in the 1990s and 2000s. It argues that Russia's turn towards a pursuit of aggressive memory politics vis-à-vis its neighbours and its increased mnemo-political militancy in 2010s (see next chapters in this Part[1]), have been nurtured in the legislative discourse of the Russian legislature since the 1990s. The contribution of the chapter stems from its close focus on the politics of commemorative declarations in Russia's parliament in the first two post-Soviet decades – with particular attention given to how Russian law-makers developed the 'rehabilitation of Nazism' trope in these declarations and what implications this law-making had for the direction of memory politics in later decades. In doing so, the chapter highlights the ethical dilemma over historical memory lying at the core of the Russian dynamics.

Political processes regarding historical memory in post-Soviet, newly democratic, Russia, and more narrowly, the output of parliamentary law-making, can be conceptualised via the distinction between democratic and authoritarian views about the Soviet past. The conceptual distinction builds upon a point by Nikolay Koposov, who notes that the main fault-line in the dynamics of historical memory in Russia has demarcated the opposing interests of 'protecting the memory of the oppressive regime … of the state against that of its victims'.[2] The

[1] See: G Bogush, 'Putin's Memory Policies in the Context of Military Aggression in Ukraine' Chapter 3 and I Nuzov, 'Memory Laws and Policies in Russia After the Annexation of Crimea and Occupation of Donbas' Chapter 2 in this volume.

[2] N Koposov, *Memory Laws, Memory Wars. The Politics of the Past in Europe and Russia* (Cambridge University Press, 2018) 295. On Russia's totalitarian past, see also: N Koposov, *Pamiat' strogogo rezhima. Istoriia i politika Rossii* (NLO, 2011).

authoritarian view emphasises positive rapprochement with the Soviet past and the protection of the memory of the Soviet regime in the legislation despite the historical record of state abuses and mass terror. The democratic view, instead, is about the condemnation of the Soviet totalitarian era, and, more generally, about pursuing 'politics of regret'[3] regarding the Soviet-Russian past.

This dichotomous dynamic between the two views about the past can already be traced at the level of legislative texts and discourses by 'memory entrepreneurs' in the wake of Perestroika[4] in the late 1980s and again later, in the post-transition era. The authoritarian view of the Soviet past adopted the more 'populist' undertone of protecting the people's memory in the discourse of the Communist Party of the Russian Federation (KPRF) in 1990s, followed by explicit mnemo-militant undertones within legislative work by Konstantin Zatulin and Vladimir Zhirinovskiy, memory moguls of Dmitry Medvedev and Vladimir Putin's era in the State Duma, in the 2000s.[5] Within the authoritarian paradigm of the past in particular, legislative engagement with the interpretation of Soviet-Russian experiences during World War II (WWII) contributed to a 'self-exculpatory' view[6] of the national past. In this light, the political dynamics of historical memory are thoroughly and fundamentally about the ethics of engagement with the past.[7] Much of the chapter's argument foreshadows the contributions by Ilya Nuzov and Gleb Bogush in this volume, which showcase how the former, authoritarian, view not only remained politically viable over the years, but came to dominate Russian politics and memory law-making more decisively in the authoritarian era of President Vladimir Putin.

The chapter is structured as follows. Section II situates the case of memory law-making in the broader context of scholarship focused on social and political memory developments in Russia since 1991. Section III turns to the analysis of parliamentary legislation voted for by Russian law-makers in the 1990s and 2000s. By putting a spotlight on previously overlooked commemorative declarations by the State Duma, the section underscores how the 'rehabilitation of Nazism' trope appeared in the work of parliamentary memory agents. Specifically, it traces the political dynamics attached to law-making activities when passing legislation in parliamentary sessions and the arguments put forth in these commemorative declarations from the legislative discourse on historical memory. The chapter's conclusions (section IV) point to the problematic political

[3] JK Olick, *The Politics of Regret: On Collective Memory and Historical Responsibility* (Routledge, 2007).

[4] The Perestroika is a term describing the reform movement initiated by Mikhail Gorbachev, the leader of the Soviet Union in 1985–91.

[5] A Shekhovtsov and A Umland, 'Vladimir Zhirinovsky and the LDPR' (2011) 102 *Russian Analytical Digest* 14; P Polian, 'For Whom the Tsar-Bell Has Tolled?' (2009) 3 *Ab Imperio* 54.

[6] E Heinze, 'Should Governments Butt out of History?' (*Free Speech Debate*, 12 March 2019): https://papers.ssrn.com/sol3/papers.cfm?abstract_id=3355963.

[7] A Margalit, *The Ethics of Memory* (Harvard University Press, 2002); J Dixon, *Dark Pasts: Changing the State's Story in Turkey and Japan* (Cornell University Press, 2018).

potential and the perilous effects of memory laws by putting the Russian case into comparative perspective.

II. DYNAMICS OF HISTORICAL MEMORY IN RUSSIA: POLITICAL AND SOCIAL CONTEXT

This section aims to contextualise the central theme of the chapter, which is the early presence of the authoritarian position of memory politics in parliamentary discourse, within the current memory scholarship landscape pertaining to Russia. At the same time, the argument of this chapter finds itself embedded in the social and political history of Russia's development in the first two post-Soviet decades.

Trauma and mourning are described as pivotal aspects of Russian memory history by Aleksander Etkind in his work *Warped Mourning: Stories of the Undead in the Land of the Unburied*.[8] At the heart of Etkind's research stands the memory of the millions of victims of revolution, terror and repression that the country suffered over the course of the twentieth century. His comparison with the culture of remembrance in Germany, where millions also fell victim to totalitarianism, resulted in the development of the concepts of hard and soft memory. He noted that intellectual and artistic discourse in Russia, which he refers to as 'soft memory', grappled with the topic of mass terror and mourning intensively. Numerous, often disturbing, novels and feature films picked up the topic and were extremely popular in the late '80s and early '90s. The 'Memorial Society' movement was able to collect and document impressive oral history collections. In fact, the overall societal relevance and attention that was devoted to this discourse showcase the important function that soft memory fulfilled in Russia from the *Perestroika* until at least the 2000s.[9] At the same time, what Etkind calls the 'hard memory' of terror and suffering – the emotional and symbolical narrative enshrined and institutionalised into official and permanent structures like museums, monuments, state holidays or sites of remembrance – has been, and very much remains, underdeveloped in present day Russia.[10]

Etkind expands on the metaphor of 'hard memory' and develops the argument that the constant search for consensus, which is necessary for a pronounced 'hard memory', leads to a hardening over time, a mnemonic 'crystallization'. This necessary, socially and politically firmly established consensus, of which he claims the German culture of remembrance is a prime example, is rather absent

[8] A Etkind, *Warped Mourning: Stories of the Undead in the Land of the Unburied* (Stanford University Press, 2013).

[9] A Etkind, 'Hard and Soft in Cultural Memory: Political Mourning in Russia and Germany' (2004) (16) *Grey Room* 36, 43 f.

[10] ibid 47–57.

in the case of Russia.[11] The absence of a state and institutionalised memory of repression, terror, war and suffering in the twentieth century in Russia is obvious, and is clearly the result of politics that see history primarily as a resource from which to gain legitimacy, by reproducing triumphalist heroic narratives and creating a stable national identity in reference to the nation's collective great deeds. Although Etkind declares 'interpretations of history'[12] to be the most political issue in Russia at the beginning of the twenty-first century, the actual political actors, practices and laws that led to said outcomes are largely absent in his analysis, an aspect noted by some of his critics.[13]

Thus, the politics surrounding historical trauma and remembrance, is by no means a research gap per se, as Russian historical and memory politics are generally well-studied. Still, Etkind's theses provide a solid starting point for establishing the terminology that underpins the discussion of historical memory dynamics in Russia. One premise of the following argument is that Russian memory politics can be analysed along a cleavage that emerges between a democratic, critical, and repentant position – focused on remembering the victims – and the triumphalist, glorifying, and Soviet-nostalgic narratives that seek to celebrate national heroes. While the former – here referred to as the democratic position – gained prominence during *Perestroika* and throughout the 1990s, particularly within 'soft culture' and in highbrow cultural expressions, the latter position – the authoritarian interpretation – has been dominant in 'hard culture' at least since the Brezhnev era.

It is not without reason that the existing memory studies scholarship on Russia has a clear dual focus: on the one hand, the massive changes that have taken place during the quarter-century of Vladimir Putin's rule in Russia, and on the other, the prominent role that the so-called 'Great Patriotic War' now holds in identity formation, memory culture, and historical politics.

The Soviet Union's victory in WWII serves as 'a pillar of national identity' for post-Soviet Russia.[14] This is closely linked to the fact that the ideological significance of the victory grew immensely in the late Soviet Union. Under Leonid Brezhnev, in particular, Victory Day became perhaps the most important holiday, with the triumphalist narrative and hero worship becoming foundational pillars of the Soviet identity. In the mid-1960s to mid-1980s, the memory of the war grew more significant than that of the Revolution and the Civil War.[15] The symbolic and discursive appropriation of the war undoubtedly resonated

[11] ibid 56 f.

[12] Etkind, *Warped Mourning* (n 8) 244.

[13] E Zaretsky, 'Collective Memory and Narrative: A Response to Etkind' (2009) 16 *Constellations* 201.

[14] J Fedor, '"Historical Falsification" as a Master Trope in the Official Discourse on History Education in Putin's Russia' (2021) 13 *Journal of Educational Media, Memory, and Society* 109.

[15] DL Hoffmann, 'Introduction: The Politics of Commemoration in the Soviet Union and Contemporary Russia' in DL Hoffmann (ed), *The Memory of the Second World War in Soviet and Post-Soviet Russia* (Routledge, 2022) 1.

with the population.[16] In Putin's global project of history and memory politics, the cult of victory is at least as central as it was in the Soviet Union. The regime continually invokes the victory on all levels and through every available channel, using it to legitimise itself and construct the Russian people as heirs of this heroic feat.[17] From this 'master narrative' or 'meta-event', as the 'Great Patriotic War' might be called, a supposed national character is derived.[18]

The second central focus in existing research is the analysis of the practices, goals, and methods of Putin's memory politics. The historical foundation of Putinism is not the idea of a 'New Russia', defined *in contrast* to the Soviet empire, but rather the concept of a 1,000-year-old Russia, *including* Soviet history. Naturally, the glaring ruptures in this history can only be bridged through historical eclecticism. In this 'post-Soviet bricolage',[19] the focus lies on state structures. This statist perspective allows for the interpretation of opposing regimes, the Tsarist Empire and the Soviet Union, as aspects of one continuous and glorious great-power history, with the 'Great Patriotic War' functioning as the culmination that cemented Russia's great-power status in Europe.[20] In accordance with this view, the 1990s are seen as a dark age, ended by Vladimir Putin,[21] and the collapse of the Soviet Union is portrayed as the catastrophic outcome of treacherous conspiracies.[22] Compared to Boris Yeltsin's policies, Putin's project represents the first comprehensive and systematic historical-political initiative in post-Soviet Russia.[23]

Important studies have explored local practices of memory, how memory is mediated within the education system, how products of the culture industry shape collective memory, what the interaction of state authorities with other actors, such as grassroots movements or the Orthodox Church, looks like in practice, and many other aspects. The detailed findings of this research cannot be fully discussed here. However, two aspects are particularly relevant to the argument at hand. First, from a long-term perspective, it becomes clear that the regime seeks to expand its control over historical narratives and discourses in every sphere examined. For example, where local memory practices are more pluralistic and less political than at the national level,[24] the 'military glory'

[16] J Fedor, S Lewis and T Zhurzhenko, 'Introduction: War and Memory in Russia, Ukraine, and Belarus' in J Fedor, M Kangaspuro, J Lassila, and T Zhurzhenko (eds), *War and Memory in Russia, Ukraine and Belarus* (Palgrave MacMillan, 2017) 13 f.

[17] Hoffmann, 'Introduction: The Politics of Commemoration' (n 15) 3 f.

[18] O Malinova, 'Political Uses of the Great Patriotic War in Post-Soviet Russia from Yeltsin to Putin' in J Fedor, M Kangaspuro, J Lassila, and T Zhurzhenko (eds) *War and Memory in Russia, Ukraine and Belarus* (Palgrave MacMillan, 2017) 62.

[19] ibid 56.

[20] ibid 46.

[21] Fedor, 'Historical Falsification' (n 14) 109 f.

[22] Malinova, 'Political Uses of the Great Patriotic War' (n 18) 56.

[23] ibid 46.

[24] T Zhurzhenko, 'World War II Memories and Local Media in the Russian North: Velikii Novgorod and Murmansk' in DL Hoffmann (ed), *The Memory of the Second World War in Soviet and Post-Soviet Russia* (Routledge, 2022) 217.

programme has been implemented to embed the global narrative within local communities.[25] History education has been systematically reformed, with the democratic interpretation of Russian history already being undermined in school textbooks.[26] The Ministry of Culture increasingly commissions patriotic war films from loyal directors, and the 'Great Patriotic War' is ever more prominent on Russian screens.[27] Former grassroots movements, like the Immortal Regiment, have been co-opted, serving as unified rituals for regime legitimation and propaganda,[28] while the Orthodox Church was completely incorporated into the regime's identity-building project.[29]

Second, existing research demonstrates that this development has never been static, rather, it has continually evolved. The political trajectory towards greater control over societal discourses has not been linear.[30] Putin did not begin his political legacy as a revisionist; initially, in the early 2000s, he held somewhat critical views of the Soviet past.[31] The regime's increasing urge for total control was propelled by internal and external political developments, such as democratic revolutions in Georgia and Ukraine in 2003–2005, and the 'conservative turn' following the Bolotnaya protests in Moscow against electoral fraud in 2012.[32]

The fact that research focuses so heavily on developments under Putin's administration is due to the relatively rapid, politically motivated, and systematically driven transformations that took place during this period. This often results in a periodisation that constructs Putin's policies as standing in stark contrast to Yeltsin's. Such approaches describe a 'revival' of the triumphalist narrative of the 'Great Patriotic War' under Putin or even proclaim an 'authoritarian turn'.[33] In this context, it is often noted that Boris Yeltsin, in his power struggle with Mikhail Gorbachev, invoked the democratic interpretation of Russian history and at times portrayed himself as an anti-imperialist. Indeed, the liberal camp to which Yeltsin belonged in the early 1990s was characterised by this 'democratic' interpretation, in which de-Sovietisation and decolonisation were crucial concepts.[34]

[25] ibid 223.

[26] Fedor, 'Historical Falsification' (n 14) 118 f.

[27] SM Norris, 'The War Film and Memory Politics in Putin's Russia' in DL Hoffmann (ed), *The Memory of the Second World War in Soviet and Post-Soviet Russia* (Routledge, 2022) 303.

[28] J Fedor, 'Memory, Kinship, and the Mobilization of the Dead: The Russian State and the "Immortal Regiment" Movement' in J Fedor, M Kangaspuro, J Lassila, and T Zhurzhenko (eds) *War and Memory in Russia, Ukraine and Belarus* (Palgrave MacMillan, 2017) 327.

[29] Hoffmann, 'Introduction: The Politcs of Commemoration' (n 15) 3; C Basar, 'War and Faith: Memories of the Great Patriotic War in the Russian Orthodox Church' (2016) 7 *Constellations* 56, 65.

[30] Fedor, 'Historical Falsification' (n 14) 110.

[31] Malinova, 'Political Uses of the Great Patriotic War' (n 18) 56.

[32] T Zhurzhenko, 'The Geopolitics of Memory' (*Eurozine*, 10 May 2007) 2; Norris, 'War Film' (n 27) 299.

[33] Hoffmann, 'Introduction: The Politcs of Commemoration' (n 15) 1.

[34] MR Beissinger, *Nationalist Mobilization and the Collapse of the Soviet State* (Cambridge University Press, 2002) 137.

There is evidence to support the construction of Yeltsin's time in office as a countermodel to Putin's approach in terms of memory and historical politics. It has been pointed out, for instance, that Yeltsin cancelled the Victory Day parade in 1992 and, in 1995, ordered the removal of Soviet symbols from Victory Park before its opening.[35] However, such an approach overlooks the fact that 1995 can also be seen as a memory political turning point. Yeltsin, who had stripped the Victory Day parade of Soviet connotations by moving the celebrations to Poklonnaya Hill, had the parade return to the symbolically charged Red Square for the fiftieth anniversary of WWII victory. This represented a symbolic retreat on this highly charged issue.[36] 1995 was also the year that cooperation between the state and the Orthodox Church in matters of memory was institutionalised, with the establishment within the Church of the Department for Relations with the Armed Forces and Law Enforcement Agencies.[37] In general, from the mid-1990s onward, one can speak of a slow and gradual rehabilitation of authoritarian positions and Soviet symbolism. Given that Yeltsin's administration increasingly relied on the victory in the 'Great Patriotic War' for legitimacy,[38] how, then, can we explain the developments during the 1990s?

In the literature, one argument is particularly prevalent when explaining why the democratic interpretation failed to take hold: it is often asserted that, in the Russian case, it was not possible to 'externalize' the Soviet past.[39] This refers to the ability of other post-Soviet states, in contrast with Russia, to mark Soviet rule as foreign through a process of discursive 'othering' and to frame the Soviet period as one of occupation. The implicit self-victimisation accompanying this process allowed for the formation of a positive national identity that excluded the Soviet era in other former Soviet republics. A similar approach was not possible in the former Russian Soviet Federal Socialist Republic RSFSR, as it contained the imperial centre itself. Therefore, the only alternative would have been a narrative of atonement, involving a conscious confrontation with guilt and perpetrators, and ultimately a process of reckoning. This explains why Etkind's comparison with German memory culture makes sense. However, this explanatory approach claims that such a path, especially in the absence of an obvious defeat, would have been too painful and politically costly for Russia, which accounts for the gradual return to Soviet-era narrative patterns and symbolism.

This mechanism – the inability to critically assess the Soviet past due to the impossibility of 'externalisation' – is fundamentally plausible and further

[35] Hoffmann, 'Introduction: The Politcs of Commemoration' (n 15) 1 f.

[36] Malinova, 'Political Uses of the Great Patriotic War' (n 18) 51 f.

[37] Basar, 'War and Faith' (n 29) 7.

[38] Malinova, 'Political Uses of the Great Patriotic War' (n 18) 51 f.

[39] See, eg: ibid; 44 f., Zhurzenko, 'Geopolitics of Memory' (n 32) 3; Fedor, Lewis and Zhurzhenko, 'Introduction' (n 16) 14.

illustrated in this chapter. The political process in the Russian parliament and the continuities between memory discourses of the 1990s and 2000s can be embedded in the narrative developed by sociologist Katharina Bluhm. The remainder of this section outlines Bluhm's narrative on the genesis of Russian illiberal conservatism in the 1990s in order to situate the subsequent examination of parliamentary discourses within this intellectual history.

Bluhm interprets the 1990s as a formative period for the political debates and positions that continue to shape discourse in Russian society and politics today. During this time, two fundamental patterns of thought emerged which persist to this day: the 'liberal' position and the illiberal conservative-nationalist countermovement that developed in opposition to it. To fully understand these camps and their perspectives, it is essential to study their origins in the 1990s,[40] as this period functioned as an 'intellectual laboratory'.[41] In Bluhm's view, both currents, including the 'liberal' one, have specific manifestations in the Russian context and do not have clear equivalents in the standard Western political models or party spectrum. The former, Russian 'liberalism', can be categorised within the terminology used here as part of the democratic interpretation, while the latter, illiberal conservatism, encompasses the proponents of the authoritarian interpretation. The seedbed for illiberal conservatism – which, under Vladimir Putin's presidency, gradually evolved first into a party project and then into a state ideology[42] – was the parliamentary opposition that formed in the 1990s. Reconstructing the memory-political discourse of this opposition, as this study does, is therefore necessary to overcome the paradigm of a 'course shift' under Putin and to highlight the continuities that stretch from the 1990s to the present.

It should be noted that Yeltsin, at the beginning of the 1990s, was part of a 'liberal' camp that had already emerged during the so-called 'war of reforms'. He advocated radical changes and a rapid transition to a market economy. While this was the primary objective, ideological positions from the neoliberalism prevalent in Western Europe and the USA at the time were blended with ideas from the 'Westernisers' in Russian intellectual history, converging into a discourse on market economy, Russia's place in Europe, sovereignty, and democracy. Boris Yeltsin, as President of the RSFSR, skilfully instrumentalised this discourse in his conflict with Gorbachev. It is crucial to recognise that large sections of the elite at that time, including staunch communists and other opponents of reform, did not partake in this discursive development.[43] Many opponents of this reform were found in the Supreme Soviet, which, while agreeing in principle on the necessity of economic reforms, did not endorse them in the radical form.

[40] K Bluhm, *Russland und der Westen: Ideologie, Ökonomie und Politik seit dem Ende der Sowjetunion* (Matthes und Seitz, 2023) 11 f.
[41] ibid 121.
[42] ibid 124.
[43] ibid 59–66.

The privatisation policy, known as 'shock therapy', was never formally approved by the parliament.

In the Supreme Soviet, which initially backed Yeltsin after the August 1991 coup, a strong opposition soon emerged. This anti-reform opposition can be seen as the 'incubator' of the 'authoritarian' interpretation. In 1992, it sent a clear signal by openly defying the President and declaring Khrushchev's 1954 transfer of Crimea to Ukraine illegal. A significant hub for this opposition was the National Salvation Front (NSF), dominated by figures such as Zyuganov, Lapshin, and Prokhanov.[44] The constitutional crisis of 1993 marked a watershed moment for subsequent discursive developments, accompanied by a radicalisation of the anti-reform movement which can be regarded as the birth of new illiberal conservatism. At the same time, the so-called 'liberals' demonstrated their willingness to use violence and other undemocratic means to achieve their objectives.[45] The unconstitutional dissolution of the parliament was followed by a temporary ban on the most important opposition parties. The new constitution granted the President significant powers while weakening the parliament.[46]

In his initial dealings with the newly named Duma (formerly the Supreme Soviet), the President struck a conciliatory tone, and relations between the Duma and Yeltsin were relatively peaceful in early 1994. Meanwhile, the moderate democratic opposition, the Civic Union, did not recover from the party ban, leaving the opposition dominated by the converging nationalist and communist forces.[47] The ongoing socioeconomic crisis did not subside but worsened in many respects: by 1994, industrial production had fallen to 51 per cent of its 1990 level. The recession and social crisis reached enormous proportions. Wages and pensions were often unpaid, GDP fell by 40 per cent, and male life expectancy dropped to levels last seen in the 1950s. Between 1992 and 1993, the Gini coefficient, a measure of social inequality, rose from 28.9 to 40.7. Large segments of the population became victims of either everyday or organised crime.[48]

The truce between the Duma and the government ended in April 1994, when the parliament decisively rejected the final wave of privatisations, which were then implemented by decree.[49] The Duma of 1993–95 (its first term was set for only two years) saw the emergence of popular ultranationalist politicians, such as Vladimir Zhirinovskiy and Konstantin Zatulin, and the outbreak of the first war in Chechnya. Zhirinovsky had won the election as head of the Liberal Democratic Party (LDPR) with 22 per cent of the vote. Overall, the first State Duma's political composition was highly fragmented, with numerous independent deputies. Despite his radical nationalist rhetoric, which would have fit well

[44] ibid 71 f.
[45] ibid 83–85.
[46] ibid 86–88.
[47] ibid 91 f.
[48] ibid 92 f.
[49] ibid 94.

within this environment, Zhirinovskiy did not join the NSF, dominated by the communists under Zyuganov.[50]

The post-voucher privatisation[51] in Russia was implemented through the 'loans-for-shares' model. In exchange for lending money to the state, bankers received shares of state-owned companies – primarily in the communications and raw materials sectors, along with access and favourable terms in later auctions, which allowed them to then fully acquire these enterprises. This process established the entrenched oligarchic structures that, in some cases, still exist today. Oligarchs like Boris Berezovsky also gained control over major media outlets, such as the ORT television channel. The combination of oligarchic wealth and media influence enabled Yeltsin to win the 1996 presidential election against all odds, despite having almost no chance of re-election at the start of his campaign.[52]

Gennady Zyuganov's Communist Party had won the 1995 parliamentary elections, and victory in the presidential election seemed assured. However, the new oligarchs financed Yeltsin's lavish campaign, which was supported by numerous celebrities and used the spectre of a communist return as a scare tactic. Berezovsky's control of ORT also turned the race into a smear campaign aimed at discrediting Zyuganov. Yeltsin's increasing shift towards 'authoritarian' memory politics can be explained by his desire to appeal to additional voters in this tough election.[53]

The establishment of Zyuganov's platform, the National-Patriotic Union (NPSR), during this campaign marked a crucial moment in the development of Russian illiberal conservatism. The discourse of the NPSR was influenced by elements of Russian conservatism from the nineteenth and twentieth centuries, Eurasianism, national communism, and the Christian Orthodox faith. What remained from Soviet communism, were its symbols, anti-Americanism, and the claim to great power status. Understanding this ideological amalgam is key to analysing the emergence of illiberal Russian conservatism. Although Yeltsin won the election, the financial crisis that followed shortly after deeply discredited both him and the 'liberal' faction, along with the economic reforms.[54]

The national-communist opposition then succeeded in having Yevgeny Primakov appointed as prime minister, who in turn tried to initiate a geopolitical reorientation of Russia.[55] This was the political environment in which Putin rose to power. Under his rule, the illiberal conservatives, whose ideas had first emerged in parliamentary opposition to Yeltsin's policies and economic liberalisation reforms, saw their ideology gradually become the state's official doctrine.

[50] Bluhm, 'Russland' (n 40) 95 f.

[51] Voucher privatisation was a privatisation method whereby citizens were given or could buy cheaply a book of vouchers representing potential shares in any state-owned company.

[52] ibid 99–103.

[53] ibid 104.

[54] ibid 104–17.

[55] ibid.

It is against this ideological backdrop that memory law-making proceeded in early post-Soviet Russia.

III. LEGISLATIVE DISCOURSE REGARDING 'REHABILITATION OF NAZISM' AND DECLARATIONS BY THE STATE DUMA IN 1990S–2000S

To examine memory law-making in the Russian parliament, the section covers the period from 1993 to 2014. The year 1993 signifies a juncture in Russian political history marked by the events of the violent dissolution of Russia's Soviet-era legislature. In a violent twist of events, President Boris Yeltsin (incumbent 1991–99) ousted the Supreme Soviet of the Russian Federation.[56] Subsequent elections to the State Duma in 1993 defined the main political constellation of the Yeltsin-era presidency, ranging between communists and pro-president parliamentarians in the new Russian legislature.

Constellations following the State Duma elections of 1999 and 2003 were similarly motivated with distinction between a major pro-presidential force and other parliamentary factions which were gravitating towards the major incumbent force in the mnemo-political field. The elections of 2007 marked the beginning of the period in which President Vladimir Putin's 'Yedinaia Rossiia' party has enjoyed an overwhelming majority in the parliament. As this chapter shows, aided by its political satellites in the mnemo-political field, the Liberal-Democratic Party of Russia (LDPR), the KPRF, and the 'Spravedlivaia Rossiia', the Yedinaia Rossiia' party defined the authoritative context of memory work as well as the content of the commemorative policy of the parliament.[57]

The institutionalisation of the Soviet war memory in post-Soviet Russia occurred in a sequence of major legislative acts in 1995 (these were: the Veterans Law, the Law on the Days of Military Glory, and the Law on the Perpetuation of the Victory of the Soviet people in the Great Patriotic War of 1941–45). The legislative history of these major laws and their role in institutionalisation of the Soviet-Russian approach to the commemoration of WWII has been discussed elsewhere already.[58] Yet, proper attention has not been paid to the politics of commemorative declarations in the 1990s and 2000s that became crucial for the moulding of historical discourse in the later periods, as well as the authoritarian view about the Soviet past enjoying a preponderant role in memory law-making.

The political rationale for commemorative declarations in the 1990s was often concerned with projecting Soviet-Russian war memory onto Russia's

[56] For broader political ramifications of the event, see: V Gel'man, 'Escape from Political Freedom: The Constitutional Crisis of 1993 and Russia's Political Trajectory' (2024) 50 *Russian History* 1, 1–20.

[57] V Gel'man, *Authoritarian Russia: Analyzing Post-Soviet Regime Changes* (University of Pittsburgh Press, 2015).

[58] Koposov, *Memory Laws, Memory Wars* (n 2) 220–37.

neighbours in the region – notably, Ukraine, Estonia and Latvia. By addressing separate developments in the neighbouring nations, the 'rehabilitation of Nazism' trope selectively reduces the dynamics of historical memories in the region to a simplified black-and-white narrative to exert a political backlash on Russia's neighbours. It should be noted that the interpretation of the memory of WWII expressed in the 'rehabilitation of Nazism' denies any possibility to address the Soviet totalitarian past. Hence in this authoritarian view, equating Soviet and Nazi totalitarianisms, and making suggestions about the repressive character of the conduct of the Soviet regime in Central-Eastern Europe is deemed revisionist and seen as trivialising Soviet victory over Nazism.

The legislative discourse about historical revisionist aspirations of former Soviet nations was introduced by leftist parliamentarians during the Boris Yeltsin era. With the passage of the 2000s and 2010s, legislative work on memory came increasingly under the oversight of the 'Yedinaia Rossiia' faction and its satellite party factions (KPRF and LDPR). The memory moguls of these party factions were, then, responsible for further developing the theme of 'rehabilitation of Nazim' in the late 2000s.

In the summer of 1998, parliamentarians of the 'Narodovlastie', a group affiliated with the KPRF at the time, prompted the State Duma to adopt a declaration addressing the Latvian authorities on matters related to WWII.[59] The declaration was prompted by the Duma committee on relations within the Commonwealth of Independent Nations (CIS), headed at the time by Vladimir Nikitin of the 'Narodovlastie'.[60] In the document, parliamentarians argued that political leaders in Latvia were engaging in the denial of the memory of the Soviet-led partisan movement against Nazis in the country. In particular, the parliamentarians were concerned with Latvia's decision to preclude veterans of the Soviet partisan movement from obtaining the requisite travel documents to travel to Latvia from Russia to take part in annual festivities dedicated to the movement's history. The voted declaration claimed that 'idealisation of the Nazi past' was occurring in the country due to the Latvian government's decision to commemorate the veterans of the 'Latvian SS', and alleged that it was actively 'forgetting of the results of the Second World War'.[61]

The mnemo-political consensus around the theme of historical revisionism originating in the discourse of the KPRF in the 1990s has travelled into subsequent legislative cycles of the State Duma. In April 2005, the Russian parliament adopted a declaration dedicated to the '60th Anniversary of the Victory of the Soviet People in the Great Patriotic War of 1941–1945' (that is, the Soviet-German conflict of WWII). This time, the impetus behind the

[59] State Duma of the Russian Federation, 1998, *O zabvenii itogov Vtoroi Mirovoi voiny rukovodstvom Latviskoi Respubliki* (2 July 1998).
[60] V Nikitin, 'Speech at the Plenary Session of the State Duma' (1 July 1998) Stenogramma zasedania 1 iuilia 1998.
[61] ibid.

commemorative declaration originated in the State Duma's committee on veterans' affairs, and was favoured by Yuriy Rodionov, the head of the committee from the 'Yedinaia Rossiia' faction.[62] The text of the declaration emphasised adherence by the Russian government to the protection of the memory of the 'Great Patriotic War', which was a common trope in the Putin-era memory law-making. Similarly to the KPRF-led declaration of 1998, it claimed that some nations in the former Soviet region had chosen to commemorate Nazi collaborators, thus, grossly trivialising and denying the significance of the Soviet Union's victory over Nazism. The vote on the declaration was supported by almost full memberships of all incumbent factions in the parliament, which at the time included 'Yedinaia Rossiia', KPRF, LDPR, and 'Spravedlivaia Rossiia'.

The same year, Russian parliamentarians continued with legislative work denying the mnemonic sovereignty of other nations in the region. In November 2005, the State Duma adopted a declaration blaming Estonia for 'neo-Nazi and revanchist aspirations'. The declaration was initiated by Russian parliamentarians on behalf of two parliamentary committees – the foreign affairs committee and the interparliamentary grouping on relations with the Riigikogu, the Estonian parliament. At the crux of the question was a legislative initiative by Estonian parliamentarians dealing with the monumental legacy of the Soviet Union in the territory of the Estonian republic.[63] The initiative concerned a ban on the erection of monuments dedicated to the occupation of Estonia (meaning the period of the Soviet rule over Estonia). From the perspective of Russian parliamentarians, the Estonian initiative was to be seen as aimed at the 'heroisation of fascism'[64] in the Baltic nation and not as a legitimate move by a sovereign nation to deal with the legacy of the Soviet totalitarian regime that occupied an independent nation in 1944–91. The passage of the Russian declaration relied on the votes of the 'Yedinaia Rossiia', LDPR, and 'Spravedlivaia Rossiia' factions.

In April 2011, the State Duma parliamentarians voted for a separate declaration devoted to the theme of historical revisionism. The LDPR faction, a 'Yedinaia Rossiia' satellite in the State Duma, initiated a declaration condemning the negative attitude towards the common historical past in the former republics of the Soviet Union.[65] The declaration originated in the workings of the committee on relations with the CIS, though this time headed by Aleksei Ostrovskiy of the LDPR faction.[66] The parliamentarians specifically addressed the governments of Estonia, Georgia, Latvia, and Lithuania in the declaration.

[62] Y Rodionov, 'Speech at the Plenary Session of the State Duma' (20 April 2005) Stenogramma zasedania 20 aprelia 2005 g., N95 (809).

[63] S Smirnova, 'Speech at the Plenary Session of the State Duma' (15 November 2006) Stenogramma zasedania ot 15 noiabria 2006 g., N193.

[64] ibid.

[65] K Zatulin, 'Speech at the Plenary Session of the State Duma' (22 April 2011) Stenogrammy obsuzhdenia proekta postanovlenia N526752-5.

[66] A Ostrovskiy, 'Speech at the Plenary Session of the State Duma' (22 April 2011) Stenogrammy obsuzhdenia proekta postanovlenia N526752-5.

They claimed a deliberate policy of the four nations aimed at 'derogatory expressions against the Russians, Russophobia ..., [and the] dissolution of monuments dedicated to Red Army soldiers involved in the liberation of these nations from the Nazi occupation'.[67] The passage of the declaration also relied on the political sponsorship of Konstantin Zatulin of 'Yedinaia Rossiia' – an influential 'memory entrepreneur' behind the politics of the Russian parliament of the 2000s and 2010s.[68]

The discourse surrounding the adoption of the declaration in speeches by parliamentarians was embodied in Russia's denial of the mnemonic sovereignty of former Soviet nations to address their Soviet past. In the debate preceding the adoption of the declaration, a plethora of historical arguments were put forward – all attesting to mnemo-militant stances regarding developments in the neighbouring nations. The claim was made that Russia should resist 'falsification of history' and that the Russian rule over other nations and territories historically was conducive to these nations 'greater self-determination'.[69] One of the main reasons given for the adoption of the declaration was the argument that former Soviet nations (especially Ukraine) were trying to diminish Russia's historical greatness in education and public discourse.[70] The political rhetoric and the content of historical argumentation pointed to the parliamentarians' reception of the authoritarian view of the Soviet past, that deemed revisionist any alternative views about the Soviet-era experiences by other nations.

In March 2012, the State Duma adopted a declaration on the impermissibility of 'rehabilitation of Nazism' in Latvia.[71] This time, the narrative of the rehabilitation of Nazism was explicitly put in the text of the declaration prompted by the 'Yedinaia Rossiia' faction.[72] The declaration condemned public events held in memory of the Latvian combatants on the German side during WWII which happened in Riga the same year. According to Russian parliamentarians, a memory policy to vindicate Nazi collaborators was adopted in Latvia, the purpose being to revise the results of the Nuremberg Tribunal that had condemned the forces of the Nazi SS and its affiliated units.[73] The declaration claimed that the Latvian authorities gave a 'tacit consent to rehabilitation

[67] Zatulin, 'Speech at the Plenary Session of the State Duma' (n 65).

[68] In the beginning of the 2010s, the initiative by Konstantin Zatulin and his affiliates in the State Duma became instrumental in developing the first version of Russia's punitive memory law of 2014, banning the 'rehabilitation of Nazism'. See Chapter 2 by Ilya Nuzov in this volume; also N Koposov, *Memory Laws, Memory Wars* (n 2) 260–68.

[69] ibid.

[70] Ostrovskiy, 'Speech at the Plenary Session of the State Duma' (n 66).

[71] State Duma of the Russian Federation, 2012, *O narusheniah prav cheloveka v Latviiskoi Respublike i nedopustimosti reabilitavii nazisma* (23 March 2012).

[72] A Pushkov, 'Speech at the Plenary Session of the State Duma' (23 March 2013) Stenogrammy obsuzhdenia proekta postanovlenia N40860-6.

[73] ibid.

of fascism and [revision of] the results of the Second World War'.[74] Thus, this declaration is a landmark as it demonstrates that the Russian legislative approach to the memory of WWII in the 2010s became narrowly concerned with conflating the interpretation of the war memory with official documents adopted by the Nuremberg Tribunal. This approach has resurfaced in the texts of Russia's full-fledged punitive laws, adopted in the mid-2010s, punishing historical speech (see Chapter two by Ilya Nuzov in this volume).

IV. CONCLUSIONS

The chapter has mapped out the evolution of legislative policy on historical memory from the Russian parliament by focusing on previously over-looked commemorative declarations. The chapter, first, positioned memory law-making in Russia in the milieu of memory scholarship demonstrating how the ideological backdrop of the Boris Yeltsin era parliament influenced Russia's dynamics of historical memory into the authoritarian era of Vladimir Putin. The chapter's key argument pertains to the ethical dilemma that lies at the core of law-making on historical memory in Russia – a dilemma which played out between the democratic and authoritarian views about the Soviet past in the Russian memory legislation. It pertains to the failure by Russia's political class in the 1990s to address the Soviet era in Russian history and to ensure a broad constituency for the democratic view of the Soviet past, its political viability and relevance in legislation and memory policy. The origins of this failure in the Russian case have been aptly summarised by Olga Malinova, who argued that:

> In Russia, the awareness that the destructive Soviet regime was a homegrown phenomenon made building a positive collective self-image somewhat problematic. Those attempts that have been made to find an external scapegoat for the shape of Russia's twentieth century tend to be based on conspiracy theories and a reluctance to confront the past honestly and openly.[75]

In this light, the legislative work in the Russian parliament concerning the claim of historical revisionism perpetrated by former Soviet nations became a convenient way for incumbent political elites not to deal with Russia's own totalitarian past. Since the late 1990s, Russian law-makers have introduced the 'rehabilitation of Nazism' trope in legislative work and discourse about WWII that reduces the dynamics of historical memories to a simplified claim about anti-Soviet revisionism happening in Russia's immediate neighbourhood. This interpretation of the memory of WWII denies any possibility to address the Soviet totalitarian past, as it ignores the repressive character of historical experiences of the Soviet

[74] State Duma of the Russian Federation, '*O narusheniah prav cheloveka v Latviiskoi Respublike i nedopustimosti reabilitavii nazisma*' (n 71).

[75] Malinova, 'Political Uses of the Great Patriotic War' (n 17) 44–45.

rule. For Russia, this interpretation externalises historical discussion about the Soviet past towards blaming Russia's neighbours for negative portrayal of Soviet-Russian experiences of WWII or the Soviet Union's conduct during the war, which is then used to equate Soviet discredit with Nazi veneration. The instrumentalisation of 'rehabilitation of Nazism' became particularly evident in the events of Russia's 2022 full-scale invasion of Ukraine, enshrined in the denial of mnemonic sovereignty of this nation (see Chapter three by Gleb Bogush in this volume).

In conceptual terms, Russia's case is emblematic of the notion of historical whitewashing, making that country's legislative discourse on historical memory comparable to other cases globally. The politics of whitewashing usually means efforts to eliminate certain historical events or periods from the historical narrative about the nation's past.[76] Equally, the concept refers to the personalisation of historical events and engagement in historical 'whataboutism', ie, precluding a historical inquiry by making disingenuous discursive arguments (based on conveniently selected facts) directed towards an interlocutor in an historical dialogue. In the literature, the politics of whitewashing is dependent on the lack of reflexive ethical engagement with the past.[77] The case of memory politics in Russia is about the country's failure to ensure the political viability of the democratic view of the Soviet past, which has led to detrimental consequences for Russian society, first, in the form of mnemonic repression at home, and soon after, in aggression against Russia's neighbours.

[76] Y He, *The Search for Reconciliation: Sino-Japanese and German-Polish Relations since World War II* (Cambridge University Press, 2009).

[77] ibid. See also: Dixon (n 7).

2

Memory Laws and Policies in Russia after the Annexation of Crimea and Occupation of Donbas

ILYA NUZOV*

I. INTRODUCTION

SOVIET HISTORY PERMEATES Russia's present to the extent that when a friend told me she had observed Lenin and Stalin get into a fistfight near the Red Square it didn't come as a surprise. Lurking between the Kremlin Wall, the State Historical Museum, souvenir shops and glitzy shopping malls, Soviet leader lookalikes often pose for pictures with tourists for a handout, especially around the time of the annual 9 May Victory Day Parade. But turf wars ensue when foreign tourists become scarce in Russia and local demand for kitsch does not make up for the shortfall, despite Stalin's soaring popularity. Indeed, since Russia's 2014 annexation of Crimea, the Soviet leader who oversaw international crimes including the Great Terror, or Great Purge (1936–38), *Holodomor*, or Ukrainian famine (1932–33), and the Katyń Massacre of Polish POWs (1940), has been viewed positively by Russians; more than half of respondents to a *Levada* poll viewed him favourably in 2016, whilst over 70 per cent held a similar opinion in 2019.[1] Most respondents attributed Stalin's popularity to his role in winning WWII, or the 'Great Patriotic War', as it is known in Russia. Conversely, acceptance of the view that Stalin was responsible for millions of murders committed during the Great Terror and as part of other Soviet crimes was almost 30 per cent lower in 2018 than in 2016.[2]

*The views expressed in this chapter do not represent those of the International Federation for Human Rights (FIDH), to which the author is affiliated.

[1] 'Stalin's Approval Rating Among Russians Hits Record High – Poll' (*The Moscow Times*, 16 April 2019): https://www.themoscowtimes.com/2019/04/16/stalins-approval-rating-among-russians-hits-record-high-poll-a65245.

[2] This figure having dropped from 62 to 44%. 'The Perception of Stalin' (*Levada Center*, 17 April 2018): https://www.levada.ru/en/2018/04/17/the-perception-of-stalin/.

These statistics are telling. During the period spanning 2014–21, the state has progressively monopolised historical memory, particularly the Soviet past, in order to pursue political objectives. Domestically, President Putin and the ruling political elites have seized on the mobilising potential of Soviet victory in WWII to consolidate Russians around a heroic collective identity. Politics of memory has served the current regime by legitimising these political elites as descendants of Soviet power structures and implementing policies to perpetuate their hold on power – for instance, by adopting constitutional changes allowing Putin to potentially serve until 2036. Historical memory policy has also been employed by Russia to ward off perceived threats to this identity stemming from abroad, to promote and justify irredentist policies,[3] and particularly to annex Crimea and other regions of Ukraine.

I argue in this chapter that to achieve these overarching political objectives, Russia has pursued a historical memory policy since 2014[4] that can be distilled into the following four aims: (i) to prioritise historical memory, particularly around victory in WWII, as a matter of both domestic and foreign strategic importance – including in matters of national security; (ii) to protect and selectively propagate Russia's principal historical narrative, which revolves around Russia's power, heroism and its special path; (iii) to downplay, obfuscate, deny or justify Soviet crimes against its own and other populations; and (iv) to persecute and stigmatise as enemies those that promote an alternative narrative or undermine the 'official' narrative.

Different policy-making tools have been employed by the Russian authorities to pursue these policy objectives. This chapter focuses primarily on legal measures that protect the dominant historical narrative and lay the ground for war propaganda, namely 'memory laws', though Russia has also

resorted to a slew of other methods. The legislative regulation of history has been accompanied by denial of access to Soviet-era archives, censorship, inculcation of patriotism through education, smear campaigns, intimidation against independent civil society actors, malicious prosecutions and other forms of judicial harassment of historians and civil society organisations like Yuri Dmitriev and International Memorial, respectively.[5]

At least until 2020 this historical memory policy was counter-balanced by meaningful efforts to pursue victim-centred mnemonic initiatives from Russia's

[3] The concept of irredentism describes a political and ideological movement aiming at unifying the nation by reclaiming (annexing) lost territories and populations. 'Irredentist claims intend to liberate from foreign control areas which are believed to belong to the motherland because of ethnic (Ethnicity) or linguistic ties, for geographical or historical reasons, or due to a previous possession', F Palermo in *Max Plank Encyclopedia of Public International Law* (2010): https://opil.ouplaw.com/display/10.1093/law:epil/9780199231690/law-9780199231690-e838.

[4] Here, the term refers to a set of techniques and methods by which political forces in power, using the administrative and financial resources of the state, seek to affirm certain interpretations of historical events as dominant.

[5] 'Russia: "Crimes Against History"' (*FIDH*, June 2021): https://www.fidh.org/IMG/pdf/russie-_pad-uk-web.pdf, 4–5.

civil society activists, like *Memorial*.[6] With the injection of new laws and the acceleration from 2020 onwards of the implementation of repressive measures aiming to stifle civil society and historical research, however, the formation of collective memory has fallen almost exclusively within the domain of state authorities. By the time of the full-scale invasion in February 2022, the focus had shifted to suppression of any undesirable historical expression and creation of a climate of intolerance and animosity against those with alternative viewpoints; Russia's civil society was unable to push back.

The case of International Memorial's liquidation is illustrative of the historical narrative that emerges from, and reinforces, the historical memory policy during this time period. On 28 December 2021, the Supreme Court of the Russian Federation heard the closing arguments of parties to an administrative proceeding initiated by the federal Prosecutor General against International Memorial,[7] Russia's leading non-governmental organisation specialising in truth-seeking, reparations and accountability for the benefit of victims of Soviet-era repressions. The Prosecutor General sought the NGO's liquidation for systematic violations of the so-called 'Foreign Agents' law,[8] one of Russia's most potent legislative measures of control, harassment and stigmatisation of Russia's civil society.[9] The case concerned International Memorial's failure to label a handful (amongst its thousands) of publications, in print and online, as items produced by a 'Foreign Agent'.[10]

Although the sole formal ground for liquidation was repeated violations of the non-labelling requirement, the politically motivated thrust of the lawsuit became evident during the Federal Prosecutor's closing remarks. He accused Memorial of engaging in activities that:

> are in fact primarily aimed at falsifying our country's history, at gradually *reformatting the collective consciousness* of the population from the *memory of victors* into

[6] Prior to their judicial liquidation, there were at least two Memorial organisations, collectively referred here as 'Memorial' – International Memorial (https://www.memo.ru/en-us/memorial/mission-and-statute/) and Human Rights Defence Centre 'Memorial' (https://memorialcenter.org/en).

[7] Known as, 'The International Historical Educational, Charitable and Human Rights Society "Memorial"', prior to its liquidation in 2022.

[8] 'Chronicle of a Death Foretold: The Liquidation of Legendary Human Rights Organizations in Russia' (*FIDH*, July 2022): https://www.fidh.org/IMG/pdf/fidh_chronicle_of_a_death_foretold_liquidation_of_memorials.pdf, 9.

[9] ECtHR, *Ecodefence and Others v Russia*, App nos 9988/13 and 60 others, Judgment 10 October 2022, paras 136, 159.

[10] In its original formulation, the Law required all NGOs receiving 'foreign funding' and engaged in 'political activities' to register with the Ministry of Justice as 'carrying out functions of a foreign agent' resulting in increased reporting obligations, audits and fines. Federal Law dated 20 July 2012 No 121-FZ 'On Introducing Amendments to Certain Legislative Acts of the Russian Federation Concerning Regulation of Activities of Non-Commercial Organizations that Perform Functions of a Foreign Agent'. The Law has resulted in over 800 entities and individuals, including human rights NGOs, journalists, activists and politicians, being added to the registry at the time of the writing of this article. Obtained from *OVD Info*: https://data-scripts.ovd.info/agents/?lang=en.

> one with a need to repent for the Soviet past ... It is obvious that Memorial, by speculating on the theme of political repression in the 20th century, is creating a false image of the Soviet Union as a terrorist state, whitewashing and rehabilitating Nazi criminals, who had the blood of Soviet citizens on their hands. ... Why should we, *descendants of the victors*, now be forced to sit back and watch rehabilitation of traitors to their Motherland and Nazi collaborators occurring with impunity? Why, instead of pride in our country, which won the terrible war and liberated the world from fascism, are we being encouraged to be ashamed and to repent, as it turns out, for our tenebrous past? (emphasis added).[11]

Having been made just two months prior to Russia's full-scale invasion of Ukraine, the statement is perfectly reflective of Russia's historical memory policy prevailing at the time with respect to the Soviet past. In the first place, it establishes a link between the past and the present by asserting the importance of historical memory of the Soviet past in the formation of Russia's present-day collective identity ('collective consciousness'). This identity is rooted in pride for the Soviet Union's victory in WWII – 'the terrible war' that 'liberated the world from fascism'. There is no room in this narrative for any actions of the Soviet Union that could cause Russians, 'descendants of the victors', 'to be ashamed' or 'repent'. Focusing on such actions, whether or not they are true, would amount to 'falsifications of history' because they would create a 'false image' of the Soviet Union as a 'terrorist state'.

The inescapable conclusion of this narrative is that one who tarnishes the Soviet past is likened to a Nazi collaborator, a traitor, a 'Foreign Agent'. By characterising International Memorial as being in the business of 'rehabilitation of ... Nazi collaborators' – a spurious allegation grounded only in the inadvertent inclusion of the names of three alleged WWII Nazi collaborators in International Memorial's database of over four million victims of Soviet political repressions[12] – the Prosecutor not only seeks to discredit the 2022 Nobel Peace Prize winner's achievements in the defence of human rights, he aims to portray these achievements as the very reason why the NGO should be viewed as a traitorous enemy of Russia. Russia's justice system was effectively signalling that if not for violations of the 'Foreign Agents' law, International Memorial must be punished for furthering justice for victims of Soviet crimes.

As aptly described by Andrii Neloliak and Paul Primbs in the previous chapter, Russia's historical memory policy since President Putin's second term in office has been built on policing interpretations of primarily the Soviet past. This was done in order to legitimise the ruling political elites – many of whom, like Putin, are former members of Soviet power structures – and to ward off any attempts to challenge the formation of Russia's identity around the sacrosanct WWII

[11] *FIDH*, 'Chronicle of a Death Foretold' (n 8) 9.

[12] N Sologub, 'Three errors amid millions of political repression victims' names. Nobel prize winner Memorial accused of "Nazism rehabilitation" in Russia' (*Mediazona*, 21 March 2023): https://en.zona.media/article/2023/03/21/memorial.

victory. In this chapter, I take stock of developments between 2014 and 2022 to show how Russia's historical memory policy has undergone a substantial evolution due to injection of new policies, particularly in the number of new 'memory laws'. Whilst it was at first a policy that was tempered by some victim-centred measures – albeit halfhearted and primarily defensive, focused on preserving the self-legitimisation and nation-building potential of 'mnemonic security' measures – by 2021 it had turned into a more offensive, purely political use of historical memory in order to create a climate conducive to the silencing or elimination of Russia's enemies.

More concretely, we will see from examples of memory laws and the chronology of their adoption – and to a lesser extent from the accompanying restrictions on access to archives, censorship, campaigns of persecution of 'memory producers', inculcation of patriotic education, and the creation of institutions to protect the overarching narrative – that Russia has created a climate where proponents of alternative viewpoints are stigmatised, harassed and intimidated, where propaganda of aggression by conflating the present and past has become possible. Since 2014 this policy has unleashed a mass campaign of human rights abuses against independent historians, journalists, activists and NGOs domestically, which by today's standards might amount to crimes against humanity. Furthermore, this campaign has underpinned the propaganda machine driving Russia's annexation of Crimea, its aggression and the perpetration of other international crimes against Ukraine.

II. HOW COLLECTIVE MEMORY INFLUENCES DOMESTIC AND FOREIGN POLICY

Historical memory policy can have an important impact on human rights and matters of international peace and security. This relationship hinges on the way that a nation's collective memory of past cataclysmic events is formed and expressed by historical narratives.[13] Domestically, if a state perceives that the 'official' historical narrative is threatened by other collective memory shaping-initiatives, such as those stemming from the grassroots levels, it might penalise historical expression and 'producers' of alternative historical viewpoints to ensure the inviolability of the state-endorsed narrative.[14]

With respect to foreign policy, states with unstable identities in the aftermath of a regime change or armed conflict often look for ways to secure a new state identity by aligning their historical narratives with their interests and

[13] See, eg BJ Steele, *Ontological Security in International Relations: Self-Identity and the IR State* (Routledge, 2008).

[14] M Mälksoo, 'Militant memocracy in International Relations: Mnemonical status anxiety and memory laws in Eastern Europe' (2021) 47 *Review of International Studies* 489, 505.

relationships in international relations.[15] Historical narratives are thus instrumental to a state's stability and continuity in the global order, and states might react strongly when they perceive that their vision of the past is threatened, misunderstood or assaulted by other states. In such cases, they might resort to so-called 'mnemonic security' measures like memory laws and, in extreme circumstances, physical force.[16]

What was the prevailing historical narrative in the years 2014–21 with respect to the Soviet past? In the previous chapter, Andrii Nekoliak and Paul Primbs have described the 'role of the cult of the Great Patriotic War' in the formation of Russia's collective memory.[17] They observed that the 'cult' of victory had become entrenched as the 'foundational myth' of modern Russia's collective identity well before 2014.

Despite Putin's obsession with WWII, which during the time period in question became nothing short of 'victorymania',[18] considering Russia's collective memory as built solely around the narrative of victory of WWII would be an oversimplification of the complex mechanism that can effectively underpin domestic and foreign policy decisions that range from criminalising 'Foreign Agents' to intervening militarily in Syria.

To understand the mobilising potential of historical narratives in pursuance of various policy objectives, sociologist James Wertsch suggests applying a 'schematic narrative template' rather than viewing the narrative in terms of a single theme, such as the 'Great Patriotic War'. Distilling the dominant narrative in Russia's collective memory to that of 'expulsion of foreign enemies', which can be manipulated at will, offers a clearer understanding of the myth's catalysing potential.[19]

In her recent book on politics of memory in Russia, Jade MacGlynn has gone even further, to define this schematic template as revolving around three broad arguments. Namely, that: (i) Russia needs a strong state; (ii) Russia has a special path of development; and (iii) it is a messianic great power with something unique to offer to the world.[20] She suggests that victory in the 'Great Patriotic War' underlies these overarching principles.[21] The victory might serve as a sort of pivot which impels the different narrative schemes, including that of an 'expulsion of foreign enemies', by often conflating the present and the past.

[15] M Mälksoo, '"Memory Must Be Defended": Beyond the Politics of Mnemonical Security' (2015) 46 *Security Dialogue* 221.

[16] ibid.

[17] N Koposov, *Memory Laws, Memory Wars: The Politics of the Past in Europe and Russia* (Cambridge University Press, 2018) 248–49.

[18] D Khapaeva, 'Memory purge: The amendment to the Constitution on "historical truth" finally kills free thought in Russia: there will no longer be another point of view other than the official one' (*Novaya Gazeta*, 17 June 2020): https://novayagazeta.ru/articles/2020/06/17/85880-zachistka-pamyati.

[19] JV Wertsch, 'The Narrative Organization of Collective Memory' (2008) 36 *Ethos: Journal of the Society for Psychological Anthropology* 120, 124.

[20] J McGlynn, *Memory Makers: The Politics of the Past in Putin's Russia* (Bloomsbury, 2023) 12.

[21] ibid.

We see this dynamic in play with respect to the war in Ukraine. During Putin's 'reunification of Crimea' speech on 18 March 2014, he justified the peninsula's annexation, citing a threat to the ethnic Russians and Russian speakers in Crimea stemming from encroaching Ukrainian 'nationalists, neo-Nazis, Russophobes and anti-Semites' and the 'ideological heirs of [Stepan] Bandera – Hitler's accomplice during the Second World War'.[22] It is difficult to judge just how much Putin regarded Ukrainians as posing a real threat to Crimeans rather than a threat to Russia's diminishing sphere of influence and righteous identity; nevertheless, the rhetoric device employed by Putin is grounded in an analogy with WWII and alludes to the need to repel the Nazi enemy.

The years 2014–21 saw a discursive shift to a more *offensive* use of historical narratives in Putin's politics of memory. What was, prior to 2014, a haphazard reliance on historical memory policy as a defensive identity-building and 'mnemonic security' measure, gradually turned into a concerted effort to cultivate an image of 'enemy' of those advocating a different historical interpretation of the Soviet period, one which focused on victims or Soviet crimes vis-à-vis its own citizens or other nations.

The fact that historical memory has become one of Russia's national security concerns is confirmed by numerous policy instruments and statements of Russia's political elites. Russia's 2014 Military Doctrine,[23] its 2015 and 2021 National Security Strategy, all refer to the need to counteract attempts at 'falsification of history', citing the need to defend 'historical memory as a strategic priority for the nation's security'.[24] These efforts have been accompanied by Putin's growing obsession with identifying and destroying modern-day 'collaborationists'. In the *National Interest* article titled 'The Real Lessons of the 75th Anniversary of World War II', he again presented the Soviet Union as the saviour of 'the entire world' and lamented ongoing attempts to 'equate liberators with occupants', regarding them as a 'betrayal of the ideals that united peoples in the fight against Nazism'.[25] On the eve of the adoption of Constitutional amendments – on 1 September 2020, the Day of Knowledge – when pupils resumed their studies, Putin condemned 'wartime collaborators' and charged those who distort history as modern-day equivalents of Nazi collaborators.[26]

[22] 'The Address of the Russian President of the Russian Federation' (*President of Russia*, 18 March 2014): http://kremlin.ru/events/president/news/20603.

[23] 'Military Doctrine of the Russian Federation' (*Rossiiskaia Gazeta*, 30 December 2014): https://rg.ru/documents/2014/12/30/doktrina-dok.html.

[24] Order of the President of the Russian Federation of 02.07.2021 No 400 on the Strategy for National Security of the Russian Federation' (2 July 2021): http://www.kremlin.ru/acts/bank/47046.

[25] V Putin, 'The Real Lessons of the 75th Anniversary of World War II' (*The National Interest*, 18 June 2020): https://nationalinterest.org/feature/vladimir-putin-real-lessons-75th-anniversary-world-war-ii-162982.

[26] 'The transcript of Putin's intervention during an open lesson: "To Remember means to know"' (1 September 2020): http://prezident.org/tekst/stenogramma-vystuplenija-putina-na-otkrytom-uroke-pomnit-znachit-znat-01-09-2020.html.

In addition to the 'historical framing'[27] of current political developments by referencing events from the past, the Russian authorities have employed a range of other measures to promote the historical memory policy and the overarching narrative. The imposition of administrative and criminal punishments for the 'incorrect' interpretation of historical events has served as a way to mould and augment the main narrative, 'chilling' opposing or victim-centred views of the past with dozens of 'show' prosecutions, including of notable political opposition leaders and human rights defenders.

III. THE CENTREPIECE OF RUSSIA'S HISTORICAL MEMORY POLICY – MEMORY LAWS

Memory laws play a key role in the formation of the 'correct' narrative, its legal protection, and the penalisation of alternative viewpoints. Depending on how 'memory laws' are defined,[28] Russia has adopted at least four such legislative measures between 2014 and Russia's full-blown invasion of Ukraine in February 2022.

During this time, Russia has been at the forefront of legal innovation with respect to the most nefarious types of memory laws: ones that 'exculpate' the state from grave human rights abuses while reinforcing national identity or another objective. These memory laws outright protect perpetrators affiliated with the state, or the state itself, from accusations of committing or facilitating international crimes, or more broadly protect the honour or good name of the state.[29] Elsewhere, I have also argued that Russia's memory laws form part and parcel of the propaganda of aggression and other speech crimes under international law.[30] Russia has perfected the art of offensive use of memory laws, or, 'militant memocracy'.[31]

Domestically, the enforcement of these laws has impeded the work of local NGOs that advance justice and seek reparations for victims of Stalinist and other Soviet-era atrocities, has led to the liquidation of International Memorial, resulted in dozens of prosecutions, chilled freedom of expression,

[27] McGlynn (n 21) 52.

[28] 'Memory laws' generally refers to laws governing the regulation of historical memory. For an overview of definitions, see e.g.: U Belavusau and A Gliszczyńska-Grabias (eds), *Law and Memory: Towards Legal Governance of History* (Cambridge University Press, 2017) 3. See also: Koposov, *Memory Laws, Memory Wars* (n 18) 253.

[29] See, eg U Belavusau and A Gliszczyńska Grabias, 'The Remarkable Rise of "Law and Historical Memory" in Europe: Theorizing Trends and Prospects in the Recent Literature' (2020) 47 *Journal of Law and Society* 325.

[30] I Nuzov, 'Legislating Propaganda: Russia's Memory Laws Justify Aggression Against Ukraine' (2022) 20 *Journal of International Criminal Justice* 805.

[31] Mälksoo (n 15) 505.

and contributed to attacks against holders of alternative viewpoints by private actors.[32] Internationally, these laws, and the rhetoric they help amplify, have also facilitated Russia's aggression by perpetuating a false rhetoric equivalency between the war Russia now wages in Ukraine and the Soviet Union's drive to liberate European territories occupied by Nazi Germany 80 years ago.

IV. SPECIFIC LAWS – REHABILITATION OF NAZISM (ARTICLE 354.1)

The memory laws adopted between the years 2014 and 2021 have established administrative or criminal liability for the expression of views about WWII that undermine the official narrative; ie, they protect the sanctity of the victory and the honour and reputation of the Soviet Union, including against accusations of its own responsibility for international crimes. The central tenet of this legal framework is Article 354.1 of the Criminal Code ('Rehabilitation of Nazism').

The original formulation of Article 354.1 ostensibly prohibited statements denying or glorifying the crimes of the Nazis, but it actually prohibited a much broader range of expression, including the negative commentary on the role of the Soviet Union in WWII, Russia's military history in general, and state symbols. Adopted just after Russia's annexation of Crimea in May 2014, the first paragraph of Article 354.1 criminalised: (i) 'denial of facts established by the judgment of the [Nuremberg] International Military Tribunal'; (ii) 'approval of crimes established by the said judgment'; and (iii) public 'dissemination of knowingly false information about the activities of the USSR during the Second World War'.[33] This offence was punishable by up to a maximum of three years in prison (Article 354.1.1.), or up to five years for statements made in an official capacity (Article 354.1.2.). Moreover, paragraph 3 of Article 354.1. criminalised the 'dissemination of information expressing manifest disrespect toward society regarding Russia's days of military glory and the commemorative dates associated with the defence of the Fatherland or public insults to the symbols of Russia's military glory'.[34]

The legislative history of the law is worth recounting. The initial bill was submitted to Russia's parliament by a group of deputies in the State Duma, the Lower Chamber of the Russian Parliament, back in May 2009.[35] The bill was met with widespread disapproval, including by the Cabinet of Ministers. It lay dormant for several years until it was revived, revised, and swiftly adopted in

[32] See, eg *FIDH*, 'Chronicle of a Death Foretold' (n 8), and *FIDH*, 'Russia: "Crimes Against History"' (n 5).

[33] Article 354.1. Penal Code of the Russian Federation, the original version, http://ivo.garant.ru/#/document/77307186/paragraph/264755760:0.

[34] ibid, Article 354.1.3.

[35] Explanatory note to the original Bill No 197582-5 on Amending the Criminal Code of the Russian Federation, https://sozd.duma.gov.ru/download/04956086-0E9A-4E6B-9B23-D0EB54F935BA.

May 2014 just after Russia's annexation of Crimea and the Maidan Revolution,[36] which was branded by Russia's official media as a 'fascist junta'[37] coup.

The enforcement of the law shows that its aim was not to counteract the alleged danger of the rise of Nazism, but to stem any critique of the Soviet Union. The first person convicted under Article 354.1 was Vladimir Luzgin, an auto mechanic from Perm, who was fined 200,000 Rubles (at the time roughly €2,800) in July 2016 for re-posting, on the popular Russian social networking site *vkontakte*, a link to an online article containing numerous assertions in defence of Ukrainian nationalist paramilitaries that fought during WWII.[38] The Nuremberg International Military Tribunal did not adjudicate on the crimes of Ukrainian nationalists, so the sole basis for Luzgin's conviction lay in the statement that unlike the Ukrainian nationalists, 'the Communists … actively collaborated with Germany in dividing Europe according to the Molotov-Ribbentrop Pact', and 'Communists and Germany jointly attacked Poland and started the Second World War on 1 September 1939!'.[39] Although these statements are factually accurate, as confirmed by the Soviet Union itself in 1989,[40] in 2016, Russia's Supreme Court ruled that they contained knowingly false information about the activities of the USSR during WWII, and were contrary to the Nuremberg Tribunal judgment. This was in spite of the fact that the latter never adjudicated on any aspect of the Soviet Red Army's invasion of Poland in September 1939.[41] Since 2017, Luzgin's case has been pending at the European Court of Human Rights.[42]

In the first five years of its implementation, prosecutions under Article 354.1 resulted in 25 convictions and only one acquittal.[43] The targets of prosecutions were usually persons of nationwide or local prominence, which ensured the resonance of such attacks. For instance, in 2019, Alekseĭ Volkov, coordinator for Russian opposition politician Alexei Navalny's Volgograd office, was convicted under Article 354.1 for posting several collages on social media in 2017 that showed the face of the Motherland Statue, commemorating the sacrifice of

[36] The Maidan Revolution or Ukrainian Revolution of February 2014 resulted in the ousting of the then President, Victor Yanukovych, who sought closer ties to Russia and rejected a political association with the EU. Widespread 'decommunisation' or de-Sovietisation of Ukraine followed.

[37] S Sokol, 'Russian Disinformation Distorted Reality in Ukraine. Americans Should Take Note'. (*Foreign Policy*, 2 August 2019): https://foreignpolicy.com/2019/08/02/russian-disinformation-distorted-reality-in-ukraine-americans-should-take-note-putin-mueller-elections-antisemitism.

[38] G Bogush and I Nuzov, 'Russia's Supreme Court Rewrites History of the Second World War' (*EJIL:Talk!*, 28 October 2016): https://www.ejiltalk.org/russias-supreme-court-rewrites-history-of-the-second-world-war.

[39] 'Supreme Court of the Russian Federation, appeal judgment of 1 September 2016, case No. 44-APU16-17, *Luzgin Vladimir Vladimirovic*': http://vsrf.ru/stor_pdf.php?id=1470274.

[40] 'Resolution of the Congress of People's Deputies of the USSR on the Molotov-Ribbentrop Pact of 9 September 1989': http://doc20vek.ru/node/3261.

[41] 'Supreme Court of the Russian Federation, appeal judgment of 1 September 2016, case No. 44-APU16-17, *Luzgin Vladimir Vladimirovich*': http://vsrf.ru/stor_pdf.php?id=1470274.

[42] *Luzgin v Russia* Application no 17942/17 (ECtHR, 26 September 2017).

[43] Official statistical data by the Judicial Department of the Supreme Court of Russia: http://www.cdep.ru/index.php?id=79.

Soviet soldiers during WWII, painted in green. The images were meant to call attention to an assault against Alexei Navalny – who has since been imprisoned and was likely murdered in captivity – by pro-Government activists using a green antiseptic dye (known as '*zelënka*'). The court ruled that Volkov had desecrated a military monument, although the statue itself had not been harmed in any way.[44]

In the same year, Konstantin Ishutov, an opposition blogger in Russia's Chuvash Republic, was convicted of two counts of 'Rehabilitation of Nazism' based on his posts on social media. Firstly, he had shared a 1941 German propaganda leaflet that promised Soviet citizens the restoration of private property and religious freedom in the event of a Nazi victory, commenting that 'the Third Reich had treated the Soviet people better than Putin treats Russians'. Secondly, he blamed the local authorities for abandoning a mass grave of German prisoners of war, and compared the treatment of mass graves and war memorials in Russia and Germany. The court found that he had 'downplayed the importance of the Soviet people's victory in the Great Patriotic War'.[45]

In addition to prosecutions, Article 354.1 has been used to threaten holders of opposing viewpoints. In 2015, Evgeniī Dzhugashvili, Joseph Stalin's grandson, requested that the authorities launch criminal proceedings under Article 354.1 against historian David Feldman, who had spoken on Russian television about the mass execution in 1940 of Polish prisoners of war by the Soviet authorities (the Katyń massacre).[46] This case appears to have been dismissed, but Feldman was not the only historian targeted for prosecution under Article 354.1. In November 2020, the Russian Military Historical Society (RMHS) – a government-sponsored institution – held a conference to deny the responsibility of the Soviet Union for the Katyń massacre. According to the final document of the conference, the historical consensus around Katyń 'should be considered as one element of a more general propaganda campaign to declare the USSR responsible for starting the Second World War'.[47] Reacting to the announcement of the conference, Alexander Guryanov, historian and head of the Polish Programme at International Memorial, wrote a letter to the conference organisers expressing his view about the responsibility of the Soviet Union for the war crimes at Katyń, and identifying the underlying political nature of the RMHS's conclusions. In response, conference delegates threatened him with Article 354.1 prosecution.[48] However, the Russian regulators didn't find

[44] M Krutov, 'Zelenka for the "Motherland." Penalty for "desecrating graves" in Photoshop' (*Radio Svoboda*, 15 March 2019): https://www.svoboda.org/a/29823414.html.

[45] 'Konstantin Ishutov sentenced to three and a half years in prison' (SOVA Center for Information and Analysis, 24 December 2019): https://www.sova-center.ru/misuse/news/persecution/2019/12/d41882.

[46] S Golubev, 'Looking for Excuses' (*Mediazona*, 15 May 2015): https://zona.media/article/2015/15/05/codex-354-1.

[47] A Gurianov and K Konoplianko, 'Military historical oblivion' (*Novaia Gazeta*, 10 December 2020): https://novayagazeta.ru/articles/2020/12/10/88317-voenno-istoricheskoe-bespamyatstvo.

[48] FIDH, 'Crimes Against History' (n 5) 10.

the restrictions encompassed by Article 354.1 sufficient to cover all undesirable historical expression. Major new 'memory laws' were introduced in 2020, including a Constitutional amendment.

V. MNEMONIC CONSTITUTIONALISM AND THE 2020 MEMORY LAWS

Russia's historical memory policy should not be seen in isolation from mnemonic initiatives of other states and international organisations which have contributed to destabilising Russia's 'mnemonic security'. In September 2019, the EU adopted a declaration 'on the importance of European remembrance for the future of Europe', which also placed responsibility for the breakout of WWII in equal parts on the Soviet Union and Nazi Germany.[49] The Resolution clearly targeted Russia's historical memory policy, including Article 354.1, and caused a vitriolic reaction inside Russia's highest political circles, including from Putin himself.[50]

The 2020 constitutional amendments were arguably one of the legislative responses to the EU Resolution. They were introduced by Putin on 15 January 2020,[51] only four months after the Resolution's adoption. Among the most significant provisions the amendments prioritised domestic law over international, institutionalised marriage as being only between a man and a woman, and annulled the current President's previous terms, allowing him to run for office again in 2024. Overall, the amendments introduced over 200 changes to 41 articles of the Constitution; yet soon after, on 11 March 2020, the State Duma adopted the draft amendments during the third and final reading. On the same day, these draft amendments were approved by the Federation Council.[52] On 14 March, President Putin signed the amendments into law, even though their official promulgation would be subject to the Constitutional Court's approval and a subsequent referendum, originally scheduled for the following month but postponed because of the outbreak of Covid-19. It ultimately took place between 24 June and 1 July 2020.[53]

[49] 'European Parliament resolution of 19 September 2019 on the importance of European remembrance for the future of Europe (2019/2819(RSP))': https://www.europarl.europa.eu/doceo/document/TA-9-2019-0021_EN.html.

[50] 'Putin shared his attitude towards the EU Parliament's Resolution on World War II' (*Izvestiia*, 20 December 2019): https://iz.ru/956706/2019-12-20/putin-rasskazal-o-svoem-otnoshenii-k-rezoliutcii-evroparlamenta-po-vtoroi-mirovoi-voine.

[51] 'Amendments to the Constitution: What did the President Propose?' (*TASS*, 15 January 2020): https://tass.ru/obschestvo/7526895.

[52] 'European Commission for Democracy Through Law (Venice Commission), Interim Opinion on Constitutional Amendments and the Procedure for their Adoption, Opinion No 992/2020' (*Venice Commission*, 23 March 2021): https://www.venice.coe.int/webforms/documents/default.aspx?pdffile=CDL-AD(2021)005-e.

[53] Law of the Russian Federation of 14 March 2020 on the Amendment to the Constitution of the Russian Federation 'On improvement of regulation of certain issues of organisation and functioning

On the eve of the voting, on the Day of Russia, President Putin gave a speech in which he drew attention away from the most politically sensitive amendments, for instance, the one which would allow him to stay in power for an additional 12 years after the expiration of his record fourth term in office. He focused on the need to enshrine 'historical memory' in the Russian Constitution as the main impetus behind the amendments.[54] Indeed, historical memory and the main tenets of the narrative encompassed in the Rehabilitation of Nazism would now become cemented in the nation's most important legal document. The Constitution now declared the Russian Federation as the 'successor' of the Soviet Union (Article 67.1 § 1) which 'shall honour the memory of the defenders of the Fatherland and shall defend historical truth. Diminishing the significance of the heroic feat of the people in defending the Fatherland shall not be permitted'.[55]

The amendments thus instilled some permanent protections of Russia's historical memory: firstly, the notion that Russia's past is necessarily 'heroic'; secondly, as is made clear by reference to the memory of the defenders of the Fatherland, the victory in the 'Great Patriotic War' officially became the cornerstone of this heroism and the 'historical truth' which the main law now aims to protect. Continuity with the Soviet Union, the sacredness of Soviet victory in WWII, and the state monopoly on history are among the foundations of Russia's political system today. Nevertheless, on 16 March 2020, the Constitutional Court ruled that the Law on amendment to the Constitution was in conformity with the Constitution, holding, in relevant part, that the new norm is: 'non-political … in character … and cannot be assessed, interpreted or applied as establishing a state or obligatory ideology' or undermining fundamental rights and freedoms.[56]

According to the Russian Government's response to the Venice Commission, which issued an interim and a final opinion on the amendments, the Constitutional provision on historical memory was intended to,

> suppress the rehabilitation of Nazism, and is in line with international obligations of the Russian Federation, notably the UN General Assembly Resolution 72/156 of 19 December 2017, which, inter alia, calls on states to take concrete measures to

of public authorities', No 1 – FKZ (14 March 2020): http://publication.pravo.gov.ru/Document/View/0001202003140001.

[54] 'Putin: most Russians support amendments to the Constitution' (*Kommersant'*, 12 June 2020): https://www.kommersant.ru/doc/4378170.

[55] 'Constitution of the Russian Federation': http://publication.pravo.gov.ru/Document/View/0001202007040001.

[56] Para 3, Conclusion of the Constitutional Court of the Russian Federation on the compliance with the provisions of Chapters one, two and nine of the Constitution of the Russian Federation of the provisions of the Law of the Russian Federation on the amendment to the Constitution of the Russian Federation 'On improving the regulation of certain issues of the organisation and functioning of public authorities', as well as compliance with the Constitution of the Russian Federation procedure for the entry into force of Article One of this Law in connection with the request of the President of the Russian Federation (16 March 2020): https://rg.ru/documents/2020/03/17/ks-rf-popravki-dok.html.

> prevent the denial of crimes against humanity and war crimes committed during the Second World War.[57]

Moreover, in arguing that the provision does not amount to a violation of freedom of opinion or expression, the Russian authorities underscored that 'the feat of the Russian people in defending the Fatherland is an objective fact and cannot be subject to revision'.[58]

Whilst the Venice Commission refrained from harshly criticising the new law in respect of these particular provisions, it remarked on the unusual nature of Constitutional provisions targeting matters of historical research.[59] The provision was also widely criticised by Russia's civil society and academics, particularly because the notion of 'historical truth' is often subjective, fluid and open to debate.[60] The norm's ambiguity thus makes it impossible to predict just what kind of conduct might be in violation of its elements. Moreover, the new norm must invariably interfere with freedom of expression, since it is impossible to 'diminish' the feat of the defenders without using some form of speech. Thus, the amendments would reinforce a 'chilling effect' on academic freedom, and would further restrict the space for historical expression, including research.

VI. NEW AMENDMENTS TO ARTICLE 354.1

As framing legislation with no sanctions specified, the updated Constitution merely provided an impetus for criminalising opposing viewpoints and 'legislating propaganda'. In September 2020, following Putin's 'Day of Knowledge' speech, where he denounced 'rewriters of history' as 'collaborationists of today',[61] Aleksandr Bastrykin, head of the Russian Federation's Investigative Committee, established a department dedicated to the 'investigation of crimes relating to rehabilitation of Nazism and falsification of history'.[62]

In November 2020, Bastrykin proposed new legislative amendments to toughen sanctions and expand the reach of Article 354.1, which were swiftly embraced by lawmakers. Irina Yarovaia, a Duma deputy who was the main protagonist behind Article 354.1 back in 2014, proposed new amendments to the law that would make 'Rehabilitation of Nazism' online an aggravated

[57] European Commission for Democracy Through Law (Venice Commission), Interim Opinion on Constitutional Amendments and the Procedure for their Adoption, Opinion No 992/2020, 23 March 2021, CDL-AD(2021)005: https://www.venice.coe.int/webforms/documents/default.aspx?pdffile=CDL-AD(2021)005-e.

[58] Venice Commission Opinion (n 57) 127.

[59] ibid 128.

[60] Crimes Against History (n 5) 99.

[61] 'People who cooperate with the enemy during a war are called and have always and everywhere been called collaborationists. *Those who agree with the re-writers of history can easily be called the collaborationists of today*' (emphasis added): 'Remembering is Knowing open lesson' (Kremlin, 1 September 2020): http://en.kremlin.ru/events/president/news/63983.

[62] 'A unit created in the Investigative Committee to investigate crimes of falsification of history' (*TASS*, 10 September 2020): https://tass.ru/obschestvo/9423583.

form of the crime, punishable by up to five years' imprisonment.[63] Secondly, the new law would introduce public liability for legal entities based on 'Rehabilitation of Nazism'.[64] In February 2021, Yarovaia proposed yet another amendment which would criminalise defamatory or denigrating statements about war veterans, punishable by up to five years' imprisonment.[65] The development was prompted by the then-recent court verdict against Alexei Navalny. He had been convicted of 'slandering' a Soviet veteran who was featured in a promotional video in support of the 2020 constitutional amendments. Navalny had described the people in the video as 'traitors' and 'corrupt lackeys'.[66] Yarovaia emphasised that the law would apply to statements not only about living but also deceased veterans. In March 2021, the Duma adopted the amendment.[67] All amendments to Article 354.1 proposed by Yarovaia officially became law on 5 April 2021.[68]

Thus, in its current version, Article 354.1 establishes two additional crimes: (iv) 'dissemination of information expressing manifest disrespect toward society regarding Russia's days of military glory and the commemorative dates associated with the defence of the Fatherland or public insults to the symbols of Russia's military glory', and (v) 'the insult of memory of the defenders of the Fatherland or degrading the honour and dignity of the veterans of the Great Patriotic War'. These additions practically outlaw any discussion of crimes committed by any Soviet servicemen and servicewomen during WWII, as well as critical statements or accusations of international crimes in relation to more recent conflicts, such as the war in Ukraine.

Russian civil society and international organisations have repeatedly denounced the 'Rehabilitation of Nazism' law as being contrary to international human rights and Russia's own Constitution, in as far as it violates freedom of expression.[69] Experts say Article 354.1 of the Criminal Code 'criminalizes the "wrong" views on Russia's Soviet-era history'.[70] While enforcement of the

[63] 'Bill No. 1050812-7 on Amending Article 354.1 of the Criminal Code of the Russian Federation': https://sozd.duma.gov.ru/bill/1050812-7.

[64] 'Bill No. 1050733-7 on Amending Article 3.5 and 13.5 of the Code of Administrative Offences of the Russian Federation': https://sozd.duma.gov.ru/bill/1050733-7.

[65] Interfax, *The Duma proposed to punish defamation of veterans with imprisonment of up to 5 years*, 24 February 2021: https://www.interfax.ru/russia/752288.

[66] 'Back In Court, Navalny Tells Russian Judge To "Stop Disgracing Yourself"' (*Radio Free Europe*, 12 February 2021): https://www.rferl.org/a/russia-navalny-veteran-slander-case/31098983.html.

[67] 'Bill No. 1050812-7 on Amending Article 354-1 of the Criminal Code of the Russian Federation': https://sozd.duma.gov.ru/bill/1050812-7.

[68] 'Federal Law dated 5 April 2021 No. 58-FZ': http://publication.pravo.gov.ru/Document/View/0001202104050008?index=3&rangeSize=1.

[69] 'The law on "Rehabilitation of Nazism" has been signed' (*SOVA Center for Information and Analysis*, 5 May 2014): https://www.sova-center.ru/misuse/news/lawmaking/2014/05/d29466; 'OSCE media freedom representative calls recent legislative initiatives in Russia potentially harmful to freedom of expression and freedom of the media' (*OSCE*, 26 June 2013): https://www.osce.org/fom/103121.

[70] Bogush and Nuzov (n 38).

law has affected not only historians but also political activists and laypersons, experts argue that the sweeping interpretation of Article 354.1 by courts and law enforcement authorities represents a very serious threat for history studies.

As of the time of writing of this chapter, over 120 cases have been initiated under Article 354.1 of the Criminal Code,[71] most of which have resulted in convictions, including for historically accurate statements regarding the Soviet Union's period of collaboration with Nazi Germany during WWII.

Even though International Memorial was not liquidated on the basis of 'Rehabilitation of Nazism' charges, those accusations, stemming from the inadvertent inclusion in the database of Soviet victims of political repression of three WWII Nazi collaborators,[72] were already being formulated during the liquidation proceedings, which were instituted under the 'Foreign Agents' Law.[73] On 28 December 2021, the Supreme Court of the Russian Federation ruled in favour of the lawsuit from the Prosecutor General's Office to liquidate International Memorial.[74] On 28 February 2022, the Presidium of the Supreme Court of the Russian Federation dismissed International Memorial's appeal, and the decision of the Supreme Court of the Russian Federation to liquidate International Memorial became final. Even though 'Rehabilitation of Nazism' was not formally charged during this trial, a series of subsequent prosecutions against individual members of Memorial were launched after Russia's full-scale invasion of Ukraine and will be addressed in the following section. In March 2023, on the basis of Article 354.1, Russia's Investigative Committee opened a criminal investigation against employees of Memorial, who have worked since the 1990s to commemorate victims of Soviet-era repressions.

VII. ANOTHER MEMORY LAW IN THE MAKING

As if neither the amended Article 354.1 nor the new constitutional provision was explicit enough with respect to the types of prohibited speech surrounding WWII, in May 2020, Aleksei Zhuravlev, a Duma deputy, proposed a new provision to the Law that would make it a crime to 'declare the USSR responsible for starting the Second World War', 'deny the leading role of the USSR in the victory over the Axis countries in the Second World War', or 'equate' Communism and Nazism.[75]

[71] Statistics compiled from https://ovd.info/.

[72] Sologub (n 13).

[73] *FIDH*, 'Chronicle of a Death Foretold' (n 8) 9.

[74] United Nations, 'Concluding observations on the fifth periodic report of China, CAT/C/EN/CO/5' (*United Nations*, 3 February 2016): https://tbinternet.ohchr.org/_layouts/15/TreatyBodyExternal/Download.aspx?Lang=en&symbolno=CAT%2FC%2FCHN%2FCO%2F5.

[75] 'Bill No. 963440-7 on Amending the Criminal Code of the Russian Federation': https://sozd.duma.gov.ru/bill/963440-7.

Another obvious response to the EU's September 2019 Resolution, which effectively equated the Nazi and Soviet totalitarian regimes,[76] the new law would expressly prohibit incorrect opinions putting into question the exorbitant human cost of the Soviet victory, Stalin's leadership – including cooperation with Hitler to divide Eastern Europe as foreseen by the Secret Protocol to the Molotov-Ribbentrop Pact – and the Soviet Union's atrocities against its own population and in the territories it occupied between 1939 and 1945, and since.

Despite its blatant infringement on freedom of expression, in January 2021, President Putin formally urged the Duma to adopt a law that would 'prohibit making public statements that equate the role of the USSR and fascist Germany during the Second World War (1939–1945),' consequently, a bill to that effect was formally introduced in the Duma on 5 May 2021.[77] A co-author of the law from the ruling United Russia party, Elena Yampol'skaia, explained the logic behind the legislation as a response to the recent attempts by Ukraine, Poland, and the Baltic States 'to slander the history of the Second World War and the Great Patriotic War' and, by extension, Russia's Armed Forces, who 'are fighting for the denazification and demilitarization of Ukraine'. 'When we fight these fakes', the lawmaker remarked,

> we are protecting the honor of our soldiers, and this is the least we can do for them. When we are fighting slander against the Great Patriotic War, we are defending the honor of our grandfathers and great-grandfathers, who can no longer stand up for themselves.[78]

The law was ultimately adopted as an amendment to the 1995 Federal Law 'On the commemoration of the Victory of the Soviet people in the Great Patriotic War of 1941–1945', prohibiting public comparisons of the 'goals, decisions and actions' of the leadership of the USSR with that of Nazi Germany, as well as the denial of the 'decisive role of the Soviet people in the defeat of Nazi Germany and the humanitarian mission of the USSR during the liberation of European countries'.[79] The implementing legislation for this law would ultimately be adopted in the form of an administrative offence. It would serve as a formidable addition to the arsenal of laws used to silence critics of Russia's aggression and other international crimes committed after its full-scale invasion of Ukraine on 24 February 2022.

[76] 'Joint Motion for a Resolution Resolution on the importance of European remembrance for the future of Europe: RC-B9-0097/2019' (*European Parliament*, 18 September 2019): https://www.europarl.europa.eu/doceo/document/RC-9-2019-0097_EN.html.

[77] Order of the President of the Russian Federation, List of Instructions Following the Meeting of the Council for Culture and Arts, 23 January 2021: http://www.kremlin.ru/acts/assignments/orders/64925; https://sozd.duma.gov.ru/bill/1166218-7.

[78] 'Punishment for equating the actions of USSR and Nazi Germany is introduced' (6 April 2022): http://duma.gov.ru/news/53971/.

[79] Federal Law of 1 July 2021 No. 278 – FZ, 'On the introduction of amendments to Federal Law "On the commemoration of the Victory of the Soviet people in the Great Patriotic War of 1941–1945"': http://publication.pravo.gov.ru/Document/View/0001202107010008?index=2.

VIII. OTHER MEASURES TO ADVANCE RUSSIA'S HISTORICAL MEMORY POLICY BETWEEN 2014 AND 2021

Memory laws have been effective in advancing the historical memory policy, primarily by protecting Russia's revisionist historical narrative and setting the proper framework in order to persecute and stigmatise as enemies those that promote an alternative narrative or undermine the 'official' narrative. But other measures have helped to accomplish these policy objectives.

In a comprehensive 2021 study of all acts of persecution against historians, activists or NGOs that work on commemorating the victims of Soviet-era atrocities, in other words, those whose work advances an 'alternative' historical narrative, the International Federation for Human Rights found a wide range of practices over the last decade that amount to systematic 'crimes against history'. This includes a crackdown on independent voices; the expulsion of independent historians from public institutions; malicious prosecutions; and condoning intimidation and violence by pro-Government non-state actors.[80] Laws other than 'memory laws', including anti-terrorism and hate speech prohibitions in the Criminal Code have also been used to target activists and historians.[81]

The prosecution of Yuri Dmitriev became an emblematic case. Since the 1990s, Dmitriev, head of a local Memorial office in Karelia, northwest Russia, has worked to uncover mass graves from Stalin's Great Terror, and to identify individual victims. In 2016, Dmitriev was arrested on charges of sexual misconduct and production of child pornography (under Articles 135 and 242.2 of the Criminal Code), based on several private photos of his adoptive daughter that he made to monitor her health, made fragile by years in an orphanage.[82] In July 2017, Human Rights Centre 'Memorial' concluded that the criminal case against Dmitriev was fabricated, recognising him as a political prisoner.[83] Dmitriev was acquitted in April 2018, only to be rearrested in June 2018 on charges of sexual abuse, which could send him to prison for between 12 to 20 years. In July 2020, Dmitriev was sentenced to three and a half years in prison, a sentence one quarter of the length recommended by the Criminal Code.[84] However, in September 2020, following an appeal by the prosecution, and in the absence of his lawyer, the appellate court increased his sentence to a draconian 13 years.

Smear campaigns and intimidation against independent civil society actors like Memorial, including from non-state actors, have also been common.

[80] FIDH, 'Crimes Against History' (n 5) 65.

[81] ibid 35–40.

[82] 'Russia must quash wrongful accusations against historian and human rights defender Yuri Dmitriev' (*FIDH*, 21 July 2020): https://www.fidh.org/en/issues/human-rights-defenders/russia-must-quash-wrongful-accusations-against-historian-and-human.

[83] 'On the Yury Dmitriev Affair' (*Memorial*, 20 January 2020): https://www.memo.ru/en-us/texts/yury-dmitriev-affair/.

[84] ibid.

In 2016, members of the radical National Liberation Movement attacked the participants and jury attending the awards ceremony for 'A Person in History. Russia – Twentieth Century', International Memorial's all-Russia annual historical school essay competition.[85] The attackers verbally abused the attendees and assaulted some of them with eggs and '*zelënka*', including the head of the jury, prominent Russian novelist Liudmila Ulickaia.[86]

Practices of censorship have likewise been prevalent by making it impossible to publish research on certain undesirable topics, like collaborationism with Nazi Germany, and through media propaganda broadcasting the regime's meta-narrative through the establishment of patriotic institutions – including the RMHS and the Russian Historical Society – inculcating a patriotic vision of the past.[87] For instance, in July 2020, shortly after the approval of the amendments to the Constitution, Russia's Parliament adopted President Putin's bill on the inculcation of patriotism. The new version of the Federal law titled 'On Education' mandates that educational institutions inculcate in their students, 'the sense of patriotism and civil consciousness, respect towards the memory of the Homeland's defenders and courageous acts of the Homeland's heroes'.[88]

At the same time, Russia has done its utmost to downplay, obfuscate, deny or justify Soviet crimes against others and its own populations. This has been accomplished by restricting access to archives relating to Soviet crimes and various forms of censorship. Almost 30 years after the collapse of the Soviet Union, and after a brief period of relatively open access to archives regarding Soviet state terror, the authorities continue to keep secret most of the historical records of the Soviet security services.[89] This policy seriously hampers the work of historians and NGOs who document the Soviet Union's human rights violations and international crimes.

IX. CONCLUSION

During Putin's tenure as Russia's President, Russia's identity has become more deeply rooted in the Soviet past and the depiction of the USSR as a just and heroic state that has banished Nazism. If, prior to 2014, Russia's historical memory policy was aimed primarily at securing this identity in order to consolidate Russians around Soviet achievements, Russia's zeal for sanitising history to prove exclusive heroism and Soviet victimhood became nothing short of obsessive by 2021.[90]

[85] FIDH, 'Crimes Against History' (n 5) 89.
[86] ibid.
[87] ibid, 4.
[88] Article 2 of the Federal Law 'On Education' as amended by the Federal Law dated 31 July 2020 No 304-FZ.
[89] FIDH, 'Crimes Against History' (n 5) 50–57.
[90] McGlynn (n 21) 2.

The increasing need to protect and police the enforcement of the meta-narrative arose firstly because of the growing instability of Putin's regime domestically. Following the 2011–12 mass protests against mass election fraud and corruption all over Russia, and then again after the diminishing euphoria of 'reunification' with Crimea, the state needed to find something of an ideological compass to offer to a constituency growing increasingly weary of the political, social and economic course undertaken by the country. On the other hand, the regime's 'mnemonic' security' was threatened by the changing geopolitical alignment of Ukraine and worsening relations with the West, which in turn has challenged and undermined Russia's vision of itself.

The singularly most significant event – the bedrock of Russia's great power status – victory in WWII, provides a justification and motivation for Russia to pursue both its internal and foreign policy objectives. Consequently, any challenges to Russia's status as a righteous, victorious state and a liberator, could damage its political ambitions and sense of identity.[91]

Russia thus needed to reassert its identity in order to justify domestic repressions and aggressive foreign policy. The historical memory policy has been employed to further these overarching objectives by better promoting and protecting the historical narrative that emphasises Russia's power and uniqueness, and its dominant role in the post-Yalta world order, especially in the Soviet sphere of influence.[92] At the same time, the policy sought to minimise communist crimes, and perhaps most significantly since at least 2014, the policy also aimed to cast anyone undermining or opposing it in any way as Russia's 'enemy', laying the ground for domestic repressions, aggression propaganda and other international crimes.

The historical memory policy was somewhat ambivalent between the years 2014 and 2020, with some meaningful victim-centred initiatives tolerated, even supported. Indeed, in 2015, the Government adopted the Policy for the Memorialisation of Victims of Political Repression.[93] As part of that policy, the authorities maintained official remembrance institutions, funded state museums, and created memorials. Subsequent to its adoption, Russia sponsored the construction of the new GULAG museum in Moscow, and erected new memorials such as the Wall of Grief.[94]

However, even in this mildly repressive period, the state made no effort to investigate Soviet-era atrocities, or to name those responsible for the grave

[91] I Torbakov, 'The Past as Present: Foreign Relations and Russia's Politics of History' in S Eliaeson, L Harutyunyan and L Titarenko (eds), *After the Soviet Empire: Legacies and Pathways* (Brill, 2016) 358–80.

[92] N Koposov, '"The Only Possible Ideology": Nationalizing History in Putin's Russia' (2022) 24 *Journal of Genocide Research* 205, 211.

[93] 'Directive to Confirm the Attached "Policy of the Russian Government No. 1561-p, About the Memorialization of Victims of Political Repression"' (15 August 2015): http://static.government.ru/media/files/AR59E5d7yB9LddoPH2RSlhQpSCQDERdP.pdf.

[94] FIDH, 'Crimes Against History' (n 5) 107.

atrocities committed by the Soviet regime. Given that Soviet state crimes were sanctioned by the country's top leadership, doing so would mean condemning the entire Soviet regime, and, by implication, would shake the foundation of the current regime, which portrays itself as the Soviet Union's successor, and whose leader is a former KGB officer. The authorities instead embraced politically neutral, innocuous actions, such as the decision to erect anonymous monuments like the aforementioned Wall of Grief, installed in 2017 in an unremarkable Moscow location, away from the notorious headquarters of the former Soviet security services. The issues of accountability and remedies play no part in the official narrative. In addition, the state tolerates and increasingly supports the once-marginal negationist and revisionist views that are now prevalent among pro-Government conservative groups.

Russia's significant grassroots memorial efforts to commemorate victims of these and other Soviet crimes have been systematically marginalised, giving the state the unhindered ability to whitewash the Soviet past. Today this narrative rejects any attempts to portray the Soviet Union as an aggressor or occupying power, responsible for international crimes like the intentional starvation of Ukrainians during the 1932–33 *Holodomor*, the deportations of Lithuanians, Latvians, Poles, Chechens and Crimean Tatars to GULAGs, the execution of Polish prisoners of war in Katyń and other international crimes in the USSR and territories it controlled.[95] The 'zero tolerance' policy towards any aspersions cast against the Soviet past is necessary in order to conflate the past and the present, to justify the ongoing aggression and the annexation of Ukrainian territories.[96]

[95] For a thorough account of these, see, e.g.: T Snyder, Bloodlands: Europe Between Hitler and Stalin (Basic Books, 2010).

[96] I Nuzov, 'The Dynamics of Collective Memory in the Ukraine Crisis: A Transitional Justice Perspective' (2017) 11 *The International Journal of Transitional Justice* 132.

3

Putin's Memory Policies in the Context of Military Aggression in Ukraine

GLEB BOGUSH

I. INTRODUCTION

As shown in the preceding chapter, the Putin regime's memory politics were instrumental in providing a pretext for Russia's full-scale aggression against Ukraine and legitimising the use of military force since 2014. The manipulation of history played a crucial role in formulating the agenda that ultimately led to the aggressive actions of the Putin regime. Putin's narratives of collective memory have become increasingly radical, and his apparent obsession with Ukraine has become a central element in Russia's conception of history. Denial of the very possibility of independent Ukrainian statehood, assertions of the artificial character of Ukrainian identity and culture, and the old idea of Russia as a 'besieged fortress' all played a direct role in the fateful decision to invade the neighbouring country.

As Putin's war of aggression progresses, memory politics and memory legislation have been used to promote the objectives of the aggression, in particular to assert Russia's 'historical' right to occupy part of the territory of Ukraine. The imposition of historical narratives, reinforced by the state's repressive policies, has contributed to the 'defensive consolidation' of a significant part of the Russian population, which has been provided with irrational 'historical' arguments to circumvent uncomfortable questions and contradictions. At the same time, punitive memory laws have been used as an additional tool against political opposition and anti-war resistance. Contamination of Russian collective memory with essentialist historical myths[1] presents one of the serious obstacles to the peaceful settlement of the conflict and the democratic transition of Russia. With these sentiments in mind, this chapter analyses the steps taken by

[1] Essentialism in history as a field of study entails discerning and listing essential cultural characteristics of a particular nation or culture. Sometimes such essentialism leads to claims of a praiseworthy national or cultural identity, or to its opposite, the condemnation of a culture based on presumed essential characteristics.

Putin's regime in the period following the full-scale invasion of Ukraine in the sphere of memory policy and legislation.

II. MEMORY POLITICS AS A TOOL IN FULL-SCALE AGGRESSION

Putin's regime memory politics have been used as a key tool in preparing, initiating, and waging the war of aggression against Ukraine. Russian 'Ukrainian policy', in its more radical version, has been largely driven by promoters of a very specific version of Russian history, such as Vladimir Putin's advisor and alleged ghost-writer, Vladimir Medinskiĭ.[2]

From the outset, Russia's aggression has been justified based on the abusive instrumentalisation of historical memory.[3] Putin's narrative suggests that Ukraine as an independent state has become, at least since 2014, 'anti-Russia' and, thus by its very existence, represents a threat to the Russian state. This narrative portrays any independent Ukrainian statehood as having an 'anti-Russian character'. The image of Russia as a 'besieged fortress', the notion that Russia was a 'victim' of the Cold War, and the 'geopolitical catastrophe' that Putin sees as the collapse of the USSR, have been imposed on a large part of Russian society through propaganda and manipulation.

According to the official Kremlin version, which also served as a putative legal justification, Putin was forced to attack Ukraine to prevent an imminent threat to Russia and the 'people's republics' of Donbas.[4] At the same time, 'geopolitical' grounds were put forward based on historical perceptions of the threat posed by the very existence of an 'artificial' Ukrainian state, at least in Putin's view. The idea of subjugating Ukraine by various means (including through open military force, political and economic control, and even dismemberment of the state) was based on a bizarre historical picture of the 'historical Russia'.

Putin's article on the 'historical unity of Russian and Ukrainian people',[5] published in July 2021, has been widely perceived as part of a preparation campaign for launching a large-scale invasion of Ukraine. The article itself was a compilation of historical myths and poorly supported ideas about the development of modern Ukraine, premised on the denial of Ukrainian independent statehood and a separate *national* identity. In the article, Putin explicitly

[2] M Zygar, 'The Man Behind Putin's Warped View of History' (*The New York Times*, 19 September 2023): https://www.nytimes.com/2023/09/19/opinion/putin-russia-medinsky.html.

[3] Leading historians of genocide, Nazism, and World War II called the 'historical' justification of Putin's military aggression a 'cynical abuse of history' See I Tabarrovsky, 'Statement on the War in Ukraine by Scholars of Genocide, Nazism and World War II' (*Jewish Journal*, 27February2022):https://jewishjournal.com/news/worldwide/345515/statement-on-the-war-in-ukraine-by-scholars-of-genocide-nazism-and-world-war-ii/.

[4] 'Address by the President of the Russian Federation' (*President of Russia*, 24 February 2022): http://en.kremlin.ru/events/president/news/67843.

[5] 'Article by Vladimir Putin "On the Historical Unity of Russians and Ukrainians"' (*President of Russia*, 12 July 2021): http://en.kremlin.ru/events/president/news/66181.

stated: 'We will never allow *our historical territories and people* close to us living there to be used against Russia' (emphasis added).[6] In essence, the article is a collection of arguments, which, in a more articulated form, were used to justify the decision to invade Ukraine in 2014.

By order of the Russian Minister of Defence, all Russian armed forces members were sent Putin's article for mandatory study. Putin's spokesperson, Dmitry Peskov, said that the article is 'an important conceptual document' and therefore it is 'completely natural that the armed forces are studying it'.[7] It is unlikely, however, that the Ministry of Defence undertook such an initiative *proprio motu*. Modest Kolerov, the ultraconservative publicist, posted a commentary accompanying Putin's article entitled 'Putin will not give up either Crimea or the Donbas. And this is only beginning'.[8] Kolerov recalled the 'political testament' of Putin's former superior in St Petersburg, Mayor Anatoliĭ Sobchak, to see a return to a 'Ukraine with the borders of 1922'.[9]

Putin himself detailed the immediate reasons for the full-scale invasion in his televised addresses on 21 and 24 February 2022. These speeches contained a large number of references to history, historical injustice against Russia, and the 'betrayal' of Russia by the West. The central gist of Putin's narrative is symbolically codified in the '*denazification* of Ukraine' war aim. In making this argument, Putin transposed linguistic tropes associated with World War II (WWII) onto the current geopolitical situation, accusing Ukrainian 'Nazis' of committing 'genocide'[10] in the Donbas and claiming that Kyïv was planning a '*Blitzkrieg*' against separatist enclaves in the Donbas with the support of Western powers.

Putin went even further in his second address,[11] when he equated the United States and NATO to Nazi Germany, referencing Stalin's failed attempts at appeasing Hitler and vowing that 'we will not make this mistake a second time'. The connection between the past and present could not have been more explicit: 'Your fathers, grandfathers, and great-grandfathers', Putin emphasised, 'did not

[6] Putin repeatedly claims that the occupied Ukrainian territories are 'historically Russian', so, according to his logic, they should belong to Russia.

[7] *Regnum News Agency*, 'Peskov: Study of Putin's article in the Russian Armed Forces is quite understandable' (*IA Regnum*, 16 July 2021): https://regnum.ru/news/polit/3324032.html.

[8] M Kolerov, 'Putin will not give Crimea or Donbas to Ukraine. And this is just the beginning' (*IA Regnum*, 12 July 2021): https://regnum.ru/news/polit/3319975.html.

[9] There was no 'political testament' by Sobchak, who mysteriously died during Putin's first presidential campaign in 2000. However, there were some, primarily oral, statements in which Mr Sobchak referred to the status of Crimea as being a part of Ukraine as a 'joke' and considering the existence of Ukrainian armed forces to be threatening to Russia. (Anatoliĭ Sobchak's Interview, *RTR TV*, 8 January 1992): https://www.youtube.com/watch?v=JkmP4mZnDIA.

[10] The reference to genocide as justification for the military attack constitutes a significant part of the subject-matter in the Russia-Ukraine dispute before the International Court of Justice.

[11] The address of Putin of 24 February 2022 (frequently referred to as a 'declaration of war speech') was submitted as an annex to Russia's Article 51 Notification to the UN Security Council, S/2022/154.

fight the Nazi occupiers and did not defend our common Motherland so that today's neo-Nazis could seize power in Ukraine'.

The invasion of Ukraine was preceded by a long period of whipping up hysteria around the issue of Ukraine and the threat of its entry into NATO. The history-laden rhetoric that preceded and accompanied Russia's February 2022 invasion of Ukraine illustrates the salience of these arguments. Indeed, Putin's framing of the incursion in the language of WWII demonstrates just how much Russia's leadership believes such analogies are persuasive.[12]

'Denazification' has become one of the officially stated goals of Putin's aggression. It is based on unsupported claims regarding the 'Nazi' character of the Ukrainian authorities. In reality, denazification, despite the Kremlin's awkward efforts to explain it, was about regime change in Kyïv, and the de facto dismantling of Ukrainian statehood and identity. In a notorious article by Kremlin publicist Timofeĭ Sergeĭcev, which is still displayed on the website of the state-run *RIA Novosti* news agency, denazification is defined, among other things, as 'de-Ukrainisation'.[13]

Legal scholars supporting the Putin regime have proposed expanding the punitive mechanism and introducing special 'denazification' norms into Russian legislation. Professor Leonid Golovko, of Moscow State University, offered in his article in the journal *International Affairs* a 'legal concept of the denazification of Ukraine', placing particular emphasis on the use of memory laws such as the 'rehabilitation of Nazism'.[14] In other words, denazification is understood by this lawyer primarily as the punishment of people with 'wrong' historical attitudes that 'deny' the 'right' interpretation of WWII.

Russian propaganda actively uses clichés and narratives based on the memory of WWII when covering the war in Ukraine. Russian state bodies and media portray individual units of the Ukrainian army as Nazi or 'Banderite' units. Support for the Ukrainian nation-state is thus absolutely equated by propaganda with collaboration with the Nazis. The Ukrainian military is usually referred to as 'Nazi' or 'nationalist'. Occupation of Ukrainian cities and towns were exposed by propaganda as 'liberation' from the Nazis. Thus, the historical memory of the WWII is actively used not only to justify the war but also to commit crimes against prisoners of war and the civilian population.[15]

As the investigation by the UN Independent Commission of Inquiry shows, the Russian armed forces constantly use the rhetoric of denazification and derogatory language when committing crimes, including torture, in the occupied

[12] F Krawatzek and G Soroka, 'Putin's Home Front: A War on Time' (*PONARS Eurasia Policy Memo No 784*, 11 July 2022): https://www.ponarseurasia.org/putins-home-front-a-war-on-time/.

[13] T Sergeĭcev, 'What Russia should do with Ukraine?' (*RIA NOVOSTI*, 3 April 2022): https://ria.ru/20220403/ukraina-1781469605.html.

[14] L Golovko, 'Denazification of Ukraine: The Need of Forming a Legal Mechanism' (*International Affairs*, 1 December 2022): https://interaffairs.ru/jauthor/material/2758.

[15] See: J Friedrich and N Masuhr, 'Why Is Russia Being So Brutal in Ukraine?' (*Global Public Policy Institute*, 23 May 2022): https://gppi.net/2022/05/23/why-is-russia-being-so-brutal-in-ukraine.

territories of Ukraine.[16] The designation of Ukrainians as Nazis, in fact, seemingly gives Russian soldiers a licence to commit all kinds of atrocities with the promise of impunity.

Historical references accompany the criminal prosecution of Ukrainian prisoners of war captured in the occupied territories of Ukraine in violation of the provisions of the Geneva Convention on Prisoners of War. They are accused of Nazism and 'extermination of the civilian population', with prosecutors using numerous clichés from the vocabulary of WWII.[17]

III. PUTIN'S WARTIME MEMORY POLICY

The full-scale invasion of Ukraine did not significantly change the Putin regime's memory policies but represented a pivotal moment in terms of their *radicalisation* and impact on society. Under the new political and legal framework, there is no alternative to acquiescence to the official historical narrative. Succumbing to Putin's views on history is now expected of all Russian subjects.[18] The state has fully embraced a somewhat bizarre version of history and placed it under full statutory protection with no dissent allowed.

The narratives of collective memory have been used intensively throughout the entire campaign. In its public discourse, Putin's Russia actively uses the method of 'mirror accusations' while using the categorical and rhetorical apparatus of war-crimes trials based on the memory of WWII. These narratives have been projected onto actual warfare situations, especially in the occupied territories.

In his speech at the military parade on the occasion of Victory Day, on 9 May 2022, Putin directly presented his war on Ukraine and the West as a continuation of the 'Great Patriotic War': 'There is no place in the world for executioners, punishers, and Nazis'. Putin described Russia's invasion of Ukraine as a 'pre-emptive response' to NATO actions, which he described as aggression and as fuelling false histories of prior wars.[19]

[16] UN Human Rights Office of the High Commissioner, 'A/HRC/52/CRP.4: Conference Room Paper of the Independent International Commission of Inquiry on Ukraine' (29 August 2023): https://www.ohchr.org/en/documents/reports/ahrc52crp4-conference-room-paper-independent-international-commission-inquiry, paras 489, 523.

[17] M Koroleva, 'More than 200 Ukrainians Tried in the Occupied Territories' (*Justice Info*, 8 February 2024): https://www.justiceinfo.net/en/128240-200-ukrainians-tried-occupied-territories.html.

[18] Putin's spokeperson Peskov admitted the existence of the state censorship, prohibited by the Russian Constitution, 'at the time of war': '"Unacceptable pressure": Kremlin denounces US for targeting Russian media' (*Al Jazeera*, 6 September 2024): https://www.aljazeera.com/news/2024/9/6/unacceptable-pressure-kremlin-denounces-us-for-targeting-russian-media.

[19] R Dixon et al, 'On Victory Day, Putin defends war on Ukraine as fight against "Nazis"' (*The Washington Post*, 9 May 2022): https://www.washingtonpost.com/world/2022/05/09/russia-victory-day-putin-speech-ukraine/.

The central state-founding myth of the 'Great Patriotic War' has continued to be strengthened. Russian officials have freed themselves from the previous unofficial ban and now speak approvingly of Stalin. In practice, the 'rehabilitation' of the Molotov–Ribbentrop Pact started a long time before the invasion of Ukraine.[20] The Kremlin even deemed the deal with Hitler a 'diplomatic achievement'. However, after the invasion, to stop any embarrassment, the Kremlin openly embraced the Stalinist version of WWII history.[21]

Rehabilitation of Stalinism extends beyond the events of WWII. In June 2024, the Russian government changed the 'Concept for Perpetuating the Memory of the Victims of Political Repression' (the Concept), which had been in effect since 2015.[22] The amended document removed the term 'mass' to characterise the repressions in the USSR. It also included a statement that the amnesty of 1955 led to 'the rehabilitation and whitewashing of Nazi accomplices and traitors to the Motherland who served in the Baltic, Ukrainian, and other punitive units'. With some specifics removed from the document, the Concept now refers to vague notions such as 'national interests', 'strengthening traditional spiritual and moral values', and the need to protect society from 'destructive information and psychological influence'.[23]

Following that, in September 2024, the Prosecutor General's Office published a draft order according to which certain decisions on the rehabilitation of victims of Soviet repression were to be reviewed and reversed. This move by the Prosecutor General's Office is astonishing, as it has been the body responsible for rehabilitation decisions since 1991, and persons responsible for grave crimes were, in principle, not eligible for rehabilitation. It seems that the goal of the authorities is not only to discredit the very idea of rehabilitating the victims of Stalinism but to downplay the mass repression in the collective memory.[24]

Another critical pillar of Putin's concept of memory is the continuity of the Russian Federation, Soviet Union, and Russian Empire. In Putin's imagination, those states are the same country and even the same state, with the narrative of the unity of the Soviet Union and Russia, and Russia as a legal continuator of the Soviet Union, even shared by the majority of legal scholars. The idea of continuity with the Soviet Union, and in a more subtle way, with the Russian Empire, has become an absolute imperative for the Russian regime. It is also

[20] On quite a notable exhibition in 2019, see: A Roth, 'Molotov-Ribbentrop: why is Moscow trying to justify Nazi pact?' (*The Guardian*, Moscow, 23 August 2019): https://www.theguardian.com/world/2019/aug/23/moscow-campaign-to-justify-molotov-ribbentrop-pact-sparks-outcry.

[21] See, eg 'Foreign Minister Sergey Lavrov's interview with Channel One's The Great Game political talk show, Moscow' (*The Ministry of Foreign Affairs of the Russian Federation*, 10 March 2023): https://mid.ru/en/press_service/minister_speeches/1857681/.

[22] Order of the Government of the Russian Federation No 1564-r dated 20 June 2024: http://publication.pravo.gov.ru/document/0001202406210044?ysclid=m0zex4tgk3140847481&index=1.

[23] O Romashova, 'Repress posthumously' (*Mediazona*, 13 September 2024): https://zona.media/article/2024/09/13/re-repression.

[24] G Sova, 'De-rehabilitation of victims of mass repression' (*OVD-Info*, 16 September 2024): https://ovd.info/2024/09/16/derehabilitation?amp.

strongly connected with the idea of Russia as 'a country-civilization', which Putin repeatedly propagates and proclaims in doctrinal documents.

An apparent 'manifesto' of this new historical policy is a new textbook on modern Russian history (since 1945) for secondary schools, authored by the former Minister of Culture and current Presidential Adviser, Vladimir Medinskiĭ. This textbook contains a one-sided view of history with a distinct imperialistic character.[25] To elaborate, the history of Russia, including the Soviet period, is presented as exclusively positive and peace-loving. This textbook reflects the general direction of Russia's educational policy, which is already being implemented in the occupied territories of Ukraine.[26]

The narrative of history spelled out in the textbook is also exclusively militaristic. The expansion of the territory justifies any crimes, even if they lead to vast 'collateral damage' for Russia itself. A disproportionately large amount of attention is devoted to Ukraine. According to the new Russian 'official' history, Ukraine does not have a tradition of independent statehood, and it has no cultural identity independent of Russia. Contrary to scientific data, it is claimed that the Ukrainian language has a very recent history and owes its origin to the 'Polonisation' of the 'southern Russian' lands. Despite the absence of any scientific support, this theory has become dominant in Russian discourse.

Putin's vision of memory has also shaped an openly anti-European vector in Russia's foreign policy. There is no acceptable alternative to the assertion of the civilisational uniqueness of the country. Putin himself, as is well-known, previously held somewhat different ideas about the place of Russia in the world, considering it an integral part of Europe and European civilisation. Now, the idea of a country-civilisation has no alternative. This was finally enshrined in the Foreign Policy Concept approved in March 2023. It proclaimed Russia a unique 'country-civilization' and officially approved the concept of the 'Russian world' without clear geographical boundaries.[27]

The memory policy has a distinct external dimension, especially with respect to post-Soviet states and Eastern Europe. One manifestation of this policy was the aggressive reaction to dismantling Soviet-era monuments in the Baltic states as well as in other states of Central and Eastern Europe. It was precisely such episodes that became the basis for Russia initiating a criminal case against Estonian Prime Minister Kaja Kallas and putting her on the wanted

[25] M Ilyushina, 'Russia's new history textbooks teach Putin's alternate reality' (*Washington Post*, 13 August 2023): https://www.washingtonpost.com/world/2023/08/13/russia-history-textbook-revision-ukraine/.

[26] R Dixon, 'Russia sending teachers to Ukraine to control what students learn' (*Washington Post*, 18 July 2022): https://www.washingtonpost.com/world/2022/07/18/russia-teachers-ukraine-rewrite-history/.

[27] 'The Concept of Foreign Policy of the Russian Federation' (*The Ministry of Foreign Affairs of the Russia Federation*, 31 March 2023): https://mid.ru/en/foreign_policy/fundamental_documents/1860586/.

persons list – ignoring the personal immunity of heads of government – along with other officials of these states (the norm of the Russian Criminal Code on the 'rehabilitation of Nazism' (Article 354.1) was used as a legal basis for this action).[28]

Putin's regime continues today to try to 'manage' history by pseudo-legal means, again based around WWII as the foundation. In particular, Russia recognises certain crimes of the Nazis during their occupation of Soviet territories as 'genocide of the Soviet people'. This practice of managing history began long before 2022 but has taken on a unique dynamic and been widely covered in the recent press. In 2023, one of the prestigious St Petersburg International Legal Forum panels was even dedicated to this topic. To date, decisions on the recognition of 'genocide against the civilian population of the USSR' have been made by eight Russian regional courts: Novgorodskaia oblast′, Pskovskaia oblast′, Stavropol′skiĭ kraĭ, Rostovskaia oblast′, Volgogradskaia oblast′, Krasnodarskiĭ kraĭ, Kareliia, and the occupied Crimea.

In July 2023, the Smolensk Regional Court, at the request of the Prosecutor's Office, was asked to recognise as

> war crimes and crimes against humanity, genocide of the peoples of the Soviet Union, established and newly revealed crimes committed by the Nazi invaders in the territory of the Smolensk region occupied in the period from July 1941 to September 1943.[29]

In these reports, it is emphasised that,

> archival documents and materials on the facts of the mass extermination of the civilian population by the German invaders and accomplices, natives of Ukraine, Poland, the Czech Republic, Austria, and France, who were distinguished by particular cruelty in their reprisals, have been studied.

It is remarkable that the Court's decision to accept the request placed a particular emphasis on the activities of the collaborators, who, operating on the territory of Soviet Russia, were allegedly distinguished by exceptional cruelty, in comparison with the German Nazis themselves – precisely corresponding to the propaganda and statements of Putin himself, who, in the course of a conversation with religious leaders, said that the Holocaust in Ukraine was carried out mainly by local nationalists, and not at all by the SS Einsatzgruppen.[30] This, despite the post-war Nuremberg trials having firmly established the central role of the SS in the massacres.

The most recent and remarkable case, however, is the one of wartime 'genocide' in Kareliia and other occupied territories of the Soviet Union, considered by the

[28] 'Wanted in Russia. Mediazona scraped and analyzed the entire Ministry of Internal Affairs' wanted database – and developed a user-friendly search tool' (*Mediazona*, 13 February 2024): https://en.zona.media/article/2024/02/13/wanted-trl.

[29] 'Statement of the Prosecutor General Office of the Russian Federation' (19 July 2023): https://epp.genproc.gov.ru/web/gprf/mass-media/news?item=89096117.

[30] 'Putin said that the Banderites and collaborators in Ukraine killed 1.5 million jews' (*TASS*, 5 September 2023): https://tass.ru/politika/18661207.

Supreme Court of Kareliia. The judgment rendered on 1 August 2024, recognised as fact that,

> the crimes committed by the German fascist invaders and the occupation authorities and troops of Finland on the territory of the Republic of Kareliia during the Great Patriotic War from 1941 to 1944 against at least 86 thousand Soviet citizens, constituted genocide of national, ethnic and racial groups representing the population of the USSR.[31]

Such judicial decisions in response to 'administrative claims', made under the rules of civil procedure by judges who do not specialise in criminal law, are aimed at judicial confirmation of Putin's historical narratives and even correction of the 'insufficiently harsh' Soviet version of the history of WWII. From the point of view of international criminal law, both the judicial recognition of facts in the absence of judicial decisions on individual criminal responsibility and the classification of genocide against the rather dubious group of 'peoples of the Soviet Union' look doubtful. It is unclear which peoples are being referred to and whether those 'peoples' constituted a protected national group within the meaning of the 1948 Convention on the Prevention and Punishment of the Crime of Genocide.

It is not also easy to understand the practical need for such solutions. It seems that they are intended to consolidate further the one-sided and uncritical picture of a WWII in which Russia is solely a victim. In addition, a line of identification between Russia and the USSR, with appropriation of the former, has been developed. In general, the current practice of the application of the norms of genocide by states is somewhat contradictory: states often use this norm in order to assert their national myth, part of which is the perception of their status as victims. For this reason, ideas about history that contribute to forming and consolidating corresponding ideas about the past are embedded in the representations.

To a certain extent, these processes support the Soviet practice of attempting a sophisticated relativisation of the Holocaust: as is known, Jews were called 'peaceful Soviet citizens' in official Soviet historiography. Nevertheless, the Soviet authorities never made a serious attempt to designate the events of WWII on the territory of the USSR as genocide. Rather, the Soviet narrative was exceptionally one-sided and included viewing people of the USSR as the primary victims of the Nazis, although the Soviet version of history did not view these events through the lens of genocide.

The idea to recognise the policy of the Nazi occupiers as a 'genocide of the Soviet people' is a well-thought-out and clever strategy that exploits the lack of understanding in Western discourse of the tragedies of Soviet citizens during WWII. Although the idea of the genocide of the Soviet people has a shaky

[31] 'Finnish Prime Minister assesses genocide court ruling in Kareliia' (4 August 2024): https://www.rbc.ru/politics/04/08/2024/66af4bdb9a79475a3c39a25f.

foundation and is at odds with the understanding of this crime developed in international law, Russian authorities and propaganda have pushed it into court decisions to widely demonstrate the 'continuity' of the 'pan-European policy of genocide against Russia and Russians'.[32]

Although the manipulation of history is being used to indoctrinate the Ukrainian population under Russian occupation, the primary target audience and object of these manipulations is the Russia's own population.[33]

IV. MEMORY CRIMINAL LAW

As already noted, Russia's memory policy and legislative framework existed, and were applied, long before the full-scale invasion of Ukraine. However, the application of these laws has escalated to the extent that criminal repression has become a key tool in memory politics. Memory criminal laws, such as the one on 'rehabilitation of Nazism', are playing a significant role in the repression of Russian civil society and any anti-war resistance.

Simultaneously with the full-scale invasion of Ukraine, the state launched a repressive policy against anti-war protest and any dissent in general. Almost immediately after the invasion, laws were passed criminalising speech questioning the goals, objectives, and methods of Vladimir Putin's 'special military operation'. The Russian legislature passed a series of administrative and criminal laws designed to prevent the dissemination of 'deliberately false information' about the armed forces, which includes referring to the war in Ukraine as anything but the aforementioned 'special military operation'. Likewise, they criminalise supporting Western sanctions and prohibit the 'discrediting' of the military or other state organs operating beyond the country's borders.

Repressive criminal laws were passed regarding spreading 'fakes [fake news] about the armed forces' and 'discrediting the army'. As a matter of principle, they represent the same type of 'false speech' legislation as the law on the rehabilitation of Nazism or false equivalences. Despite their secondary role, the number of criminal cases on the rehabilitation of Nazism has increased noticeably: 23 new criminal cases were opened in the first six months of 2023 alone.[34] The increase in the number of cases has also affected various regions. Although most of the cases so far have dealt with insulting monuments and symbols

[32] O Boldyrev, 'Dig down to a verdict: Why does the Investigative Committee need genocide cases from WWII?' ('Dokopat' do verdikta: zachem Sk nuzhny dela o genocide Vtoroĭ mirovoĭ?') (*BBC News Russian Service*, 12 January 2021): https://www.bbc.com/russian/features-55486566.

[33] I Nuzov, 'Legislating Propaganda: Russia's Memory Laws Justify Aggression Against Ukraine' (2022) 20 *Journal of International Criminal Justice* 805.

[34] UN Human Rights Office of the High Commissioner, 'A/HRC/54/54: Situation of human rights in the Russian Federation Report of the Special Rapporteur on human rights in the Russian Federation, Mariana Katzarova' (15 September 2023): https://www.ohchr.org/en/documents/country-reports/ahrc5454-situation-human-rights-russian-federation-report-special.

rather than with historical dissent, the current 'revisionist' case illustrates the general nature of Russia's 'memory legislation': any statement contradicting the 'state point of view' is potentially criminally punishable. The wording of Russian legislation, and most importantly, the peculiarities of its law enforcement, make the issue of criminal repression extremely arbitrary and dependent on the authorities.

The case of Ivanovo architect Sergeĭ Volkov is an illustrative example. Volkov was fined two million Roubles (roughly 20,000 Euros) in September 2023 as a result of a second jury trial (the first jury panel was dissolved during deliberations) for making critical statements regarding Stalin's policy during the siege of Leningrad. In his statements, it is impossible to find any rehabilitation of Nazism, a denial of the crimes of the Nazis, or even a specific description of the crimes of the Soviet army (which can be deemed 'manifestly false' according to Article 354.1). Despite its controversial nature, the statement about the war for which Volkov was convicted did not contain any information about specific facts. Moreover, he in no way denied the siege of Leningrad; he merely *assessed* the policy. An examination of Volkov's case found that his 'publications contradict the "scientific paradigm of the Great Patriotic War in Russian historiography"'. Thus, according to the conclusions of the Russian authorities, contradicting the 'paradigm' is prohibited and entails criminal liability.[35]

Volkov's case illustrates the pattern of Russian memory legislation well. Contrary to the doctrine of criminal law – which requires specificity about information that is regarded as false – in practice, Russian courts punish evaluative negative statements about the policy of the Soviet leadership during the war, such as statements that Stalin was responsible for the outbreak of WWII. Under these conditions, the linguistic expert examination of the author's specific statements is paramount. As a rule, such examinations are carried out by expert institutions controlled by the authorities and by individual experts. In all cases, the courts agree with their findings. Such a system eliminates the independent role of the court in evaluating statements, which leads to entirely arbitrary law enforcement and the punishment of anyone who appears on the authorities' radar. The current system makes it possible to recognise virtually any statement about the history of WWII as representing the 'rehabilitation of Nazism'. As in the case of the new legislation on the persecution of anti-war dissidents, the courts in practice do not, contrary to the law, tend to establish the intent to 'rehabilitate Nazism'.

Another illustrative case is that of Mikhail Belousov, a historian and lecturer at St Petersburg State University. He was dismissed from the university for his negative public stance against the glorification of aggression. Belousov was denounced for the messages written by him and his students against

[35] 'The jury found a resident of Ivanovo guilty of rehabilitating Nazism. He wrote about the siege of Leningrad' (*OVD-Info*, 12 July 2023): https://ovd.info/express-news/2023/07/12/prisyazhnye-priznali-zhitelya-ivanova-vinovnym-v-reabilitacii-nacizma-pisal.

the backdrop of mourning for St Petersburg State University student Fëdor Solomonov, who had died in Ukraine. A case was subsequently commenced against Belousov and considered by the St Petersburg State University Ethics Commission.[36] As a result of this, in mid-June 2023, the university administration expelled seven of Belousov's students. The case against Belousov under the article on 'discrediting' the Russian army, however, was dismissed due to the expiration of the statute of limitations. Later, a criminal case was opened against Belousov on charges of rehabilitating Nazism. According to the Russian Investigative Committee, Belousov denied any connection between Hitler's racial theory and the course of the 'Great Patriotic War'. Belousov said he saw signs of the falsification of history in some topics about the 'Great Patriotic War'. However, it was impossible to discuss this due to it being punishable by law.[37] Belousov's case illustrates the auxiliary role that memory legislation plays in prosecuting anti-war dissent.

In March 2023, the Investigative Committee of the Russian Federation opened another criminal case against employees of the liquidated Memorial Society under Article 354.1 on 'Rehabilitation of Nazism'. The initiation of this case was based on 'suspicions that Memorial included in the lists of repressed persons those people who collaborated with the fascist occupiers during the Great Patriotic War'. The investigators believed that several Memorial employees equated collaborators with victims of political repression and knowingly disseminated false information about the activities of the USSR during WWII using the media, a mistake Memorial corrected.

Prison sentences for the 'rehabilitation of Nazism' also began to appear. For example, in Krasnoiarsk, activist Igor′ Orlovskiĭ was sentenced by a regional court for the 'rehabilitation of Nazism' and spreading 'military fakes' to seven and a half years in prison, two of them based on the former charge. The reason for the prosecution under the article on the rehabilitation of Nazism was a comment he made that compared the political courses of Hitler and Stalin before WWII, stating, 'Stalin was just as much an aggressor as Hitler'.[38] Among other victims of the 'rehabilitation of Nazism' provision was Alexei Navalny, who was convicted under the most recent version of the article, criminalising false statements about the veterans of WWII, amongst other 'crimes'. The grotesque charge, in a certain way, contributed to the killing of the opposition politician within the Russian prison system.

[36] St Petersburg University, 'On the decision of St. Petersburg State University Ethics Commission about the actions of Mr. Belousov': https://spbu.ru/news-events/novosti/o-reshenii-komissii-po-etike-spbgu-po-voprosu-o-deystviyakh-m-s-belousova.

[37] Official site of the Investigative Committee of the Russian Federation *Kommersant*: 'A criminal case has been opened against an ex-docent of St Petersburg State University "on rehabilitation of Nazism"': https://sledcom.ru/press/smi/item/1805157.

[38] 'The Krasnoiarsk resident was sentenced to 7.5 years for anti-war posts, taking into account the previous sentence' (*OVD-Info*, 13 December 2023): https://ovd.info/express-news/2023/11/13/krasnoyarca-prigovorili-k-75-godam-za-antivoennye-posty-s-uchetom.

On the personal instruction of Vladimir Putin,[39] the 2021 legislation prohibited statements equating Nazism and Stalinism and denying the decisive role that the Soviet people played in countering the Third Reich and the 'humanitarian mission of the USSR in the liberation of European countries'.[40] Although it provides for 'just' an administrative punishment, such punishment may include heavy fines as well as 15 days' detention.[41]

A liberal politician, Leonid Gozman, has become perhaps the most well-known victim of this new provision. He was sentenced to 15 days' detention for his 2020 Facebook post, in which he mocked the Russian legislation that banned linking the Soviet Union to Nazi Germany, saying that 'it is wrong to put an equal mark between them – Hitler was an absolute evil and Stalin even worse'. By 'worse', Gozman meant that, unlike Hitler, Stalin predominantly destroyed his *own* country's population. In the 'offending' post, Gozman criticised the Russian authorities' desire to write into law the very ban he now stands accused of violating: the ban on comparisons between the Soviet Union and Hitler's Germany. He wrote,

> [Actually,] in this case, I want to express support: they cannot be compared. Hitler was an absolute evil, but Stalin was even worse. The SS were criminals, but the NKVD were even more terrible because the Chekists murdered their own. Hitler unleashed a war against humanity; the communists declared total war against their own people.[42]

Gozman had left Russia when the campaign started, but returned in June 2023 in what he described as a 'moral' choice. The Russian Ministry of Justice listed him as a 'foreign agent', a description that carries a solidly pejorative meaning and implies additional government scrutiny. Police briefly detained him in July after the Russian Ministry of the Interior issued a warrant for his arrest while investigating a criminal case against him. Gozman's case is remarkable, as he was convicted for criticising the very provision under which he was charged.

As practice shows, these provisions were used as a 'backup' for the persecution of anti-war and opposition figures. The secondary role of Article 354.1 on the rehabilitation of Nazism against the backdrop of the mass persecution of anti-war activists explains why there has been no increase in the number of convictions for this particular crime.[43] Andrii Nekoliak and Elizaveta Klochkova note that

[39] 'Putin supported the idea to ban comparing actions of USSR and Nazi Germany' (*Kommersant*, 27 October 2020): https://www.kommersant.ru/doc/4549480.

[40] Federal Law 'On Amendments to the Federal law "On Memorialization of the Victory of the Soviet People in the Great Patriotic War of 1941–1945"' № 278-FZ of 1 July 2021, https://rg.ru/documents/2021/07/06/fz278.html.

[41] Federal Law 'On Amendments to the Code of Administrative Offences' № 103-FZ of 16 April 2022.

[42] 'Russian politician Leonid Gozman arrested for calling Stalin "worse than Hitler"' (*Meduza*, 29 August 2022): https://meduza.io/en/news/2022/08/30/russian-politician-leonid-gozman-arrested-for-calling-stalin-worse-than-hitler.

[43] A Golubeva, 'Criminal Cases on Rehabilitation of Nazism in Russia: Authorities' Attempt to Get Rid of Discussions about the Past' (*Ugolovnye dela o reabilitacii nacizma v Rossii: popytka*

> [w]hile cases involving Article 354.1 [of the Russian Criminal Code] present a fraction of a larger number of cases to prosecute anti-war dissent, they provide an important insight in the operation of the criminal justice system and memory politics in Russia.[44]

Nevertheless, the role of these norms in the overall strategy of the Putin regime should be considered. They have perpetuated the existing trend of restricting freedom of speech in memory politics. Along with other norms, the 'rehabilitation of Nazism' has been used to stigmatise the political opposition, along with accusations of 'betrayal' manifested in protests and disagreements with Putin's decisions to attack Ukraine.

V. REPRESSIONS AGAINST ORGANISATIONS AND INDEPENDENT HISTORIANS

Repressive actions have also been launched against organisations. Following Memorial, Russia also liquidated the SOVA Center for Information and Analysis, which used to carry out research and monitor developments relating to countering extremism, including the application of memory laws.[45] The Free Historical Society, an association uniting independent historians, also had to cease its work. This organisation had been subject to a coordinated campaign of slander for a long time before that decision.

Furthermore, several historians and writers have been declared 'foreign agents' and have been forced into exile in other countries. The most recent case of such 'academic repression' includes the dismissal of Ivan Kurilla, a well-known independent critical historian,[46] from the European University in St Petersburg.

Any meaningful international discussion with global partners, including academic discussion, has thus become impossible. Along with the established censorship, it has been deemed essential to declare almost all Western countries (in particular, the EU Member States, the United Kingdom, Norway, the United States, Canada, and Japan) 'unfriendly'. A growing number of organisations, including universities (Central European University), thinktanks (Chatham House), and scientific associations, such as the German Association for East European Studies (DGO),[47] have been declared 'undesirable' and even 'extremist' organisations; cooperation with them is criminalised.

vlasti izbavit'sia ot diskussiĭ o proshlom) (*BBC News Russian Service*, 15 March 2023): https://www.bbc.com/russian/features-64967805.

[44] A Nekoliak and E Klochkova, 'Weaponizing Russia's Memory Law: On Russia's Mnemonic Dissidents' (*Verfassungsblog*, 11 July 2023): https://verfassungsblog.de/weaponizing-russias-memory-law/.

[45] Sova Research Center, 'About the liquidation of the Sova Centre and our further work' (17 August 2023): https://www.sova-center.ru/about-us/nashi-slozhnosti/2023/08/d78342/.

[46] 'Americanist Ivan Kurilla has been fired from the European University in St. Petersburg' (*Kommersant'*, March 2024): https://www.kommersant.ru/doc/6553034.

[47] 'DGO Declared an "Undesirable Organisation" in the Russian Federation' (Zentrum für Osteuropa- und internationale Studien, 6 March 2024): https://www.zois-berlin.de/en/about-us/

VI. LEGAL PROTECTION OF PUTIN'S WAR MYTHS

An important feature of Putin Russia's politics of memory is the cultivation of myths about the past that have taken root in the public consciousness, as well as the creation of new myths about the recent past and ongoing events, such as the war against Ukraine.

Thus, according to the official doctrine voiced by Putin and his closest associates, Crimea peacefully 'reunited' with Russia in 2014 under mortal threat from the 'nationalist regime' in Kyïv, which came to power with the help of a 'coup d'état'. The same happened with four other regions of Ukraine. Despite Putin's promises that the purpose of his war 'is not the occupation of Ukrainian territories', they were annexed in September 2022. This was executed following the same annexation playbook through staged 'referendums', 'recognition of dependence', and the conclusion of 'treaties on admission to the Russian Federation'. The Russian authorities justified their actions not only by the mythical threat to the Russian-speaking population of Ukraine but also by the fact that these regions are 'primordially Russian, ours'.

The central myth of the war is not only manipulative but also directly contradicts the facts: in all four regions, the majority of the population were ethnic Ukrainians, and in the Kherson and Zaporizka oblast, their predominance was especially significant. In addition, there were no separatist sentiments in the Kherson and Zaporizka oblast until 2022.

The Russian Constitutional Court, headed by its chairman, Valeriĭ Zor'kin,[48] has played an unexpected role in shaping the historical narrative of the Russian authorities. In its decisions on the legality of treaties on the 'acceptance' of 'new regions' into the Russian Federation, the Constitutional Court has used non-legal considerations and reproduced, uncritically, most of Putin's propaganda myths in the form of judicial decisions.[49]

Criminal law has also played a role in consolidating Russia's 'new history'. The criminal law provision punishing 'calls for the violation of Russia's territorial integrity', first introduced to the Criminal Code after the occupation of Crimea, now applies also to the newly annexed territories. It should be noted that this provision now enjoys constitutional support. The 2020 amendments prohibit the 'alienation of the territories of the Russian Federation, and even

news/archive-2024/translate-to-englisch-einstufung-der-dgo-als-unerwuenschte-auslaendische-organisation-in-der-russischen-foederation; 'DGO listed as an "extremist organization" in Russia' (*Deutsche Gesellschaft für Osteuropakunde*, 30 July 2024): https://dgo-online.org/informieren/aktuelles/dgo-extremist-organization-russia/.

[48] 'Valeriĭ Zor'kin on the decision of the Russian constitutional court: We could not ignore that people's lives were put under a catastrophic threat' (*RGRU*, 2 October 2022): https://rg.ru/2022/10/02/sootvetstvuet-konstitucii.html.

[49] S Masol, 'Orwellian Rulings of the Russian Constitutional Court on the Donetsk, Kherson, Luhansk, and Zaporizhzhia Provinces of Ukraine' (*EJIL:Talk!*, 25 October 2022): https://www.ejiltalk.org/orwellian-rulings-of-the-russian-constitutional-court-on-the-donetsk-kherson-luhansk-and-zaporizhzhia-provinces-of-ukraine/.

'calls' for such 'alienation'. It is possible that these amendments had in mind not only Crimea but also 'new territories' in Ukraine.

VII. CONCLUSIONS

The politics of memory have played a significant role in the war unleashed by the Putin regime against Ukraine. The mechanism of aggression, the manipulation of history and the suppression of dissent on a broad range of issues play a significant, or even essential, role. They strengthen public indifference, undermine anti-war resistance efforts, and disorient and divide not only Ukraine's allies but the anti-war resistance in Russia itself.

This 'parallel reality' created by the Kremlin is far from harmless. It has a tangible impact on the state of Russian society and paralyses the will to resist. False 'mirror' historical narratives facilitate the commission of international crimes. In an even greater sense, Putin's regime's historical policies have been aimed at Russia and its people. They falsify facts in colossal proportions and legitimise similar practices in other countries, especially those under Russian influence, providing a blueprint for repressive memory policies.

Russia's war against Ukraine is closely linked to and dependent on the historical myth of Putin's Russia. In contrast to the Soviet universalist narrative, the Russian authorities offer a purely isolationist myth of Russia as a 'besieged fortress'. From being purely marginal in the 1990s and, so to a large extent, in the 2000s, this discourse has now evolved and completely taken over the public discourse controlled by authorities, which in turn has led to an intensification of repressive policies in the field of historical memory. Any international conflict is linked to a confrontation based on memory. In this case, Russia seeks to impose on its citizens and neighbouring states a historical picture that is not based on an objective view of history.

Putin's 'memory politics' and 'memory laws' have already caused, and are continuing to cause, enormous harm to Russia both within and beyond the context of the war against Ukraine. Correcting this situation will be possible only after the elimination of the Putin regime; doing so will require significant efforts.

Part II

Memory Laws and Policies in Ukraine

4

Ukrainian Memory Laws and Policy before 2014: Overcoming the Past

ALINA CHERVIATSOVA

I. INTRODUCTION

THE CHAPTER TRACES the development of Ukrainian memory laws and policy[1] throughout the first two decades of Ukrainian independence – from 1991 (the collapse of the Soviet Union) to 2014 (the Euromaidan[2] and the Revolution of Dignity). Between these two historical milestones, Ukraine's memory policy can be divided into three periods. The first period, 1991–2004, embraces the circumspect memory policy of Leonid Kravchuk (1991–94) and Leonid Kuchma (1994–2005), the first Ukrainian presidents. Each sought to sidestep discussion about the communist crimes by adopting a multi-vector memory policy[3] and playing – depending on the political situation – with both Ukraine's national sentiments and the Soviet nostalgia. During the second period, in the aftermath of the Orange Revolution,[4] Ukraine's third president, Victor Yushchenko (2005–10), introduced a controversial narrative surrounding the fighters for Ukraine's independence, and aimed to form a national consensus around the *Holodomor*. However, these mnemonic initiatives were opposed during the third period by subsequent president, Victor Yanukovych

[1] Under the concept 'memory policy', this article refers to varied complex social practices designed to preserve, shape or (re)construct collective memories. Engaging with historical events – commemorating or discarding them – memory policy frames the public vision of the past to forge national identity and/or legitimise current internal or external political decisions. Accordingly, memory laws are the tools of memory policy through which a state regulates what should be remembered and how.

[2] Euromaidan was a wave of demonstrations and civil unrest in Ukraine, which began on 21 November 2013 with large protests in Maidan Nezalezhnosti (Independence Square) in Kyiv. The protests were sparked by President Viktor Yanukovych's sudden decision not to sign the European Union–Ukraine Association Agreement, instead choosing closer ties to Russia and the Eurasian Economic Union.

[3] N Koposov, *Memory Laws, Memory Wars: The Politics of the Past in Europe and Russia* (Cambridge University Press, 2017) 181.

[4] The Orange Revolution was a series of protests that led to political upheaval in Ukraine from late November 2004 to January 2005. The protests were sparked by reports that the 2004 Ukrainian presidential election run-off was marred by mass corruption, voter intimidation and electoral fraud.

(2010–14), who revived the Soviet/Russian narratives framed around the 'Great Patriotic War'.

In fact, from 1991–2014, Ukraine grappled with implementation of two incompatible projects: one anticolonial (national, anti-Soviet), and the other neocolonial (pro-Soviet, pro-Russian).[5] This is the reason why 'historical amnesia and amnesty of the soviet past' and, at the same time, 'nationalisation of history' were identified as the main shortfalls of Ukraine's memory policy.[6] This chapter maps the turning points in Ukraine's memory policy from 1991 to 2014 to reveal how Ukraine was constructing its national identity whilst dealing with its traumatic past and controversial historical narratives. It identifies two key trends within Ukraine's memory policy:[7] a negative trend that involved deconstructing Soviet narratives and transforming former heroes into villains, and a positive trend, that entailed creating a new pantheon of national heroes, who had been forgotten or even condemned during the Soviet times, thereby turning former villains into heroes.[8] Accordingly, the chapter is divided into two main sections. Section II scrutinises the decommunisation process, focusing on its origins, the fate of the Communist Party and the 'Lenin-fall' phenomenon. Section III traces the (re)construction of national identity through the new set of state symbols and the *Holodomor* narrative. Section IV concludes.

II. DECONSTRUCTING SOVIET NARRATIVES – A 'NEGATIVE' TREND IN UKRAINE'S MEMORY POLICY

A. Too Soviet to be Post-Soviet

Ukraine (re)emerged as an independent state following the collapse of the Soviet Union in 1991.[9] While this event reshaped the global political landscape, it did not result in a turnover of political leadership across most post-Soviet nations. Ukraine was no exception. The collapse of the Soviet Union did not prompt parliamentary elections, lustration[10] or other change of political elites: the same

[5] M Ryabchuk, *Heroyi i lykhodiyi. Rozshcheplenist' natsional'noyi pam'yati ta problema symvolichnoyi legitymizatsiyi derzhavy* // Kul'tura istorychnoyi pam'yati: yevropeys'kyy ta ukrayins'kyy dosvid / [YU Shapoval, L Nahorna, O Boyko ta in.]; za zahal'noyu redaktsiyeyu YU Shapovala (Kyiv, 2013). 600 s.

[6] See generally: O Hrytsenko, *Prezydenty i pam'yat'. Polityka pam'yati prezydentiv Ukrayiny (1994–2014): pidgruntya, poslannya, realizatsiya, rezul'taty* (Vydavnyts̄tvo 'KIS', 2017) 1136 s.

[7] A Cherviatsova, 'On the Frontline of European Memory Wars: Memory Laws and Policy in Ukraine' (2020) 5 *European Papers* 119, 119–36.

[8] DR Marples, *Heroes and Villains: Creating National History in Contemporary Ukraine* (Central European University Press, 2007).

[9] The chapter uses the term 're-emerged' to stress the historical ties between different reincarnations of Ukraine's statehood – (i) Kyiv Rus' (862–1240), (ii) the Cossack Hetmanate (1648–1764), and (iii) the Ukrainian People's Republic (1917–21).

[10] Lustration is the restoration of credibility to a government by the purging of perpetrators of crimes committed under an earlier regime. In Central and Eastern Europe it is the official procedure

individuals who had, for decades, built socialism became the architects of an independent state and remained in power. Adapting to the new political landscape, they changed their political colours and rhetoric (former communists transformed into fervent democrats),[11] yet preserved the Soviet state machinery and apparatus. The parliament and the government of the Ukrainian Soviet Socialist Republic (Ukrainian SSR) continued with their functions, however under new banners: the Supreme Soviet became the Verkhovna Rada of Ukraine,[12] while the Council of Ministers was called the Cabinet of Ministers, accordingly.[13] Hence, for the subsequent decades, Ukraine was being governed by institutions it had inherited from the Soviet state.

The Communist Party also survived. After the collapse of the Soviet Union its political profile included a ban in August 1991,[14] revival in 1993[15] and years of political prosperity when the party not only participated in the elections but held a dominant position in Ukraine's political system.[16] Moreover, in December 2001, the Constitutional Court of Ukraine fully rehabilitated the Communist Party of Ukraine by ruling the party's 1991 ban unconstitutional.[17]

of scrutinising a public official or a candidate for public office in terms of their history as a knowing collaborator (informant) of the former communist secret police.

[11] Ukraine's first presidents, Leonid Kravchuk (1991–94) and Leonid Kuchma (1994–2005) were previously the communist functionaries: Leonid Kravchuk served as a former secretary of the Communist Party of the Ukrainian SSR, while Leonid Kuchma held positions as chairman of the Ukrainian Supreme Soviet and as a former director of Yuzhmash, a prominent Ukrainian machine-building enterprise. Neither of them has ever been associated with any dissident movement, whether democratic or nationalist.

[12] It should be noted that the numbering of parliamentary convocations was not set to zero after Ukraine's independence – a small detail which proves that the parliament of independent Ukraine saw itself as a successor and continuator of the Supreme Council of the Ukrainian SSR. Only the parliament elected in 1998, as the Verkhovna Rada of the fourteenth convocation, changed this numbering and proclaimed itself the parliament's third convocation (by that time Ukraine had already had two parliamentary elections). See: Zakon Ukrayiny *'Pro vyznachennya poryadku obchyslennya sklykan'* (1 February, 2000).

[13] Zakon Ukrayiny *'Pro pravonastupnytstvo Ukrayiny'* (5 October, 1991).

[14] In August 1991, the Communist Party of Ukraine was banned for its involvement in the coup d'état (that is, the so-called GKChP); its assets were seized. Yet, the ban didn't challenge the Soviet past or dismantle communist ideology. Remarkably, no investigations or trials followed, enabling the party's legal resurrection within two years. See: Ukaz Prezydiyi Verkhovnoyi Rady Ukrayiny *'Pro zaboronu diyal'nosti Kompartiyi Ukrayiny'* (30 August 1991).

[15] In 1993, the Presidium of the Verkhovna Rada, revisiting the 1991 ban, concluded that since no criminal charges had been filed against the Communist Party for its role in the August coup, its members should not be considered complicit. Accordingly, the citizens of Ukraine who espouse communist ideals should have the right to establish a party in accordance with the Ukrainian legislation. See: Postanova Prezydiyi Verkhovnoyi Rady Ukrayiny *'Pro Ukazy Prezydiyi Verkhovnoyi Rady Ukrayiny "Pro tymchasove prypynennya diyal'nosti Kompartiyi Ukrayiny" ta "Pro zaboronu diyal'nosti Kompartiyi Ukrayiny"'* (14 May 1993).

[16] In the 1998 Ukrainian parliamentary elections, communists secured 25.65% of the vote becoming the largest party in the Verkhovna Rada. In the 1999 presidential elections, Petro Simoneko, the party's leader, advanced to the second round but was defeated by Leonid Kuchma.

[17] The Court determined that the parliament's decision to ban the party in August 1991 constituted a violation of the principle of separation of powers, as it encroached upon the judiciary's authority. See: Rishennya Konstytutsiynoho Sudu Ukrayiny u spravi pro ukazy Prezydiyi Verkhovnoyi Rady Ukrayiny shchodo Kompartiyi Ukrayiny (27 December, 2001).

However shortly after this, on the wave of decommunisation triggered by the Orange Revolution, the Communist Party of Ukraine witnessed a sharp decline, transforming into a conservative and pro-Russian rather pro-working class grouping by the 2010s. Finally, in 2015, the party was prohibited in accordance with the decommunisation package adopted after the annexation of Crimea and the onset of Russia's hybrid war in Ukraine's Donbas.

These developments indicate that after the collapse of the Soviet Union there was no distinct line between the 'Soviet past' and the 'post-Soviet present'. The burden of the Soviet legacy, including collective memories and historical narratives, precluded a rapid transition to democracy, making Ukraine's decommunisation a prolonged, contentious, and challenging process. This section provides an overview of Ukraine's decommunisation efforts, examining how the nation addressed two critical issues – communist symbols and communist crimes.

B. Dealing with Soviet Symbols in the Public Space: An Enduring Saga

Communist symbols dominated the public space in the Soviet Ukraine. Indeed, with over 5000 Lenin statues at the beginning of the 1990s,[18] Ukraine was the most 'Leninised' country in the world, a consequence of the so-called Bolshevik monumental policy.[19] For more than 70 years, Lenin monuments and other communist symbols were used to build the Soviet identity symbolising the glory of the past, the strength and unity of the USSR in the present, and the ideal communist society in the future. As Vladymyr Mayakovsky famously expressed: 'Lenin-lived./ Lenin – lives./ Lenin – will live'.[20]

What happened to all these symbols following Ukraine's independence? This chapter will address this question by focusing on the fate of the communist symbols displayed in the Ukrainian parliamentary building as a case study. Constructed between 1936–38, this building was a quintessential example of

[18] The exact number of Lenin monuments is unknown. The catalogue, 'Monuments of history and culture of the Ukrainian SSR', issued by the Institute of History of the Academy of Science of USSR in 1987, mentions more than 4000 monuments to Lenin. Victor Akulenko refers to 5015 Lenin monuments, stressing that these monuments constituted the overwhelming majority of the monuments in Ukraine (out of 8248 monuments). See: V Akulenko, 'Tin'ovyy bik Leniniany, abo nezareyestrovanyy u Hinnesa rekord' (1991) 2 *Pam'yatky Ukrayiny* 53.

[19] On 12 April 1918, the Council of People's Commissars of the Soviet Russia issued the Decree 'On the Monuments of the Republic' which mandated the replacement of tsarist monuments with those commemorating 'the great events of the Russian Socialist Revolution'. See: Dekret *'O pam'yatnikakh Respubliki'* (18 April 1918) in Dekrety Sovetskoy vlasti. Tom II. 17 marta–10 iyulya 1918 goda (Moskva, Gos. izdat-vo politicheskoy literatury, 1959). Notably, the Decree reflected Lenin's ideas on what to do with 'bourgeois' monuments and, more broadly, how to use art for the purpose of communist propaganda. See more in: Lunacharskiy's *Memories and Impressions*, chapter 'Lenin on Monumental Propaganda'. AV Lunacharskiy, *Vospominaniya i vpechatleniya* (Sovetskaya Rossiya, 1968), 197–200.

[20] Reprinted many times, Mayakovsky's poem 'Komsomol'skaya', was first published in *Molodaia Gvardiia* (1924) nos 2–3, 10–14.

Stalinist architecture,[21] hosting an array of communist symbols, including the coat of arms of the Soviet Ukraine prominently displayed on its facade, and a big statue of Lenin dominating the presidium in the plenary hall.

Discussion about communist symbols commenced in May 1990. Then, on the wave of Gorbachev's reforms,[22] the Soviet Ukraine held partially free elections ending the Communist Party's political monopoly. A new political force – the so-called 'Democratic Bloc' consisting of various parties (the People's Movement of Ukraine (Rukh), the Helsinki Watch Committee of Ukraine, and the Party of Greens of Ukraine, among others) – emerged as an opposition. Thus, this parliament differed from its predecessors.[23] Its political makeup alongside broader democratisation in the late 1980s enabled genuine parliamentary debates on previously suppressed issues.

For instance, during its inaugural session, Mykola Porovsky, a Rukh deputy, called on the newly-elected parliament to 'de-ideologise' the plenary hall of the Verkhovna Rada by removing Lenin's monument. He stressed that with various political parties (not only communists) represented in the parliament, the meetings should adhere to the principle of political pluralism, while Lenin's monuments created an 'atmosphere of ideological dictate'.[24]

It is interesting that Leonid Kravchuk (who in December 1991 would be elected as president of independent Ukraine) also participated in this discussion. Being a member of the communist majority at that time, Kravchuk accused Porovsky of violating the 'spiritual rights' and 'dignity' of millions of communists. In particular, Kravchuk said:

> Lenin is a global figure beyond question … An attack on Lenin's memory disrespects those who believe in his teachings … This affects the dignity and beliefs of communists and millions worldwide … Calls for removing monuments or burning books always end in bloodshed.[25]

The debate persisted as Levko Lukyanenko, a Soviet dissident, challenged Kravchuk's position:

> While communists have a right to believe in Lenin, the Verkhovna Rada includes individuals of various beliefs. Why should communists claim exclusive rights? People of diverse ideologies, like us, deserve equal respect. Transitioning from totalitarianism to democracy necessitates acknowledging differing beliefs. Without this recognition, progress toward a free democratic republic is hindered.[26]

[21] Its architect, Volodymyr Zabolotny (1898–1962) received the Stalin Prize in 1941.

[22] Gorbachev's reforms are defined by three signature policies – *perestroika* ('rebuilding'), *glasnost* ('open speech'), and new political thinking (a foreign policy doctrine that envisioned the end of the Cold War).

[23] This parliament was destined to play a decisive role in the history of Ukraine's state-building. It adopted the Declaration of State Sovereignty and the Act of Independence of Ukraine.

[24] Zasidannya tretye Verkhovnoyi Rady Ukrayins'koyi RSR, 16 travnya 1990 roku, Byuleten' № 3, pp 6–7.

[25] Zasidannya desyate Verkhovnoyi Rady Ukrayins'koyi RSR, 21 travnya 1990 roku., Byuleten' № 10, pp 26–29.

[26] ibid.

As evidenced by this debate, in 1990, even the anti-communist opposition considered the Communist Party of Ukraine a part of democratic society. The statue of Lenin in the parliamentary hall was questioned not as a symbol of communist crimes but as a symbol of an 'ideological dictate'. Moreover, the idea that communist ideology should be constitutionally protected due to political pluralism prevailed until 2014–15, changing only with the decommunisation package. Thus, the Lenin monuments and other communist symbols were protected by law. However, this did not prevent sporadic destruction of Lenin statues.

The first Lenin monument removal in the USSR occurred in Chervonohrad, in the L'viv region, in August 1990. It was spurred by a large protest of miners, who, in addition to socio-economic demands, called for the 'de-partyisation' of the coal industry and nationalisation of Communist Party's property. The protestors' demand to remove Lenin's monument from Chervonohrad's city centre was unanimously supported by local deputies. Unlike the Soviet Ukrainian parliament in Kyiv, Chervonohrad's city council was clear in its stance on Lenin. Here are excerpts from the city council's session:

> Lenin's actions targeted Ukrainians, leading to the deaths of the nation's finest. It's shameful that his monument remains in our city.
>
> The figure on the central square is an insult. The Communist Party's actions are crimes.
>
> Shouldn't a monument to Hitler be placed beside the Lenin's monument? There should be a Nuremberg-style trial against the Communist Party to expose its crimes.[27]

Notably, some cities in the L'viv region followed suit and also removed Lenin's monuments. The central government was uncertain how to respond. Unable to use force in the atmosphere of Gorbachev's *perestroika*, it resorted to condemning the dismantlement of monuments as constituting 'illegal' and 'barbarian' acts. On 11 September 1990, the Presidium of the Verkhovna Rada declared the decisions of the Chervonograd council and other city councils[28] to be in violation of the Ukrainian SSR's Law 'On the Protection and Utilisation of Historical and Cultural Monuments', emphasising that monument removals needed approval from the Council of Ministers of the Ukrainian SSR, and urging local authorities to reconsider their decisions.[29] It was an attempt to safeguard the Lenin monuments and other communist symbols by using legal arguments.

However, following the 1991 August coup (less than a year later) the Presidium of Verkhovna Rada showed less concern about rules and formalities when it came to removing the Lenin statue from the parliamentary hall. On 24 August 1991, after adopting the 'Act of Declaration of Independence

[27] Quoted under: V Semkiv, 'Paday, Lenine, paday' (*Zbruc*, 10 August 2015).

[28] The Decree mentions five cities in the L'viv region (oblast').

[29] Postanova Prezydiyi Verkhovnoyi Rady Ukrayins'koyi RSR *'Pro porushennya Zakonu Ukrayins'koyi RSR "Pro okhoronu i vykorystannya pam'yatok istoriyi ta kul'tury"'* (11 September 1990).

of Ukraine', the parliamentary session closed with Lenin's statue standing in the parliamentary hall.[30] However, on 3 September 1991 when the Verkhovna Rada opened a new session, the statue was no longer in place. It is known that Lenin was removed overnight, between 2 and 3 September. Yet, it remains unclear how, when and by who, this decision was made. Indeed, it was a 'secret mission', as a witness to and participant in the statue's removal described it. Notably, the people's deputies did not express any surprise or outrage at the removal of the main communist symbol. Only Volodymyr Marchenko, a communist from the Sumy region, raised the question:

> [W]e pretend that nothing happens. I am speaking about the decisions of the Presidium of the Verkhovna Rada to remove the Lenin's statue. We started this session without Lenin. Yesterday, we had a discussion with Mykola Homenko [Secretary of the Presidium] about this. However, he neither handed over the decision of the Presidium of the Verkhovna Rada, nor informed us about the terms of its implementation.[31]

Between 24 August and 3 September 1991, the Presidium of Verkhovna Rada made several significant decisions, such as the ban on the Communist Party and nationalisation of its property. Yet, the decision to remove the Lenin statue from the parliament hall was not documented in the parliamentary records, thus confirming that it was indeed a 'secret mission',[32] performed to avoid the unpredictability of parliamentary debates. Soon after, the flag of independent Ukraine replaced the Lenin statue, a practice commonly known as, 'Lenin down, Ukraine's bicolour up'.[33]

The Soviet coat of arms was also removed from the parliamentary hall, but not from the facade of the parliamentary building where it remained until 2015, sparking occasional discussions. For instance, in the midst of the parliamentary crisis in January 2000,[34] the pro-presidential majority (primarily composed of former communists) voted for the removal of the Soviet coat of arms. Interestingly, the decision was made during an 'alternative' session held in the Ukrainian House instead of the parliamentary building. In this political context,

[30] The statue survived the extraordinary session despite its presence in the parliamentary hall being challenged. Volodymyr Kolinets, a deputy from Ternopil, called to remove the statue before the beginning of the session saying: 'There is no greater shame than having a monument to someone who is a theorist of the coup in the very hall where we work, particularly during the days of suppression and the coup itself'. See: Zasidannya Verkhovnoyi Rady Ukrayins'koyi RSR, 24 serpnya 1991 roku, Byuleten' № 1, pp 9–10.

[31] Zasidannya Verkhovnoyi Rady Ukrayiny, 3 veresnya 1991 roku, Byuleten' № 1, p. 24.

[32] See: A Bondarchuk, 'Tayemnytsya parlaments'koyi nochi: yak iz Verkhovnoyi Rady vynosyly Lenina' (*Volyn'*, 28 June 2020).

[33] Interesting detail: it appeared that the Lenin statue, which looked monolithic, was made of pressed cardboard. See: S Ryabenko, 'Paperovyy "vozhd" z sesiynoyi zaly: yak dekomunizovuvaly Verkhovnu Radu' (*Istorychna Pravda*, 28 December 2020).

[34] The majority aimed to change the parliament's leadership and oust two communists, Oleksandr Tkachenko (Speaker) and Adam Martynuk (Vice-Speaker), who were opposed to Leonid Kuchma, the newly re-elected president. Leaving aside a detailed analysis of this crisis, it should be noted that both sides to the conflict violated Ukraine's Constitution.

this decision was not solely about decommunisation. Rather, it primarily served as a demonstration of power – a symbolic gesture to assert control over the parliamentary space, even though the majority was not physically present in the parliamentary building. For the next 15 (!) years this decision was not executed for 'technical reasons', according to the official explanation.[35] However, the fact that the symbols were replaced in 2015, right after the Revolution of Dignity, proves that the main reason for delaying the removal was a lack of political will and not technical constraints.

The case of the parliamentary building is reflective of all the issues associated with the decommunisation process in Ukraine: society was not ready to reflect on the communist past. It preferred to avoid or postpone a discussion, rather than admit and accept responsibility. It was Yanukovych's misuse of power, the annexation of Crimea and Russia's hybrid war against Ukraine that ultimately made communist symbols unacceptable for Ukrainian society. This shift transformed a sporadic destruction of the Lenin monuments into a widespread phenomenon known as *Leninopad* ('*ленінопад*' – in Ukrainian), a pun literally translated as 'Leninfall' '*-пад*' meaning 'fall' in English (as in 'waterfall', 'snowfall', etc). With the adoption of the decommunisation package in April 2015, dismantlement of Soviet monuments and removal of communist symbols became a part of the state-sponsored memory policy. Russia's full-scale invasion accelerated this process.

C. Dealing with Communist Crimes: Not Calling a Perpetrator by Name

The first timid attempts to condemn the communist past at the state level were made by the Ukrainian SSR in April 1991, when the Law 'On Rehabilitation of Victims of Political Repressions in Ukraine' was adopted.[36] The Law's preamble read as follows:

> After 1917, during the Civil War and subsequent decades, Ukraine experienced immense bloodshed. A lot of human blood has spilled on the land of Ukraine. Millions were persecuted for political activities, statements, and religious beliefs due to inhumane, anti-democratic policies and despotism. The Stalinist regime's mass repressions left a heavy legacy in the Republic … The Verkhovna Rada of Ukraine condemns these repressions, distances itself from the terrorist methods and expresses condolences to the victims and their families. It commits to restoring justice,

[35] As Deputy Sergiy Gavrysh put it: 'The symbols are attached to the building by complicated metal constructions. To remove them we need to turn the building into a huge site of reconstruction. It was decided to approach this matter carefully, and in the near future the symbols will be replaced. For this, we have already received the architectural plan proposals'. See: Zasidannya pershe vid 01 lutogo 2000 roku (Zal zasidan' Natsional'noho kompleksu 'Ekspotsentr Ukrayiny' ('Ukrayins'kyy dim'), Byuleten' № 1.

[36] Zakon Ukrayins'koyi Radyans'koyi Sotsialistychnoyi Respubliky *'Pro reabilitatsiyu zhertv politychnykh represiy na Ukrayini'* (17 April 1991).

> eliminating civil rights violations, providing compensation, and ensuring that such abuses will never be repeated, and that human rights and the rule of law will be sacredly respected.[37]

Though the Law condemned 'political repressions' it did not call the perpetrator – the communist regime – by name. Additionally, even though the Law provided justice for the victims of 'state terror', it did not raise any questions about responsibility for the political repressions. Although, rehabilitating and compensating victims had an important political and symbolical meaning, without clear condemnation of the communist regime, it was merely a half-measure. Only in 2018, following the line of the decommunisation package, was the Law 'On Rehabilitation of Victims of Political Repressions in Ukraine' transformed. Amendments to the law changed its title and preamble, introduced new articles and redrafted existing ones. A new version of the Law, entitled 'On Rehabilitation of Victims of the Repressions of the Communist Totalitarian Regime of 1917–1991', addresses the crimes of the communist regime and condemns the Soviet era as totalitarian.[38] It explains the meaning of political repression by defining its different forms (deprivation of life, liberty and property, exile, expulsion, deportation etc), yet similarly to the 1991 edition, the Law 'On Rehabilitation of Victims of the Repressions of the Communist Totalitarian Regime of 1917–1991' seeks justice for the victims but not for their perpetrators. The Law remains silent about holding those involved in communist crimes accountable, just as it did over 30 years ago.

III. (RE)CONSTRUCTING UKRAINE'S NATIONAL IDENTITY – A 'POSITIVE' TREND IN UKRAINE'S MEMORY POLICIES

A. Memory Policy Through State Symbols

The historical record of decommunisation in Ukraine reveals the country's hesitance to confront its communist past. Against this backdrop, Ukraine's success with constructing its new state symbols free from Soviet legacies within the first year of independence appears particularly remarkable. However, the fact that some of these symbols remained half approved for several years – eg, music without lyrics for the state anthem; the so-called 'small coat of arms' instead of the 'normal' coat of arms – reflected the high degree of polarisation of Ukraine's society and controversies in the collective memory.[39]

[37] ibid.

[38] ibid.

[39] Notably, more than 30 years later, Ukraine is still in the process of institutionalisation of its state symbols (for instance, the so-called, 'Great State Coat of Arms of Ukraine' has not been approved despite many attempts). By (re)constructing its state symbols, Ukraine has had to think about its past in order to answer challenging questions: where it comes from and what it really stands for.

As with the negative trend in Ukraine's memory policy, the positive one was rooted in Gorbachev's reforms. In the late 1980s, these reforms triggered the so-called 'parade of sovereignties' – a series of sovereignty declarations by Soviet republics and subunits.[40]

Ukraine's Declaration of State Sovereignty, adopted on 16 July 1990, outlined fundamental principles (such as the principle of self-determination, the rule of law, territorial supremacy, economic independence, political pluralism etc) based on which Ukraine would reform its political and socioeconomic systems, and modernise its international relations within the Soviet Union and beyond. It was clear that this new Ukrainian SSR – democratic and sovereign – would need a new constitution and new state symbols. The parliamentary Decree 'On Measures Regarding Ukraine's State Symbols'[41] adopted on 3 August 1990, advised that the new symbols should 'reproduce the symbols of the Ukrainian statehood' and 'implement the idea of national immortality'.[42] The Decree opened the way for official recognition of the symbols from Ukraine's pre-Soviet history, reflecting its centuries-old fight for independence.

(i) National Anthem

Ukraine started to create a new set of the state symbols from the state anthem. On 15 January 1992, the Presidium of Verkhovna Rada[43] approved music by Mykhailo Verbytsky (1815–70) to a national song, Pavlo Chubynsky's patriotic poem, known by its first line '*Shche ne vmerla Ukraina*' ('Ukraine has not yet perished, neither her glory, nor her freedom').[44] Written in 1862, the poem expressed the mixture of hope and desperation felt by Ukrainians over their struggle to rule their own land; it became popular in territories that now comprise the western regions of Ukraine. In 1863, Mykhailo Verbytskyi set it to music and in 1917, the song became the national anthem of the short-lived Ukrainian People's Republic. Suppressed in the Soviet Ukraine, '*Shche ne vmerla Ukraina*' was approved as the state anthem of the Carpathia Ukraine in 1939. The song was also popular among the Organisation of Ukrainian Nationalists–Ukrainian Insurgent Army (OUN-UPA). At the end of 1980s, the song revived

[40] Over a short period of time, from November 1988 (Estonia's declaration) to July 1991 (Adygea's declaration), 41 Soviet units declared sovereignty. This movement peaked in mid-1990 with Soviet Russia's declaration on 12 June 1990.

[41] Postanova Prezydiyi Verkhovnoyi Rady Ukrayins'koyi RSR '*Pro derzhavnu symvoliku Ukrayins'koyi RSR*' (3 August 1990).

[42] Postanova Prezydiyi Verkhovnoyi Rady Ukrayins'koyi RSR '*Pro zakhody shchodo vyrishennya pytannya pro derzhavnu symvoliku Ukrayiny*' (24 June 1991).

[43] It is noteworthy that this decision was made not by the entire parliament but by its Presidium. Ironically, the Presidium used the authority granted by the still-in-force Soviet Constitution to replace the Soviet anthem with a song that had been a symbol of the Ukrainian national movement and banned during the Soviet era.

[44] Ukaz Prezydiyi Verkhovnoyi Rady Ukrayiny 'Pro Derzhavnyy himn Ukrayiny' (15 January 1992).

with the People's Movement of Ukraine (Narodnyi Rukh Ukrayiny), a Ukrainian political party, the first opposition to the Communist Party in Soviet Ukraine.

Given the song's historical meaning, approving it as Ukraine's state anthem, even without lyrics, was a significant departure from Soviet symbols and legacy. However, the Soviet influence persisted, and for the next 10 years, Ukraine's state anthem remained wordless.

In 1996, the Constitution of Ukraine (Article 20) confirmed the status of Verbytskyi's music as the state anthem. It also prescribed that the lyrics should be introduced by law if adopted by no less than two-thirds of the constitutional composition of Ukraine's parliament. This norm reflected a compromise between pro-Soviet (pro-communist, pro-Russian) and pro-Ukrainian nationalistic forces: on the one hand, the Constitution guaranteed that Verbytsky's music would not be replaced (ie, neither Soviet state symbols nor any modification of them could be used), on the other hand, the norm made it more difficult to endorse the original Chubynsky's lyrics of '*Shche ne vmerla Ukraina*'. Following the adoption of the Constitution, numerous parliamentary commissions were created to work on the lyrics, and several drafts were presented. All these drafts were framed around two ideas – returning to the Soviet anthem (these drafts suggested different variations of the Soviet Ukraine anthem) or pushing forward the national song (these drafts suggested different variations of lyrics of '*Shche ne vmerla Ukraina*').[45] Notably, it was President Kuchma who ended the debate in March 2003, when his slightly modified version of Chubynsky's poem (draft no 1073-2)[46] was approved by 334 votes (the 'communist' version of the state anthem – the Soviet Ukraine's anthem with the amended lyrics[47] – received 62 votes).

Initially, Ukrainian society was indifferent towards the new state anthem. In 2003, Valeriy Mishura, a deputy from the Communist Party noted that a part of Ukraine's society had not accepted the state symbols proclaimed in the Constitution as their own. Yet, this attitude quickly changed. The song gained immense popularity during the 2004 Orange Revolution and the 2013–14 Revolution of Dignity, uniting protesters against Yanukovych's pro-Russian regime. Following Russia's full-scale invasion in February 2022, the song, 'Ukraine's freedom has not yet perished, nor Ukraine's glory' along with the state flag, became symbols of Ukraine's resistance.

[45] See text from some of the drafts in: *Derzhavnyy himn Ukrayiny*: istoryko-pravovi aspekty: zbirnyk dokumentiv i materialiv / LV Zaslavs'ka, VS Holubovs'ka, SO Dorohykh (Vydavnychyy dim 'ArtEk', 2020).

[46] The first line of the original song 'Ukraine has not yet perished, neither her glory, nor her freedom' was changed to 'Ukraine's freedom has not yet perished, nor Ukraine's glory'.

[47] Some of the former Soviet Republics followed this path: they kept the melody of their Soviet anthems and discarded or re-wrote the lyrics: this is the case for Russia (uses melody of the USSR state anthem), Uzbekistan (uses melody of the anthem of the Uzbek SSR), Kazakhstan (uses melody of the anthem of the Kazakh SSR), Turkmenistan (uses melody of the anthem of the Turkmen SSR), and Belarus (uses melody of the anthem of the Belorussian SSR).

(ii) Flag

Ukraine's blue and yellow bicolour emerged as a new (old) political symbol at the end of the 1980s. Suppressed as a symbol of Ukraine's fight for independence, it entered political practice as 'the national flag' before it was officially recognised as the state flag of Ukraine. For instance, in April 1989, in L'viv, a rally commemorating the Chernobyl tragedy was held under the national flag; the following month, in Kyiv, the national flag was raised during celebrations devoted to Taras Shevchenko, a Ukrainian poet.[48]

In April 1990, the L'viv city council adopted a decision 'On the Use of the Ukrainian National Flag in L'viv'. In accordance with this decision, the national flag of Ukraine was raised over the city council's building. To avoid cancellation by central authorities, the decision detailed the historical significance of the flag and stressed that the need for its official recognition emerged from the process of democratisation, ie, the main achievement of *perestroika*:

> The Ukrainian blue-yellow combination has a long history. In the XIII century, it was on the coat of arms of the Kingdom of Galicia-Volhynia as an original symbol of the west-Ukrainian lands. The Dnieper Ukraine also has a tradition to use these colours – they were on the Ukrainian Cossacks' flags during the liberation wars. At the beginning of the XX century, the blue-yellow flag spread around Ukraine and was officially recognised as the state symbol of the Ukrainian People's Republic ... Blue and yellow colours symbolised unification of the Ukrainian people in January 1919.

Based on this historical record,[49] L'viv's city council concluded that 'revival and recognition of the National Ukrainian Flag expressed the will and aspirations of the Ukrainian people'. To pre-empt any negative reaction from the Soviet government, the document stressed that the national flag would not replace the state flag, instead, it would be used alongside it. At the same time, L'viv's deputies urged the central government to officially recognise and legally protect Ukraine's national symbols. Soon afterward other cities in the western Ukraine also raised the national flag.[50]

For several years, Ukraine had two flags with opposing symbolic meanings. The state flag of Soviet Ukraine, which represented the country's affiliation to the Soviet Union, was officially recognised, protected by law, and popular in the Eastern regions. In contrast, the national flag, symbolising Ukraine's struggle for independence, though not recognised officially, was championed by the Western

[48] B Kostyuk, 'Udar po imperiyi. Yak nad Kyyevom 28 rokiv tomu pidnimaly syn'o-zhovtyy prapor' (*Radio Svoboda*, 24 July 2018).

[49] Notably, the document does not mention that Ukrainian nationalists also used the bicolour during WWII. Only 15 years later, Yushchenko would make the first attempt to introduce the historical narrative of the fighters for Ukraine's independence.

[50] On 24 July 1990, the Kyiv City Council became the ninth member of the national flag 'coalition'.

regions. This dichotomy highlighted a profound crisis of the Soviet system and, at the same time, a resurgence of Ukraine's national identity.

Ukraine's independence did not resolve this conflict. In this context, Leonid Kravchuk offers a noteworthy example of political flexibility and evolution. As the Secretary of the Central Committee of the Communist Party of the Ukrainian SSR, he supported Soviet symbols, arguing for their respect until new symbols were officially adopted. Yet, as the first president of independent Ukraine, he advocated for the national bicolour and successfully persuaded parliament to adopt the national flag as the state flag.

Using a purely legalistic approach, Kravchuk did not allow the national flag to be raised on the parliamentary building on 24 August 1991, when the Act of Declaration of Independence of Ukraine was adopted. As he explained, the parliament had to change the relevant norms in the Constitution and upgrade the national flag's status for this to happen.[51] However, 10 days later, on 4 September 1991, it was Kravchuk who promoted the Decree 'On Raising the Blue-Yellow Flag Over the Building of the Verkhovna Rada of Ukraine'. The document read:

> With regard to the Act of Declaration of Independence and before the referendum on the state symbols and adoption of a new constitution, the historic national blue-yellow flag symbolising the peaceful Ukraine, its clear sky and grain fields, should be raised above the building of the Verkhovna Rada of Ukraine.[52]

It was stressed that this decision did not annul the existing state symbols of the Soviet Ukraine – the national flag would be raised along with the state flag.[53]

The Decree 'On the Flag of Ukraine', adopted on 18 September 1991, permitted the use of the national flag during official events.[54] However, it did not cancel the state flag of the Ukrainian SSR. The final official recognition of the national flag took place in January 1992. Kravchuk, by then President of Ukraine, urged the deputies to approve the national flag as the state flag: 'Look around!' Kravchuk said. 'Ukraine's national flag is everywhere ... It has entered our life. Any discussion about the national flag brings confrontation and contradicts the existing reality.[55] Kravchuk also stressed that he was the only president of a post-Soviet republic which did not have its own flag. His persuasive rhetoric led to the national flag's official status,[56] confirmed by the Constitution of Ukraine in 1996.

[51] Zasidannya Verkhovnoyi Rady Ukrayins'koyi RSR vid 24 serpnya 1991, Byuleten' № 2.

[52] Postanova Verkhovnoyi Rady Ukrayiny '*Pro pidnyattya nad budynkom Verkhovnoyi Rady Ukrayiny syn'o-zhovtoho prapora*' (4 September 1991).

[53] Zasidannya Verkhovnoyi Rady Ukrayins'koyi RSR, 4 veresnya 1991 roku, Byuleten' № 2.

[54] Postanova Verkhovnoyi Rady Ukrayiny '*Pro prapor Ukrayiny*' (18 September 1991).

[55] Zasidannya Verkhovnoyi Rady Ukrayiny, 28 sichnya 1992, Byuleten' № 1.

[56] Postanova Verkhovnoyi Rady Ukrayiny '*Pro Derzhavnyy prapor Ukrayiny*' (28 January 1992).

(iii) Coat of Arms[57]

In February 1992, the golden trident, a symbol linked to Kyivan Rus', the Ukrainian People's Republic and the Organisation of Ukrainian Nationalists,[58] was approved as the state symbol (the so-called Ukraine Small Coat of Arms) despite fierce opposition from the communists. With the Soviet Coat of Arms still in use, communists sought to obstruct the adoption of a new emblem by calling for extended discussions, additional commissions, more drafts, referendums, and input from local authorities, etc. They opposed any version of the coat of arms that did not include communist symbols. Meanwhile, Ukraine urgently needed a new coat of arms to assert its independence. As one of the deputies said: 'If we fail to approve the State Coat of Arms, it would mean that we do not have a state'.[59]

In the end, it was Kravchuk who proposed the idea of having two coats of arms – a big one and a small one. Kravchuk's compromise, proposing the trident as a 'small' coat of arms, which would be the main element of a future 'big' coat of arms,[60] was accepted by all parties: Ukraine's national forces were satisfied with the official recognition of the trident, while the communists got a chance to include the Soviet symbols in a big coat of arms. Considering Kravchuk's reputation as a 'wily bureaucrat and astute tactician',[61] it remains unclear whether he genuinely believed in the prospect of a big coat of arms in the near future or deceived the communist forces by hiding the intention of having the trident as the State Coat of Arms of Ukraine. In any case, the fact is that the 'small coat of arms' – the trident, initially intended as a temporal symbol, has served as Ukraine's Coat of Arms to date, while a big coat of arms has never been approved. The latest unsuccessful attempt to adopt a big coat of arms was made by President Zelenskyy in 2021.

By adopting new state symbols, Ukraine has had to reflect on its past in order to answer challenging questions about where it comes from and what it really stands for. Regionally divided Ukraine did not have an answer to this question: if the Western regions celebrated Ukraine's independence as the culmination of a centuries-long struggle for statehood, the Eastern regions, where Soviet education and propaganda had had more time to create 'a new soviet man', perceived

[57] To view the coat of arms, see: https://ukraine.ua/stories/trident-tryzub/.

[58] There are different theories which explain the meaning of trident. According to one hypothesis, it is a stylised image of bird – a falcon descending on prey. It can symbolise a pitchfork to underline Ukraine's importance as the 'breadbasket of Europe'. The trident also can be interpreted as a symbol of peace – its central part a reminder of 'a sprout, a child, a bud that grows upwards'. Some people see three Cyrillic letters in the symbol – 'В', 'О', 'Я' – which refer to prominent figures in Ukraine's ancient past – Volodymyr, Olha and Yaroslav; whereas others believe that the trident encrypts the word 'воля' – freedom. The last interpretation (which has gained popularity in the context of Russia's full-scale invasion) stresses Ukraine's democratic traditions and its aspiration of independence.

[59] Zasidannya Verkhovnoyi Rady Ukrayiny 19 lutogo 1992, Byuleten' № 21.

[60] ibid, 98.

[61] B Hall, 'Leonid Kravchuk, Ukrainian politician, 1934–2022' (*Financial Times*, 13 May 2022).

the Soviet Union's collapse as a loss. Thus, it was not an easy task to find symbols which would unite Ukrainians and be accepted all around the country. Yet, Ukraine succeeded, by constructing a national identity based on the national symbols and upgrading them to the level of the state symbols (the national song '*Shche ne vmerla Ukraina*' – the state anthem; the national bicolour – the state flag; and the trident – the coat of arms). Ukraine linked itself with its pre-Soviet historical reincarnations and, at the same time, distanced itself from the USSR and Soviet Ukraine. In this context, Ukraine's memory policy through the state symbols represented the first attempt to introduce narratives of anti-communist resistance, which had hitherto been suppressed. Later on, these narratives were developed by President Yushchenko and confirmed by the Law 'On Fighters for Ukraine's Independence' adopted in 2015 as part of the decommunisation package.

B. *Holodomor*: Constructing National Identity Through National Trauma

The *Holodomor* (Ukrainian '*Голодомор*' meaning '*морити голодом*' – torturing and murdering by hunger) refers to the Great Famine of 1932–33, when millions of Ukrainians died of starvation during a famine artificially created by the Soviet State. At that time, the Soviet Union was experiencing a rapid industrialisation. The so-called 'industrial breakthrough' required vast resources that could be obtained through the forced collectivisation and brutal implementation of grain-quotas. The *Holodomor* was especially horrific considering that this man-made catastrophe hit a region known as the 'breadbasket of Europe'.

Undeniably, Stalin's regime was responsible for this crime. Yet, until the end of 1980s the very occurrence of the Great Famine of 1932–33 was denied; there was no public awareness and no commemoration of the innocent victims. Moreover, since the 'official' memory of *Holodomor* was no memory, any discussion of the Great Famine was punishable as anti-Soviet propaganda. After the collapse of the Soviet Union, the *Holodomor* evolved from one of the most suppressed topics in Soviet history into Ukraine's trauma, which received international recognition as the Genocidal Famine. Thus, shifting from marginalised private memories to a central element of Ukraine's national identity. Despite this, the long-lasting struggle of memory over silencing and denial continues to this day.

Initially, the revival of memory of the *Holodomor* started outside Ukraine and was pushed by Ukrainian communities in the diaspora and by Western historians.[62] Robert Conquest's book *Harvest of Sorrow*, published in 1986, brought the 1932–33 Great Famine into public discourse. Many reviewers expressed astonishment that they knew so little about such a deadly tragedy.[63]

[62] See: R Conquest, *The Harvest of Sorrow: Soviet Collectivization and the Terror-Famine* (Oxford University Press, 1986).

[63] A Applebaum, *Red Famine: Stalin's War On Ukraine* (Knopf Doubleday Publishing Group, 2017) 336–37.

Knowing that the 'Harvest of Sorrow' would be echoed in Ukraine, the Soviet state tried to create an alternative narrative. In 1987, *Froud, Famine and Fascism: The Ukrainian Genocide Myth from Hitler to Harvard* was published by Douglas Tottle,[64] a Canadian labour activist. Although the book acknowledged the food shortage in Ukraine in 1932–33, it denied the Soviet state's role in orchestrating starvation. According to the author, the famine was a hoax invented by Ukrainian fascists and anti-Soviet groups in the West. Creating a link between the famine and Nazi propaganda, the book intended to smear anyone who wrote about the famine at all. This tactic was effective. Moreover, in 2014, it was employed by Russia in its memory wars with Ukraine and other European countries who challenged the glory of the Soviet past: any questions about communist crimes were deemed a rehabilitation of Nazism.[65]

Despite Soviet attempts to suppress discussion about the famine, it continued. In 1988, the US Commission of the Ukraine Famine, set up 'to expand the world's knowledge of the famine and provide the American public with a better understanding of the Soviet System by revealing the Soviet role in it' presented its findings:

> There is no doubt that a large number of inhabitants of the Ukrainian SSR and the North Caucasus Territory starved to death in a man-made famine in 1932–33, caused by the seizure of the 1932 crop by Soviet authorities [and that] Stalin and those around him committed genocide against Ukrainians in 1932–33.[66]

In response, the USSR established a counter-commission. The Ukrainian Communist Party's First Secretary, Volodymyr Scherbytsky, granted scholars access to official archives to find evidence denying the famine. Contrary to his intention, the study revealed grain confiscations, the protests of activists, corpses on the city streets, the tragedy of orphans, terror and cannibalism. The archive documents confirmed that the famine had been real, that it had happened.[67] During the years of *perestroyka* and *glasnost*, it became difficult to deny the past crimes. In 1987, in a speech dedicated to the 70th anniversary of Soviet power in Ukraine, Scherbytsky acknowledged the Great Famine.[68] This marked the first official recognition of the *Holodomor* and opened the door for commemorative civic initiatives to honour the victims.

On 26 January 1990, the Central Committee of the Communist Party of Ukraine adopted a Decree 'On famine 1932–33 in Ukraine and Publication of

[64] D Tottle, *Froud, Famine, and Fascism: The Ukrainian Genocide Myth from Hitler to Harvard* (Progress Books, 1987).

[65] See Art 354-1 'Rehabilitation of Nazism' of the Criminal Code of the Russian Federation.

[66] United States Commission on the Ukraine Famine, 'Investigation of the Ukrainian famine, 1932–1933: report to Congress, interim report of meetings and hearings of and before the Commission on the Ukraine Famine, held in 1988' (US GPO, 1988) v–vi.

[67] See more about this in: Applebaum (n 63) 343–44.

[68] V Shcherbyts'kyy, 'Pid praporom Velykoho Zhovtnya, kursom perebudovy'. (*Radyans'ka Ukrayina*, 26 December 1987).

the Relevant Archive Documents'. The Decree acknowledged the famine as 'a real tragedy of the Ukrainian people which resulted from the criminal course pursued by Stalin and those from his inner circle'. Furthermore, it condemned 'the principles and irresponsible politics of grain seizure implemented by the leaders of the Soviet Ukraine' and 'the violent methods of solving problems of the social development'.[69] This document was one of the last acts on memory adopted by the Communist Party before the collapse of the Soviet Union.

It seemed that Ukraine as a sovereign state free from Soviet bans and restrictions would take an active role in commemorating the tragic historical events, especially the 1932–33 Great Famine. However, this did not happen. Although on the level of political rhetoric, President Kravchuk called the *Holodomor* 'a well-planned administrative action' and 'an act of genocide',[70] his contribution to the *Holodomor* commemoration was limited to a single document: the Decree 'On Events in Connection with the 60th Anniversary of the Famine in Ukraine', which he signed under pressure from activists in 1993. As a former Secretary of the Communist Party of Ukraine, Kravchuk did not feel comfortable with the *Holodomor* memories, as they made him vulnerable to critics aligned with national democratic forces. Simultaneously, his former colleagues from the Communist Party criticised Kravchuk for the deep economic crisis, raising concerns about a new famine of 1993 and drawing historical parallels with the *Holodomor*.

In 1994, Kravchuk was defeated by former Prime Minister Leonid Kravchuk during the early presidential elections. Over the next four years, the state's position regarding the *Holodomor* was neutral: it did not fund any projects related to the famine, but it also did not hinder private commemorative initiatives.[71] However, in 1998 the policy changed: two documents – the Decree 'On the 65th Anniversary of the Holodomor in Ukraine' and the Decree 'On Setting the Day of Commemorating the Holodomor Victims'[72] – were adopted by the Cabinet of Ministers and President Kuchma respectively. The reason behind this mnemonic activity lay not in the *Holodomor* or its commemoration per se, but rather, in the 1998 political situation. In Spring 1998, Ukraine had parliamentary elections which were not successful for Kuchma's political party, and which unveiled the rise of the pro-communist forces. In this context, Kuchma used the *Holodomor* card against his political opponents and, first of all, against Petro Simoneko, leader of the Communist Party of Ukraine.

[69] 'O golode 1932–33 godov na Ukraine i publikatsii svyazannykh s nim arkhivnykh materialov. Postanovleniye TSK Kompartii Ukrainy' (*Pravda Ukrainy*, 7 February 1990).

[70] See more: *Holodomor 1932–33 rr. v Ukrayini: prychyny i naslidky*. Mizhnarodna naukova konferentsiya. Kyyiv, 9–10.09.1993 (1995), 10.

[71] VI Marochko, 'Holodomor-henotsyd 1932-1933 rokiv v Ukrayini: politychnyy dyskurs' (2014) *Istorychna pam'yat'* 30, 55.

[72] Nakaz Prezidenta Ukrayiny 'Pro vstanovlennya Dnya pam'yati zhertv holodomoriv' (26 November 1998).

During Kuchma's presidency there were other legal acts devoted to the *Holodomor* commemoration; however, they failed to move the Great Famine from the periphery to the forefront of Ukraine's memory. Overall, Kuchma's approach to the *Holodomor* can be described as: 'reactionary' – lacking his own initiatives, Kuchma merely responded to the initiative of others; 'situational' – the memory policy depended on the prevailing political circumstances, both internal and external, rather than consistent principles or a strategic vision of the past; and 'ineffective' – the objectives outlined in the acts were never fully realised.[73]

In 2004, the Orange Revolution – the mass protests in Kyiv against stolen presidential elections, corruption and Russia's influence – brought Victor Yushchenko to power. He elevated the *Holodomor* to a cornerstone of Ukrainian identity, making it a priority of Ukraine's memory policy. He established the National Memory Institute with the *Holodomor* designated as a primary area of study. During his five-year presidency, he issued around 20 decrees focused on the Great Famine, its commemoration and legal qualification.[74] Yushchenko initiated official recognition of the *Holodomor* as a genocide in Ukraine and lobbied for its international acknowledgment.

Yushchenko's draft 'On the 1932–33 Holodomor in Ukraine', defining the *Holodomor* as a genocide, was passed into law in 2006. Initially, the draft proposed penalties for denying the *Holodomor*, but this provision was not included in the final law.[75] It was a compromise – granting the *Holodomor* official recognition without imposing penalties for its denial – which Yushchenko had to accept, as both the Communist Party and the Party of Regions opposed the very idea that the *Holodomor* was a genocide. The Communist Party of Ukraine was reluctant to acknowledge past crimes, while the Party of Regions, a pro-Russian force, perceived the *Holodomor* as an anti-Russian narrative.

This anti-Russian connotation of the Great Famine should be explained. Despite the fact that Yushchenko undoubtedly politicised the *Holodomor*, understanding its power as a unifying memory for Ukrainians, he had never claimed that it was Russia's crime against Ukraine. Instead, he attributed blame to the Communist Party, the Communist regime and the Soviet Union. He called upon Russia to denounce the crimes of Stalinism and the totalitarian past. The problem was that Russia, perceiving itself as a 'successor' and 'continuator' of the Soviet Union, could not condemn communist crimes. On the contrary, glorification of the Soviet past became a key element of Russia's memory policy. This clash of memories between Russia and Ukraine went beyond a mere memory war; it represented an existential conflict of two

[73] O Hrytsenko, *Prezydenty i pam'yat'. Polityka pam'yati prezydentiv Ukrayiny (1994–2014)* (2017), 245.

[74] In comparison, Kuchma issued three times fewer decrees during his decade in power.

[75] Art 2 of the law recognised *Holodomor* denial as an 'illegal act' and an 'insult to the memory of millions of victims', yet, it did not specify a sanction.

mutually exclusive identities: the Ukrainian identity – associated with the *Holodomor* and resistance, and the Russian identity – based on Soviet nostalgia and imperial ambitions. Russia's war against Ukraine has highlighted this conflict, yet in the mid-2000s this memory confrontation was not as evident: paradoxically, the Eastern regions of Ukraine who suffered the most during the *Holodomor* were not inclined to acknowledge it. This ambivalent attitude towards the *Holodomor* and the Soviet past allowed Victor Yanukovych, who came to power in 2010, to make a U-turn in Ukraine's memory policy, reviving the Soviet historical narratives and suppressing both the process of decommunisation and (re)construction of Ukraine's national identity.

IV. CONCLUSION

Ukraine's memory policy before 2014 was the policy of a state in transition, torn between the communist past and unclear future, disappointments and new hopes, national aspirations and Soviet nostalgia. Regionally divided and without a well-considered strategy for forming a national identity, Ukraine continued to display a tendency towards national rebirth and, at the same time, marginalisation of the Soviet memories. Two distinct trends in Ukraine's memory policy – deconstructing the Soviet narratives (negative) and (re)constructing the national identity (positive) – despite the periods of regression, and even reversals, gradually steered Ukraine away from its Soviet past and from Russia.

Russia's full-scale invasion of Ukraine has shed light on communist crimes. As President Zelenskyy expressed:

> [E]verything became clear to all those who had been in doubt. Everyone saw literally, live, in real time, what modern Russia, which calls itself the successor to the USSR, is capable of. Which enjoys being the heir to the worst crimes and murders of that era.[76]

This understanding has sped up recognition of the *Holodomor* as a genocide not only within Ukraine but internationally, and has made the process of decommunisation irreversible.

[76] 'Address of the President of Ukraine on the occasion of the Day of Remembrance of the Victims of the Holodomors' (*President of Ukraine Volodymyr Zelenskyy Official Website*, 25 November 2023): https://www.president.gov.ua/en/news/zvernennya-prezidenta-ukrayini-z-nagodi-dnya-pamyati-zhertv-87249.

5

Ukrainian Memory Laws and Decommunisation Policies from the Euromaidan to the Full-Scale Russian Invasion

TATIANA ZHURZHENKO

I. INTRODUCTION

THE DECOMMUNISATION LAWS adopted by parliament in spring 2015 were not the first attempt to legislate on historical memory in Ukraine.[1] However, compared to previous legislative initiatives (such as those introduced by President Viktor Yushchenko during his presidency (2005–10) aimed at the official recognition of the *Holodomor* as genocide),[2] the decommunisation laws, despite their shortcomings, represent the most radical and systematic reform of the Ukrainian memory regime so far. Not only did they cover the most significant and controversial aspects of Ukraine's twentieth-century history, such as the nature of the Soviet regime, the history of World War II (WWII) from the Ukrainian perspective, and the legacy of Ukrainian nationalism, but they also manifested a radical break with the Soviet historical narrative – and with an increasingly Soviet-nostalgic Russia. Ukraine's commemorative and symbolic landscape has dramatically, yet sustainably, transformed in a relatively short period of time to such an extent that even the 2019 change of political leadership in Kyiv did not cause backlash.[3]

[1] See A Cherviatsova, 'Ukrainian Memory Laws and Policy Before 2014: Overcoming the Past', Chapter 4 in the present volume.

[2] H Kasianov, *Danse macabre: holod 1932–1933 rokiv u politytsi, masovii svidomosti ta istoriohrafii (1980-ti-pochatok 2000-kh)* (Nash Chas, 2010); V Vasylenko and M Antonovych (eds), *Holodomor 1932–1933 rokiv v Ukraini yak zlochyn henotsydu zghidno z mizhnarodnym pravom* (Kyiv Mohyla Academy Publishing, 2013); L Klymenko, 'The Holodomor law and national trauma construction in Ukraine' (2016) 58 *Canadian Slavonic Papers* 341, 341–61.

[3] See A Nekoliak, 'Ukrainian Memory Laws and Policies in the Context of 2022 Russian Aggression', Chapter 6 in the present volume.

Ukraine's decommunisation legislation has garnered quite a bit of attention in academic literature.[4] Historians, political scientists, and scholars of law have reflected on this development in multiple contexts: Ukraine's nation-building and decolonisation agenda, the European trend towards legislating on historical memory, Russian-(Eastern) European mnemonic conflicts, and transitional justice politics in post-authoritarian and post-conflict societies. Drawing on Kubik and Bernhard's theoretical framework,[5] Oxana Shevel conceptualised Ukraine's decommunisation as a shift from a fractured memory regime dominated by two types of mnemonic warriors – pro-Russian Soviet nostalgists and West-leaning nationalists – towards a more unified model where the former have been marginalised,[6] whilst Maria Mälksoo introduced the notions of 'mnemonic security' and 'militant memocracy' in order to grasp Ukraine's dilemma of securitisation versus democratisation.[7]

Drawing on existing literature and the author's previous research,[8] this chapter seeks to re-evaluate the decommunisation legislation, its implementation, and its political and societal impact in the light of the full-scale Russian invasion of Ukraine in February 2022, which Moscow justified through ample reference to historical arguments.[9] While being subject to domestic and international criticism back in 2015, Ukraine's decommunisation policy appears in this new context as a legitimate measure which has strengthened national identity and social cohesion, as well as paved the way to de-Russification and decolonisation in response to Russian aggression. At the same time, as public opinion polls

[4] N Koposov, *Memory Laws, Memory Wars: The Politics of the Past in Europe and Russia* (Cambridge University Press, 2018) 177–206; G Kasianov, 'In Search of Lost Time? Decommunisation in Ukraine, 2014–2020' (2023) 71(4) *Problems of Post-Communism* 326; I Lyubashenko, 'Between Heroes and Perpetrators: Ukraine's Ambiguous Legal Approaches to the Soviet Legacy and Independence Fighters' in K Bachmann and C Garuka (eds), *Criminalizing History: Legal Restrictions on Statements and Interpretations of the Past in Germany, Poland, Rwanda, Turkey and Ukraine* (Peter Lang, 2020) 127–42; O Grytsenko, *Dekomunizatsiia v Ukraini yak derzhavna polityka i yak sotsiokulturne yavyshche* (IF Kuras Institute of Political and Ethnonational Studies, 2019); Y Vlasenko and BD Ryan, 'Decommunization by Design: Analyzing the Post-Independence Transformation of Soviet-Era Architectural Urbanism in Kyiv, Ukraine' (2022) 50 *Journal of Urban History* 247; M Kovalov, 'When Lenin Becomes Lennon: Decommunisation and the Politics of Memory in Ukraine' (2022) 74(5) *Europe-Asia Studies* 709.

[5] M Bernhard and J Kubik (eds), *Twenty Years After Communism: The Politics of Memory and Commemoration* (Oxford University Press, 2014).

[6] O Shevel, 'No Way Out? Post-Soviet Ukraine's Memory Wars in Comparative Perspective' in HE Hale and RW Orttung (eds), *Beyond the Euromaidan: Comparative Perspectives on Advancing Reform in Ukraine* (Stanford University Press, 2016) 21–40.

[7] M Mälksoo, 'Militant memocracy in International Relations: Mnemonical status anxiety and memory laws in Eastern Europe' (2021) 47(4) *Review of International Studies* 489.

[8] T Zhurzhenko, 'Legislating Historical Memory in Post-Soviet Ukraine' in E Barkan and A Lang (eds), *Memory Laws and Historical Justice: The Politics of Criminalizing the Past* (Palgrave Macmillan, 2022) 97–130.

[9] See G Bogush, 'Putin's Memory Policies in the Context of Military Aggression in Ukraine', Chapter 3 in the present volume.

demonstrate, the war has accelerated changes in the Ukrainian mass consciousness originally initiated by decommunisation.[10]

Although the chapter focuses on decommunisation laws adopted in 2015, it also delves into a more expansive period of Ukrainian politics (spanning from the Euromaidan to Russia's full-scale invasion in February 2022) in order to analyse the origins and effects of those laws. The mass protests in winter 2013–14, which resulted in the fall of Viktor Yanukovych's regime and were followed by Russia's annexation of Crimea and the military conflict in Donbas, became a watershed in the history of independent Ukraine. The patriotic mobilisation in response to the Russian aggression, the political realignment resulting from the snap parliamentary elections in October 2014, and the marginalisation of the pro-Russian/Soviet-nostalgic political forces (the Communist Party of Ukraine and the Party of Regions) opened the way for a radical reform of Ukraine's memory regime. The pro-European majority in the Ukrainian parliament voted for the decommunisation laws, a move fully supported by President Poroshenko. The enhanced role of the Ukrainian Institute of National Remembrance (UINP, *Ukrainskyi Instytut Natsionalnoi Pamiati*) and the support of local activists have ensured the relatively smooth implementation of the new legislation. Russia's embrace of the Soviet-nostalgic (and the Russian imperialist) narrative combined with its demonisation of Ukrainian nationalism, echoed by the self-proclaimed Donetsk and Luhansk 'republics' (the so-called DNR and LNR),[11] legitimised the securitisation of memory politics by Ukraine's ruling elites and made it easier for society to accept the new memory regime. Nevertheless, Ukrainians remained divided on the issue of the Soviet past and became increasingly tired of the politicisation of memory, language and religion. Capitalising on this post-revolutionary fatigue, Volodymyr Zelenskyi, who did not prioritise memory and identity, won the 2019 presidential elections; the same year, his newly formed political party, Servant of the People, gained an outright parliamentary majority. The new leadership, however, demonstrated a remarkable continuity in terms of memory politics. Decommunisation was carried on, but with a government less militant and more open to dialogue with local communities. Zelenskyi, in particular, favoured the rhetoric of reconciliation between Ukrainians with differing attitudes to the past. There is some irony to the fact that the Kremlin has chosen him, a Russian-speaking Ukrainian Jew, as an object of 'de-Nazification'. The full-scale Russian invasion posed radically new challenges to Ukrainian politics

[10] 'The Tenth National Survey: Ideological Markers of the War' (*Rating Group Ukraine*, 27 April 2022): https://ratinggroup.ua/en/research/ukraine/desyatyy_obschenacionalnyy_opros_ideologicheskie_markery_voyny_27_aprelya_2022.html.

[11] Donetsk people's republic (DNR – *Donetskaia narodnaia respublika*) and Lugansk people's republic (LNR – *Luganskaia narodnaia respublika*) were proclaimed in May 2014 on the territories of the Donetsk and Luhansk oblasts of Ukraine partly occupied by pro-Russian separatists backed by Moscow. In February 2022, Russia recognised the state sovereignty of DNR and LNR; in September 2022, following a sham referendum, they became part of the Russian Federation.

and society and marked the end of the decommunisation era, even if decommunisation has since been carried on under the broader agenda of decolonisation.

This chapter starts with a brief recapitulation of the changes introduced by the 2015 decommunisation laws and the political context which made their adoption possible. It then outlines the arguments of domestic and international critics, before (re-)considering the consequences of decommunisation for Ukrainian politics and society. It also addresses the role of the UINP in the transformation of Ukraine's memory regime. Finally, the chapter deals with the impact of the decommunisation laws on Ukraine's relations with Poland and, in particular, with Russia from a renewed perspective in light of the Russo-Ukrainian war. In the conclusion, I will return to the dilemma of Europeanisation versus securitisation of memory under the new conditions of war, on the one hand, and Ukraine's EU integration, on the other.

II. POLITICAL CONTEXT AND ESSENCE OF THE REFORM

The decommunisation legislation of 2015 did not come out of the blue; it was the culmination of more than a decade of memory wars in Ukrainian politics and society. Viktor Yushchenko's legacy of unfinished decommunisation continued to inspire national democrats and nationalists in parliament throughout the Yanukovych presidency (2010–14). Draft laws prohibiting communist ideology and criminalising the public denial of Soviet crimes were met with counter-drafts submitted by Communists and some pro-Russian politicians from the Party of Regions, who criminalised Ukrainian nationalism as 'fascist propaganda' and 'rehabilitation of Nazism'. None of the drafts submitted from either side of the political spectrum were adopted, but the significance of this proliferation of draft memory laws before the Euromaidan should not be underestimated: first, it pointed to the internationalisation of the Ukrainian discourse on the past, reflecting the conflict between Russian and European regimes of memory; second, it showed that the idea of legislating on history and criminalising certain statements about the past was becoming widely accepted across the whole spectrum of Ukrainian politics.[12]

The Euromaidan, the annexation of Crimea by Russia, and the outbreak of the military conflict in Donbas broke the fragile equilibrium of the Yanukovych era and led to a radical shift in the Ukrainian political landscape. The Party of Regions was marginalised and lost a significant part of its constituency with the Russian occupation of Crimea and Donbas, while the Communists were heavily compromised by their sympathies with Moscow.[13] As a result of the snap parliamentary elections in October 2014, a new pro-European coalition was formed

[12] Zhurzhenko, 'Legislating historical memory' (n 8) 112.
[13] Shevel, 'No way out?' (n 6); Lyubashenko, 'Between Heroes and Perpetrators' (n 4).

consisting of the Petro Poroshenko Bloc, the People's Front (led by Arseniy Yatsenyuk), Self-Reliance (the party of the Mayor of L'viv, Andriy Sadovyi), Yulia Tymoshenko's Batkivshchyna and the Radical Party of Oleh Liashko. The Opposition Bloc which succeeded the Party of Regions showed only modest results, with the Communist Party unable to reach the election threshold. The memory laws were thus easily passed by a parliamentary majority during the first reading, and without any debate, on 9 April 2015. On 15 May 2015, President Poroshenko signed them into law.

The laws were drafted by the UINP (for more on its role, see below) and experts from the Reanimation Package of Reforms (a coalition of non-governmental organisations which had emerged from the Euromaidan protests). This set of laws contained the following legislative acts: (i) 'On Access to the Archives of Repressive Organs of the Communist Totalitarian Regime 1917–1991';[14] (ii) 'On the Commemoration of the Victory over Nazism in World War II 1939–1945';[15] (iii) 'On the Legal Status and Honouring of the Memory of the Fighters for the Independence of Ukraine in the Twentieth Century';[16] and (iv) 'On Condemning the Communist and National Socialist (Nazi) Totalitarian Regimes and Prohibiting the Propaganda of their Symbols'.[17]

Of the four memory laws, the first two were prescriptive while the other two were prohibitive and thus more controversial (here I follow the classification of memory laws espoused by De Baets).[18] The first law required free access to the former KGB archives and their centralisation under the auspices of the UINP. The second law provided for the replacement of the Soviet term 'Great Patriotic War', still popular in Ukraine back then, with the more general term 'WWII'. It referred to the European narrative of WWII as the great tragedy of the twentieth century and to the victory over Nazism as a common achievement to which Ukraine had significantly contributed. In alignment with the European tradition of VE Day, the law introduced the Day of Memory and Reconciliation to be celebrated on 8 May, but also re-affirmed the status of the old Soviet Day of Victory on 9 May as a national holiday (now the Day of Victory over Nazism). In general, the law reflected the turn away from the Soviet narrative of the 'Great

[14] 'Pro dostup do arkhiviv represyvnykh orhaniv komunistychnoho totalitarnoho rezhymu 1917–1991 rokiv' (Law of Ukraine № 316-VIII from 9 April 2015), *Verkhovna Rada Ukrainy, Zakonodavstvo Ukrainy*: https://zakon.rada.gov.ua/laws/show/316-19#Text.

[15] 'Pro uvichnennia peremohy nad natsyzmom u Druhii Svitovii Viini 1939–1945 rokiv' (Law of Ukraine № 315-VIII from 9 April 2015), *Verkhovna Rada Ukrainy, Zakonodavstvo Ukrainy*: https://zakon.rada.gov.ua/laws/show/315-19#Text.

[16] 'Pro pravovyi status ta vshanuvannia pamiati bortsiv za nezalezhnist Ukrainy v XX stolitti' (Law of Ukraine № 314-VIII from 9 April 2015), *Verkhovna Rada Ukrainy, Zakonodavstvo Ukrainy*: https://zakon.rada.gov.ua/laws/show/314-19#Text.

[17] 'Pro zasudzhennia komunistychnoho ta natsional-sotsialistychnoho (natsyskoho) totalitarnykh rezhymiv v Ukraini ta zaboronu propahandy yikhnoi symvoliky' (Law of Ukraine № 317-VIII from 9 April 2015), *Verkhovna Rada Ukrainy, Zakonodavstvo Ukrainy*: https://zakon.rada.gov.ua/laws/show/317-19#Text.

[18] A de Baets, 'Laws Governing the Historian's Free Expression' in B Bevernage and N Wouters (eds), *The Palgrave Handbook of State-Sponsored History After 1945* (Palgrave Macmillan, 2018) 55.

Patriotic War' which had been politically instrumentalised in 2014 by Kremlin propaganda for pro-Russian mobilisation in the east and south of Ukraine.

The third memory law established a long list of organisations, movements and military formations which were declared 'fighters for Ukrainian independence in the twentieth century'. Some of these organisations had already been officially acknowledged on different occasions, while others were hardly known to the public. The inclusion of the historically controversial Organisation of Ukrainian Nationalists (OUN, *Orhanizatsiia Ukrainskykh Natsionalistiv*) and the Ukrainian Insurgent Army (UPA, *Ukrainska Povstanska Armiia*)[19] in the list seemed to mark the final rehabilitation of these nationalist organisations, thus putting an end to a protracted debate. Similarly to the second, the purpose of this law was to demarcate a shift from the Soviet to a newly established, and now officially prescribed, national narrative. This narrative constructed a continuation of the country's history from the Ukrainian People's Republic to the armed fight against the Soviet regime up to the late Soviet dissident movement and *Narodnyi Rukh* (People's Movement in Support of Perestroika). In particular, the law stipulated the following:

> Public denial of the legitimacy of the struggle for independence of Ukraine in the twentieth century is recognised as insult to the memory of fighters for independence of Ukraine in the XX century, disparagement of the Ukrainian people and is unlawful.[20]

Although the law introduced no explicit sanctions for such denial, this particular provision resulted in its classification as part of the prohibitive category.

Finally, the fourth law deemed criminal both the 'communist totalitarian regime of 1917–1991 in Ukraine' and the Nazi regime. It positioned communism and Nazism as being practically identical in terms of regimes:

> that exercised the policy of state terror characterised by numerous violations of human rights in the form of individual and mass murders, slaughters, deaths, deportations, tortures, use of forced labour and other forms of mass physical terror, persecution for ethnic, national, religious, political, class, social and other reasons, inflicting mental and physical sufferings via application of psychiatric measures for

[19] The OUN, a radical nationalist organisation, was established in 1929 and acted underground using methods of political violence, sabotage and terror with the aim of establishing an independent Ukrainian state on the territory of interwar Poland. In 1942, the UPA was founded as a military formation to continue the armed fight for Ukraine's independence. The Polish–Ukrainian conflict in the Nazi-occupied territories of eastern Poland culminated in an outbreak of violence in Volyn in summer 1943, when mass killings of Polish civilians were committed by the UPA. The activities of the OUN and UPA continued well into the late 1940s as an underground resistance against the Soviet regime after the annexation of the former eastern Polish territories by the USSR. For these reasons, the role of OUN and the UPA has been seen as highly controversial in both Poland and Russia.

[20] English translation by UINP, 'The law "On the Legal Status and Honoring the Memory of Fighters for Ukraine's Independence in the Twentieth Century"' (*UINP*, 2 March 2020): https://uinp.gov.ua/dokumenty/normatyvno-pravovi-akty-rozrobleni-v-instytuti/zakony/law-of-ukraine-on-the-legal-status-and-honoring-the-memory-of-fighters-for-ukraines-independence-in-the-twentieth-century (Law № 314-VIII, Article 6.2.).

> political purposes, violation of the freedom of conscience, thought, expression, press and lack of political pluralism and due to these reasons it is condemned as incompatible with the fundamental human and citizens' rights and liberties.[21]

In equating the Nazi and communist regimes, the law referred to the respective resolutions of PACE (the Council of Europe Parliamentary Assembly), OSCE (Organization for Security and Co-operation in Europe) and the European Parliament which underlined the need to dismantle the legacy of the communist totalitarian regimes.[22] This law decreed decommunisation per se by enforcing the dismantling of remaining monuments dedicated to the leaders of the Soviet regime, the removal of Soviet symbols in the public space, and changes to geographic names and toponyms linked to the Soviet period. The law also explicitly prohibited propaganda and symbols of the communist and National Socialist totalitarian regimes, and, for the first time in Ukrainian history, introduced criminal liability, ie, restraint of liberty for a term of up to five years (up to 10 years if committed in a group or by a person holding public office) for the production, dissemination or public use of such symbols.

III. DOMESTIC AND INTERNATIONAL CRITICISM

A revolution in the Ukrainian legislation regulating the public use of history, the laws on decommunisation faced a lot of criticism from the first day they were adopted by parliament. This criticism came from traditional ideological opponents – ie, Soviet-nostalgic and pro-Russian political forces – as well as from inside the liberal democratic camp. Critical voices from inside the country were joined by international ones, including Ukraine's most significant neighbours

[21] English translation by UINP, 'The law "On the Condemnation of the Communist and National Socialist (Nazi) Regimes, and Prohibition of Propaganda of their Symbols"' (*UINP*, 2 March 2020): https://uinp.gov.ua/dokumenty/normatyvno-pravovi-akty-rozrobleni-v-instytuti/zakony/law-of-ukraine-on-the-condemnation-of-the-communist-and-national-socialist-nazi-regimes-and-prohibition-of-propaganda-of-their-symbols (Law № 317-VIII, Article 2.2.).

[22] See, eg: 'Measures to dismantle the heritage of former communist totalitarian systems' (*Resolutions of the Council of Europe Parliamentary Assembly (PACE):* No 1096, 27 June 1996): https://assembly.coe.int/nw/xml/XRef/Xref-XML2HTML-en.asp?fileid=16507; 'Need for international condemnation of crimes of totalitarian communist regimes' (*PACE*, No 1481 from 25 January 2006) http://assembly.coe.int/nw/xml/xref/xref-xml2html-en.asp?fileid=17403&lang=en;' Combating the resurrection of nazi ideology' (*PACE*, No 1495 from 12 April 2006): www.assembly.coe.int/nw/xml/xref/xref-xml2html-en.asp?fileid=17427&lang=en;'Attitude to memorials exposed to different historical interpretations in Council of Europe member states' (*UINP*, No 1652 from 29 January 2009): https://assembly.coe.int/nw/xml/XRef/Xref-XML2HTML-en.asp?fileid=17713&lang=en; 'Declaration of the European Parliament on the proclamation of 23 August as European Day of Remembrance for Victims of Stalinism and Nazism' (*European Parliament*, 23 September 2008): www.europarl.europa.eu/doceo/document/TA-6-2008-0439_EN.html; 'Commemoration of the Holodomor, the Ukraine artificial famine (1932–1933)' (*European Parliament*, 23 October 2008): www.europarl.europa.eu/doceo/document/TA-6-2008-0523_EN.html; 'European conscience and totalitarianism' (*European Parliament*, 2 April 2009): www.europarl.europa.eu/doceo/document/TA-6-2009-0213_EN.html.

and long-term mnemonic rivals: Poland and Russia[23] (see more on this aspect in the last two sections of this chapter).

For analytical purposes, the arguments underlying this criticism can be differentiated into historical (addressing the historical narrative prescribed by the law) and legal-political (concerned with the implications of the new legal norms for Ukrainian society). Quite naturally, the first type of argument has mainly been confined to debates amongst historians. The law on fighters for Ukrainian independence was criticised for failing to mention the controversial aspects of the UPA and OUN activities, and for making the struggle for independence the main aspect of Ukrainian history.[24] The law on condemning the communist and Nazi regimes came under fire for failing to differentiate between these two totalitarian regimes and between Stalinism and the late Soviet period.[25]

In practice, however, various actors merged critical arguments of different kinds. For example, the Communists and pro-Russian politicians of the Opposition Bloc protested what they saw as 'historical revisionism' and the 'rehabilitation of Ukrainian nationalism', complaining at the same time about the 'authoritarian methods' used to impose the new memory regime. Meanwhile, historians who criticised the selective or highly simplified approach to history were also concerned about possible restrictions on freedom of research and historical writing. This related in particular to the law on fighters for Ukrainian independence, where any critical inquiry into the history of Ukrainian nationalism could easily be interpreted as an unlawful 'insult to the memory' of the people in question. An open letter to the president and head of parliament, initiated by a number of Ukrainian and Western historians,[26] opposed 'the wholesale condemnation of the entire Soviet period as one of occupation of Ukraine' and argued that the content and spirit of the two punitive laws were contrary to freedom of speech. The authors advised against the passage of the laws, warning that their introduction would damage Ukraine's reputation as 'a tolerant and inclusive state'.[27]

[23] The mnemonic legislation 'entangled' in the Ukraine-Russia-Poland triangle is analysed in U Belavusau, A Gliszczyńska-Grabias and M Mälksoo, 'Memory Laws and Memory Wars in Poland, Russia and Ukraine' (2021) 69 *Jahrbuch des öffentlichen Rechts* 95. See also: H Kasianov, *Past Continuous. Istorychna polityka 1980-kh – 2000-kh. Ukraina ta susidy* (Laurus, 2018) 322–90; N Koposov, 'Populism and Memory: Legislation of the Past in Poland, Ukraine, and Russia' (2022) 36 *East European Politics and Societies and Cultures* 272.

[24] G Kasianov, 'Nationalist Memory Narratives and the Politics of History in Ukraine since the 1990s' *Nationalities Papers* (2023); JP Himka, 'Legislating historical truth: Ukraine's laws of 9 April 2015' *Ab imperio*, 21 April 2015); Koposov, *Memory Laws* (n 4) 203.

[25] Koposov, *Memory Laws* (n 4) 204.

[26] 'Letter: Experts Worry that "Decommunization" Laws Curtail Free Speech' (*Atlantic Council*, 22 April 2025): www.atlanticcouncil.org/blogs/ukrainealert/letter-experts-worry-that-decommunisation-laws-curtail-free-speech/.

[27] See, for eg, the collection of essays on decommunisation published by *Krytyka* under the heading 'The Future of Ukraine's Past' (*Krytyka*): https://m.krytyka.com/en/featured-topics/future-ukraines-past.

Overall, the coercive prescription of the official historical narrative, which excluded alternative or critical voices, worried journalists, historians and human rights activists in Ukraine and abroad.[28] An expert from the Human Rights Protection Group, an influential organisation with a long history of human rights advocacy, also called on the president to veto the most controversial laws. She argued that Ukrainian society was divided on aspects of its difficult past, and thus imposing one single view would effectively silence a significant part of the Ukrainian population.[29] According to David Marples, a historian from Canada, the decommunisation strategy was 'treated by the authorities as a social form of economic shock therapy: at breakneck speed and without much discussion'.[30] Vague definitions such as 'propaganda', 'falsification of history', and 'denial of the criminal nature of the regime' would, critics argued, open the way for the political instrumentalisation and prosecution of opponents.[31] In particular, the law on condemning the communist and Nazi regimes drew criticism from the Venice Commission[32] and the OSCE in a Joint Interim Opinion;[33] the OSCE Representative on Freedom of the Media, Dunja Mijatović, expressed her frustration at Poroshenko's signing of the laws despite calls to safeguard freedom of speech and media.[34]

Finally, it was argued that such a radical reform could further alienate that part of the Ukrainian population that did not accept the Euromaidan revolution and which is susceptible to Russian propaganda.[35] Imposing a unilateral view of history upon a divided Ukrainian society haunted by pro-Russian separatism would make reconciliation even more difficult.[36] Moreover, it could play into the hands of Moscow and exacerbate internal Ukrainian conflict. While the

[28] *cf* Kasianov, 'In Search of Lost Time?' (n 4); O Shevel, 'The Battle for Historical Memory in Postrevolutionary Ukraine' (2016) 115 *Current History* 258.

[29] H Coynash, 'Parliament ignores public opinion on Ukraine's history. Will the President?' (*Human Rights in Ukraine*, 13 April 2015): https://khpg.org/en/1428876846.

[30] DR Marples, 'The Destruction of "Colonial Remnants" in Ukraine' (*E-International Relations*, 14 July 2017): www.e-ir.info/2017/07/14/the-destruction-of-colonial-remnants-in-ukraine/.

[31] O Shevel '"De-Communization Laws" Need to Be Amended to Conform to European Standards' (*Vox Ukraine*, 7 May 2015): https://voxukraine.org/en/decommunisation-laws-need-to-be-amended-to-conform-to-european-standards.

[32] The European Commission for Democracy through Law, which meets in Venice, is the Council of Europe's advisory body on constitutional matters.

[33] 'Venice Commission Opinion no. 823/2015 ODIHR, Opinion no. FOE-UKR/280/2015' (21 December 2015): www.venice.coe.int/webforms/documents/default.aspx?pdffile=CDL-AD(2015)041-e; see also: H Coynash, 'Ukraine's Decommunisation Law hammered by Venice Commission for violating democratic standards' (*Kharkiv (Human Rights Protection Group (KHRPG)*, 21 December 2015): https://khpg.org/en/1450571329.

[34] 'New laws in Ukraine potential threat to free expression and free media, OSCE Representative says' (*OSCE*, 18 May 2015): www.osce.org/fom/158581.

[35] *cf* H Coynash, "Decommunization" Laws: Deeply Divisive and Destined for Strasbourg' (*Krytyka*, April 2015): https://krytyka.com/en/articles/decommunisation-laws-deeply-divisive-and-destined-strasbourg.

[36] I Nuzov, 'Transitional Justice in Ukraine: National Reconciliation or Reconsolidation of Post-Communist Trauma?' (*International Center for Transitional Justice*, 17 October 2016): https://ictj.org/es/node/22470.

proponents of decommunisation, such as the Director of the UINP, Volodymyr Viatrovych, referred to security as a key argument in favour of decommunisation, arguing that 'bearers of Soviet values … are today the main source of manpower for the terrorist bands of the so-called DNR and LNR',[37] critics saw the divisive potential of the decommunisation laws as a threat to national security.

As pointed out by Shevel, the reform was complicated by the fact that the

> criticism of decommunisation laws has come both from intellectual circles in the West and in Ukraine that are genuinely concerned with upholding freedom of expression and fostering free historical inquiry, and from retrograde forces in Ukraine and Russia concerned first and foremost with keeping Ukraine in the Russian sphere of influence and preserving the Soviet era memory regime.[38]

In the context of hybrid Russian aggression exploiting antagonistic memories and of the internal crisis resulting in the extreme polarisation of Ukrainian society, this criticism itself was inevitably instrumentalised as a political weapon. Despite widespread appeals to amend the controversial laws and bring them closer to European standards, neither the president, nor the political parties that had voted for the legislation, nor the UINP, have showed any interest in such amendments. Having learned from previous Ukrainian history that a political window of opportunity can close quickly, these political actors were interested first and foremost in the speedy implementation and irreversibility of the legislative changes. A less resolute approach would also have looked like a sign of weakness and of buckling under the pressure exerted by Russia and its allies in Ukrainian politics.

IV. IMPLEMENTATION AND IMPACT

Of the four decommunisation laws, it is the law on condemning the communist and Nazi regimes which has had the most far-reaching implications for Ukrainian society and given rise to especially heated debates, as it implied a radical transformation of the commemorative landscape. In this section, I will therefore focus on the implementation of this particular law. Having learnt from previous experience (Yushchenko's decree of 2008 on the removal of monuments to Soviet leaders guilty of organising the *Holodomor* was largely ignored by local authorities),[39] the architects of decommunisation built in an implementation mechanism. This time, local authorities were left with little opportunity for sabotage, as their responsibility and the strict deadlines for implementing the required changes were determined by law. If local authorities failed to decide

[37] V Viatrovych, '"Decommunization" and Academic Discussion' (*Krytyka*, April 2015): https://krytyka.com/en/articles/decommunisation-and-academic-discussion.

[38] Shevel, 'The Battle for Historical Memory' (n 28) 263.

[39] *cf* T Zhurzhenko, '"Capital of Despair". Holodomor Memory and Political Conflicts in Kharkiv after the Orange Revolution' (2011) 25 *East European Politics and Societies* 597–639.

on renaming of Soviet-linked places within a six-month period, the regional authorities were supposed to step in; in contested cases, the government had the final say.

While local authorities often referred to budget constraints and the low support for decommunisation among the population, in general they complied with the law.[40] Some, such as the Mayor of Kharkiv, came up with 'creative solutions' to minimise administrative costs (and give Kyiv the finger behind his back): the Dzerzhynskyi district was 'renamed' after the brother of the founder of the Soviet secret police, a local doctor, and the Frunze district after the son of a famous Bolshevik, a military pilot. Despite the attempts of local authorities to hijack and manipulate the public hearings prescribed by the law, local activists who supported decommunisation (eg the Kharkiv Toponymic Group) used the available democratic instruments to put forward alternative suggestions and start a public debate.[41] The pressure from below, including so-called 'wild decommunisation' – the violent tearing down of Soviet monuments by radical activists –, helped to convince local authorities that giving the process a legal form would allow better control.

Despite the low support for, and even passive opposition to, decommunisation among the population,[42] its traditional political opponents failed to capitalise on the public mood and organise visible public protests. They had other problems and were thus focused on fighting for their political survival. Following the law on condemning the communist and Nazi regimes, the Communist Party of Ukraine (and a couple of smaller parties with the adjective 'communist' in the title) were banned in December 2015. The Opposition Bloc – the much-weakened successor of the Party of Regions – sharply criticised the decommunisation laws in parliament and even appealed to the Constitutional Court, alas without much success.[43] The 'Anti-Maidan' and pro-Russian radicals active in the east and south of Ukraine from 2014 to the beginning of 2015 were either arrested or forced to leave for Russia. In this situation, the lack of popular support for the decommunisation laws and even the widespread

[40] O Shevel, 'Decommunisation in Post-Euromaidan Ukraine, Law and Practice' PONARS Eurasia Policy Memo January 2016: www.ponarseurasia.org/wp-content/uploads/attachments/Pepm411_Shevel_Jan2016-1.pdf.

[41] V Noskov, 'Kharkiv Fights Tooth And Nail Against Ukraine Decommunisation Process' (*Radio Free Europe/ Radio Liberty*, 20 November 2015): www.rferl.org/a/ukraine-kharkiv-decommunisation/27377959.html; for more on decommunisation in Kharkiv see: M Takhtaulova, 'Kharkivska toponimika: etapy dekommunizatsii' (2017) 2 *City: History, Culture, Society* 142–51.

[42] In autumn 2016, an opinion poll conducted by the Sociological Group 'Rating' confirmed the low popularity of the decommunisation policy, especially in the east and south. 'Stavlennia do okremykh istorychnykh postatei ta protsesu dekomunizatsii v Ukraini' (*Rating Group Ukraine*, 17 November 2016): https://ratinggroup.ua/files/ratinggroup/reg_files/decommunisation_rg_112016.pdf.

[43] See: A Nekoliak, 'Ukraine's Constitutional Court, Historical Narrative-Making, and the Law' (*MELA (Memory Laws in European and Comparative Perspective)*, 30 November 2020): https://melaproject.org/blog/601 for an analysis of the verdict.

(but largely non-ideological) opposition to them could not be converted into political mobilisation.[44]

Decommunisation definitely had a regional dimension, with the symbolic landscape in the east and south in particular shaped by Soviet-era urbanisation and industrialisation. The list of almost 900 localities subject to renaming, according to the UINP, was led by the Donetsk, Dnipropetrovsk and Kharkiv regions, followed by the Crimea, Odesa and Luhansk regions.[45] Thus, decommunisation implied a more radical transformation of the symbolic landscape in parts of Ukraine where there was less popular support. This regional challenge to the implementation of decommunisation was, however, reduced by Russia's annexation of Crimea and its support for the separatist 'people's republics' of Donbas. As noted by Shevel, 'where the opposition would have been strongest, the process is not going to take place due to inability of the central government to enforce the law'.[46] Despite this, in May 2016, the Ukrainian parliament renamed a number of localities in the temporarily occupied territories of the Donetsk and Luhansk regions[47] and the Republic of Crimea.[48] In Crimea, many places regained their original Crimean Tatar names; shortly after Kyiv's decision, the Google Maps service even adopted the changes. However, it restored the Russian version following protests from Moscow.[49] Decommunisation in the occupied territories is seen as part of Ukraine's comprehensive de-occupation agenda. At the same time, decommunisation, despite being only virtual, predictably prompted extremely negative reactions from 'public officials' in Donbas and Crimea and was used for the ideological consolidation of the local population around the Soviet-nostalgic and anti-Ukrainian stance.

In February 2018, UINP Director Viatrovych reported that decommunisation was 'almost completed': around 1,000 localities and 52,000 streets had been renamed, and 2,500 monuments had been removed.[50] The most controversial and debated cases – including the renaming of two oblast centres, Dnipropetrovsk as Dnipro and Kirovohrad as Kropyvnytskyi – were also closed despite the attempts of opponents to challenge the decision in court. In some

[44] Shevel, 'Decommunisation in Post-Euromaidan Ukraine' (n 40).

[45] 'Perelik mist i sil do pereimenuvannia' (UINP, n.d.): https://old.uinp.gov.ua/rename.

[46] Shevel, 'Decommunisation in Post-Euromaidan Ukraine' (n 40) 3.

[47] Postanova Verkhovnoi Rady Ukrainy № 1351-VIII from 12 May 2016 'Pro pereimenuvannia okremykh naselenykh punktiv ta raioniv na tymchasovo okupovanykh terytoriiakh Donetskoi ta Luhanskoi oblastei' in *Verkhovna Rada Ukrainy, Zakonodavstvo Ukrainy*: https://zakon.rada.gov.ua/laws/show/1351-19#Text.

[48] Postanova Verkhovnoi Rady Ukrainy № 1352-VIII from 12 May 2016 'Pro pereimenuvannia okremykh naselenykh punktiv ta raioniv Avtonomnoi Respubliky Krym ta mista Sevastopolia' in *Verkhovna Rada Ukrainy, Zakonodavstvo Ukrainy*: https://zakon.rada.gov.ua/laws/show/1352-19#Text.

[49] T Lokot, 'Here's Why Google Maps Changed Some Town Names in Crimea – And Is Now Changing Them Back' (*Global Voices*, 29 July 2016): https://globalvoices.org/2016/07/29/heres-why-google-maps-changed-some-town-names-in-crimea-and-is-now-changing-them-back/.

[50] 'Dekomunizatsiia v Ukraini faktychno zavershena – Viatrovych' (*Ukrainska Pravda*, 10 February 2018): www.pravda.com.ua/news/2018/02/10/7171212/.

cases, such as the removal of the Marshal Zhukov monument and the renaming of Zhukov Avenue after the Soviet dissident General Hryhorenko (Grigorenko) in Kharkiv, the political conflict turned into a protracted legal battle between the city authorities and local activists, which ended with the victory of the latter only after Russia's full-scale invasion.

One of the unintended consequences of decommunisation was the emergence of a public discussion about the future of Soviet monumental sculpture and public decorative art deemed 'ideologically wrong' and thus under threat of destruction. Some Soviet monuments, such as the equestrian statue of the Red Army Commander and Civil War hero Mykola Shchors (1885–1919) in Kyiv, or the Legendary Tachanka monument in Kakhovka, Kherson region, were the subject of especially heated discussions. A number of public, cultural and artistic initiatives aimed at the preservation of the Soviet cultural heritage have emerged over the last decade.[51]

Finally, the implementation of the most controversial aspect of the decommunisation legislation – its punitive component – should be briefly mentioned. As the law on fighters for Ukraine's independence was only declarative in this respect, this mainly concerns the law on condemning the communist and Nazi regimes, which resulted in a new article of the Criminal Code criminalising the production and dissemination of communist and Nazi symbols and the propaganda of these totalitarian regimes. As shown by Lyubashenko[52] and Nekoliak,[53] there has been a steady growth in the number of registered criminal cases (from two in 2015 to 53 in 2021), with only a handful resulting in an actual verdict (suspended short-term imprisonment). While human rights activists continued to argue that even one such case is one too many, one can say, however, that the courts have been reticent in applying this article of the Criminal Code, which could mean actual imprisonment for up to five years with or without confiscation of property.

V. ROLE OF THE UKRAINIAN INSTITUTE OF NATIONAL REMEMBRANCE (UINP)

The role of the UINP in the drafting, adoption and implementation of the decommunisation laws deserves special attention, as it has significantly contributed to the outcomes – positive and negative – of the reform. Due to the troubled political

[51] eg, Y Nikiforov and O Balashova, *De-communized. Ukrainian Soviet Mosaics* (Osnovy / DOM, 2017). For an overview of artistic projects and the debate, see: E Sułek, 'The Past Living in the Future: Ukrainian Politics of Memory in Visual Arts after Maidan' (*Switch on Paper*, 4 September 2020): www.switchonpaper.com/en/geopolitics/memory/the-past-living-in-the-future-ukrainian-politics-of-memory-in-visual-arts-after-maidan-2/.

[52] Lyubashenko, 'Between Heroes and Perpetrators' (n 4).

[53] See A Nekoliak, 'Ukrainian Memory Laws and Policies in the Context of 2022 Russian Aggression', Chapter 6 in the present volume.

history of post-Soviet Ukraine and its abruptly changing memory regimes, one can in fact talk about three or even four different 'Institutes' since 2006, when it was first established on the initiative of President Yushchenko, inspired by the examples of other Eastern European countries, in particular, Poland.[54] Although the Institute as a central body of executive power was helpful in implementing the Law 'On the *Holodomor* of 1932–1933 in Ukraine'[55] as well as organising commemorative, research and publishing activities, it lacked sufficient resources and became hostage to political infighting inside Ukraine's Orange government. Under Yanukovych, who had little interest in memory politics, the status of the Institute was downgraded to a research facility under the auspices of the Cabinet of Ministers. Under the newly appointed Director, historian Varerii Soldatenko, a member of the Communist Party of Ukraine, the research agenda shifted to the left. After the Euromaidan, however, the initial status of the Institute was restored and Volodymyr Viatrovych, a historian and co-founder of the Centre for Studies of the Liberation Movement in Lviv, was appointed as its new Director. As head of the Ukrainian Security Service (SBU, *Sluzhba Bezpeky Ukrainy*) Archives from 2008 to 2010, and in this capacity an important ally for Yushchenko in fulfilment of his decommunisation efforts, Viatrovych had the necessary administrative experience accompanied by a strong sense of political mission. However, his uncritical approach to the history of the OUN and the UPA earned him the reputation of a propagandist rather than a historian. Viatrovych himself eagerly assumed the mantle of an active promotor of the new historical narrative and saw the mission of the UINP as shattering the historical myths created by Soviet propaganda.

Under his leadership, the UINP played a central role in drafting the decommunisation laws, their public promotion and the supervision of their implementation.[56] The Institute developed guidelines, methodological materials and recommendations for local self-government, thus contributing to the informational support of the reform.[57] In contested cases, the Institute was proactive,

[54] A brief history of the Institute (from a rather critical angle) between 2006 and 2019 is provided by G Kasianov, *Memory Crash: The Politics of History in and around Ukraine 1980s–2010s* (CEU Press, 2022) 121–35. On the changes at the UINP after 2019 and since the Russian invasion see: A Nekoliak, 'Towards Liberal Memory Politics? Discussing Recent Changes at Ukraine's Memory Institute' (*Cultures of History Forum*, 16 January 2020): www.cultures-of-history.uni-jena.de/politics/discussing-recent-changes-at-ukraines-memory-institute, and A Nekoliak, 'Ukrainian Memory Laws and Policies in the Context of 2022 Russian Aggression' Chapter 6 in the present volume; see also: A Nekoliak, 'Institute of National Memory / Ukrainskyi Instytut Natsionalnoi Pamiati (Ukraine)' in L Stan and N Nedelsky (eds), *Encyclopedia of Transitional Justice* (2nd edn, Cambridge University Press, 2023) 1346–51.

[55] 'Pro Holodomor 1932–1933 rokiv v Ukraini' (Law of Ukraine № 376-V from 28 November 2006), *Verkhovna Rada Ukrainy, Zakonodavstvo Ukrainy*: https://zakon.rada.gov.ua/laws/show/376-V#Text.

[56] *cf* G Kasianov, 'In Search of Lost Time?' (n 4); Vlasenko and Ryan, 'Decommunisation by Design'.

[57] S Butko et al, *Dekomunizatsiia: shcho i chomu repeimenovuvaty i demontuvatu. Zbirnyk materialiv, rekomendatsii i dokumentiv shchodo vykonannia vymoh Zakonu Ukrainy 'Pro zasudzhennia komunistychnoho ta natsional-sotsialistychnoho (natsyskoho) totalitarnykh rezhymiv v Ukraini ta*

insisting on full implementation of the law and often supporting activists in their fight with local authorities. In the aforementioned conflict around the renaming of Marshal Zhukov Avenue in Kharkiv, for example, the Institute contacted the procurator's office regarding the city council's decision to revoke the renaming.[58] The Institute's role in the controversial renaming of Kirovohrad was also telling: the UINP opposed the suggestion to rename it Yelizavethrad, the name the city had under Russian imperial rule (1754–1924), a reference to Russian empress Yelizaveta. Instead, it recommended renaming the city Kropyvnytskyi after one of the founders of the Ukrainian National Theatre. While these decisions were formally taken by the respective parliamentary commission and voted on by parliament, the Institute and its Director certainly had the upper hand in such cases. This example also shows how the legacy of the Soviet regime in Ukraine was viewed by the UINP as part of a broader issue: centuries-old Russian political and cultural dominance. Although decolonisation and de-Russification were not part of the decommunisation legislation, the UINP under Viatrovych's leadership acted, in this respect, ahead of time: the Law 'On the Condemnation and Prohibition of Propaganda of Russian Imperial Policy in Ukraine and the Decolonization of Toponymy' was adopted in 2023, after the Russian invasion.[59]

Beyond the formal decommunisation agenda, the programme of commemorative events developed by the Institute on the occasion of the 100th anniversary of the Ukrainian revolution (1917–21) traced Ukraine's tradition of statehood (and revolution) from the Ukrainian People's Republic to the Euromaidan. According to Viatrovych, the lessons drawn from the failure of the newly founded Ukrainian state in the face of an attack by Bolshevik Russia were important for post-Maidan Ukraine in its fight against neo-imperial Russia, its historical enemy.[60] The concept of the 'hundred years war for independence', which frames the current Russo-Ukrainian war as just another phase in the long history of Ukraine's fight against Russian imperial oppression, was embraced by a significant part of Ukrainian society, especially after February 2022.[61]

zaboronu propahandy yikhnoi symvoliky' (Kyiv, Ukrainskyi Instytut Natsionalnoi Pamiati, 2015) https://old.uinp.gov.ua/sites/default/files/decomunizaciya-r.pdf. For more materials see the UINP website: https://old.uinp.gov.ua/page/dekomunizatsiya-0.

[58] 'Viatrovych zvernuvsia u prokuraturu cherez povernennia dekomunizovanomu prospektu v Kharkovi imeni marshala Zhukova' (*Gordon*, 6 July 2019): https://gordonua.com/ukr/news/politics/-v-jatrovich-zvernuvsja-v-prokuraturu-z-za-povernennja-dekommunizirovannomu-prospektu-v-harkovi-imeni-marshala-zhukova-1094599.html.

[59] 'Pro zasudzhennia ta zaboronu propahandy rosiiskoi imperskoi polityky v Ukraini i dekolonizatsiiu toponimii' (Law of Ukraine № 3005-IX from 21 March 2023), *Verkhovna Rada Ukrainy, Zakonodavstvo Ukrainy*, https://zakon.rada.gov.ua/laws/show/3005-IX#Text. See also A Nekoliak, 'Ukrainian Memory Laws and Policies in the Context of 2022 Russian Aggression' Chapter 6 in the present volume.

[60] T Zhurzhenko, 'The making and unmaking of revolutions: What 1917 means for Ukraine, in light of the Maidan' (*Eurozine*, 30 November 2017): www.eurozine.com/the-making-and-unmaking-of-revolutions/.

[61] T Zhurzhenko, 'Making sense of the war' (*Eurozine*, 16 June 2022): www.eurozine.com/making-sense-of-the-war/.

Looking back on his years as Director, Viatrovych named among his main achievements the opening of the former KGB archives to the public, the decommunisation of the public space, and his contribution to new projects commemorating the recent dramatic events in Ukrainian history: the Museum of the Maidan and the Memorial to the Heavenly Hundred, both in Kyiv. No less important from today's perspective of the Russo-Ukrainian war was Ukraine's distancing itself from the 'Great Patriotic War' narrative and its Soviet symbolism. The emphasis shifted from victory to reconciliation and from the years 1941–45 to 1939–45; the St George ribbon, used as a pro-Russian symbol in 2014–15, was banned; and new Ukrainian symbols were introduced, including a poppy flower as a sign of mourning and the motto 'Never again', both connecting to the European tradition of commemorating WWII. The new Ukrainian narrative of WWII promoted from 2015 onwards was consciously constructed as inclusive, accommodating the heroes of the UPA as well as those who fought in the Soviet Army, making visible the contribution of women and national minorities, and even mentioning the Holocaust. (Critics of the Institute, however, considered this merely a form of political correctness aimed at camouflaging traditional ethnic nationalism; the failure to address the controversial aspects of the UPA history only went to prove this).[62]

In sum, the UINP was extremely efficient from 2014 to 2019, but its activities were highly controversial. Decommunisation, the most radical attempt to get rid of the Soviet symbolic legacy in Ukraine, was accomplished quickly and did not lead to mass protests and political destabilisation. Even if the majority did not support the changes, the new status quo was soon accepted by Ukrainian society. But the methods which allowed for the success of the reform were heavily criticised, and the new memory regime was often seen as unfairly excluding significant parts of society. The Institute was accused of merely replacing the Soviet-nostalgic narrative with a nationalist one, instead of promoting a culture of dialogue and historical reflection.

VI. DECOMMUNISATION AND RELATIONS WITH POLAND

The decommunisation laws, and in particular the adoption of the law on fighters for Ukrainian independence, which finally granted OUN and UPA an official status, did not come as a shock to Poland, as the two countries share a long history of political tensions over their common past. While post-communist Poland and independent Ukraine embarked on a strategic partnership in the early 1990s, it repeatedly stumbled over unsolved controversies. In the mid-2010s, the memory wars between the two countries intensified. When PiS (Law and Justice Party) came to power in 2015, issues of historical memory and identity

[62] Kasianov, *Memory Crash* (n 54) 132.

became more pronounced in Polish domestic and foreign policy.[63] Though the latter also concerned Russia, Germany and Israel, it was especially damaging for Ukrainian–Polish relations. In 2016, the Polish parliament adopted a resolution declaring the Volyn massacre an act of genocide committed by Ukrainian nationalists.[64] The PiS government's commitment to strategic cooperation with Ukraine and support for Ukraine's European integration was made dependent on Kyiv's revision of its historical policy. In 2017, the Polish Minister of Foreign Affairs, Witold Waszczykowski, famously promised that 'Ukraine will not enter the EU with Bandera'.[65] In 2018, the Polish parliament adopted a new law, criminalising accusations against Poland or the Polish people of complicity in crimes committed during the Holocaust as well as the denial of crimes against the Polish population committed by Ukrainian nationalists.[66] 'Ukrainians' were the only national group explicitly stated to have carried out such crimes. In an official statement, the Ukrainian parliament condemned the Polish law as opening up 'the road to manipulation and strengthening of anti-Ukrainian tendencies in Polish society'.[67] The law was amended the same year and once again in 2019, with the controversial wording 'Ukrainian nationalist' removed; yet, it is still punishable by up to three years' imprisonment to deny crimes of 'members of Ukrainian formations that collaborated with the Third Reich'.[68]

In Ukraine, the rise of nationalism after the Euromaidan was mainly a result of Russian aggression. The growing popularity of the OUN-UPA and Stepan Bandera as symbols of national resistance in war-torn Ukraine did not reflect an anti-Polish sentiment (in fact, many Ukrainians, especially in the east and south, had little knowledge of the difficult Ukrainian–Polish past). But Ukraine's relations with Poland became collateral damage of this development. One example was the renaming of Kyiv's Moscow Avenue to Bandera Avenue in July 2016,

[63] See A Gliszczyńska-Grabias, 'Wounds Unhealed: Polish-Ukrainian and Polish-Russian Memory Wars before 2022', Chapter 7 in the present volume.

[64] 'Poland's Parliament Declares Volyn Massacres "Genocide," Ukraine Laments Move' (*Radio Free Europe / Radio Liberty*, 22 July 2016): www.rferl.org/a/poland-parliament-declares-volyn-massacres-/27874252.html. Stepan Bandera (1909–59) was a right-wing Ukrainian nationalist who led the OUN, alleged Nazi collaborator and deemed an enemy by many Poles.

[65] 'You will not enter Europe with Bandera: Polish FM Waszczykowski on Ukraine's EU integration prospects' (*Censor*, 4 July 2017): https://censor.net/en/n446466.

[66] Ustawa z dnia 26 stycznia 2018 r. 'O zmianie ustawy o Instytucie Pamięci Narodowej – Komisji Ścigania Zbrodni przeciwko Narodowi Polskiemu, ustawy o grobach i cmentarzach wojennych, ustawy o muzeach oraz ustawy o odpowiedzialności podmiotów zbiorowych za czyny zabronione pod groźbą kary' [Law from 26 January 2018 Amending the Law of 18 December 1998 on the Institute of National Remembrance – Commission for the Prosecution of Crimes against the Polish Nation]: https://orka.sejm.gov.pl/proc8.nsf/ustawy/771_u.htm.

[67] 'Ukrainian parliament condemns Polish law banning Bandera ideology' (*Ukrinform*, 6 February 2018): www.ukrinform.net/rubric-polytics/2397345-ukrainian-parliament-condemns-polish-law-banning-bandera-ideology.html.

[68] For an analysis of the law, in particular the Ukraine aspect, see: U Belavusau, 'The Rise of Memory Laws in Poland: An Adequate Tool to Counter Historical Disinformation?' (2018) 29 *Security and Human Rights* 36, 36–54.

which coincided with President Poroshenko's visit to Warsaw.[69] The law on the fighters for Ukrainian independence, which (as mentioned above) included the OUN and UPA, predictably provoked a negative response. Perhaps the biggest scandal was down to timing: Ukrainian MPs voted for the law in a package with other decommunisation laws on the day of Polish President Komorowski's visit to Kyiv and only hours after his solidarity speech in the Ukrainian parliament.[70] Former Polish Prime Minister Leszek Miller insisted that the OUN was responsible for mass murders of Poles during WWII, and challenged Ukraine to prosecute him.[71] Some Polish experts, however, took a rather balanced approach, admitting that the law is not about the OUN and UPA per se, as the two organisations are mentioned in the same breath as dozens of others, that Nazi collaborators (such as the SS-Galicia Division) are not on the list, and that the act is merely symbolic and does not grant a veteran status (and related social benefits) to anyone.[72] For sure, this aspect of the decommunisation legislation did not improve Ukraine's relations with Poland, though it did not cause a major blow to it either.

Probably more important than the legislation itself was the role of the UINP in (un-)settling Ukrainian-Polish historical controversies. Under the leadership of Viatrovych, this role was rather divisive, and not only because of his position as a historian who promoted an apologist approach to the history of Ukrainian nationalism and denied military crimes committed by the UPA. Viatrovych was a firm proponent of 'mnemonic sovereignty' and a hardliner who believed that the Ukrainian state should be assertive and, following the Polish example, not give in to pressure from outside. In this sense, the UINP, for which the Polish Institute of National Remembrance served as a model, copied to some extent its behaviour under the PiS government. Having established working contacts with its Polish counterpart from the outset, the UINP soon faced the limits of such cooperation. As the so-called war of graves escalated between the two countries, relations were frozen. Indeed, burial sites and memorials of WWII were regularly vandalised on both sides of the Ukrainian-Polish border, but in 2017, the situation was aggravated when a monument to UPA soldiers at the Hruszowice cemetery in Poland was demolished. Constructed in 1994 on the initiative of the local Ukrainian community, more than 20 years later it was deemed 'illegal' by

[69] C Bigg, 'Kyiv Renames 'Moscow Avenue' After Contentious Nationalist Hero' (*Radio Free Europe/ Radio Liberty*, 7 July 2016): www.rferl.org/a/ukraine-kyiv-avenue-renamed-moscow-to-bandera/27844918.html.

[70] 'Istorychnyi vystup prezydenta Polshchi Komorovskoho. Povnyi text' (*Yevropeiska Pravda*, 9 April 2015): www.eurointegration.com.ua/articles/2015/04/9/7032765/.

[71] 'Miller: Ukraińcy przyjęli ustawę dot. UPA? Polska powinna zareagować' (*Wprost*, 10 April 2015): www.wprost.pl/501940/miller-ukraincy-przyjeli-ustawe-dot-upa-polska-powinna-zareago.html.

[72] TA Olszański, 'The Great Decommunisation. Ukraine's Wartime Historical Policy' (*Centre for Eastern Studies*, 2017): www.osw.waw.pl/sites/default/files/pw_65_great_decommunisation_net_0.pdf, 29–34.

the Polish authorities.[73] The UINP responded with a moratorium on the search for and exhumation of Poles killed during WWII on Ukrainian territory. 'We had no choice; this step was made to stop the wave of the dismantling of Ukrainian gravestones in Poland and it worked', claimed the UINP Director.[74] The moratorium caused a stalemate in Ukrainian–Polish relations; it did not put an end to the strategic partnership and security cooperation, but a number of local infrastructure projects were stopped. The newly-elected president Volodymyr Zelenskyi, whom the Polish side saw as an eastern Ukrainian unburdened by the Ukrainian-Polish historical controversies, promised to lift the moratorium. Yet the issue remains unresolved.[75] As a gesture of concession, Warsaw restored one of the Ukrainian graves in Poland on the occasion of a meeting between the Polish and Ukrainian presidents in 2020. However, the new gravestone, which was not agreed upon with the Ukrainian side, bears neither the names of the fallen UPA soldiers nor the inscription 'Died for a Free Ukraine', which had been part of the original memorial.[76]

VII. RUSSIA'S RESPONSE

Russia's response to the decommunisation laws followed the long-established pattern (going back to the Yushchenko era) of accusing Kyiv of 'historical revisionism', 'rehabilitation of fascism' and 'falsification of history'.[77] In the context of the deep crisis in Ukrainian–Russian relations and Russia's hybrid aggression against Ukraine, decommunisation was highlighted by Russian propaganda as proof of the weak legitimacy of the 'Kyiv regime', to reveal its nationalist or even Nazi features and to showcase the low level of support it allegedly enjoyed among the Ukrainian population. The tone of comments in mainstream and Kremlin-loyal Russian media ranged from sarcastic and condescending to

[73] 'Nielegalny pomnik UPA w powiecie przemyskim rozebrany po 23 latach. Pierwsza taka akcja w Polsce' (*Portal Przemyski*, 26 April 2017): www.portalprzemyski.pl/nielegalny-pomnik-upa-w-powiecie-przemyskim-rozebrany-po-23-latach-pierwsza-taka-akcja-w-polsce-galeria-zdjec/.

[74] Cited in: Y Panchenko, 'History Still Strains Poland-Ukraine Relations' (*Institute for War and Peace Reporting*, 18 November 2020): https://iwpr.net/global-voices/history-still-strains-poland-ukraine-relations.

[75] 'Polish official: Ukraine "cannot dream" of EU without resolving Volyn victims' exhumations' (*The Kyiv Independent*, 7 November 2023): https://kyivindependent.com/polish-official-ukraine-cannot-dream-of-eu-without-resolving-volyn-victims-exhumations/.

[76] V Birchak, 'Khto pokhovanyi na hori Monastyr?' (*Istorychna Pravda*, 12 October 2023): www.istpravda.com.ua/articles/2020/10/12/158256/.

[77] T Zhurzhenko, 'In the shadow of victory: The memory of WWII in the Russian–Ukrainian conflict' (*Eurozine*, 7 May 2020): www.eurozine.com/in-the-shadow-of-victory/. On the instrumentalisation of these issues in Russian domestic politics see eg: M Luxmoore, '"Orange Plague": World War II and the Symbolic Politics of Pro-state Mobilization in Putin's Russia' (2019) 47 *Nationalities Papers* 822–39; J Fedor, '"Historical Falsification" as a Master Trope in the Official Discourse on History Education in Putin's Russia' (2021) 13 *Journal of Educational Media, Memory, and Society* 107–35.

dismissive and openly hostile. For example, *Rossiiskaia Gazeta* reported that the Ukrainian parliament had 'banned communist ideology, declared seventy years of Ukrainian history non-existent, appointed new heroes for the country and adopted a law denying Ukrainians all their rights'.[78] The law on fighters for Ukrainian independence in particular was used to remind the Russian public about the OUN and UPA's radical nationalism and fascist ideology, as well as the military crimes committed during WWII by them as historical predecessors of the 'Kyiv junta'.[79] Reporting about the changes to commemorating the end of WWII, Russian media lamented Kyiv's 'ban of Victory Day' and what they considered an attempt by Ukrainian politicians to steal victory from Russia and monopolise it.[80] Citing criticism from the West, in particular from the left, Russian media accused the Kyiv government of 'vandalism' and compared it to the Taliban and ISIS.[81]

The reaction of the Russian media by no means contradicted the official position of Moscow, summed up in the statement 'On the attempts to revise history in Ukraine', published by the Russian Foreign Ministry one day after the adoption of the laws. The statement started by saying that 'Moscow is seriously alarmed by the growing struggle against Ukraine's heroic past waged by the forces that have seized power in the Ukraine'.[82] The Ministry accused Kyiv of 'rewriting the history of Ukraine', 'suppressing political dissent', 'totalitarian methods', 'censorship', 'restriction of the right to freedom of thought, religion, opinion and expression', as well as 'government-approved acts of vandalism'. What irritated Moscow most was not, of course, the anti-Soviet message of the Ukrainian legislation as such (the glorification of the Soviet past being highly selective in Russia, with a focus on those elements which best fit the Russian imperial narrative). Rather, decommunisation was rightly seen as an attempt to dismantle the ideological concept of a 'common history', which effectively kept Ukraine in the Russian geopolitical orbit. In criticising decommunisation (and recycling arguments coming from (pro-)European and liberal democratic political forces and institutions), Moscow was fulfilling a number of tasks at once here: delegitimising the post-Maidan Ukrainian government and its politics, undermining Ukraine's image in the West, presenting Russia as a guardian of democratic values and the rights of Russian speakers, and justifying pro-Russian separatism in Donbas. Decommunisation was denounced as the 'rehabilitation

[78] 'Ukrainskaia Rada zapretila termin "Velikaia Otechestvennaia voina"' (*Rossiiskaia Gazeta*, 9 April 2015): https://rg.ru/2015/04/10/zapret.html.

[79] 'Verkhovnaia Rada priznala deiatelnost OUN-UPA borboi za nezavisimost Ukrainy' (*TASS*, 9 April 2015): https://tass.ru/mezhdunarodnaya-panorama/1891306.

[80] 'Den bez Pobedy. Kak Kiev boretsia s prazdnikom 9 maia' (*Lenta.ru*, 8 May 2016): https://lenta.ru/articles/2016/05/08/maidan_style/.

[81] 'Spasem khotia by chast naslediia, popavshego v ruki vandalov' (*Vzgliad*, 19 May 2015): https://vz.ru/politics/2015/5/19/745983.html.

[82] 'Comment by the Information and Press Department on the attempts to revise history in Ukraine' (*Ministry of Foreign Affairs of the Russian Federation*, 10 April 2015): https://mid.ru/ru/foreign_policy/news/themes/id/1507158/?lang=en.

of Nazism', which allegedly provided the ideological foundation of the 'Kyiv regime'. This paved the way for the new Russian agenda of 'de-Nazification' of Ukraine, which in February 2022 was presented as one of the main aims of, and justifications for, the 'special military operation'.

In the eyes of Moscow, some aspects of decommunisation went beyond the 'Ukraine crisis' and had broader implications for Russia's relations with the EU. Counteracting the invented threat of a return of Nazism was one of them, and Ukraine was presented as the most prominent case in a larger European tendency. This is evident from the official Report 'Neo-Nazism – a dangerous challenge to human rights, democracy and the rule of law' presented by the Russian Foreign Ministry in Russian and English on 23 April 2015, shortly before the 70th anniversary of the end of WWII. Citing examples of neo-Nazism from virtually all EU countries, as well as the USA and Canada (and omitting Russia), the report devoted a disproportionally large number of pages to the Ukrainian case. Appointing itself the guardian of the historical lesson of the Nuremberg trials, Russia proclaimed fighting Nazism on the European and global scale not only as its historical mission but as the very essence of its national identity. From this perspective, condemning Nazism and Communism as 'equally criminal' totalitarian regimes largely contributes to what Mälksoo conceptualised as 'mnemonical status anxiety'.[83] No wonder that Vladimir Putin addressed this issue in his traditional 'Direct Line' with Russian citizens, insisting that the equation of Stalinism and Nazism is historically wrong and politically inappropriate.[84] The issue remained on the top of the list of mnemonic controversies in Russian–EU relations. In 2019, the European Parliament once again condemned the Soviet–Nazi non-aggression pact, and relations with Poland in particular were strained over the question of who to consider responsible for the start of WWII. In 2021, Putin entrusted Vyacheslav Volodin, the speaker of the State Duma with drafting amendments to Russian legislation that would prohibit publicly equating the role of the USSR and Nazi Germany in WWII.[85] In April 2022, Putin signed the relevant law which provided for the penalisation of such comparisons with a fine of up to 100,000 Roubles or a 15-day detention.[86] Along with the law criminalising the rehabilitation of Nazism, adopted in 2014 following the Euromaidan, the new legal provision is now used to punish anti-war dissent in Russia.[87]

[83] Mälksoo, 'Militant memocracy in International Relations' (n 7).

[84] 'Putin vernulsia k voprosu o Stalinizme i Natsizme' (*BBC News Russkaia Sluzhba*, 16 April 2015): www.bbc.com/russian/russia/2015/04/150416_putin_phone_in_stalinism.

[85] 'Putin Seeks to Ban Nazi-Soviet Comparisons' (*The Moscow Times*, 26 January 2021): www.themoscowtimes.com/2021/01/26/putin-seeks-to-ban-nazi-soviet-comparisons-a72728.

[86] See I Nuzov, 'Memory Laws and Policies in Russia After Annexation of Crimea and Occupation of Donbas' and G Bogush, 'Putin's Memory Policies in the Context of Military Aggression in Ukraine' Chapter 3 in the present volume.

[87] A Nekoliak and E Klochkova, 'Weaponizing Russia's Memory Law: On Russia's Mnemonic Dissidents' (*VerfassungsBlog*, 11 July 2023): https://verfassungsblog.de/weaponizing-russias-memory-law/.

Finally, one more aspect of the anti-decommunisation discourse in Russia (and in the Russia-occupied territories of Ukraine) needs to be mentioned. The decommunisation of the Ukrainian past, some critics have argued, has implications for the legitimacy of Ukraine in its current borders – because these very borders are the product of Soviet history. For example, *Golos Sevastopolia* published an article titled 'Rejection of the legacy of the USSR deprives Kyiv of the right to Donbas'.[88] Others went even further, arguing that rejecting the Soviet period of history calls into question the legality of the accession of the western Ukrainian lands annexed from Poland in 1939. While Polish politicians avoided strong reactions to the law on fighters for Ukrainian independence for reasons of political pragmatism, this might change in the future, warned one Russian expert: 'one day they will present the bill'.[89]

This line of argument was neither new[90] nor was it central to Russian political discourse before 2022, as Moscow still hoped that the Minsk Agreements would result in the re-integration of Donbas into Ukraine as a pro-Russian autonomous entity. This, however, changed with the 2022 invasion, which Vladimir Putin notoriously justified with reference to his vision of Ukraine as an artificial state, 'entirely and completely created by Russia, or rather, the Bolshevik, communist Russia'. 'Do you want de-communization? Well, this quite suits us. But you must not stop halfway. We are ready to show you what genuine de-communization means for Ukraine', he threatened Kyiv in his infamous speech to the nation on the eve of the invasion.[91]

VIII. CONCLUSION

The adoption of decommunisation legislation and its implementation coincided with what is often called the 'post-Euromaidan period' of Ukraine's contemporary history:[92] a period replete with unprecedented challenges and conflicts, on the one hand, and with ambitious pro-European reforms, on the other. Russia's hybrid aggression, the annexation of Crimea and the military conflict in Donbas

[88] 'Obnulenie istorii: otkaz ot naslediia SSSR lishaet Kiev prava na Donbas' (*Golos Sevastopolia*, 22 May 2015): https://voicesevas.ru/news/13935-obnulenie-istorii-otkaz-ot-naslediya-sssr-lishaet-kiev-prava-na-donbass.html.

[89] 'Put k svetlomu proshlomu. Otritsanie sovetskogo perioda stavit pod vopros prisoedinenie zapadnoukrainskikh oblastei' (*Lenta.ru*, 18 April 2015): https://lenta.ru/articles/2015/04/18/backtothefuture/.

[90] T Zhurzhenko, 'From the "Re-Unification of the Ukrainian Lands" to "Soviet Occupation": The Molotov-Ribbentrop Pact in Ukrainian political memory' in C Karner and B Mertens (eds), *The Use and Abuse of Memory: Interpreting World War II in Contemporary European Politics* (Transaction Publishers, 2013) 229–47.

[91] 'Russia ready to show what true de-communization means for Ukraine – Putin' (*TASS*, 21 February 2022): https://tass.com/politics/1407587.

[92] See eg, V Kulyk, 'Memory and Language: Different Dynamics in the Two Aspects of Identity Politics in Post-Euromaidan Ukraine' (2019) 47 *Nationalities Papers* 1030–47; S Hosaka, 'Hybrid Historical Memories in Post-Euromaidan Ukraine' (2019) 71 *Europe-Asia Studies* 551–78.

spurred the Ukrainian political class and society to distance themselves from the 'common past' with an 'aggressor state'. While the architects of decommunisation referred to the experience of other post-communist states, Ukraine's case was unprecedented: none of the other Eastern European countries have had to deal with the legacy of communism while facing external aggression and military conflict. For this reason, memory politics and mnemonic legislation, along with other issues like the public use of language, the role of Russian mass culture and the independence of the Ukrainian Orthodox Church came to be seen through the lens of national security. But for many in Ukraine who saw the origins of the conflict not only in the Russian aggression but also in internal cleavages, decommunisation seemed a contested or even dangerous move.[93] The divisive effects on Ukrainian society and the risk of sliding into authoritarianism by curtailing freedoms had the potential to exacerbate these home-made threats. Those who hoped for a political solution to the conflict in Donbas often saw decommunisation as an obstacle to re-integration of the de-occupied territories based on political compromise and a long reconciliation process.

What came next, however, was not a resolution of the Donbas conflict but the full-scale Russian invasion and with it an imminent and existential threat to the Ukrainian state. Russia's embrace of the Soviet-nostalgic and Russian imperial narratives in justifying the military intervention, the officially proclaimed goal of Ukraine's 'denazification', and the total denial of Ukrainian statehood created a radically new context. Amid a corporeal war, little room was left for the discursive Russo-Ukrainian mnemonic conflicts of the pre-war era. From the Ukrainian perspective, the Russian invasion just proved that the decommunisation legislation of 2015 was a correct and timely political choice, having consolidated the Ukrainian political nation and demarcated it from Russia. The 2022 invasion and the imminent threat to the Ukrainian nation made internal cleavages and conflicts, including mnemonic ones, less relevant. At the same time, the re-integration of Russian-occupied Donbas and Crimea appeared a more distant prospect; if at all, it will be decided on the battlefield and not through political compromises on decommunisation. Opinion polls conducted in Ukraine after February 2022 show that the war has accelerated the shift in public attitudes initiated by the 2015 legislation. Decommunisation is perceived nowadays as less controversial; even if certain segments of the Ukrainian population (mostly older, less educated and poorer citizens) remain sceptical about it, the majority supports the denouncement of the Soviet regime as criminal and approves of the renaming of Soviet toponyms.[94] In Ukraine, where Soviet

[93] See eg, H Coynash, '"Decommunisation" Laws: Deeply Divisive and Destined for Strasbourg'; O Matsuka, 'Donbas. Operatsiia Dekomunizatsiia' (*Radio Svoboda*, 4 August 2016): www.radiosvoboda.org/a/27900539.html.

[94] See: 'How Ukrainian society will look like: De-Sovietization, Democracy, New Symbols of Freedom' (*Ilko Kucheriv Democratic Initiatives Foundation (DIF)*, 29 August 2023): https://dif.org.ua/en/article/how-ukrainian-society-will-look-like-de-sovietization-democracy-new-symbols-of-freedom.

nostalgia was until recently widespread, this is clearly the effect of Russia's war of attrition dressed in neo-Stalinist narratives.

Perhaps another reason why decommunisation appears less controversial in the context of the full-scale war is the shift of the political focus towards decolonisation and de-Russification. While monuments to Aleksandr Pushkin are falling, Ukrainians quarrel about the future place of Russian culture in Ukraine. What appears at first glance to be a new agenda – Russian imperial symbols and narratives were not formally banned by the decommunisation laws – has roots in post-Euromaidan Ukraine.[95] For some actors such as the UINP, decommunisation was part of a broader agenda aimed at the emancipation from Russian historical narratives (testified to, for example, by the objection of then Director, Volodymyr Viatrovych, to the renaming of Kirovohrad as Yelizavethrad, discussed above in section V). The entanglement of decommunisation with the decolonisation agenda is another aspect which makes the Ukrainian case a special one in post-communist Europe.

The 'Europeanisation' of Ukrainian national memory was one of the declared goals of the decommunisation legislation: in distancing itself from the Russian 'mnemonic empire', Ukraine has strived to embrace European symbols and narratives of WWII as an alternative and used the 'European template' to denounce the communist regime. At the same time, OSCE, PACE, the European Parliament and other institutions, concerned as they were with freedom of speech and democracy, played the role of arbiter and sometimes sharp critic of Ukrainian mnemonic legislation. The 'European standards' of memory politics were perceived by many Ukrainian politicians and experts as criteria for acceding to the EU – a highly desirable but rather distant future.

Since February 2022, this future has, paradoxically, become less remote: on 23 June 2022, the European Council granted candidate status to Ukraine. As the victim of Russian aggression, Ukraine enjoys a certain immunity from criticism of its memory politics. Moreover, as a gesture of solidarity, EU states like Germany, France, Italy and the Netherlands, which had previously been reluctant to do so, have now officially recognised the *Holodomor* as a genocide by the Soviet regime.[96] Ukraine's newly gained self-confidence emerging from its resilience to the Russian aggression and its new geopolitical identity as a 'bulwark

[95] See eg: T Zhurzhenko, 'Fighting Empire, Weaponising Culture: The Conflict with Russia and the Restrictions on Russian Mass Culture in Post-Maidan Ukraine' (2021) 73 *Europe Asia Studies* 1441–66.

[96] 'Germany declares Ukraine's Holodomor famine a genocide' (*Deutsche Welle*, 30 November 2022): www.dw.com/en/germany-declares-stalin-era-holodomor-famine-in-ukraine-a-genocide/a-63944665; 'French lawmakers recognize Ukraine's Soviet-era famine as "genocide"' (*Le Monde* with AFP, 29 March 2023): www.lemonde.fr/en/france/article/2023/03/29/french-lawmakers-recognize-ukraine-s-soviet-era-famine-as-genocide_6021067_7.html; 'Italy's Senate recognises Holodomor as genocide of Ukrainian people' (*European Pravda, Ukrainska Pravda*, 26 July 2023): www.pravda.com.ua/eng/news/2023/07/26/7413014/; 'Dutch House of Representatives Recognises Holodomor as Genocide of Ukrainian People' (*European Pravda*, 7 July 2023): www.eurointegration.com.ua/eng/news/2023/07/7/7165236/.

of free Europe' has challenged the traditional hierarchy in EU-Ukrainian relations. The same tendency can be observed in Ukrainian-Polish relations, where mnemonic conflicts receded into the background in favour of strategic partnership and solidarity against a common threat.

Finally, the question is often raised as to what role memory politics, and particularly the 2015 decommunisation legislation, has played in the transition from the hybrid conflict to the full-scale Russo-Ukrainian war? Can zealous legislation based on an anti-Soviet historical narrative antagonistic to the Russian narrative indeed explain the Russian invasion? In more general terms, does the escalation of memory wars inevitably lead to real, corporeal wars? While legislation of historical memory can certainly contribute to mnemonic conflicts and cause tensions in interstate relations, the hypothesis that memory laws inspire memory wars and then serve as a fuel for corporeal wars would be too simplistic and even misleading. Embracing such a line of argument risks putting equal responsibility on both sides and blaming the victim. While memory wars are a rather common phenomenon across Europe, it would be difficult to imagine their evolution into an armed conflict. Rather than being a clash of irreconcilable narratives about a common past, the multifaceted Ukrainian-Russian conflict, rooted in different geopolitical interests and opposing trajectories of political regimes, was fuelled by the Kremlin's manipulation of historical memory.

6

Ukrainian Memory Laws and Policies in the Context of 2022 Russian Aggression

ANDRII NEKOLIAK

I. INTRODUCTION

THE CHAPTER ANALYSES memory laws and policies in Ukraine following the full-scale Russian aggression in February 2022. While there is growing attention to the phenomenon of memory laws in Ukraine (especially pertaining to the case of post-Euromaidan 2015 legislation),[1] an account of how the politics of memory laws has progressed following the Russian invasion remains absent from the scholarship. Thus, this chapter sets two aims for its investigation. The first is to take a stock of changes in the field of commemorative lawmaking[2] and memory policies at the parliamentary, administrative,

[1] Lyubashenko placed the case of 2015 memory laws into the context of transitional justice scholarship and offered a theoretically valuable insight about the preconditions to, political interests behind, and the implementation of de-communisation laws since 2015. See: I Lyubashenko, 'Between Heroes and Perpetrators: Ukraine's Ambiguous Legal Approaches to the Soviet Legacy and Independence Fighters' in K Bachmann and C Garuka (eds), *Criminalizing History: Legal Restrictions on Statements and Interpretations of the Past in Germany, Poland, Rwanda, Turkey and Ukraine* (Peter Lang, 2020) 127–42. The scope of Lyubashenko's analysis ended in 2020. Drawing from international relations literature, both Mälksoo and Zhurzhenko scrutinised the case of post-Euromaidan memory politics in Ukraine using the concept of 'ontological security' and its application to Ukraine's memory politics. See: M Mälksoo, 'Militant memocracy in International Relations: Mnemonical status anxiety and memory laws in Eastern Europe' (2021) 47 *Review of International Studies* 489; and T Zhurzhenko, 'Legislating Historical Memory in Post-Soviet Ukraine' in E Barkan and A Lang (eds), *Memory Laws and Historical Justice: The Politics of Criminalizing the Past*' (Palgrave MacMillan, 2022) 97–130.

[2] For the purpose of this chapter, I define commemorative lawmaking as a lawmaking activity aimed at valorising historical events and figures, and instituting remembrance days. Bucholc offered an alternative treatment of the same term. See M Bucholc, 'Commemorative Lawmaking: Memory Frames of the Democratic Backsliding in Poland After 2015' (2018) 11 *Hague Journal on the Rule of Law* 85, 85–110. My notion of commemorative lawmaking parallels the category of declarative memory law in the works of Fronza, Heinze, and Koposov. See E Fronza, 'The Punishment of Negationism: The Difficult Dialogue between Law and Memory' (2006) 30 *Vermont Law*

and judicial levels in Ukraine. The second aim is to assess the progression of the politics of memory laws in the country analytically. In the latter regard, the chapter seeks to unveil what new political and legal developments that have occurred since the full-scale Russian invasion might say about Ukraine's politics of memory in a future post-war situation.

My core argument is that the politics of memory laws in Ukraine, since the Russian invasion, has largely preserved its non-repressive and decentralised posture. I base this argument on the empirical analysis of parliamentary politics, the policy of Ukraine's Institute of National Memory (UINP), and judicial practice pertaining to memory legislation. Foremost there is a puzzling characteristic present in Ukraine's parliamentary politics of memory. While Ukrainians fight off the malign aggressor, which enshrined its justification for the war in historical memory,[3] the absence of new historical speech laws is a curious characteristic of Ukraine's politics. Since the 2022 invasion, Ukraine's parliament has been reluctant to introduce new punitive memory laws.[4]

Thus, the chapter is concerned with what explains the reticent approach of the Verkhovna Rada to the penalisation of historical speech since the start of the full-scale Russian invasion. Moreover, it is concerned with assessing whether, and how, commemorative lawmaking by the Verkhovna Rada has built on previous trends and parameters in the legal regulation of historical memory (ie, those predating the invasion of the country in February 2022). I argue that in the absence of a hard legislative policy emanating from parliamentary politics in 2022, the development of 'soft' memory policies as well as the implementation of the 2015 legislation has subsequently devolved to regulation at the administrative level through UINP, the activities of local councils and municipalities, and the politics of Ukraine's courts. Accordingly, this chapter assesses the latter institutions' involvement in shaping the posture of Ukraine's politics of memory throughout 2022 and 2023.

The chapter proceeds around three main sections. Section II analyses commemorative legislation adopted by the Verkhovna Rada in its current (wartime) legislative cycle. In doing so, it assesses the political context surrounding the adoption of commemorative legislation in 2022 and the evolution of parliamentary memory discourse since the beginning of Russia's

Review 609; E Heinze, 'Epilogue: Beyond 'Memory Laws': Towards a General Theory of Law and Historical Discourse' in U Belavusau and A Gliszczyńska-Grabias (eds), *Law and Memory: Towards Legal Governance of History* (Cambridge University Press, 2017) 413–34; N Koposov, *Memory Laws, Memory Wars. The Politics of the Past in Europe and Russia* (Cambridge University Press, 2018).

[3] Chapter 3 by Gleb Bogush in this volume; I Nuzov, 'Legislating propaganda: Russia's memory laws justify aggression against Ukraine' (2022) 20 *Journal of International Criminal Justice* 805.

[4] A punitive memory law prescribes punishment for public instances of historical speech. For a discussion about this notion and its treatment in the scholarship, see: A Nekoliak, '"Memory Laws" and the Patterns of Collective Memory Regulation in Poland and Ukraine in 1989–2020: A Comparative Analysis' (PhD Dissertations in Political Science, University of Tartu Press, 2022) 22–40.

February 2022 invasion. While the main analysis of Ukraine's memory legislation between 2014 and 2022 is provided elsewhere in this volume,[5] this chapter asks about the fate of punitive memory laws from 2015 and examines whether, since then, any new punitive memory laws have been introduced (or attempted) in the Verkhovna Rada.

The next two sections assess the role of non-parliamentary institutions in mediating the country's 'mnemonic regime'[6] in 2022. Section III reviews the activities of UINP and assesses its overall role in the politics of memory in 2022–23, including UINP's analytical supervision of the process of grassroots de-colonisation initiated by local councils and municipalities since the February 2022 invasion. The De-colonisation Law that was passed in the spring of 2023 has simply officialised this role of UINP without aggrandising the institution with the grant of any new administrative authority or resources. Section IV surveys judicial practice regarding the implementation of Ukraine's punitive memory laws of 2015. It reflects on whether there were any changes in how Ukrainian courts engaged with, interpreted, and implemented the 2015 memory laws against the backdrop of the full-scale Russian invasion. In the conclusion (section V), I reflect on how these (post-February 2022) developments in the legal regulation of historical memory are indicative of a possible future (post-war) trajectory for the politics of memory in Ukraine.

II. THE POLITICS OF MEMORY IN THE VERKHOVNA RADA SINCE RUSSIA'S 2022 FULL-SCALE INVASION

The Russian invasion happened to catch the Verkhovna Rada in the middle of the legislative cycle of its ninth convocation, as elected in autumn 2019. After the elections, for the first time in modern Ukrainian history, a one-party faction single-handedly captured the parliamentary majority. Coupled with presidential elections that had occurred a few months prior, in spring 2019 – which also led to change in incumbent presidents – it might well be observed that Ukraine had experienced a drastic change in governing political classes, at least since the Euromaidan events of 2014. Consequently, this political change triggered questions about the relevance of post-Euromaidan memory politics which emerged after 2014 under President Petro Poroshenko and his political force in the parliament.

For years, Ukraine's memory politics were characterised by a cleavage between supporters and opponents of the pro-Soviet-era interpretation of

[5] Chapter 5 by Tatiana Zhurzhenko in this volume.

[6] Bernhard and Kubik define mnemonic regimes as 'the dominant pattern of memory politics that exists at a given moment in reference to a specific highly consequential past event or process'. See: M Bernhard and J Kubik (eds), *Twenty Years After Communism: The Politics of Memory and Commemoration* (Oxford University Press, 2014) 4.

national history.[7] The Soviet 'nostalgists' in Ukraine's politics promoted an agenda on historical memory that entailed valorising Stalinism in Ukraine's history, and denying the validity of the memory of the *Holodomor* and the Ukrainian nationalists' struggle during World War II (WWII). In contrast, since Ukraine gained independence in 1991, the anti-communist politicians of national-Ukrainian political orientation have promoted a national vision of Ukraine's past as concerned with disavowing Soviet-era transgressions and 'Europeanising' the representation of WWII in Ukraine's history. Importantly, advocates of the national-Ukrainian memory were concerned with the struggle of the Ukrainian WWII nationalists for independence in the twentieth century. In Ukrainian politics, this memory cleavage was underpinned by competing geopolitical considerations, economic integration, and language policy orientations of major political players.[8]

The political constellation of the parliament in 2022–23 can be described as manufacturing a 'fractured' memory regime characterised by the symbiosis of two 'mnemonic warriors'[9] on competing sides of parliamentary politics, with one mnemonic abnegator enjoying a majoritarian status. Ideationally and further complicating the mnemo-political landscape, there are two main political memory cleavages running through the politics of the Verkhovna Rada since the 2019 elections: the long-standing pro-/anti-Soviet memory cleavage and the cleavage within the anti-Soviet memory advocates themselves. The pro-/anti-Soviet memory cleavage persisted in parliamentary politics for decades and thus, was still relevant at the time of the full-scale Russian invasion of the country in 2022. As to the assessment of parliamentary memory politics, the significance of the pro-/anti-Soviet memory cleavage decreased due to electoral demise of the political alliance of communists and President Yanukovych's *Party of Regions*, a consequence of the Euromaidan events and the parliamentary elections of 2014. Since 2014 (and subsequently the elections of 2019), politicians of Yanukovych's (former) party formed only a minority faction in the parliament (*Opposition Platform*) while communists ceased participating in parliamentary

[7] A Portnov, 'Memory Wars in Post-Soviet Ukraine (1991–2010)' in U Blacker, A Etkind and J Fedor (eds), *Memory and Theory in Eastern Europe* (Palgrave McMillan, 2013) 233–54; O Shevel, 'Memories of the Past and Visions of the Future: Remembering the Soviet Era and its End in Ukraine' in M Bernhard and J Kubik (eds), *Twenty Years After Communism: The Politics of Memory and Commemoration* (Oxford University Press, 2014) 146–67; G Kasianov, *Past Continuous: istorychna polityka 1980-h – 2000-h. Ukraina ta susidy* (Laurus, 2018).

[8] P D'Anieri, *Understanding Ukrainian Politics: Power, Politics, and Institutional Design* (Routledge, 2015).

[9] Here, I use the terminological apparatus introduced by Bernhard and Kubik (2014) to explore politics of memory in Central and Eastern Europe. Mnemonic warriors are characterised with a 'militant' stance over national history. Politically, they put an emphasis on the issues of historical memory in political struggle with political opponents. In contrast, mnemonic pluralists argue for a civic-minded view of national history adopting an accommodating view of politics. Mnemonic abnegators avoid arguments about history pragmatically. For a full explanation of the typology of mnemonic actors, see: M Bernhard and J Kubik (eds), *Twenty Years After Communism: The Politics of Memory and Commemoration* (Oxford University Press, 2014) 7–36.

politics. Nevertheless, having lost political significance over time, the remnants of Yanukovych's party retained their activist warrior-like stance in defending Soviet-era interpretations of Ukraine's history in the parliament.

The second (albeit more politically significant) memory cleavage runs between two major political groupings supporting the national-Ukrainian version of national history. On the one hand, the parliamentary faction of *European Solidarity*, led by former President Petro Poroshenko (2014–19) in the Verkhovna Rada since 2019, has remained an active mnemonic warrior with regards to disavowing Soviet-era memory and promulgating nationalist-minded Ukrainian historical narratives. Its already activist profile was further bolstered with the election of Volodymyr Viatrovych (Head of UINP in 2014–19) to the ranks of *European Solidarity* parliamentarians in 2019. In historical memory affairs, Petro Poroshenko's political faction has primarily opposed supporters of the pro-Soviet memory faction.

President Volodymyr Zelensky's political camp is the most significant player in the mnemo-political field which can be categorised as mnemonic abnegator. The *Servant of the People* party (as well as Volodymyr Zelensky himself) runs on a catch-all party programme which has avoided the issue of historical memory within its political rhetoric, campaigns and policy since 2019.[10] Consequently, following an overwhelming majority in parliament, the politicians rallying around President Zelensky were largely uninterested in contesting Poroshenko-era achievements in relation to commemorative lawmaking tacitly agreeing on anti-Soviet legislative memory policy. Therefore, a renaissance of Soviet-era memory themes and memory legislation akin to the political developments of 2010–13 did not unfold in parliamentary politics under newly-elected President Zelensky.[11]

The Zelensky-era Verkhovna Rada voted for commemorative Acts addressing multiple historical periods at once as opposed to stand-alone commemorative declarations dedicated to separate historical figures or events. For instance, in December 2021, a few months before the Russian invasion, Ukrainian parliamentarians adopted a major Act addressing 531 anniversaries of historical figures and events, with public commemoration scheduled for the next two calendar years (2022 and 2023).[12] In comparison, in the preceding legislative cycle between 2014–19, the Poroshenko-era Verkhovna Rada adopted 33 individual commemorative declarations and only three complex commemorative declarations simultaneously addressing multiple historical events and figures (in 2015, 2018 and 2019 respectively). Over the years, there has been a trend which has seen Ukraine's parliament voting for fewer stand-alone declarations in

[10] O Onuch and HE Hale, *The Zelensky Effect* (Hurst Publishers, 2022).

[11] For a review of political events of the Soviet-era memory model renaissance in Ukraine between 2010 and 2013, see: Nekoliak (n 4) 156–60.

[12] '*Pro vidnzachenia pamiatnyh dat i yuvileiiv u 2022–2023 rokah*' (Verkhovna Rada Ukrainy, 17 December 2021).

favour of complex acts addressing multiple historical periods and anniversaries relating to events and figures of the past.[13]

A notable characteristic of the politics of memory laws in the Verkhovna Rada since 2019 is the demise of Soviet-era historical themes in commemorative lawmaking, a trend that builds upon the post-2014 movement in commemorative lawmaking. The political memory of the Soviet-era, that is the glorification of the 'Great Patriotic War of 1941–1945' as well as the celebration of foundational events and figures of the Soviet Union, ceased to be referenced in the content of anniversary legislation. As illustrated by the aforementioned commemorative Act of the Verkhovna Rada adopted in December 2021 regarding commemorative events for 2022 and 2023.[14] The Act was adopted by the ruling *Servant of the People* faction in tandem with *European Solidarity* parliamentarians. *Opposition Platform* deputies voted against it. In this Act, a majority of anniversaries addressing Soviet-era events of Ukraine's pre-WWII past were dedicated to the establishment of higher education institutions in the Soviet Ukraine from the 1920 until the 1950s, yet there were no events embracing Soviet-era political memory. Anniversaries of events pertaining to Ukraine's Soviet past after WWII provided an anti-Soviet historical interpretation of the national past. The December 2021 Act distinguished the anniversaries of Soviet-perpetrated deportations of Ukrainians to Siberia (1947), Polish communist government-perpetrated deportations connected to the 'Vistula' operation (1947), and the KGB-perpetrated appraisals of Ukrainian dissidents in the Soviet Ukraine (1972). In other words, the orientation of the commemorative policy of the parliament remained focused on the victims of Soviet-era repressions and on disavowing the Soviet past in Ukraine's history.

Prior to Russia's February 2022 invasion, the Zelensky faction in the Verkhovna Rada had accepted the anti-Soviet memory trend in commemorative lawmaking regarding the issue of Ukrainian WWII nationalists, another landmark historical theme within post-Euromaidan politics under former President Poroshenko. In this regard, the December 2021 declaration addressed both the approaching 80th anniversary of the creation of the Ukrainian Insurgent Army in 1942, and the anniversary of the birth of Vasyl Kuk – the last military commander of UPA. Politically, the adoption of this declaration relied on support of the – *Servant of the People* dominated – parliamentary committee on humanitarian and information policy charged with overseeing the legal aspects of the draft. Mykyta Poturaiev, the head of the committee and a prominent *Servant of the People* politician argued that full historical legitimacy and

[13] The record for producing the most commemorative legislation was reached in the lawmaking of the Verkhovna Rada between 2007 and 2012, coinciding with the Presidencies of Viktor Yushchenko and Viktor Yanukovych. See more: Nekoliak (n 4) 132.

[14] Verkhovna Rada Ukrainy (n 12).

justice should be granted to the topic of UPA in Ukrainian history.[15] In a parliamentary committee sitting endorsing the draft of December 2021 declaration, the committee members expressed no disagreement about the content nor the inclusion of the themes of Ukrainian WWII nationalism. Rather, the ensuing discussion among committee members concerned legal-technical aspects.

Another pre-full-scale Russian invasion declaration of 2021 established May 14 as an annual day of remembrance commemorating Ukrainians who rescued Jews during WWII.[16] This markedly 'Europeanising' move in the realm of anniversary legislation was initiated by a joint initiative of *Servant of the People* and *European Solidarity* parliamentarians and widely supported in a plenary vote. The path towards Europeanisation of the memory of WWII was originally paved by politicians arriving in parliament after the Euromaidan events of 2014, with the very first legislative moves in this direction carried out under President Petro Poroshenko.[17] In the Zelensky-era parliament, it soon became clear that this the trend would continue despite the 2019 change in governing political classes.

Russia's February 2022 invasion further solidified the interpretative stance of parliamentary factions over the memory of WWII. In May 2022, the Verkhovna Rada voted to commemorate the Allied victory in WWII and condemned contemporary Russia's 'attempts to ascribe' victory over Nazism.[18] The May 2022 declaration offered a political narrative of WWII in which victory represented the common achievement of several nations fighting against Nazi Germany across continents. It framed the ongoing Russian aggression against Ukraine as a major setback to the international order, similar in its underlying implications to the start of WWII in Europe in 1939. Furthermore, the declaration claimed that the Russian approach to WWII memory in recent decades was to mythologise the events of WWII and to engage in propaganda of war. In a separate passage, the declaration asserted the validity of Ukraine's de-communisation legislation by referring to the 2015 Law on the Commemoration of Victory over Nazism in WWII,[19] arguing that contemporary Ukraine adheres to the 'European' approach to war memory already paved previously by this memory law.

[15] M Poturaiev, 'Speech at the Sitting of the Culture and Information Policy Committee' (1 December 2021).

[16] '*Pro vshanuvania pamiati ukrainciv, yaki riatuvaly evreiiv pid chas Druhoii Svitovoii viiny*' (Verkhovna Rada Ukrainy, 2 February 2021).

[17] L Klymenko, 'Forging Ukrainian national identity through remembrance of World War II' (2020) 22 *National Identities* 130.

[18] '*Pro Zaiavu Verkhovnoii Rady Ukrainy z nahody 77-ji richnyci peremohy nad nacyzmom ta neprypustimist prysvoienia Rosiyskoiu Federacieiu peremohy nad nacyzmom*' (Verkhovna Rada Ukrainy, 5 May 2022).

[19] As discussed in the chapter by Tatiana Zhurzhenko in this volume, this law became a staple of the commemorative policy under President Poroshenko in order to create distance from the Soviet-era interpretation of WWII after the Euromaidan events in 2014.

The political events that unfolded around the adoption of the May 2022 declaration showcased the entrenchment of parliamentary politics between more lenient and more radical wings of the anti-Soviet memory camp. The lenient wing is represented by politicians from the pro-presidential *Servant of the People* faction. The radical wing is represented by mnemonic warriors of the *European Solidarity* faction. In a sitting of the parliamentary committee on humanitarian and information policy – entrusted with providing an opinion on the declaration project before it could be moved to the plenary voting stage – the majority of the committee members represented by the *Servant of the People* faction members supported the declaration draft. At the same time, three *European Solidarity* parliamentarians voted against not only the declaration itself, but also placement of the item on the committee's agenda and the accompanying discussion regarding the regulatory approach to legislation on historical memory. The *European Solidarity* parliamentarians démarche was aimed at persuading other committee members to choose stronger legislative measures to deal with WWII commemoration, but not about opposing the narrative of the proposed declaration.

During a committee sitting on 3 May 2022, Volodymyr Viatrovych argued that adopting a symbolic declaration of the parliament dedicated to the 77th anniversary of victory over Nazism was too lenient as a legislative measure.[20] Instead, Viatrovych urged committee members to support his legal project regarding amendments to the 2015 Law on Commemoration of Victory over Nazism in WWII. The project had been introduced to the committee a few weeks prior in April 2022 from the *European Solidarity* faction in the parliament. The draft law envisaged cancellation of 9 May as a remembrance day and preserved only 8 May as a single public holiday dedicated to victory over Nazism in Ukraine. *European Solidarity* members of the committee urged the timely support of Viatrovych's initiative, especially in view of anniversary of the end of WWII approaching in May.[21] In other words, mnemonic warriors of the Poroshenko's faction pushed for stronger regulatory intervention in the domain of WWII remembrance that went beyond merely adopting a symbolic commemorative declaration. However, ultimately it was the hold of the *Servant of the People* politicians over the committee which was instrumental to the more lenient approach to war memory being supported and the concerns raised by *European Solidarity* politicians being waived.

A major parliamentary politics development of 2022 concerned the normalisation of de-colonisation discourse in the legislative work of the Verkhovna Rada, a direct consequence of Russia's February 2022 invasion. Again, the political

[20] V Viatrovych, 'Speech at the Sitting of the Culture and Information Policy Committee' (3 May 2022).

[21] S Fedyna, 'Speech at the Sitting of the Culture and Information Policy Committee' (3 May 2022); M Kniasytsky, 'Speech at the Sitting of the Culture and Information Policy Committee' (3 May 2022).

constellation of the Verkhovna Rada, structured between radical and lenient wings of the national-Ukrainian memory advocates on the matter of historical memory, played a decisive role in modelling the de-colonisation legislation in parliamentary work. In a nutshell, while the *European Solidarity* parliamentarians were successful in initiating the discussion over a de-colonisation law, the *Servant of the People* politicians seized this idea, having appropriated control over any further legislative work on the topic.

Thus, a look into the political events and parliamentary discourse regarding de-colonisation is in order. De-colonisation discourse entered the political mainstream thanks to UINP in 2019.[22] As distancing from Soviet-era commemorative legacy had already been largely achieved with the adoption and implementation of the 2015 memory laws, the next step was to stimulate public discussion about the place of the Russian imperial legacy in modern Ukraine whilst also re-conceptualising Ukraine's history in such debates.[23] However, the topic faded from the policy agenda with the change of the leadership of UINP in autumn 2019 (alongside the demise of Poroshenko's presidency and his political camp in the parliament earlier the same year). Prompted by the Russian invasion, politicians in Poroshenko's political camp saw an opportunity to push the parliament to embrace the discourse of de-colonisation, thus resurrecting and furthering their 2019 agenda.

Legislative discourse over de-colonisation found its way into three projects regarding a framework law, which were tabled before parliament in September 2022. Two were tabled by notable *Servant of the People* parliamentarians (the Fedir Venislavskyi et al project of March 2022, and Mykyta Poturaiev's project of September 2022) and one by a group of *European Solidarity* parliamentarians (the Kniazhytskyi et al project of September 2022). While an extended version of Venislavskyi's project was eventually voted on in the spring of 2023, a protracted legislative debate between Poroshenko's and Zelensky's camps over the draft laws ensued in parliamentary work. This competition around alternative projects showcased the political dynamics of the parliament, which is likely to keep shaping the mnemo-political dynamics of Ukraine beyond 2022, and competing ideational perspectives on how legislative memory policy for the country should proceed.

In April 2022, Fedir Venislavskyi, joined by a group of parliamentarians, offered to ban the use of references to Russia's imperial past in public space and monument-building. Thus, the project of the law became a major legislative step in the realm of public remembrance since the 2015 De-communisation Laws adoption. The Venislavskyi project consisted of a single article amending Ukraine's legislation on geographical names (proper names of geographic sites). It forbade naming geographical sites (for instance, cities, settlements,

[22] V Viatrovych, '*Dekomunisatsia – pershyi etap dekolonizacii Ukrainy*' (*Radio Svoboda*, 10 May 2018).
[23] UINP, '*Kruhlyi stil 'Imperska spadschyna: sczho z neiu robytu?*' (*Ukrinform*, 14 March 2019).

railway stations, ports, etc) in ways that 'glorify, symbolize or propagate' Russia or use 'memorial, historical, cultural' references to Russian events, places, and figures responsible for imperial conquest in the past.[24] The Venislavskyi et al project proceeded into the workings of the regional development committee of the Verkhovna Rada given that it sought to amend a technical sphere of legislation.

In early September 2022, a group of *European Solidarity* parliamentarians introduced a draft law on the de-colonisation of public space in Ukraine. The main co-authors were key figures of Poroshenko-era memory politics from a previous legislative cycle of the Verkhovna Rada in 2014–19. Mykola Kniasytskyi, a *European Solidarity* parliamentarian and the main co-author of the draft law, also served as head of the cultural affairs committee of the Verkhovna Rada in 2014–19. As this committee was responsible for legal work connected to all commemorative legislation, Kniasytskyi played one of the crucial roles in developing the commemorative policy of the Poroshenko-era parliament. Since 2019, Kniazhytskyi remained an ordinary member of the abovementioned committee.

The *European Solidarity*-initiated draft law defined de-colonisation as the 'riddance of imperial, post-imperial, Soviet-era symbolism, other symbols of the Russian imperial hegemony in public space of Ukraine, in culture, education, architecture, mass media etc'.[25] At the policy level, the draft law envisaged administrative measures regulating how renaming in public spaces should be conducted. In addition, it defined principles of monument-building, naming of educational institutions, cultural establishments, and religious organisations. It was deemed forbidden to use the names of historical personalities or events, in instances where such naming,

> glorifies, memorializes, propagates or symbolizes the aggressor-state or its memorial, historical, cultural places, dates, events, or its persons, who conducted military aggression against Ukraine or other sovereign nations, who conducted or glorified colonial policy, imperial expansion, totalitarian policy and practice.[26]

The draft entrusted the government, via the Ministry of Culture and Information Policy, with the responsibility for supervising the process of renaming. On a punitive dimension, the law prescribed administrative fines for the violation of legal provisions of the ban o 'anti-Ukrainian, pro-Russian propaganda'.[27]

A few weeks later, a group of *Servant of the People* deputies headed by Mykyta Poturaiev introduced a second, alternative draft law on de-colonisation to circumvent the Kniazhytskyi et al draft. This draft developed a different

[24] F Venislavskyi et al, *Proekt Zakonu pro vnesenia zmin do Zakonu Ukrainy 'Pro heohraficzni nazvy* (2022).

[25] M Kniasytskyi et al, *Proekt Zakonu pro dekolonizaciu humanitarnoii sfery Ukrainy* (2022).

[26] ibid Article 5.

[27] ibid Article 12.

terminological apparatus regarding the 'Russian imperial and totalitarian practice', speaking about 'decolonization, deoccupation and sovereignization' of Ukraine.[28] However, the biggest difference in comparison to the *European Solidarity*-promoted draft concerned the scope of de-colonisation measures. In this regard, the draft law offered a more lenient approach towards the renaming and removal of the Russian imperial legacy from the public space. The caveat of Article 7 allowed for the preservation, and erection, of (new) monuments and memorials to historical personalities if the contentious historical personality in question had made a 'significant contribution' to the Ukrainian and the 'world culture' or sciences. The draft law offered a decentralised mechanism for the process of making decisions about the removal of existing monuments. It was foreseen that local councils would be tasked with supervising and sponsoring the removal of contentious memorial legacies from the public space. No fines or other types of legal liability were referenced in the draft introduced by the *Servant of the People*.

In late autumn 2022, the work of the committee headed by Mykyta Poturaiev over the two competing bills came to a halt. In parallel, the regional development committee, dominated by the *Servant of the People* parliamentarians, proceeded with the Venislavskyi et al project having posited a significantly developed version of the draft. In November 2022. The new version was modelled after the 2015 De-communisation of Public Space Law having repeated the structure, content of administrative procedure on renaming, and overall approach of the 2015 Law. The original formulation of Venislavskyi's ban was preserved in the core of the draft. The regional development committee pushed the draft for a successful plenary vote in March 2023 which was achieved by votes of the *Servant of the People*, *European Solidarity*, and other smaller groupings of parliamentarians. In other words, enjoying the upper hand in the parliament and using procedural technicalities of the legislative process, the *Servant of the People* faction was able to neutralise the *European Solidarity* legislative initiative and push for a preferred version of the de-colonisation legislation.

To sum up, the way in which de-colonisation legislation entered the parliamentary agenda in 2022 reflects the mnemo-political dynamics of the Zelensky-era parliament at large. Ideationally, the memory cleavage between pro- vs anti-Soviet memory partisans has a longstanding current in the politics of post-independence Ukraine. Since 2022, the partisans of Soviet-era memory are no longer able to alter the direction of commemorative policy of the parliament due to their political marginality. A more politically relevant memory divide runs between the Poroshenko and Zelensky political factions. This memory divide is more political than ideational, as showcased by the passage of the de-colonisation legislation – prompted by Russia's full-scale invasion, both

[28] M Poturaiev, E Kravchuk and O Sanchenko, *Proekt Zakonu pro podalshu dekolonizaciu, deokupaciu ta suverenizaciu kulturnoho prostoru Ukrainy* (2022).

political camps agreed on the need for such legislation with the ruling party being successful in instrumentalising the legislative process to its benefit. As there was no intellectual or political opposition raised against the legislation coming from the Soviet-era memory supporters in the parliament, legislative work on the issue has been firmly aligned with Poroshenko and Zelensky politicians. Most likely, this political constellation around historical memory issues will persist in parliamentary politics in the observable future.

III. MEMORY POLICIES OF UINP IN 2022 AND 2023

Russian aggression resulted in the disruption of the pattern of work carried out by UINP in 2022, with the endorsement of the annual plan for UINP's activities delayed until June 2022. In addition, Anton Drobovych, head of the Institute since December 2019, joined the Armed Forces in order to defend Ukraine and has since remained on active military duty. As for assessing the political situation regarding UINP. political support for its activities lasted through 2022 and 2023.[29] Despite initial hiccups in months following the February 2022 invasion, UINP was able to recuperate later.

In 2022, though the commemorative function remained at the core of UINP's activities, a new activity was brought to life due to the Russian aggression, namely, memorialisation of the victims of the Russian war against Ukraine. In the latter regard, UINP was tasked with the development of a conceptual narrative about the memorialisation of the victims of war as well as oral history projects – including collecting eyewitness accounts of the Russian aggression in spring 2022.[30] UINP holds an advisory role regarding the removal of the monumental legacies of the Soviet totalitarian and Russian imperial eras of Ukraine's past. According to the 2022 plan of activities, endorsed by the Ministry of Culture, UINP was charged with the development of 'conceptual approaches to toponymic decolonization' as well as a list of place-names to be renamed.[31]

For 2022, the administrative work of UINP remained primarily analytical. In July 2022, in response to societal pressure and a wave of renaming conducted by local authorities,[32] and in order to streamline the process of

[29] The positioning of UINP in the administrative system of the Ukrainian government has not changed since 2019. The Institute retains its status of a central body of executive power, whose activities are closely coordinated with the Ministry of Culture and Information Policy. Moreover, the annual budget for the UINP has been growing steadily since the political changes of 2019, having almost tripled between 2020 and 2022.

[30] '*Plan roboty Ukrianskoho Instytutu nacionalnoii pamiati na 2022 r, zatverdzeno Ministrom kultury ta informaciinoii polityky*, No 05/18/756-22' (Ministry of Culture and Information Policy, 13 July 2022).

[31] ibid 10.

[32] For a case study of Kyiv Council decisions to de-colonise the city's landscape, see: O Betlii, 'The Identity Politics of Heritage: Decommunization, Decolonization, and Derussification of Kyiv Monuments after Russia's Full-Scale Invasion of Ukraine' (2022) 4 *Journal of Applied History* 149.

grassroots de-colonisation, the Institute, together with the Ministry of Culture, drafted recommendations on renaming policy. The policy document differentiated between two types of monumental Soviet/Russian imperial legacy: monuments to personalities related to Russian history and culture, and WWII memorials. The Institute offered a pluralistic approach by engaging local authorities in the process of dealing with both types of memorial legacy. For the Soviet-era legacy, the policy document referred to the respective provisions of the 2015 Law to be followed, and issued a reminder about the need to remove inscriptions referring to the 'Great Patriotic War' or the 'Soviet people' (but not memorial objects themselves). For monuments dedicated to personalities marking Russian imperial presence in Ukraine, the recommendations advised the relocation of contentious objects to local museums. If such an option was not available for local authorities, it was advised that the presence of such monuments in public spaces should be re-conceptualised into art objects, supplemented with informative inscriptions explaining the historical context of an event or personality.[33]

In 2023, the De-colonisation Law officialised this advisory-analytical role of UINP in the process of renaming. According to the 2023 Law, UINP can issue recommendations to local authorities on how to carry out changes in public space. It is unclear if recommendations have binding effect under the new law. At the time of writing, there is no evidence of significant executive aggrandisement on the part of the UINP or its attempts to intervene in public memory.[34]

IV. THE POLITICS OF LAW ENFORCEMENT AND COURTS SINCE 2022

A punitive component of the 2015 de-communisation laws consisted of legal provisions stemming from two laws, namely, the Law on Freedom Fighters and the Law on the Condemnation of the Communist and National Socialist (Nazi) Regimes and Prohibition of Propaganda of their Symbols. It should be noted that the Freedom Fighters Law is defunct in its criminal-punitive capacity, having only a declaratory provision outlining the unlawfulness of public denial of the independence struggle of Ukrainians in the twentieth century. Since the adoption of this law in 2015, there have been no instances of prosecutions for public denial of the memory of the Ukrainian WWII nationalism within academia,

[33] '*Rekomendacii Ekspertnoi Rady MKIP shodo okremyh katehorii pamiatnykiv i monumentiv, poviazanyh iz rosiyskoiu ta radianskoiu imperskoiu istorieiu*' (Ministry of Culture, UINP, 28 October 2022).

[34] For instance, in 2015–16, the Institute took a proactive role in monitoring decisions by local authorities and collected data about the removal of Soviet-era symbols. In the same years, the public visibility of UINP and its activities were somewhat higher. See A Nekoliak, 'Institute of National Memory / Український інститут національної пам'яті (Ukraine)' in L Stan and N Nedelsky (eds), *Encyclopedia of Transitional Justice* (Cambridge University Press, 2023) 1346–51.

media, or the public discourse whatsoever.[35] At the same time, the second 2015 memory law incorporated an amendment into the Criminal Code with actual punitive capacity. Back in 2015, the newly introduced Article 436-1 of the Criminal Code criminalised production and dissemination of communist or Nazi symbols, and of propaganda of communist and National Socialist (Nazi) totalitarian regimes.[36] The legal sanctions for violating this norm ranged from restraint of liberty, to actual terms of imprisonment (up to five years) with or without confiscation of property, depending on the gravity of the crime.

Since the adoption of the Criminal Code amendment in 2015, the politics of law enforcement agencies and courts regarding its implementation have remained uneven. Table 1 presents information about the number of investigations in relation to violation of Article 436-1, collated from the General Prosecutor's Office data. In 2015–19, there was a steady growth in how often criminal investigations involving Article 436-1 were initiated, ie, since the introduction of the legal provision into the Criminal Code. According to a previous analysis by Lyubashenko, there were two criminal cases initiated in 2015, 20 in 2016, 26 in 2017, and 38 in 2018.[37] As Table 1 demonstrates, this trend continued uninterrupted despite political changes in 2019, including changes in terms of who held the position of Prosecutor General under President Zelensky.

Table 1 *Number of Registered Investigations Regarding the Violation of Article 436-1 of Ukraine's Criminal Code 2019–22**

Year	Registered Criminal investigations	Reasonable suspicions handed out in pre-trial investigations
2019	31	6
2020	72	18
2021	53	8
2022	233	91

* Compiled based on descriptive statistics provided by the General Prosecutor's Office; however, there is a limit to the data. Descriptive statistics do not differentiate between events of propaganda of Nazi and Soviet totalitarian regimes. In other words, there is no data on the content of registered criminal cases and, consequently, no ability to evaluate charges on what parts of the criminal offence prevail in the overall statistics. However, based on previous observations by Lyubashenko, cases of propagating or condoning the Soviet regime outweighed the number of cases of neo-Nazi propaganda or usage of Nazi Germany symbols in 2015–19. There is no reason to suspect that matters have changed since.

[35] '*Pro pravovyi status ta vshanuvania pamiati borciv za nezaleznist Ukrainy u 20 stolitti*' (Verkhovna Rada Ukrainy, 9 April 2015).

[36] '*Pro zasudjenia komunistycznoho ta nacional-socialistycznoho (nacystskoho) totalitarnyh rezymiv v Ukraini ta zaboronu propagandy ihnioi symvoliky*' (Verkhovna Rada Ukrainy, 9 April 2015).

[37] Lyubashenko (n 1) 138.

Two hypotheses can be put forward to explain the sudden growth in recorded cases in 2022 based on existing (albeit limited) data. Firstly, a higher number of registered cases might indicate a change in the approach of law enforcement agencies to the implementation of the 2015 amendment to the Criminal Code. Structurally, Article 436-1 belongs to the chapter of the Criminal Code dealing with crimes against peace, humanity and the international legal order. This chapter forms the backbone of the war crimes regime within Ukrainian criminal law. Among other things, the chapter deals with the violation of the rules and customs of warfare, propaganda of war, the crime of aggression and so on. Naturally, since the Russian invasion, this group of crimes has gained renewed focus in the Ukrainian criminal justice system. It might be hypothesised that the law enforcement agencies entrusted with pre-trial investigations of the crimes envisaged by this chapter of the criminal law started to deploy more logistical and investigatory resources to unveil and investigate this group of crimes, including the violation of Article 436-1 amongst others (eg, by monitoring instances of propaganda on social media platforms).

Another hypothesis to explain the high number of recorded cases involving Article 436-1 in 2022 concerns instances in which charges are brought based on multiple articles of the Criminal Code. It may be that the charges for violating Article 436-1 are related to investigations into the violation of Article 436-2 (justification, legitimisation and facilitation of Russia's armed aggression against Ukraine and glorification of its participants), which was introduced in March 2022.[38] It might be that the instances of local Ukrainian collaborationists justifying Russian aggression in public simultaneously involve historical speech propagating and justifying the Soviet totalitarian regime. However, the hypotheses presented here should be approached with caution as their basis can only be corroborated when pre-trial investigations into ongoing criminal investigations are complete and courts' verdicts describing the content of the cases are made publicly available.

Verdicts issued by Ukrainian courts in 2022 offer an insight into the approach of the criminal justice system to prosecuting the violation of Article 436-1. In 2022, 45 verdicts were punishing the production or dissemination of propaganda of the Soviet totalitarian regime. With certainty, it can be concluded that there has been no change in the severity of punishments prescribed by judges in criminal cases since February 2022. In this regard, the analysis of the 2022 verdicts confirms previous findings by Lyubashenko, who has analysed the implementation of Article 436-1 in practice since the introduction of the norm in 2015. Short terms of imprisonment handed down in the form of suspended sentences were the punishment most often chosen by judges in 2015–19.[39] Among 45 verdicts issued in 2022, the vast majority continued this practice of

[38] As of late December 2022, there were 1,313 investigations launched involving charges based on Article 436-2 according to General Prosecutor's Office data.

[39] Lyubashenko (n 1) 140–41.

sentencing with suspended punishment, identified by Lyubashenko before, and only two verdicts prescribed actual terms of imprisonment.[40] Once the legal practice of the courts has accumulated further, a more definite assessment can be made about the prevalence of the violation of Article 436-1, the context of the criminal cases and the legal reasoning of the Ukrainian judges.

V. CONCLUSIONS

This chapter had two aims. On an empirical level, it sought to provide an analysis of how Ukraine's politics of memory laws have progressed at the parliamentary, administrative, and judicial levels since the start of Russia's February 2022 invasion. In times of war, the chapter argued that the politics of memory laws in Ukraine largely preserved its non-repressive and decentralised characteristics. In terms of non-repressiveness, there was no progression towards the adoption of new punitive memory laws in 2022 nor any tangible punitive crackdown in the implementation of the 2015 memory laws so far. The explanation for this reticent approach of the Verkhovna Rada to historical speech regulation is the political constellation driving parliamentary politics of memory – there is no political constituency that could drive the adoption of the legislation reminiscent of the 2015 memory laws. In parliamentary politics, the adoption of the Freedom Fighters Law in 2015 fulfilled the impetus to protect the memory of Ukrainian WWII nationalists – achieved mainly through symbolic legal measures. While back in 2015 the historical topic of Ukrainian WWII nationalists was associated with scholarly and political controversies, the actual punitive dimension of the Freedom Fighters Law was oblique, as were legal prospects of implementing the law from the very beginning. Since 2022, Ukraine's parliament has not sought to amend this 2015 law.

The current (wartime) legislative cycle of the Ukrainian parliament is characterised by a cleavage between the political groupings of mnemonic abnegators and mnemonic warriors, who nevertheless agree on the underlying paradigm of Ukrainian national history. This is in contrast to previous decades of parliamentary politics, which were defined by a competition between pro- and anti-Soviet memory partisans, exposing antagonistic (and consequently much less reconcilable) approaches to the interpretation of the national past and legislative policy on memory. The political struggle between Soviet-era and national-Ukrainian memory partisans shaped the commemorative policy of the parliament before. At the same time, political marginality of the Soviet-era memory partisans in the wake of Russian aggression has become the state of affairs nowadays. It is justified to suggest that the dominant pattern of memory politics (which

[40] '*Vyrok u spravi N127/10958/22*' (Vinnytsia City Court, 31 August 2022); '*Vyrok u spravi N345/4027/22*' (Kalush City Court, 2 February 2023).

is underlined by existing political constellations in the parliament) on the issue of Ukrainian historical memory became more thoroughly and fundamentally 'National-Ukrainian' over time. The embracement of the topic of de-colonisation of public space across political aisles in legislative work is a sign of this pattern. It is worth pointing out that Russia's February 2022 invasion of Ukraine has directly contributed to the normalisation of the legislative agenda on de-colonisation policy. As the discussion around de-colonisation legislation in 2022 in parliament showcased, there was no ideational disagreement over the need to deal with the legacy of Russian imperial presence in public space.

Furthermore, on the parameter of being decentralised, it might be said that Ukrainian society has taken the lead in forming the contours of the post-war memory landscape of the country. In the absence of actual legislative policy emanating from the Verkhovna Rada, societal de-colonisation has started taking shape throughout the country, in the form of decisions by local authorities (eg, Kyiv City Council) to reform the memorial landscape of local vicinities and municipalities. The 2023 De-colonisation Law has bolstered these grassroots processes by streamlining the administrative framework. Yet it did so without aggrandising the administrative authority of UINP much. The rise in convictions punishing propaganda of the Soviet regime is the only realm that provides some evidence that Ukraine's approach to historical memory offences became more indignant. Still, while there is a rise in recording of offences of Article 436-1 of the Criminal Code, actual punishments meted out for these offences are rather lenient, the preference of courts being to issue suspended verdicts sentences.

Finally, the chapter sought to unveil what new political and legal developments since Russia's February 2022 say about the future of Ukraine's politics of memory. Much will depend on the progression of the current war. The orientation of political-discursive work over historical memory depends on how much the country is able to preserve its democratic politics (especially regarding the degree of democratic deliberation and decision-making). So far, Ukraine has been successful in the latter regard, having preserved the essential features of a democratic polity while Ukraine's society undergoes unprecedented societal and ideational change caused by the war. If Ukraine prevails in the war, the dominant pattern of parliamentary politics is likely to hold, with official remembrance politics shifting towards memorialisation of today's victims of the war.

Part III

Neighbours Actively Involved in the Regional Memory Wars

7

Wounds Unhealed: Polish-Ukrainian and Polish-Russian Memory Wars before 2022

ALEKSANDRA GLISZCZYŃSKA-GRABIAS

> Every way of thinking about the past is linked to some way of valuing and understanding the contemporary world. The divergence of value judgements, if only in the form of different assessments of validity, is always present in disputes over the interpretation of historical processes. This is why these disputes are not fully resolvable.
>
> (Karol Modzelewski, *Barbarzyńska Europa*)[1]

I. INTRODUCTION

IN A PROPAGANDA-SERVING interview in February 2024, by Trump fan Tucker Carlson, Putin once again presented his falsified version of history. In addition to his repeated narrative of the lack of a historical basis for Ukrainian statehood and national secession, he also commented on Poland.[2] According to Putin, it was Poland that once reached for Kyiv and other

[1] K Modzelewski, *Barbarzyńska Europa* (Wydawnictwo Iskry, 2004).

[2] In response to the interview, the Polish Foreign Ministry issued a special statement refuting Putin's main claims relating to history, namely that: Poland collaborated with Nazi Germany; Poles forced Hitler to start WWII: Hitler was left with no other option in carrying out his plans [but] to start with Poland; Poland became a victim of the policy pursued towards Czechoslovakia because, under the famous Ribbentrop-Molotov Protocols, part of these territories fell to Russia, including western Ukraine, and thus Russia, under the name of the Soviet Union, returned to its historical territories; Ukraine is a de facto an artificial entity created by Lenin and Stalin; the left bank of the Dnieper, including Kiev, is historically Russian land; the idea of Ukrainians as a separate nation emerged in Poland. See: 'Oświadczenie MSZ ws. 10 kłamstw prezydenta Władimira Putina nt. Polski i Ukrainy, których nie prostował Tucker Carlson' (*Ministerstwo Spraw Zagranicznych*, 9 February 2024): https://www.gov.pl/web/dyplomacja/oswiadczenie-msz-ws-10-klamstw-prezydenta-wladimira-putina-nt-polski-i-ukrainy-ktorych-nie-prostowal-tucker-carlson-wywiad-z-dnia-8-lutego-2024-r.

'Russian lands'. It was Poland that in 1938, as Hitler's accomplice, carried out a 'partition of Czechoslovakia', and thus bears blame for the outbreak of World War II (WWII) and yet at the same time, was deserving of the invasion. As commented by Carl Bildt, former Prime Minister of Sweden: 'It is indeed true that in 1939 Poland didn't bend to Hitler. For Putin, that seems to justify Hitler's decision to invade and try to annihilate the country. His historical revisionism is breathtaking in all its implications'.[3] At the same time, this is nothing new. In December 2019, in an attempt to justify the rationale behind the alliance between Stalin and Hitler known as the Molotov-Ribbentrop Pact, Putin pointed to the 'hyena of Europe' – ie, Poland – as the culprit behind the war and the extermination of the Jews.[4]

For centuries, Poland, Ukraine and Russia have had a difficult historical relationship, burdened by successive dramatic conflicts, crimes and geopolitical reshuffles.[5] The consequences of these tensions also emerged sharply after the breakthrough of 1989, when the collapse of the USSR and the Iron Curtain initially permitted hopes and plans for a new opening, including overcoming the conflicts accumulated around the common past. These hopes were quickly dashed. In recent years the dispute which began as primarily political and academic has extended to the legal field, sanctioning national 'historical truths' and, in the case of Russia, falsifying those concerning the entire history of twentieth-century Europe.[6] At the same time, tensions between Russia and Ukraine took a dangerous turn. Ukraine's strengthening of its identity, democracy and statehood, including through mnemonic constitutionalism, was a threat to authoritarian Russia. This is because authoritarian leaders fear the influence of their neighbours, which could lead to democratisation in their own country and thus the erosion of the authoritarian power base. This is not to say that Ukraine, invaded by Russia in 2014 and then in 2022, was an exemplary liberal democracy, but the contrast in the political and constitutional systems of the two countries was clear. In the last year before the war, 2021, Ukraine was classified by civil liberties monitor Freedom House as 'partly free' with a 'transitional or hybrid' regime, while Russia has been classified as a 'captive' autocracy since 2005. Russia's trajectory has been

[3] C Bildt 'It is indeed true that in 1939 …' (X, @carlbildt, 9 February 2024): www.twitter.com/carlbildt/status/1756032801550279019?ref_src=twsrc%5Egoogle%7Ctwcamp%5Eserp%7Ctwgr%5Etweet.

[4] W Radziwinowicz, 'Putin przystroił się w piórka jastrzębia pokoju. Carlson na tureckim kazaniu' (*Gazeta Wyborcza*, 9 February 2024): www.wyborcza.pl/7,75399,30681368,putin-przystroil-sie-w-piorka-jastrzebia-pokoju.html.

[5] On the historical dimension of this relationship, see eg: M Rady, *Russia, Poland and the Ukraine 1462–1725* (Hodder and Stoughton, 1990). See also a recent essay on this issue: R Nyberg, 'Russia, Ukraine, and Poland: The End of a Tragic Triangle' (*Carnegie Endowment for International Peace*, 28 July 2023): www.carnegieendowment.org/politika/90289.

[6] Extensively on this turn see: U Belavusau, A Gliszczyńska-Grabias and M Mälksoo, 'Memory Laws and Memory Wars in Poland, Russia and Ukraine' (2021) 69 *Jahrbuch des Öffentlichen Rechts der Gegenwart* 95.

the opposite to the extent that, as Timothy J Colton concluded, 'If, from a democratization perspective, Ukraine prior to the war had been a work in progress, Russia was the inverse: a work in regress'.[7] Each successive term of President Vladimir Putin (with a brief hiatus for Dmitry Medvedev, but with Putin in charge) has resulted in the systematic deterioration of democracy and the spread of authoritarian practices in Russia. The steady erosion of any semblance of competitive elections (with the brutal persecution and murder of the only viable opposition candidate, Alexei Navalny), and of individual rights (symbolised by Russia's withdrawal from the Council of Europe (CoE) and the European Convention on Human Rights (ECHR) system); the expansion of classifications and sanctions against the category of 'foreign agents', which affected many NGOs and activists and journalists; and the 2020 constitutional amendments which ratified further restrictions on freedom of expression and effectively ensured Putin a lifetime presidential term,[8] are just some of the symptoms of the democratic decline of the Russian political system over the past decades. The legally approved distortion of history can be seen as another such symptom.[9]

At the same time, it is worth emphasising that the use of memory laws by those in power is neither a new phenomenon nor characteristic only of selected jurisdictions such as the ones in the present chapter. However, the visible proliferation of these regulations in Central and Eastern Europe (CEE) over the last few decades, as well as the European origin of the most classic memory laws, such as the criminal prohibitions on Holocaust denial, warrant in-depth analysis precisely in the context of the European legal space. Post-war Europe, in its democratic and liberal part, laid the foundations of a newfound remembrance around the crimes of the Holocaust and a commitment to stop any authoritarian, criminal regimes in the future that could lead to a repeat of the Holocaust. Such a circumscribed field of remembrance, focusing on regulations that are closely related to the doctrine of 'militant democracy', including, for example, bans on negationism, the functioning of totalitarian political parties and associations, and the use of Nazi symbols, was confronted over time not only with the challenge of legal regulation of the aftermath of a different past – that of Stalin and communism – but also with attempts at a populist takeover of memory to serve particular political interests.[10] These challenges were also confronted by the constitutional courts of some European states, as well as by

[7] TJ Colton, 'Ukraine and Russia: War and Political Regimes' (2022) 33 *Journal of Democracy* 27.

[8] Although the Constitution allows for two presidential terms in a lifetime, a clever provision reset Putin's presidential clock to start counting from 2024, meaning he can seek re-election for six-year terms in 2024 and 2030. Accordingly, he can sit as president until 2036, or age 84.

[9] The most comprehensive description of this symptom was provided by Nikolay Koposov. See N Koposov, *Memory Laws, Memory Wars: The Politics of the Past in Europe and Russia* (Cambridge University Press, 2017).

[10] A Gliszczyńska-Grabias, 'Stalinism and Communism equals or versus Nazism? Central and Eastern European Unwholesome Legacy in ECtHR' (2016) 30 *East European Politics and Societies* 74.

the European Court of Human Rights (ECtHR) and, finally, the Court of Justice of the EU, which in 2021 ruled that Polish courts had no jurisdiction to hear an action against a German publisher for the use of the phrase 'Polish extermination camp', initiated by a Polish survivor of German Nazi concentration camps, because the plaintiff could not be considered a direct victim of a violation of personal rights on the basis of the contested publication.[11]

The rest of this chapter, which focuses on the last decade of mnemonic constitutionalism in Poland, Ukraine and Russia, is designed as follows: firstly in section II, the focus is placed on the analysis of legal aspects of the remembrance policy implemented by Polish authorities over the last decade in relation to Ukraine and Russia. Secondly, in section III the chapter discusses memory laws adopted in Ukraine and Russia, which stood in sharp opposition to those adopted in Poland, showing the deep duality – or contradiction – in the ways of remembering, and at the same time, proving the need to legally decree one's own truth about the past. Next, the chapter reflects in section IV on possible (though extremely difficult) ways to discuss history legally, in a way that not only protects historical truth but also secures the proper implementation of human rights and freedoms. Section V concludes.

II. POLISH–UKRAINIAN HISTORICAL NARRATIVES AND LEGAL ENTANGLEMENTS

The Russian aggression of 2022, at least in the first months of the invasion, dramatically changed the mutual perception of Polish-Ukrainian historical relations. They were not the important ones, giving way at a dramatic time to the imperative of saving lives and providing shelter to those fleeing the war.[12] With the passage of time, however, the word-symbol and word-code clear to every Pole – *'Volhynia' (Wołyń)*[13] – began to return more and more frequently to the Polish political narrative, including in its mainstream dimension. This example proves that historical identity issues are stronger than current threats, and that the political implications of past wrongdoings can obscure even the most immediate security-related challenges.

[11] Case C-800/19 *Mittelbayerischer Verlag KG v SM*, ECLI:EU:C:2021:489, 17 June 2021.

[12] In May 2022, President Zelenskyy said: 'February 24 changed everything. It changed our nations. Changed our countries. Although this is not accidental. I do not know whether our astronomers Drohobych and Copernicus studied this phenomenon, but the stars are always formed in such a way that during the most difficult periods of eclipse Ukrainians and Poles unite and stand side by side, despite past quarrels and "nebulae"'. See 'Speech by President of Ukraine Volodymyr Zelenskyy during the joint participation with President of the Republic of Poland Andrzej Duda in the plenary session of the Verkhovna Rada' (*President of Ukraine*, 22 May 2022): www.president.gov.ua/en/news/vistup-prezidenta-ukrayini-volodimira-zelenskogo-pid-chas-sp-75261.

[13] G Motyka, *From the Volhynian Massacre to Operation Vistula: The Polish-Ukrainian Conflict 1943–1947* (Brill, 2022).

Polish-Ukrainian relations bear a heavy historical burden that each side presents differently. The 'centre of gravity' for the Ukrainian side is related to centuries of economic exploitation of Ukrainians by the Polish nobility and attempts to suppress their identity, which, as claimed, partly provoked the heinous acts of mass ethnic cleansing of Poles by the Ukrainian Insurgent Army (UPA) and Stepan Bandera's faction of the Organisation of Ukrainian Nationalists (OUN) in Volhynia and eastern Galicia in 1943–45 (then in Nazi German-occupied Poland). Several former Ukrainian governments treated OUN members and leaders as national heroes. This narrative, particularly in the recent upsurge of discussions on Europe's colonial past, comes close to the question of the colonialist character of the Polish presence in those territories and the colonial exploitation of the Ukrainian population.[14] In 2015, these narratives and sentiments were translated into binding Ukrainian law.[15] Enacted as a package of four laws, and heralded by the Ukrainian Institute of National Memory (UINP, Ukrainskyi Instytut Natsionalnoi Pamiati), Ukrainian memory laws included: (i) legislation condemning the communist and National-Socialist totalitarian regimes in Ukraine and criminalising production and dissemination of their symbols and propaganda; (ii) and (iii) commemoration of fighters for Ukraine's independence in the twentieth century and Ukraine's victory over Nazism in WWII; and (iv) guarantees of access to the archives of repressive Soviet era institutions.

The official justification for adopting this package of memory laws that refers to the need to remove the threats to Ukraine's independence, sovereignty, territorial integrity and national security is well summarised by Lina Klymenko:

> Initiated by various political parties – some stemming from the aftermath of the 2013–2014 Euromaidan revolution – these laws became the Ukrainian response to Russia's annexation of Crimea and support for the pro-Russian insurgency in the Ukrainian Donbas. The Ukrainian policymakers included the laws in a 'national memory bloc', thus underlining the importance of the state in consolidating the Ukrainian nation through the creation of a common historical consciousness.[16]

The second most important explanation for the necessity of these memory laws focuses on the fact that they constitute an act of breaking from communism, a

[14] On a very little-known aspect of colonialism with regards to Poland, see: M Skulimowska, 'Poland's Colonial Aspirations and the Question of a Mandate over Liberia, 1933–1939' (2022) 65 *The Historical Journal* 730.

[15] For a detailed analysis of the package see: T Zhurzhenko, 'Legislating Historical Memory in Post-Soviet Ukraine' in E Barkan and A Lang (eds), *Memory Laws and Historical Justice: The Politics of Criminalizing the Past* (Springer, 2022) and I Nuzov, 'The Dynamics of Collective Memory in the Ukraine Crisis: A Transitional Justice Perspective' (2017) 11 *International Journal of Transitional Justice* 132.

[16] L Klymenko, 'Cutting the Umbilical Cord: The Narrative of the National Past and Future in Ukrainian De-communization Policy' in U Belavusau and A Gliszczyńska-Grabias (eds), *Law and Memory: Towards Legal Governance of History* (Cambridge University Press, 2017) 310.

condemnation of Nazism, and an expression of Ukraine's readiness and willingness to join Western Europe as a member of the EU and NATO. Law (iii) – 'On the commemoration of the victory over Nazism in the Second World War in 1939–1945', perceives the condemnation of communism as a path to Ukraine's Europeanisation and democratisation. In a bid to guarantee that a true version of historical events will be presented and disseminated, Law (iii) established measures aimed at preventing distortion of the history of WWII and the role of the Soviets. As explained by the former Head of the UINP, Volodymyr Viatrovych (quoted by Klymenko):

> Today is the best time to finally complete the de-communization of the country. In contrast to other post-Communist countries of Eastern Europe, Ukraine did not do this at the beginning of the 1990s. In countries such as the Czech Republic, Poland and the Baltic countries, similar laws were adopted in the early 1990s … In this way, in these countries the process of democratic revolutions was completed and this allowed these countries to become EU and NATO members … I am convinced that the break with the totalitarian past is an incredibly important condition for Ukraine's development as a normal democratic state.[17]

However, from the perspective of Polish-Ukrainian relations, Law (ii), 'On the legal status and honouring of the fighters for Ukraine's independence in the twentieth century', remains difficult, if not essentially impossible, to accept. Furthermore, public allegations have been raised, in connection with the adoption of this provision, about whitewashing the crimes by Ukrainian nationalists as well as the crimes and collaboration of SS Galizien and the OUN with Nazi Germany.[18] The Law lists the names of fighters in the struggle for the independence of Ukraine, underlines their service for the homeland, grants them a unique legal status, and commands that their memory be honoured. The public denial of the legitimacy of such a struggle is considered an unlawful insult to the respective memory and a disparagement of the Ukrainian people. Honouring the memory of those involved in the murder of the Polish population must have met with obvious opposition from the Polish side, which promptly, in the following year, responded with Polish MPs adopting a resolution calling the 1940s Volhynian massacre a 'genocide'.[19] It was also rightly criticised as an attempt to establish historical truth by legislation and to police freedom of speech, with significant potential for shutting down scholarly discussions by

[17] ibid 319.

[18] J McBridge, 'How Ukraine's New Memory Commissar Is Controlling the Nation's Past' *The Nation* (13 August 2015): www.thenation.com/article/archive/how-ukraines-new-memory-commissar-is-controlling-the-nations-past/.

[19] Uchwała Sejmu Rzeczypospolitej Polskiej z dnia 12 lipca 2013 r. w sprawie uczczenia 70. rocznicy Zbrodni Wołyńskiej i oddania hołdu Jej ofiarom [Resolution of the Sejm of the Republic of Poland of 12 July 2013 on the commemoration of the 70th anniversary of the Volhynian Crime and payment of homage to its victims].

legally prescribing a state-endorsed narrative.[20] This criticism was deepened by the highly controversial views on the past expressed by Viatrovych. Today, however, after the 2022 invasion, we should probably revise at least some of the criticism levelled at these laws. The factor of mnemonic security, named, defined and comprehensively discussed in the context of Ukraine by Maria Mälksoo,[21] and the pro-European aspirations in the outcome of these laws should be factors taken into account when discussing mnemonic constitutionalism in Ukraine. As observed by Tatiana Zhurzhenko, also in the context of the 2014 Crimea annexation:

> Being involved in a military conflict on its own territory, Ukraine has struggled to preserve both democratic freedoms and national sovereignty. Therefore, another important context of the debate on de-communization legislation concerns the tension between two political priorities: democracy, freedom of speech and human rights, on the one hand, and national security, and more specifically, 'mnemonic security,' on the other.[22]

Nevertheless, the commemoration of UPA fighters by the Ukrainian mnemonic constitutionalism remains problematic despite the changed circumstances. It should be seen as a classic, painful paradox of heroes and defenders of a nation who were at the same time murderers responsible for massacres and pogroms. Significantly, this is also the case in Poland: there is a broad social, and – under the Law and Justice rule[23] – also official, cult of the so-called *cursed soldiers* [*żołnierze wyklęci*], ie, anti-communist partisans who fought against the communists at the end of, and after, WWII, despite the fact that their involvement in the crimes of some of their commanders against the civilian population, including in particular Jews and other ethnic minorities, is undisputable.[24] However, this did not prevent the implementation of the resolution issued by the Polish parliament commemorating 'the heroes of the fallen, murdered, and persecuted members of the "Freedom and Independence" organisation'.[25] What is more, the National Day of Remembrance of the Cursed Soldiers, was established as a

[20] Some authors have challenged this argument, at least in regard to the part of the law that equally condemns the Nazi and Soviet regimes: AJ Motyl 'Facing the Past: In Defense of Ukraine's New Laws' (2015) 178 *World Affairs* 58.

[21] M Mälksoo, '"Memory Must Be Defended": Beyond the Politics of Mnemonical Security' (2015) 46 *Security Dialogue* 221.

[22] Zhurzhenko (n 15) 121.

[23] The Law and Justice Party was in power in Poland between 2015 and 2023.

[24] J Kułak, 'Pacyfikacja wsi białoruskich w styczniu 1946' (*Biuletyn Instytutu Pamięci Narodowej*, 2001). The cult of the Polish Underground Home Army has recently been challenged by researchers. See eg: JD Zimmerman, 'The Polish Underground Home Army (AK) and the Jews: What Postwar Jewish Testimonies and Wartime Documents Reveal' (2020) 34 *East European Politics and Societies and Cultures* 194.

[25] 'Komunikat Sejmu, Narodowy Dzień Pamięci 'Żołnierzy Wyklętych' [Official Announcement of the Polish Sejm, National Day of Remembrance of 'Cursed Soldiers'] (1 March 2023): www.sejm.gov.pl/sejm9.nsf/komunikat.xsp?documentId=3E923019C61766EAC1258964004583A0&symbol=M_WYDARZENIA_KOMUNIKAT.

national holiday[26] and the one-sided, whitewashing version of history concerning the 'cursed soldiers' became part of the school curriculum.

Despite these similarities in the attitude towards 'one's own heroes', Ukrainian policy and memory laws, representative of an attempt to consolidate its own identity within statehood and to strengthen mnemonic security, were not met with understanding in Poland, but rather with protest, denial and countermeasures. The degree of tension between Poland and Ukraine prior to 2022 is best illustrated by the following example. Just a few words uttered by Olga Tokarczuk, the most prominent Polish author and 2019 Nobel Prize Winner in Literature, about the Poles' shared responsibility for the fate of Jews and crimes committed against Ukrainians in the past, triggered a wave of hatred against her, including death threats. All that Tokarczuk stated was the, seemingly, obvious characteristic of almost all nations in the world burdened with difficult pasts and brutal conflicts:

> We contrived a narrative of Polish history depicting Poland as a tolerant, open country, one which has never disgraced itself with any wrongdoing towards its minority groups ... Meanwhile, as colonisers and an ethnic majority, we did appalling things, suppressing minorities; we were slaveholders and murderers of Jews.[27]

The legal dimension of these anti-Tokarczuk emotions was expressed by the adoption by the Polish Sejm of the resolution of 2016 commemorating the murders in Volhynia committed by Ukrainians against Poles, labelling and qualifying these crimes as genocide. This sparked international tensions, but it was first in 2018 when these tensions reached the level of legislation. The so-called Polish Holocaust Bill of January 2018 caused international and domestic turmoil – mostly due to its Holocaust-related implications and its legal censorship of the difficult truth about the involvement of parts of Polish society in crimes committed against the Jews during and after WWII. The less publicised thread of this controversy is that concerning legal governance over the Polish-Ukrainian past. In January 2018, an amendment to the Institute of National Remembrance Act (*Ustawa o Instytucie Pamięci Narodowej*, INRA) was passed by the Polish parliament.[28] With the amendment, the catalogue of crimes falling under the

[26] Ustawa z dnia 3 lutego 2011 r. o ustanowieniu Narodowego Dnia Pamięci 'Żołnierzy Wyklętych' Dz.U. 2011 nr 32 poz. 160 [Act of 3 February 2011 on the establishment of the National Day of Remembrance of 'Cursed Soldiers' *Journal of Laws* 2011 No 32 item 160].

[27] Tokarczuk's words were widely quoted in the press. See: J Słodkowski, 'Mordowaliśmy Żydów, kolonizowaliśmy Ukrainę. I co was tak w tym boli?' *Gazeta Wyborcza* (19 October 2015): www.wyborcza.pl/1,75410,19043800,mordowalismy-zydow-kolonizowalismy-ukraine-i-co-was-tak-w.html.

[28] Ustawa z dnia 26 stycznia 2018 r. o zmianie ustawy o Instytucie Pamięci Narodowej – Komisji Ścigania Zbrodni przeciwko Narodowi Polskiemu, ustawy o grobach i cmentarzach wojennych, ustawy o muzeach oraz ustawy o odpowiedzialności podmiotów zbiorowych za czyny zabronione pod groźbą kary [The Act of 26 January 2018 amending the Act on the Institute of National Remembrance – Commission for Investigating Crimes Against the Polish Nation, the Act on Military Graves and Cemeteries, the Act on Museums and the Act on Corporate Liability for Proscribed Punishable Conduct].

scrutiny of the INRA was expanded to include crimes by 'Ukrainian nationalists' and 'Ukrainian groups collaborating with the Third Reich'. This provision came with the new Article 2a of the Act, which defined crimes by Ukrainian nationalists and organisations collaborating with the Third Reich as acts committed by Ukrainian nationalists in the years 1925–50, involving the use of violence, terror, or other forms of human rights violation directed against individuals or groups of people, in particular against the Polish population. 'Crimes by Ukrainian nationalists and Ukrainian organisations collaborating with the Third Reich' also includes their involvement in the extermination of the Jewish population and the commission of genocide against the citizens of the Second Polish Republic in the areas of Volhynia and Eastern Małopolska. The provision in its 'Ukrainian nationalists' part was subsequently repealed by the Constitutional Tribunal as insufficiently precise for criminal legislation.[29] The Tribunal stated in particular, that the provision was incompatible with the principles concerning the specificity of legal provisions and the restriction of rights and freedoms, inferred from Article 2 and Article 42.1 of the Polish Constitution, and that it could not be clearly stated, on the basis of the disputed law, who were the 'Ukrainian nationalists'.[30] At the same time, the amendment introduced another change that resulted in a situation where the denial of 'crimes by members of Ukrainian formations collaborating with the Third Reich' has become a criminal offence punishable by up to three years' imprisonment. Thus, this form of denialism has been equated with the criminalisation of Holocaust denial. The inconsistency with international standards of free speech protection led to legal controversies and strong objections. Additionally, it has been claimed that the law would remain completely ineffective, as there are no legal instruments by which to actually penalise and incarcerate citizens of Ukraine, Germany or Canada who would question the commission of crimes by the UPA in Volhynia. These legal developments were accompanied by some negative political implications. The Ukrainian government reacted by declaring that the legislation undermines Polish-Ukrainian relations and the strategic partnership between the two states.[31]

The Polish-Ukrainian conflict of memory has certainly never reached the stage of a 'war of remembrance' in which the steps taken by either side, including legal steps, could not be reversed or rectified. Even the Polish Constitutional Tribunal, infected by the systematic destruction of the rule of law, proved this by invalidating the legislation concerning the Ukrainian crimes. This is why it seems that, despite all the difficulties, dialogue and adjustments to the

[29] Wyrok Trybunału Konstytucyjnego z 17 stycznia 2019 r., K 1/18, Nowelizacja ustawy o Instytucie Pamięci Narodowej [Judgment of the Constitutional Tribunal of 17 January 2019, Amendment of the Act on the Institute of National Remembrance].

[30] Judgment of the Constitutional Tribunal of Poland, 17 January 2019, K 1/18, otk ZU A/2019.

[31] 'Польські депутати вночі прийняли закон про заборону 'бандерівської ідеології' (*Dzerkalo Tyzhnia*, 1 February 2018).

position are possible. And they are certainly necessary, above all in the context of Mälksoo's reference to mnemonic security threats. The question of sorting out the Ukrainian attitude to the crimes of Volhynia and the crimes of the Ukrainian Insurgent Army must now be put on the back burner, but certainly not forgotten. After all, a revision of its own legislation can benefit not only political and social relations, but also Ukrainian democracy itself. What matters now are symbolic gestures.[32] Ukraine's President Zelensky congratulated Poland on the 104th anniversary of its independence in November 2022, stressing the need to overcome historical disputes. And perhaps most importantly, the 'reconciliation process' has also been noticed at the grassroots level. For instance, residents of Volhynia cleaned Polish cemeteries to demonstrate their gratitude to the Poles for their help in defending the country. Such gestures should form the basis for the healing of mutual relations, with respect for historical truth, which can nevertheless name the murderers by their true names.

III. HISTORICAL TRUTH(S), HISTORICAL LIES AND MNEMONIC CONSTITUTIONALISM IN POLISH-RUSSIAN MEMORY WARS

Presenting the results of an extremely interesting and important study on the relationship between Russians and Stalinism through the Polish lens, centred around the issues of remembrance and oblivion, Ewa Pogonowska, a Polish literature scholar, notes that the only almost universally undisputed historical fact in Russia concerns the Russian victory in the 'Great Patriotic War' and the assumption that the evil (Nazism) was defeated by the Good (Soviet Army). As she claims: 'Here, in the clash between good and evil, the good won. Cultivating the memory of heroic events is the duty of descendants'.[33] But the key aspect of the mnemonic war between Russia and almost the whole of the European continent is well captured in another observation by Pogonowska:

> The mythology of the Great Patriotic War has taken hold of the collective memory of the inhabitants of first the Soviet Union, then the Russian Federation. In general, they eagerly picked up the attractive discourse of glory, providing a sense of pride, a conviction of the uniqueness of their own experience, ergo possessing an identity- and bond-building value.[34]

While the 'mnemonic discrepancies' between Poles and Ukrainians mainly concern interpretation of the causes and responsibility for the crimes committed, the Russian mnemonic constitutionalism in its very essence contradicts the Polish policy of remembrance, also enshrined in law. Leaving aside the

[32] Resolution of the Sejm of the Republic of Poland of 23 February 2022 on the aggression of Russia against Ukraine.

[33] E Pogonowska, 'Rosja – między pamięcią a zapomnieniem (w świetle polskich dyskursów)' (2020) LXIX *Slavia Orientalis* 15, 20.

[34] ibid 27.

distortions of this policy during the Polish Law and Justice administration, which nevertheless focused almost entirely on Polish-Jewish relations and the expression of various kinds of hostility towards Germany, it remains a stable Polish *raison d'état* to shape the historic consciousness of Europe (and beyond) as to the true nature of the wartime crimes of the Soviet Army, as well as its aftermath under the Stalinist and communist regime. Polish memory laws refer to these crimes, prohibiting the denial of crimes committed against persons of Polish nationality or Polish citizens of other nationalities during the period from 8 November 1917 to 31 July 1990, including the communist crimes and other crimes constituting crimes against peace, humanity or war crimes.[35] Mnemonic constitutionalism in Poland also directly outlaws political parties that apply methods and practices of both Nazism and communism. Article 13 of the Constitution prohibits the formation and operation of parties and organisations,

> referring in their programmes to the totalitarian methods and practices of Nazism, fascism and communism, as well as those, the programme or activities of which presuppose or permit racial and national hatred, the use of violence to gain power or influence state policy, or which envisage secrecy of their structures or membership.[36]

Numerous resolutions of the Polish parliament adopted during the four decades of democracy since the fall of communism, also refer to Soviet and communist crimes, including the latest ones condemning Russia's attempts to distort these historical facts.[37]

'Russian memory', however, seems to remain in a state of denial and amnesia, strengthened by the authority of the national law.[38] One of the most relevant explanations of this phenomenon was aptly described by Uladzislau Belavusau:

> A plethora of Russian citizens still believe a specific ideological image, one nurtured by populist politicians and old-regime historians: the Soviet empire as a source of ontological security … Central to this ideology, is the pompous heroic narrative regarding World War II, embraced in Russian settings as the 'Great Patriotic War'

[35] Article 55 of the INRA.

[36] Konstytucja Rzeczypospolitej Polskiej z dnia 2 kwietnia 1997 r. [Constitution of the Republic of Poland of 2 April 1997].

[37] Uchwała Sejmu RP z dnia 9 stycznia 2020 r. w sprawie wyrażenia sprzeciwu wobec manipulowania faktami i zakłamywania historii przez polityków Federacji Rosyjskiej w celu dyskredytowania Polski i pogarszania relacji rosyjsko-polskich [Resolution of the Sejm of the Republic of Poland of 9 January 2020 on objecting to the manipulation of facts and falsification of history by politicians of the Russian Federation to discredit Poland and worsen Russian–Polish relations].

[38] Scholars specialising in the field of mnemonic constitutionalism and memory laws have been raising the alarm regarding Russian governance of the past. In particular, this threat has been defined and addressed by Belavusau and Mälksoo. See the remarks of these authors in: U Belavusau, 'Final Thoughts on Mnemonic Constitutionalism' *Verfassungsblog* (15 January 2018): www.verfassungsblog.de/final-thoughts-on-mnemonic-constitutionalism/; and M Mälksoo, 'In Search of a Modern Mnemonic Narrative of Communism: Russia's Mnemopolitical Mimesis during the Medvedev Presidency' (2015) 1 *Journal of Soviet and Post-Soviet Politics and Society* 317.

(Великая Отечественная Война) that supposedly single-handedly liberated the nations of Central and Eastern Europe.[39]

The ground for the current historical manipulations – allowing Putin to talk about the need for armed denazification of Ukraine and Polish responsibility for the outbreak of WWII – had been prepared by, among other things, the 2020 constitutional referendum on amendments to the Constitution of the Russian Federation. Envisaged primarily as a tool to extend Putin's power, the referendum also introduced an amendment directly linked to the mnemonic constitutional reading of the past by the Kremlin. In the newly introduced Article 67.1, the Russian Constitution prohibits 'diminishing the importance of the heroism of the people in the defence of the Fatherland'. Thus, a historical misrepresentation has been introduced into the Russian Constitution itself, allowing the constitutionally embedded denial of Soviet culpability for war crimes.

However, the project described by Nikolay Koposov in 2022 as 'neo-imperial reconstruction',[40] was already clearly visible in 2009, with a parliamentary proposal for a bill that would criminalise acts violating historical memory of events which took place during WWII and with the establishment by then President, Dmitry Medvedev, of a Presidential Commission to Counter Attempts to Falsify History to the Detriment of Russia's Interest.[41]

The situation in this regard, however, significantly intensified at the time of the Russian military intervention in Ukraine and the annexation of Crimea in 2014. Following these events, new provisions of the Criminal Code were introduced, including Article 354 paragraph 1, which provides for liability for denying:

> facts established by the Judgment of the International Military Tribunal for the trial and punishment of major war criminals of European countries of the Axis, the approval of crimes established by the above-mentioned Judgment, as well as public dissemination of knowingly false information on the activities of the USSR during the Second World War.[42]

The law also protects against insult to Russia's 'military glory':

> public distribution of information expressing manifest disrespect toward society regarding Russia's days of military glory and the commemorative dates associated with the defence of the Fatherland or public insults to the symbols of Russia's military glory which are punishable by a fine up to three hundred thousand rubles.

[39] U Belavusau, 'Mnemonic Constitutionalism and Rule of Law in Hungary and Russia' (2020) *Interdisciplinary Journal of Populism* 16, 22.

[40] N Koposov, 'Populism and Memory: Legislation of the Past in Poland, Ukraine, and Russia' (2022) 36 *East European Politics and Societies* 272.

[41] I Nuzov, 'Freedom of Symbolic Speech in the Context of Memory Wars in Eastern Europe' (2019) 19 *Human Rights Law Review* 231, 245.

[42] The law increases the punishment to a maximum of 5 years of imprisonment if the same deeds have been committed by using one's official position or via mass media, as well as with the artificial fabrication of prosecution evidence.

Importantly, even the provisions concerning the condemnation of Nazism bring Soviet heroism to the forefront: Federal Law 80-FZ of 19 May 1995, that includes prohibition of the usage of Nazi symbols and of the denial of facts established by the Nuremberg Tribunal, in its very name stresses Soviet innocence: 'On the Entrenchment of the Victory of the Soviet People in the Great Patriotic War of 1941–1945'. Therefore, in the Russian narrative translated into the language of the law, there is no room for any sincere confrontation with one's own past.

Just as in Polish-Ukrainian relations, the symbolic word referring to the name of the place marked by the mutually significant crime remains Volhynia, in the case of Poland and Russia it is 'Katyń'. The Katyń Massacre entailed the murder of nearly 22,000 citizens of the Polish state by the political police of the Union of Soviet Socialist Republics (NKVD) in the spring of 1940.[43] The victims of the crime included some 14,500 prisoners of war and 7,300 civilians.

The Katyń Massacre was of an unprecedented nature. Thousands of prisoners of war, whose lives were under the protection of international law, were murdered. Part of the patriotic and intellectual elite of the Polish state was murdered at Katyń in order to stop their involvement in the fight for a free Poland: among those murdered were numerous scholars, doctors, engineers and artists. 'Katyń', however, is also a symbol of the decades-long falsification of history. Until 1990, the Russian authorities denied responsibility for the murder of Polish citizens and falsely attributed such blame to the Germans. The end of Soviet rule and the beginning of attempts to normalise historically fraught Polish-Russian relations also brought some progress with regard to the Katyń massacre. In November 2010, the State Duma, the lower house of the Russian parliament, adopted a resolution on the Katyń massacre, officially recognising it as a crime of the Stalinist regime.[44] This step was heavily influenced by the work of the Polish-Russian Group on Difficult Matters, established in 2002. These events, however, did not bring a fundamental breakthrough regarding full explanation of this crime, and the judgment of the Grand Chamber of the ECtHR in *Janowiec v Russia*[45] was a kind of legal culmination of Polish aspirations for the truth, hampered by the Russian will to conceal it. The case concerned the alleged failure of Russia to conduct an effective investigation into the fate of the relatives of the applicants, and the inhuman and degrading treatment of the applicants resulting from the lack of information and the dismissive

[43] G Sanford, *Katyn and the Soviet Massacre of 1940: Truth, Justice and Memory* (Routledge, 2005).

[44] 'Rosyjska Duma przyjęła uchwałę ws. Katynia: To zbrodnia reżimu stalinowskiego' (*Dziennik Gazeta Prawna*, 26 November 2010): www.gazetaprawna.pl/wiadomosci/artykuly/467867,rosyjska-duma-przyjela-uchwale-ws-katynia-to-zbrodnia-rezimu-stalinowskiego.html.

[45] *Janowiec v Russia*, App nos 55508/07 and 29520/09 (ECtHR, 21 October 2013).

attitude of the Russian authorities to their requests for such information. The Grand Chamber concluded that it has no temporal jurisdiction in the case, as the massacre occurred in 1940 before the ECHR was adopted over a decade later in 1953, and Russia ratified it only in 1998. Though the ECtHR criticised Russia for failing to provide evidence and a satisfactory rationale for classification of the documents, the outcome of this symbolic case was highly unsatisfactory for historical truth.[46]

IV. *SINA QUA NON* CONDITIONS FOR PROPER LEGAL GOVERNANCE OVER MEMORY IN POLAND, UKRAINE AND POST-WAR RUSSIA

The very concept of appealing to 'historical truth' seems to preclude any negotiation over the past and historical facts. The Soviet Army carried out atrocities and murders; UPA fighters carried out the Volhynia massacre; and on 10 March 1944, Polish partisan units (of the Home Army and Peasant Battalions) slaughtered the Ukrainian population in Sahry.[47] Acknowledging that these events took place and that their perpetrators remain unquestionably identified and named is an indisputable and unavoidable starting point for any debates on historical – and legal – interpretations of the past. Thus, this counts as *sine qua non* condition number one. Number two seems to be the abandonment of a nationalistically tinged historical narrative and its use for political ends. This threshold is most difficult to reach under autocracy modelled on the Orwellian vision of totalitarianism:

> In the realm of fiction as in reality, the totalitarian intention is essentially the same; to ensure that power has control over minds and, in particular, over collective memory, which is considered a key element. The techniques of exercising this control are essentially the same: subjecting all information about the past to strict censorship, erasing certain historical facts, creating new 'facts', constantly updating different perceptions of the past according to current political or ideological needs, creating new historical mythologies, fabricating the charisma of the 'leader' etc.[48]

[46] Importantly, in his dissenting opinion, Judge Krzysztof Wojtyczek pointed to one of the fundamental aspects of the relationship between the law and past crimes committed by the Stalinist regime. Judge Wojtyczek argued that time does not always flow in the same way in different places, and decades spent in a totalitarian state cannot be compared to the same period of time in a democratic state governed by the rule of law. Therefore, the question of when the legal obligations to investigate the most drastic human rights violations expire should take into account the individual context of the place and time in question.

[47] I Iljuszyn, *UPA i AK. Konflikt w Zachodniej Ukrainie (1939–1945)* (Warszawa, 2009) 148.

[48] B Baczko, *Wyobrażenia społeczne. Szkice o nadziei i pamięci zbiorowej* (Warszawa, 1994) 202 quoted by Pogonowska (n 33) at 17. This corresponds well with remarks by Mark Tushnet raised in the context of constitutionalism, particularly in his writing about the nature of authoritarian constitution-making and constitution-amending by authoritarian rulers who enforce their vision of the nation, the state and the past. See: M Tushnet, 'The Politics of Constitution-Making' in M Tushnet and D Kochenov (eds), *Research Handbook on the Politics of Constitutional Law* (Routledge, 2023) 143–62.

Other prerequisites are perhaps easier to achieve as they concern more 'technical' aspects of mnemonic constitutionalism: national memory laws must be drafted and applied in accordance with constitutional and international standards for the protection of human rights, and the contents of the most problematic legal drafts should be consulted with counterparts before they reach the level of international public feuds, tinged with xenophobia and blocking dialogue and reconciliation, sometimes for decades. International tribunals also have an important role to play, most notably the ECtHR, which has already repeatedly ruled on cases with a strong mnemonic element, such as the *Janowiec* case. Although, in principle, they should avoid stepping into the role of historians and reflecting on very strong nationally-linked emotions about the past, in practice this is quite often the reality. Among the starkest examples of such an attitude is the judgment in *Vajnai v Hungary*,[49] which concerned a ban on the public display of the communist red star symbol. The ECtHR found the Hungarian government to have violated the right to freedom of expression, explaining as follows:

> The Court is of course aware that the systematic terror applied to consolidate communist rule in several countries, including Hungary, remains a serious scar in the mind and heart of Europe. It accepts that the display of a symbol which was ubiquitous during the reign of those regimes may create uneasiness among past victims and their relatives, who may rightly find such displays disrespectful. It nevertheless considers that such sentiments, however understandable, cannot alone set the limits of freedom of expression.[50]

Keeping in mind all the differences between the historical and social perception of Stalinism/communism v Nazism, it is truly hard to imagine a similar judgment being handed down on the public display of Nazi symbols in today's Warsaw, where the 'uneasiness among past victims and their relatives' would be a sacrifice for the greater good of free speech. Therefore, courts such as the ECtHR should strive to avoid this kind of discourse and assessment and, if unable to do so, should apply similar criteria for assessing historical conditions to all totalitarian regimes. They must react in the cases of historical misrepresentations supported by legal and judicial instruments at the national level, very often in violation of the standards of protection of freedom of expression. As noted by Judge Garlicki in his dissent in *Adamsons v Latvia*,[51] judges are 'experts in law and legality, but not in politics and history' and therefore must not 'venture into these territories unless in cases of absolute need'.[52]

[49] *Vajnai v Hungary* App no 33629/06 (ECtHR, 8 July 2008).

[50] ibid para 57.

[51] *Adamsons v Latvia* App no 3669/03 (ECtHR, 24 June 2008).

[52] ibid, para 3 of the dissenting opinion of Judge Garlicki, joined by Judges Zupančič and Gyulumyan. ('Nous sommes des experts en droit et en légalité, mais non en politique et en histoire, et nous ne devrions nous aventurer dans ces deux derniers domaines que lorsque cela se révèle absolument nécessaire'.).

At the interstate level, this catalogue of demanded prerequisites is, it seems, fully acceptable and presentable for Polish-Ukrainian relations. In the case of Polish-Russian relations, however, none of these prerequisites stands a chance of fulfilment on the Russian side. As long as the armed aggression against Ukraine – triggered by, among other things, Putin's historical lies – continues, any room for negotiation remains closed. The purely hypothetical and (today) unrealistic scenario that assumes the collapse of Putin's Russia and the rebirth of Russian democracy on its territory, would include, in the context of Polish-Russian relations, the re-establishment of the Polish-Russian Commission for Difficult Matters. The Commission also would appear to be the right place to discuss the revision of Russia's mnemonic legislation, with one of the most important aspects of this revision being the compatibility of the Russian memory laws with the CoE's human rights standards – again, if Russia was to regain its membership.

V. CONCLUSIONS

In times as geopolitically and axiologically volatile, polarised and fragile as the present, it is crucially important to make sure that the law, grounded in its social functions and roles, remains immune to attempts to abuse it for political and ideological purposes. However, putting particular interests and political gains above constitutional guarantees and principles is a pattern becoming more frequently visible, even in fully-fledged democracies, not to mention the authoritarian regimes or states on their way towards autocracies, systematically violating the foundations of the rule of law and constitutional order.[53]

One of the most sensitive points on the European memory map, outlined by the contours of the law, seems to be Polish-Ukrainian relations. The vividness and relevance of the still existing controversies is demonstrated by the recently published results of a study tellingly entitled 'Poles and Ukrainians 1989–2023: why still entangled in the past?'.[54] As concluded by its authors, in Ukraine and Poland today, images of the past, historical narratives and the politics of remembrance serve different political projects, corresponding to different social consciousnesses, including historical consciousnesses. As they note, these 'projects' in Ukraine serve to build a better, pro-European future, while in Poland, they are oriented towards confirming Poland's past greatness and fostering nostalgic attitudes. Thus, 'the difference in the functions fulfilled by images of the past, historical narratives and the politics of remembrance in both countries

[53] Examples of this process are described by Wojciech Sadurski. See: W Sadurski, *A Pandemic of Populists* (Cambridge University Press, 2022).

[54] J Konieczna-Sałamatin and T Stryjek, 'Polacy i Ukraińcy 1989–2023: dlaczego nadal uwikłani w przeszłość?' *Batory Foundation* (Warsaw, 2023): www.batory.org.pl/publikacja/polacy-i-ukraincy-1989-2023-dlaczego-nadal-uwiklani-w-przeszlosc/.

indicates the most significant barrier to overcoming the dispute about the past between them'.[55] It is thus worth considering the idea of setting up a Truth and Reconciliation Commission, which would try to overcome these differences and develop one common project, including revising national memory laws.

The main challenge, however, remains the question of Poland's and Ukraine's (and more broadly, the European states and institutions) response to Russia's distorted fake historical narrative, which bears no chances for correction or change in the foreseeable future. The CEE region in particular, and in essence, all of Europe, should reflect on how to counteract Russia's hypocrisy over history that led to war crimes. Perhaps the collective European re-reading and dissemination of the European Parliament's resolution of 19 September 2019 on the importance of European remembrance for the future of Europe can serve as a starting point for such urgently necessary reflection.[56] As it importantly reminds us:

> [A]s a direct consequence of the Molotov-Ribbentrop Pact, followed by the Nazi-Soviet Boundary and Friendship Treaty of 28 September 1939, the Polish Republic was invaded first by Hitler and two weeks later by Stalin – which stripped the country of its independence and was an unprecedented tragedy for the Polish people – the communist Soviet Union started an aggressive war against Finland on 30 November 1939, and in June 1940 it occupied and annexed parts of Romania – territories that were never returned – and annexed the independent republics of Lithuania, Latvia and Estonia.

Lastly, one of the crucial issues to be continuously discussed is the future of the phenomenon of mnemonic constitutionalism. As evidenced by the example of Russia on a total scale, as well as Poland and Ukraine on a much more minor and non-violent scale, it is most often used as a tool to create a particular narrative about the past whilst bypassing difficult parts of the history of a given state and nation. At the same time, it is problematic to point to effective legal mechanisms to prevent such abuses – they are subject to and dependent on political will and decisions. When these are taken by populists or autocrats, the role of the law is often reduced to the stamped will of those in power, with no respect for the rule of law or even the principles of proper legislation. In this way, the law inevitably ceases to serve as a shield against historical misrepresentations.

[55] ibid 14.

[56] European Parliament resolution of 19 September 2019 on the importance of European remembrance for the future of Europe [2019] OJ C 171.

8

Memory Laws and Policies in Belarus in the Context of the Russo-Ukrainian War

ULADZISLAU BELAVUSAU

> We dream that it will be a country full of warmth and advantageous to live in. This is a noble idea, concordant with the global ideas of civility. We are not dreaming of something special or extraordinary, we just want "to be called human", as our classic Yanka Kupala said. It implies respect for ourselves and for others, it implies human rights, a democratic way of life, the recognition of the Belarusian language and of our history.
>
> (Aleś Bialacki, Noble Prize Lecture, 2022)[1]

I. INTRODUCTION

FOR A LONG time, Belarus remained on the periphery of Europe's memory wars, avoiding a dynamic discussion on memory laws and staying in the mnemonic shadow of its more geopolitically active neighbours.[2] However,

[1] The Nobel Prize, 'Aleś Bialacki (Ales Bialiatski) Nobel Lecture' (10 December 2022): www.nobelprize.org/prizes/peace/2022/bialiatski/lecture/.

[2] Regarding memory laws in these neighbouring countries in the period preceeding the fully-fledged Russo-Ukrainian war of 2022, see U Belavusau, A Gliszczyńska-Grabias and M Mälksoo, 'Memory Laws and Memory Wars in Poland, Russia and Ukraine' (2021) 69 *Jahrbuch des öffentlichen Rechts* 95. Some notable exceptions on general memory politics in Belarus prior to 2022 in Anglophone academic literature include: S Lewis, 'The "Partisan Republic": Colonial Myths and Memory Wars in Belarus' in J Fedor, M Kangaspuro, J Lassila and T Zhurzhenko (eds), *War and Memory in Russia, Ukraine and Belarus* (Palgrave Macmillan Memory Studies, 2017) 371–96; DR Marples, 'History, Memory, and the Second World War in Belarus' (2012) 58 *Australian Journal of Politics and History* 437; A Lastouski, 'The Politics of Memory in Belarus: Narratives and Institutions'(*CBEES State of the Region Report 2020: Construction and Instrumentalization of the Past: A Comparative Study on Memory Management in the Region*, 2020): www.academia.edu/44921433/The_Politics_of_Memory_in_Belarus_Narratives_and_Institutions; N Bekus, 'Historical Memory and Symbolism in the Belarusian Protests' (*Cultures of History Forum*,

the full-scale Russian invasion of Ukraine, carried out substantially through Belarusian territory in February 2022,[3] brought renewed focus on Belarusian governance of historical memory, which this chapter examines through the lens of memory laws and policies. Following social upheaval after Alaksandr Łukašenka's[4] sham elections in August 2020, and the use of Belarusian territory by the Russian military in its war against Ukraine, Łukašenka's government solidified its position as a staunch ally of Putin. Yet, the majority of Belarusian citizens have remained either distinctly anti-war, displaying strong pro-Ukrainian and – to varying degrees – anti-Russian sentiments, or indifferent and ambivalent to the regime's latest wave of historical propaganda, which can be attributed to the complexities of local memory politics and cultural narratives.[5]

The chapter begins with an analysis of memory policies in Belarus following the collapse of the Soviet Union, with developments categorised into four distinct periods. These periods illustrate Belarus's rapid transformation from an independent state – experiencing cultural, linguistic, and historiographical renaissance in the early 1990s – into the totalitarian dictatorship it is today (focused on promoting the Russification of its citizens). The first section thus

16 February 2021): www.cultures-of-history.uni-jena.de/politics/historical-memory-and-symbolism-in-the-belarusian-protests; A Kotljarchuk, 'The Tradition of Belarusian Statehood: Conflicts about the Past of Belarus' in E Rindzeviciute (ed), *Contemporary Change in Belarus* (Baltic and East European Graduate School, 2004) 43–44; A Marková, 'Institutional Historical Memory and History in Post-Soviet Belarus' (2020) 1 *Journal of Belarusian Studies* 51; A Marin, 'Belarusian Nationalism in the 2010s: a Case of Anti-Colonialism? Origins, Features and Outcomes of Ongoing "Soft Belarusianisation"' (2020) 1 *Journal of Belarusian Studies* 27.

[3] 'Belarus' Involvement in Russia's War of Aggression against Ukraine: New EU Restrictive Measures Target Trade, Services, Transport and Anti-circumvention' (*Press Release of the Council of Europe*, 29 June 2024): www.consilium.europa.eu/en/press/press-releases/2024/06/29/belarus-involvement-in-russia-s-war-of-aggression-against-ukraine-new-eu-restrictive-measures-target-trade-services-transport-and-anti-circumvention/.

[4] In this chapter, the Belarusian Latin alphabet (*łacinka*) is used for Belarusian names, toponyms and titles in the footnotes, as opposed to the Cyrillic-based systems of transliteration from Belarusian. This explains the usage of *Alaksandr Łukašenka*, in contrast to *Alyaksandr Lukashenka* (from Cyrillic Belarusian, Аляксандр Лукашэнка) or *Aleksandr Lukashenko* (from Cyrillic Russian, Александр Лукашенко), which are more common in Anglophone media and literature about Belarus. Unlike Russian and Ukrainian, the Belarusian language historically developed both Cyrillic and Latin scripts. See I Ivanou, 'Three Alphabets of the Belarusian Language' (*European Studies Blog: British Library*, 22 January 2018): https://blogs.bl.uk/european/2018/01/three-alphabets-of-the-belarusian-language.html; Y Jung and B Kim, 'Coexistence of Multiple Writing Systems: Classifying Digraphia in Post-Socialist Countries' (2023) 14 *Journal of Eurasian Studies* 139; T Kamusella, 'Who is Afraid of Letter Ł? Łacinka and the Belarusian Dictator' (*New Eastern Europe*, 11 April 2021): www.neweasterneurope.eu/2021/04/11/who-is-afraid-of-the-letter-l-lacinka-and-the-belarusian-dictator/.

[5] T Astrouskaya, 'Culture as a Battlefield: Belarus's Struggle Over Culture and Identity, SCEEUS Guest Commentary No 12, 2024' (*Stockholm Centre for Eastern European Studies*, 17 May 2024): www.sceeus.se/en/publications/culture-as-a-battlefield-belaruss-struggle-over-culture-and-identity/; A Rudnik, 'Whom do Belarusians Actually Support in the Russia-Ukraine War?' (*Belarus Digest*, 23 March 2022): www.belarusdigest.com/story/whom-do-belarusians-actually-support-in-the-russia-ukraine-war.

covers two pre Russo-Ukrainian war periods; that is, between 1991 (marking the collapse of the Soviet Union) and 1994 (when Łukašenka first came to power), as well as between 1994 and 2020 (the year of mass political unrest in Belarus preceeding the war in Ukraine). The second section focuses on the period after the presidential elections of 2020, providing a detailed account of the most recent ideologically-driven memory law in Belarus, namely, the January 2022 introduction of a criminal provision mimicking memory laws found in Poland and Russia. This Belarusian memory law of 2022 prescribes punitive measures for denying the 'genocide of the Belarusian people' during, and in the aftermath of, the 'Great Patriotic War', a term clearly rooted in Soviet and Russian ideological narratives.

The third section examines the present period, beginning in February 2022, with a focus on both the 'Year of Historical Memory' proclaimed by the government and the subsequent constitutional amendments of 2022 which placed a populist emphasis on historical memory. In doing so, this section explores the intensification of Russification policies, particularly through the politics of history, as well as the impact of recent memory politics for the representation of Jewish, Lithuanian, Polish and Ukrainian minorities.

The conclusion will demonstrate the existence of two parallel sets of Belarusian historical memory policies – one cultivated by the regime and the other by civil society (the latter largely operating in exile)[6] – each reflects divergent attitudes towards the ongoing Russo-Ukrainian war: the same war which has seen the regime intensify its reliance on both Soviet and, to some extent, Russian myths and propaganda clichés in its memory politics, even incorporating constitutional and criminal law to shape a dystopian narrative that frames the democratic opposition as neo-Nazis.

II. MEMORY POLICIES BETWEEN THE COLLAPSE OF THE SOVIET UNION IN 1991 AND THE UPRISING IN 2020

Compared to other Central and Eastern European (CEE) countries reviewed in this volume, the politics of historical memory in Belarus has been closely tied to the ontological security of the Łukašenka dictatorship, rather than to the ontological security of Belarus as a sovereign entity.[7] His dictatorship has already lasted over a quarter of a century (1994–2024), making Belarus a radically different country study compared to the analysis of other constitutional models and memory laws in the region. Thus, four distinct periods are crucial

[6] See: A Coakley, 'Belarusian Exiles are Running out of Hope' (*Coda*, 22 August 2023): www.codastory.com/rewriting-history/belarusian-exiles-battle-for-democracy/.

[7] Compare M Mälksoo, '"Memory Must be Defended": Beyond the Politics of Mnemonical Security' (2015) 46 *Security Dialogue* 221.

for understanding the politics of memory and related legal aspects in Belarus following its independence in 1991:

(a) From the proclamation of Belarusian independence amidst the collapse of the Soviet Union (1991) to the first presidential elections (1994);
(b) From the first presidential elections, when Łukašenka came to power (July 1994), to his sixth presidential elections (9 August 2020);
(c) From the mass upheaval following the sixth presidential elections (August 2020) to the start of the Russo-Ukrainian war (February 2022);
(d) The present period following the full-scale Russian invasion of Ukraine in February 2022 (demarcated, for the purposes of this chapter, as 2022–24).

The follow-up to this initial part of the analysis will collectively cover two of the aforementioned periods; that is, from 1991 to 2020. These two periods (1991 to 1994, and 1994 to 2020) were characterised by a competition between Soviet-centric and Belarusian-centric policies of historical memory, though with different dynamics and power plays in between those narratives.

A. The Years 1991–94

The first timespan covers the period between 1991 and 1994, which marked the transition from communism with a cautious optimism about revival of the Belarusian national identity following the collapse of the Soviet Union, where Belarus had been one of the most Russified Soviet republics along with Ukraine and Kazakhstan.[8] Belarus, during this time, operated as a parliamentary republic with a vocal and active democractic opposition in its parliament despite communists preserving the majority of seats. This vibrant opposition championed core democratic values such as sovereignty, national revival, human rights, economic liberalisation, and the rule of law. This brief but critical period led to a cultural and political renaissance that sought to redefine Belarusian national identity and fostered pride in the country's diverse historical legacy.[9]

A central focus during this period was the revival of the Belarusian language, which had been suppressed under Soviet rule for the benefit of Russian.[10] Efforts to restore the national language were accompanied by a resurgence in Belarusian

[8] A Marková, 'Institutional Historical Memory and History in Post-Soviet Belarus' (2020) 9 *Journal of Belarusian Studies* 51.

[9] A Kazharski, 'Belarus' Entry into International Society: Between a Small Nation-State and Big Narratives' in F Ejdus (ed), *Memories of Empire and Entry into International Society* (Routledge, 2017); N Bekus, 'Reassembling Society in a Nation-State: History, Language, and Identity Discourses of Belarus' (2023) 51 *Nationalities Papers* 98.

[10] D Marples, *Belarus: A Denationalized Nation* (Harwood Academic Publishers, 1999).

culture, arts, and historiography.[11] Historians and scholars turned (or rather re-turned) their attention to the Grand Duchy of Lithuania,[12] recognising it as a formative period for the early (pre-)Belarusian identity within this medieval statehood.[13] Equally significant was the rehabilitation of the Belarusian People's Republic (Biełaruskaja Narodnaja Respublika), proclaimed in 1918, as a symbol of early Belarusian independence.[14] The narratives surrounding the People's Republic, previously marginalised during the Soviet era, were re-established as key elements in the nation's collective memory.[15] Cultural figures, including poets, novelists, artists, and intellectuals who had been repressed or exiled during the Soviet era,[16] were rehabilitated, with their works and contributions celebrated in emerging memory and cultural policies.[17]

This short era of identity revival also extended to minority cultures within Belarus, including Jewish, Lithuanian, Polish, Roma and Ukrainian communities.[18] These groups experienced a renaissance in cultural, political, and religious representation, contributing to a broader and more inclusive national identity within the independent Belarusian state. Jewish cultural and religious life, for example, began to re-emerge in Minsk and other major cities, while the Polish minority gained political visibility, particularly in areas like the Hrodna (Grodno) region.[19]

This initial period of Belarusian independence can be linked to similar national revivals and de-Sovietisation processes witnessed across the former Soviet Bloc. Countries such as Estonia, Latvia, Lithuania, and Ukraine also

[11] S Zaprudski, 'Language Policy in the Republic of Belarus in the 1990s' in P Kazanecki and M Pejda (eds), *Belarus – The Third Sector People, Culture, Language* (East European Democratic Center, 2002) 33–40.

[12] U Arloŭ, *Belarus: The Epoch of The Grand Duchy of Lithuania* (Technalohija, 2018).

[13] On this aspect, see: N Davies, *Litva: The Rise and Fall of the Grand Duchy of Lithuania* (Penguin Tracks, 2012); L Bazan, *A History of Belarus: A Non-Literary Essay That Explains the Ethnogenesis of the Belarusians* (Glagoslav Publications, 2014).

[14] Per A Rudling, *The Rise and Fall of Belarusian Nationalism: 1906–1931* (University of Pittsburg Press, 2014).

[15] Technically, the government of the Belarusian People's Republic has continued to function in exile and has officially become the longest to do so, though more so symbolically nowadays. With current President Madame Ivonka Survilla, residing in Canada. See the website of this entity: 'Rada of the Belarusian Democratic Republic' (*Council of the Belarusian People's Republic*, 2024): www.radabnr.org/english/.

[16] AB McMillin, *Belarusian Literature of the Diaspora* (University of Birmingham Central Printing Services, 2002). See also: A McMillin, 'Language, Place and History in Belarusian Literature' (2015) 6 *Przegląd Wschodnioeuropejski* 97.

[17] N Bekus, *Struggle Over Identity: The Official and Alternative 'Belarusianness'* (Central European University Press, 2010).

[18] A Kotljarchuk, 'World War II Memory Politics: Jewish, Polish and Roma Minorities of Belarus' (2013) 7 *The Journal of Belarusian Studies* 7.

[19] I Kabzińska, 'The Ethnic Identity of the Polish Population in Belarus: A Research Note' in R Taras (ed), *National Identities and Ethnic Minorities in Eastern Europe: Selected Papers from the Fifth International Congress of Central and East Europian Studies* (Palgrave Macmillan, 1998) 148–50; M Frėjutė-Rakauskienė, O Sasunkevich and K Šliavaitė, 'Polish Ethnic Minority in Belarus and Lithuania: Politics, Institutions, and Identities' (2021) *Nationalities Papers* 1132; A Miarka, 'Social Mobilization in Belarus – The Polish Perspective' (2022) 71 *Problems of Post-Communism* 84.

embarked on efforts to reclaim their historical narratives, having stripped away Soviet influences, and affirmed their distinct identities.[20] However, this period in Belarus was cut short with the ascent of Alaksandr Łukašenka to power in 1994, who would steer governance of the nation and memory politics in a very different direction.

B. The Years 1994–95 and the Period Until 2020

The second timespan, starting from 1994–95 and running until 2020, is particularly important as this is the period after Łukašenka won the first (and so far, the last transparent) presidential election in Belarus. Since then, he has built an authoritarian state including full expulsion of the democratic opposition from parliament, suppression of the rule of law and media freedoms, mass repressions and state-sponsored violence, and the embedding of machinery consistently falsifying all of its (by now, six)[21] elections and four referenda.[22] The very first referendum he staged in 1995 made Russian the second state language de jure;[23] de facto, it has become the only fully protected official language. He re-introduced the Soviet-Belarusian flag and coat of arms (instead of the historic 'white-red-white' flag that was used in Belarus from 1991–94),[24] and constitutionally imposed closer economic ties with the Russian Federation. The starting point between 1994 and 1995 proved crucial for the entire subsequent period up until 2020, which can be characterised by a peculiar competition of two sets of memory politics in the country. The first is built upon the existing national historiography, stressing the uniqueness of the Belarusian identity and its historical development. To a certain, albeit limited, extent, its soft promotion has been made possible through the activism of history educators in schools and universities, who have long resisted Russification and re-Sovietisation in their teaching of Belarusian history. This has been complemented by the mobilisation of cultural activists,[25] as well as the necessity for the formally independent state to maintain some minimal differentiation from Russia. This includes, among

[20] G Gill, *Democracy and Post-Communism: Political Change in the Post-Communist World* (Routledge, 2002). For an analysis of 'ethnic democracy', see: Y Peled, *The Challenge of Ethnic Democracy: The State and Minority Groups in Israel, Poland and Nothern Ireland* (Routledge, 2014).

[21] According to current official announcements, the seventh presidential elections are expected to take place on 26 January 2025.

[22] A Wilson, *Belarus: The Last European Dictatorship* (Yale University Press, 2021).

[23] A Piletski, 'The Day Belarus Lost its Language, White-Red-White Flag and Pahonia Coat of Arms' (*EuroRadioFM*, 14 May 2016): www.euroradio.fm/en/day-belarus-lost-language-white-red-white-flag-and-pahonia-coat-arms/.

[24] A Kotljarchuk, 'The Flag Revolution: Understanding the Political Symbols of Belarus' in N Mörner (ed), *Constructions and Instrumentalization of the Past. A Comparative Study on Memory Management in the Region* (CBEES: Södertörns högskola, 2020) 45–54.

[25] S Oushakine, 'How to Grow out of Nothing: The Afterlife of National Rebirth in Postcolonial Belarus' (2017) 28 *Qui Parle* 423.

other aspects, the use of national toponyms,[26] the Belarusian spelling of names in official documents,[27] and modest investments in the restoration of historical monuments.[28]

Yet the second competing politics of memory,[29] with its cult of World War II (WWII) (or rather, the 'Great Patriotic War', the post-Soviet vocabulary and chronology transplanted from the Russian analogues)[30] and a promulgated image of Belarus as an anti-Nazi partisan republic has been incomparably more powerful, due to its sustainment – including financial – by Łukašenka's state machinery.[31] It has encompassed not only the explicit linguistic Russification of all major social networks (from teaching at schools and universities, to Russian becoming de facto the sole language of court proceedings), but also showcased Belarusian historiography and cultural representation as derived from the Soviet hagiography of Belarusian statehood. Several historical themes were either ignored in educational and official cultural policies or addressed only sporadically and subjected to censorship. These include the history of the Holocaust of Belarusian Jews, the mass genocide of the Roma, the histories of Ostarbeiters, Soviet military defeats and errors, non-communist resistance to Nazism, the Jewish partisan movement, controversial and violent episodes of the Soviet partisan movement for the Belarusian population, and the history of the national movement during the war period (which was exclusively portrayed as collaborationist). Also overlooked were the repressive policies of the Soviet political regime before, during, and after WWII, analysis of regional historical differences within Belarus (particularly between Western and Eastern Belarus), state violence and Stalinist crimes in the twentieth century, the post-war history of the national movement, and the memory of the 1986 Chernobyl disaster.[32]

While imperial Russian concepts have been permitted to compete in the *non*-free market of historical ideas in Belarus, the state's memory politics have primarily favoured Soviet elements of historical narratives. This includes

[26] UN Economic and Social Council, 'The Roman Alphabet Transliteration of Belarusian Geographical Names' (*Tenth United Nations Conference on the Standardization of Geographical Names*, 13 July 2012): https://unstats.un.org/unsd/geoinfo/ungegn/docs/10th-uncsgn-docs/crp/E_CONF.101_CRP2_The%20Roman%20alphabet%20transliteration.pdf/.

[27] R Astapenia, 'Getting Belarusian Names and Places Right' *BelarusDigest* (Belarus, 20 July 2015): www.belarusdigest.com/story/getting-belarusian-names-and-places-right/.

[28] S Stureika, 'Developing the Cultural Heritage Sector in Belarus' (*Culture Partnership Europe*): www.culturepartnership.eu/en/article/report-stureika.

[29] Lastouski (n 2).

[30] For socio-legal implications stemming from the usage of 'World War II' and the 'Great Patriotic War' in the (post-)Soviet context, as well as the differentiation between these terms, see the chapters on Russia in this volume (in particular, Chapter 1 by Andrii Nekoliak and Paul Primbs, and Chapter 2 by Ilya Nuzov).

[31] A Goujon, 'Memorial Narratives of WWII Partisans and Genocide in Belarus' (2010) 24 *East European Politics and Societies: and Cultures* 6.

[32] A Bratačkin, '2022-y – hod "histaryčnaj pamiaci" i palityčnaha vykarystańnia historyi ŭ Biełarusi' (*Biełaruski PEN*, 13 February 2023): www.penbelarus.org/2023/02/13/2022-y-god-gistarychnaj-pamyaczi-i-palitychnaga-vykarystannya-gistoryi-u-belarusi.html.

the pompous military parades celebrating victory in the 'Great Patriotic War' on 9 May,[33] rather than shifting focus to the outright Russian imperialist constructs which deny Belarusians and Ukrainians any historical agency or independent identity.[34] Civil society, with its mnemonic practices,[35] has continued to function inside the country, though under quasi-dissident conditions.[36]

Nonetheless, authorities permitted civil society activists to hold anniversary events in honour of the centenary of the formation of the Belarusian People's Republic in 2018,[37] and even attempted to depoliticise the memory of Stalinist repressions by erecting a monument at the site of mass executions from the late 1930s in Kurapaty,[38] near Minsk.[39] This period of short-lived 'liberalisation' in memory policies came to an end in 2020.

III. THE SHIFT IN MEMORY POLITICS BETWEEN 2020 AND 2022: MEMORY LAW ON THE 'GENOCIDE OF BELARUSIAN PEOPLE' (2022)

Between 2020 and 2022, Belarusian memory politics underwent significant changes, particularly in the context of state-controlled narratives about the nation's past, the turning point being the mass protests in the aftermath of the 2020 presidential election, which resulted in the tightening of control over historical discourse.[40] This culminated in the 2021 memory law on the 'Genocide of the Belarusian People',[41] a key legislative development that marks a profound shift in how the past is officially framed and used by Lukašenka's regime.

[33] U Belavusau and M Karliuk, 'The State of Denial Amidst a Military Parade: COVID-19 in Belarus' (*Verfassungsblog*, 20 May 2020): www.verfassungsblog.de/the-state-of-denial-amidst-a-military-parade-covid-19-in-belarus/. The parade is held every 5 years.

[34] M Mälksoo, 'The Postcolonial Moment in Russia's War Against Ukraine' (2022) 25 *Journal of Genocide Research* 471.

[35] Oushakine (n 25).

[36] 'Human Rights Situation in Belarus: December 2020' (*Viasna*, 31 December 2020): www.spring96.org/en/news/101166. See also: 'European Parliament Resolution of 10 March 2010 on the Situation of Civil Society and National Minorities in Belarus, 2010/C 349 E07' (*EU Parliament Resolution*, 10 March 2010): https://eur-lex.europa.eu/LexUriServ/LexUriServ.do?uri=OJ:C:2010:349E:0037:0039:EN:PDF.

[37] Regarding this historical entity, see the previous section of this chapter (II.B), covering the years 1991–94.

[38] DR Marples and V Laputska, 'Kurapaty: Belarus' Continuous Debate' (2020) 79 *Slavic Review* 521, 521–43; N Bekus, 'Agency of Internal Transnationalism in Social Memory (2018) 70 *The British Journal of Sociology* 1602.

[39] Bratačkin (n 32).

[40] A Kazharski, 'Belarus' New Political Nation? 2020 Anti-authoritarian Protests as Identity Building' (2021) 29 *New Perspectives* 69; T Kulakevich, 'National Awakening in Belarus: Elite Ideology to "Nation" Practice' (2020) 40 *SAIS Review of International Affairs* 97.

[41] Law of the Republic of Belarus of 5 January 2022, No 146-Z 'About Genocide of the Belarusian People' (Закон Республики Беларусь от 5 января 2022, номер 146-З, «О Геноциде белорусского народа»): https://pravo.by/document/?guid=12551&p0=H12200146 (on the website of the National Legal Portal of Belarus). See also Instructional and Methodological Letter from the Ministry of Education of the Republic of Belarus, 'On the Study of Materials about the Genocide of the

A. Context of the Shift in Memory Politics

The unsuccessful mass protests of 2020 triggered the start of a new period in Belarusian memory politics which is crucial for understanding the escalation of Łukašenka's equating the democratic opposition with Nazi collaborationists.[42] This period was marked by its failed, though impressively massive and peaceful,[43] uprising against the dictatorship of Łukašenka after the presidential elections in August 2020.[44] Despite their seemingly fraudulent result,[45] the elections demonstrated the unequivocal victory of a democratic – albeit then completely accidental – candidate, Ms Sviatłana Cichanoŭskaja (Tsikhanouskaya),[46] with all the major opponents of Łukašenka (including her husband),[47] having already been imprisoned that summer. The peaceful uprising was brutally suppressed (with Russia backing Łukašenka's massacres);[48] several people lost their lives (including those under circumstances that were not investigated); thousands of people were tortured and imprisoned;[49] and hundreds of thousands left the country in the two years following[50] (as political refugees and, even more so, as economic migrants escaping the dictatorship and potential escalation of the Russo-Ukrainian war on Belarusian territory).[51]

Belarusian People during the Great Patriotic War in General Secondary Education Institutions', 30 August 2024 (Инструктивно-методическое письмо Министерства Образования Республики Беларусь «Об изучении в учреждениях общего среднего образования материалов о геноциде белорусского народа в годы Великой Отечественной войны», от 30 авуста 2024).

[42] U Belavusau (interviwed by M Steinbelis), 'Corona Constitutional #45: Europas letzter Diktator?' (*Verfassungsblog*, 19 August 2020): www.verfassungsblog.de/corona-constitutional-45-europas-letzter-diktator/.

[43] M Karliuk and Y Miadzvetskaya, 'The Kafkaesque Edifice of Law: Belarusian Presidential Elections 2020' (*Verfassungsblog*, 7 August 2020): www.verfassungsblog.de/the-kafkaesque-edifice-of-law/.

[44] 'Statement: the Democractic Oppostition in Belarus' (*European Parliament*, 2020): https://www.europarl.europa.eu/cmsdata/215921/.

[45] J Kinnear, 'Fraudulent Presidential Election in Belarus: Joint Statement to the OSCE' (*UK Government – Foreign, Commonwealth and Development Office*, 2 September 2022): www.gov.uk/government/speeches/fraudulent-presidential-election-in-belarus-joint-statement-to-the-osce/.

[46] Although I use the Belarusian Latin alphabet throughout this chapter, the name and surname of Cichanoŭskaja are more widely used in their transliteration from Cyrillic Belarusian (like in Ms Tsikhanouskaya's passport) in Anglophone literature and media, including on her official website, see: 'Official Website' (*Sviatlana Tsikhanouskaya*, 2024): www.tsikhanouskaya.org/en/.

[47] 'Belarus Opposition Leader Tsikhanouski Jailed for 18 Years' (*Euractiv*, 14 December 2021): www.euractiv.com/section/europe-s-east/news/belarus-opposition-leader-tsikhanouski-jailed-for-18-years/.

[48] A Leukavets, 'Russia's Game in Belarus: 2020 Presidential Elections as a Checkmate for Lukashenka?' (2021) 29 *New Perspectives* 90.

[49] BBC News, 'Belarus Jails: Stories of Fear and Violence' (*BBC News* London, 27 May 2021) www.bbc.com/news/world-europe-57238628.

[50] A McMillan, 'The Recent Belarusian Exodus Seen against the Background of Earlier Belarusian and Russian Emigrations' (2023) 15 *Białorutenistyka Białostrock* 111; M Gaučaitė-Znutienė, 'Thousands of Belarusians Flee to Lithuania for Fear of Repressions and Conscription *LRT.lt* (Lithuania, 27 July 2022): www.lrt.lt/en/news-in-english/19/1745790/thousands-of-belarusians-flee-to-lithuania-for-fear-of-repressions-and-conscription.

[51] A Główczewski, 'Zaryn: Belarusians are Fleeing the Country' *Polish Press Agency* (Poland, 17 June 2022): www.pap.pl/en/news/news%2C1251774%2Czaryn-belarusians-are-fleeing-country.html.

Widespread use of the white-red-white flag,[52] and other historical symbols during the protest,[53] constituted a trigger for the impulsive turn in Łukašenka's politics of memory regarding not only *re-Sovietisation* of the historical policies, but also – to a large degree – their substitution with Russian historiographic myths.[54] Furthermore, support extended by Poland and Lithuania to the Belarusian democratic opposition led to Łukašenka's notoriously aggressive stance not only towards activists of the Polish[55] and Lithuanian[56] minorities, but also the periods of Belarusian historiography shared with these nations. These include the Grand Duchy of Lithuania and the Commonwealth of Poland and Lithuania, as well as the later period up until 1939. In addition, Łukašenka orchestrated the refugee crisis on the Polish and Lithuanian borders as part of his broader political tactics.[57] Putin's economic and political support of Łukašenka's suppression of the mass peaceful protest led to daily arrests, as well as gigantic political and social repression on various levels.[58]

It was during this period of instability, which began in the summer of 2020, that historical memory became a central battleground for state officials.[59] They portrayed the democratic opposition as heirs to the collaborationist faction among Belarusians who had cooperated with the Nazi regime during the 'Great Patriotic War'.[60] This narrative involved not only the suppression of alternative historical perspectives – particularly those linked to the national independence movement and opposition figures – but also the amplification of Soviet-era commemorations and the accelerated Russification of historical discourses. The latter process had been comparably slower and less pervasive between 1994 and 2020. In fact,

[52] Regarding the white-red-white flag (dating back to 1918) being briefly restored as the state symbol in the period between 1991 and 1994 – before Lukašenka returned the Soviet flag of the Belarusian Soviet Socialist Republic (with minor adjustments) – and its cultural and political significance for Belarusian independence and democracy, see the previous section of this chapter (II.B.), covering 1994–2020, and the literature cited in footnotes therein.

[53] Bekus (n 2); Kotljarchuk (n 24).

[54] G Ioffe, 'Belarus's Politics of Memory Swing Back Toward Russo-Centrism' (*Eurasia Daily Monitor*, 26 January 2022): https://jamestown.org/program/belaruss-politics-of-memory-swing-back-toward-russo-centrism/.

[55] 'Minsk Regime Began to Oppress the Polish Minority in Belarus' (*InformNapalm*, 19 May 2021): https://informnapalm.org/en/minsk-regime-began-to-oppress-the-polish-minority-in-belarus/.

[56] R Jakubauskas, 'Belarus Bans Lithuanian Instruction in Minority Schools, Prompting Protests from Vilnius' *LRT.lt* (Lithuania, 25 April 2022): www.lrt.lt/en/news-in-english/19/1680264/belarus-bans-lithuanian-instruction-in-minority-schools-prompting-protests-from-vilnius.

[57] A Kubal, 'Why is There a Humanitarian Crisis at the Polish-Belarusian Border?' (*Georgetown Journal of International Affairs*, 17 November 2021): https://gjia.georgetown.edu/2021/11/17/why-is-there-a-humanitarian-crisis-at-the-polish-belarusian-border/.

[58] Belsat.eu, 'Genocide of Belarusian People' (*Belsat ENG Video*, 16 November 2021): https://belsat.eu/en/programs/16-11-2021-genocide-of-belarusian-people-eng-video/; see publications of *Viasna* on human rights situation in Belarus, 'Publications' (*Viasna*, 2023–24): https://spring96.org/en/publications.

[59] SM Norris, 'History, Memory, and the Art of Protest in Belarus' (*Origins: Current Events in Historical Perspective*, February 2021): https://origins.osu.edu/article/history-memory-and-art-protest-belarus. See also M Kranz, 'Belarusian Leader Writes Poles, Jews, Other Minorities out of WWII History in a Bid for National Unity' (*Coda*, 23 September 2022): https://www.codastory.com/rewriting-history/belarus-war-on-historical-memory/.

[60] Bratačkin (n 32).

up until 2020, Łukašenka did not base his memory politics explicitly on the Russian colonial myth.[61] His propaganda neither resisted nor explicitly endorsed Russian imperialist doctrines, despite his regime's full dependence on the Kremlin, the linguistic Russification of the country and Łukašenka's periodic slip of the tongue about Belarusians being 'the quality version of Russians'.[62] Nevertheless, much like Putin – arguably even more so – Łukašenka became notorious in the post-Soviet space for his rhetoric of whitewashing[63] and denying communist-era crimes.[64] He promoted various cultural policies that effectively perpetuated the cult of the Soviet state and the hagiography of the 'Great Patriotic War' (1941–45).[65] Despite this, the spectrum of Belarusian memory laws (mostly non-punitive) under his presidency until 2020 remained relatively modest compared to the veritable boom of such legislation in neighbouring Poland, Russia, and Ukraine,[66] as demonstrated in various chapters of this volume. In these countries, memory laws have largely been converted into instruments of offence and defence during so-called 'memory wars'.[67] The failed peaceful uprising of 2020, however, led to increasingly neurotic political rhetoric, which accelerated the discussion and adoption of memory policies by Łukašenka's puppet parliament. Among these, the most controversial was a punitive memory law concerning the denial of the genocide against the Belarusian people.

B. The Law on the 'Genocide of the Belarusian People' (2022)

The most significant legislative development in this shift was the passage of the 2021 Bill on the 'Genocide of the Belarusian People'.[68] This Bill was passed by

[61] See A Kazharski and K Lozka, 'Belarus-Russia Relations: Identity as Product and Factor' in A Moshes and R Nizhnikau (eds), *Russian Policy Toward Belarus after 2020: At a Turning Point?* (Lexington Books, 2023) 11–28.

[62] See CTVBY, 'Lukashenko: "Belorus – eto russkij so znakom kachestva"' (*STB TV Channel*, 18 January 2019): www.youtube.com/watch?v=k5HqUfOIQr8. This narrative has been picked up again in a recent interview with Russian media, see: 'Interview with Rossiya TV Channel' (*President of the Republic of Belarus*, 15 August 2024): https://president.gov.by/en/events/interv-u-telekanalu-rossia-1723807637.

[63] C Bigg, 'Lukashenka Comes to Praise Stalin, Not to Bury Him' (*RadioLibertyEurope/ RadioLiberty*, 17 October 2012): www.rferl.org/a/lukashenka-belarus-russia-stalin-lenin/24742548.html/.

[64] A Sannikov, 'The Accidental Dictatorship of Alexander Lukashenko' (2005) 25 *SAIS Review of International Affairs* 75; N Leshchenko, 'The National Ideology and the Basis of the Lukashenka Regime in Belarus' (2008) 60 *Europe-Asia Studies* 1419; K Matzuzato, 'A Populist Island in an Ocean of Clan Politics: The Lukashenka Regime as an Exception among CIS Countries' (2004) 56 *Europa-Asia Studies* 235; M Frear, *Belarus Under Lukashenka: Adaptive Authoritarianism* (Routledge, 2019).

[65] DR Marples, *Our Glorious Past': Lukashenka's Belarus and the Great Patriotic War* (Columbia University Press, 2014).

[66] G Baranowska and L Castellanos-Jankiewicz, 'Historical Memory in Post-Communist Europe and the Rule of Law' (2020) 5 *European Papers* 95. See also: 'Debate: Memory Laws' (*Verfassungsblog*, 2017–2018): www.verfassungsblog.de/category/debates/memory-laws-debates/.

[67] Belavusau, Gliszczyńska-Grabias and Mälksoo (n 2).

[68] Law of the Republic of Belarus of 5 January 2022 (n 41). In Russia, the 'genocide of the Soviet people' has been commemorated annually, on 19 April, since 2019. See A Weiss-Wendt, '"Genocide

Parliament on 14 June 2021 and signed into law by Łukašenka on 5 January 2022, that is, only a month before the fully-fledged 'de-Nazifying' – as framed by Putin – Russian invasion into Ukraine. The officially announced primary aim of this law was to establish a legal framework that recognises the mass killings of Belarusians during WWII as genocide. This includes crimes committed by Nazi Germany, ignoring Soviet repression and other controversial aspects of Belarus's twentieth-century history.

According to this memory law, the 'genocide of the Belarusian people' includes atrocities committed by Nazi criminals and their collaborators, as well as by nationalist formations during the 'Great Patriotic War' and the post-war period. These actions, according to the law, were aimed at the systematic physical extermination of the Belarusian people through killings and other acts recognised as genocide in accordance with legislative acts and international law.[69]

By introducing this law, the Belarusian parliament appears to have drawn inspiration from both Polish[70] and Russian precedents,[71] elevating memory populism in criminal law to a level of explicit demagogy. The 2022 Belarusian memory law added a new crime to Article 130 of the Criminal Code of Belarus (essentially extending an existing provision on hate speech), stipulating a prison sentence of five to ten years for the denial and trivialisation of the 'genocide of the Belarusian people' during WWII and up until December 1951.[72] Thus, this law also covers the period of anti-Soviet national Belarusian resistance after 1945 on the communist-occupied territory of Belarus. Similarly to Putin's version of memory governance,[73] this law promulgates the heading, 'Great Patriotic War', transplanting post-Soviet Russian historiographic imagery and denialism of the joint Soviet-German aggression

of the Soviet People": Putin's Russia Waging Lawfare by Means of History, 2018–2023' (2023–2024) 17 *Genocide Studies and Prevention: An International Journal* 1.

[69] Art 1 of Law of the Republic of Belarus of 5 January 2022, No 146-Z 'About Genocide of the Belarusian People' (Закон Республики Беларусь от 5 января 2022, номер 146-З, «О Геноциде белорусского народа»).

[70] A Gliszczyńska and W Kozłowski, 'Calling Murders by Their Names as Criminal Offence: a Risk of Statutory Negationism in Poland' (*Verfassungsblog*, 1 February 2018): www.verfassungsblog.de/calling-murders-by-their-names-as-criminal-offence-a-risk-of-statutory-negationism-in-poland/.

[71] G Bogush and I Nuzov, 'Russia's Supreme Court Rewrites History of the Second World War' (*EJIL:Talk*, 28 October 2016): www.ejiltalk.org/russias-supreme-court-rewrites-history-of-the-second-world-war/.

[72] Art 2 of this Law stipulates that: '(1) The denial of the genocide of the Belarusian people, whether expressed in a public speech, a printed or publicly displayed work, in mass media, or in information posted on the global computer network Internet, another public telecommunications network, or a private telecommunications network, shall be punishable by arrest, or by restriction of liberty for a term of up to five years, or by imprisonment for the same term. (2) The act specified in part 1 of this article, if committed by a person previously convicted of denying the genocide of the Belarusian people, or by an official using their official authority, shall be punishable by imprisonment for a term of three to ten years'.

[73] N Koposov, '"The Only Possible Ideology": Nationalizing History in Putin's Russia' (2022) 24 *Journal of Genocide Research* 205.

towards Poland in 1939. Furthermore, this Belarusian memory law seems to almost mock the 2018 Polish memory law[74] (often – erroneously, in my opinion[75] – referred to in the press as the 'Polish Holocaust Law'). The Polish law refers to the 'Polish Nation', that should not be accused of atrocities committed by the Third Reich, including those connected to the Holocaust.[76] The Belarusian law of 2022 applies the political ethnonym of 'Belarusian people' (*biełaruski narod*) against whom a genocide was committed during the 'Great Patriotic War'. The asterisked note to 'Belarusian people' in Article 1 contains the definition that '[f]or the purposes of this Article, the term "Belarusian people" refers to Soviet citizens who resided within the territory of the Belarusian Soviet Socialist Republic during the Great Patriotic War and/or the post-war period'. In doing so, the law certifies the Soviet narrative about the heroic victimhood of the Belarusian people, considering that every fourth Belarusian inhabitant perished during WWII.[77]

Nonetheless, most 'Belarusian' victims of the *systemic* annihilation in Nazi-occupied Belarus were Jews, who are not even mentioned one single time in this law. Before the Holocaust, Belarus hosted one of the most dense Jewish Ashkenazi populations and was even where the renaissance of the Yiddish-language culture unfolded.[78] Unsurprisingly, the law has been criticised by Israeli historians and press (yet comparatively less so than the analogous Polish legislation of 2018).[79] In reply to criticism addressed to the earlier Bill of this law, the Belarusian embassy in Tel Aviv delivered an op-ed to *Haaretz*, where it insisted that the ethnonym of the Belarusian people sufficiently encompasses all nations living on Belarusian territory.[80] This rhetoric seems to reanimate the old Soviet approach of silencing the crimes against Jews, by emphasising that

[74] U Belavusau and A Wójcik, 'Polish Memory Law: When History Becomes a Source of Mistrust' (*New Eastern Europe*, 19 February 2018): www.neweasterneurope.eu/2018/02/19/polish-memory-law-history-becomes-source-mistrust/.

[75] U Belavusau and A Wójcik, 'La criminalisation de l'expression historique en Pologne: la loi mémorielle de 2018' (2018) *Archives de politique criminelle* 30.

[76] BELTA English, 'MFA Hosts Exhibition about Genocide of Belarusian People During War' (18 July 2022): https://eng.belta.by/society/view/mfa-hosts-exhibition-about-genocide-of-belarusian-people-during-war-151843-2022/.

[77] Per A Rudling, '"For a Heroic Belarus!": The Great Patriotic War as Identity Marker in Lukashenka and Soviet Belarusian Discourses' (2008) 32 *Nationalities Affairs* 43.

[78] E Bemporad, *Becoming Soviet Jews: The Bolshevik Experiment in Minsk* (Indiana University Press, 2013) (see in particular, the chapter on 'Soviet Minsk: The Capital of Yiddish', 81–111).

[79] L Smilovitsky, 'The Real Reason Belarus' Dictatorial Regime is Downplaying the Holocaust' (*Haaretz*, 12 January 2022): www.haaretz.com/world-news/2022-01-12/ty-article-opinion/.premium/the-real-reason-belarus-dictatorial-regime-downplays-the-holocaust/0000017f-e9f7-dc91-a17f-fdff62590000/. See also L Rozovsky, 'Belarus Under Fire for Law Equating Holocaust with Nazi Crimes Against Nationals' (*Haaretz*, 19 December 2021): https://www.haaretz.com/jewish/2021-12-19/ty-article/.premium/israeli-historians-belarus-blurring-holocaust-with-genocide-legislation/0000017f-ef3a-d8a1-a5ff-ffba160f0000.

[80] E Vorobyev, 'We Will Never Separate Jewish Victims from the Nazi Genocide against the Entire People of Belarus' (*Haaretz*, 22 December 2021): www.haaretz.com/world-news/2021-12-22/ty-article-opinion/.premium/we-will-never-separate-jewish-victims-from-the-nazi-genocide-against-belarus/0000017f-dc84-db5a-a57f-dceec14c0000. See also L Allwork, 'At Engagement Edge:

'all Soviet citizens' were targeted.[81] In the meantime, Łukašenka himself has been accused on several occasions of anti-Semitic statements.[82]

By no means has the law been a sleeping monster; instead, it has been utilised as a weapon against independent media,[83] leaders of the Polish minority in Belarus,[84] cultural figures, historians and even tour guides.[85] Furthermore, propaganda agencies and history educators explicitly link the 'genocide of the Belarusian people'[86] to the 'rehabilitation of Nazi collaborationism' by the democratic opposition.[87] Such allegations are explicit, in particular, in the book edited by the Prosecutor General, *The Genocide of the Belarusian People* (published in the summer of 2022) with a cover collaging an image from WWII with a photo of the 2020 protestors.[88] The Belarusian Prosecutor's Office has launched official criminal proceedings and orchestrated an almost theatrical investigation into this 'international crime of genocide', collecting evidence and periodically suggesting that perpetrators of that genocide share the same political ideologies as current opponents of the Belarusian regime.[89] In March 2024, the first person accused of the crime of denying the 'genocide of the Belarusian people' was detained.[90]

Amendments introduced in 2021 to the laws 'On Countering Extremism' and 'On the Prevention of the Rehabilitation of Nazism', alongside provisions on hate speech (Article 130) and the denigration of state symbols (Article 370) in the Criminal Code, have been transformed into instruments for persecuting individuals based on their political views expressed through historical narratives. These

Heritage Experts and Holocaust Education in Belarus' (2023) 30 *Holocaust Studies: A Journal of Culture and History* 1.

[81] R Weinberg, 'The Politics of Remembering: The Treatment of Holocaust in the Soviet Union' (2006) 7 *The Holocaust in International Perspective* 414.

[82] See L Gershovich, 'Anti-Semitism in the Propaganda and Public Discourse in Russia, Ukraine, and Belarus during the Russian-Ukrainian War (February-August 2022)' (2023) 41 *Analysis of Current Trents in Antisemitism* 1. See also S Asatiani, 'Belarus: Lukashenka Comments Draw Accusations of Anti-Semitism' (*RadioFreeEurope/ RadioLiberty*, 22 October 2007): www.rferl.org/a/1079002.html; TO Fritzhand, 'Katz Calls Belarus President's Remarks "Clear" Antisemitism' (*Jewish News Syndicate*, 16 June 2024): www.jns.org/belarus-president-blames-jews-for-political-corruption/; L Nevzlin, 'The Silence over Lukashenko's Antisemitism' (*Haaretz*, 20 December 2021): https://www.haaretz.com/opinion/2021-12-20/ty-article-opinion/.premium/the-silence-over-lukashenkos-antisemitism/0000017f-f226-d497-a1ff-f2a659e90000.

[83] 'Sud nad mastakom Alesiem Puškinym zrabili adkrytym' (*Viasna*, 10 March 2022): www.spring96.org/be/news/107036.

[84] 'Andrzej Poczobut pačaŭ znajomicca z materyjałami spravy' (*Naša Niva*, 8 April 2022): www.nashaniva.com/297212.

[85] 'Nia možaš raskazvać, što dumaješ: jak režym ciśnie na ekskursavodaŭ' (*Naša Niva*, 10 August 2022): www.nashaniva.com/297141.

[86] 'Henprakuratura źviazała henacyd z padziejami 2020 hoda ŭ Biełarusi' (*Naša Niva*, 27 January 2022): www.nashaniva.com/?c=ar&i=283701.

[87] 'Vyjšła kniha pra hienacyd biełaruskaha Naroda' (*Naša Niva*, 8 April 2022): www.nashaniva.com/?c=ar&i=287917.

[88] ibid.

[89] For investigation materials in Russian, see, the website of the Belarus Prosecution Office: http://prokuratura.gov.by/ru/activity/rassledovanie-ugolovnogo-dela-o-genotside/.

[90] See: 'Chto toj biełarus, jakoha pieršym zatrymali za "admaŭleńnie henacydu biełaruskaha narodu"' (*Naša Niva*, 4 March 2024): www.nashaniva.com/337758.

measures include explicit prohibitions on the use of the historical white-red-white flag and the coat of arms of the Grand Duchy of Lithuania ('Pahonia') – both official state symbols in Belarus from 1991 to 1994 – as well as the slogan 'Long Live Belarus' (*Žyvie Biełaruś*), which dates back to the early twentieth century.[91]

On 26 March 2021, the General Prosecutor's Office of Belarus initiated a criminal case against renowned Belarusian artist Aleś Puškin,[92] for displaying a portrait of the anti-Soviet underground figure Aŭhien Žychar at an exhibition in the Hrodna Centre for Urban Life. The prosecutor's office interpreted this as a 'rehabilitation of Nazism', despite the fact that the painting had been created in 2014 and subsequently exhibited in both Russia and Belarus. Although Puškin was aware of the criminal case, he did not cancel his return flight from Ukraine, where he had been holding an exhibition. He returned home that evening and on 30 March 2022, Puškin was sentenced to five years in prison for 'incitement to racial, national, or religious hatred' – the same provision of the Criminal Code, concerning hate speech, to which the 2022 memory law added extensions relating to the denial of the 'genocide of the Belarusian people'. On 11 July 2023, Puškin tragically passed away at the age of 57 in a hospital to which he had been urgently transferred from a prison facility after being allegedly denied adequate medical treatment for several days.[93]

The memory law on the 'Genocide of the Belarusian People' (2022) is emblematic of a broader trend in Belarusian memory politics under Łukašenka, where historical narratives and symbols have been weaponised to bolster regime legitimacy. This shift – which intensified after the 2020 election protests that

[91] Bratačkin (n 32). It should be noted that the link between counteracting the rehabilitation of Nazism and counteracting extremism is a feature of both Russian and Belarusian legislation. The crime of Holocaust denial, for example, is never a self-standing provision as in Germany and other European countries, but rather part of the general prohibition of the Nazi ideology and its glorification or rehabilitation. See in particular, R Shulga, 'Pravovyje aspiekty otvietstviennosti za otritsaniye Kholokosta v Rossii (na primierie sudiebnogo diela Romana Yushkova)', *Viestnik Sankt-Pieterburgskogo univiersitieta: Pravo*, 3, 2023. 595–609; Ma Sovetova, 'O sodierzhanii ponyatiya "reabilitatsyi Natsizma": fakticheskiy, sotsialno-pravovoy i ugolovno-pravovoy askpiekty', Trudy *Akademii Upravlieniya MVD Rossii*, 1, 65, 2023. 164–71. See also, Postanovlieniye Parlamientskoy Assambliei Organizatsii Dogovora o Kolliektivnoy Biezopastnosti, 'O Proiektie Rekommendatsiy po soviershenstvovaniyu natsionalnogo zakonodatielstva gosudarstv-chlenov ODKB v sfierie protivodieystviya rasprostranieniyu natsizma i jego projavlieniy' no 12-5.3 (5 November 2019); ODKB: 'Resolution of the Parliamentary Assembly of the Collective Security Treaty Organization, "On the Draft Recommendations for the Improvement of the National Legislation of the CSTO Member States in the Sphere of Countering the Spread of Nazism and Its Manifestations"' (available at: https://pacsto.org/documents/rekomendatsii-po-sovershenstvovaniyu-natsionalnogo-zakonodatelstva-gosudarstv-108).

[92] 'Who was Ales Pushkin?' (*Euroradio*, 12 July 2023): www.euroradio.fm/en/who-was-ales-pushkin-artist-who-died-captivity.

[93] A Williams, 'Ales Pushkin, Dissident Artist in Belarus, is Dead in Prison' (*New York Times*, 25 July 2023): www.nytimes.com/2023/07/25/world/europe/ales-pushkin-dead.html; R Svaboda, 'U špitali pamior palitźniavoleny mastak Aleś Puškin' (*New York Times*, 11 July 2023): https://www.nytimes.com/2023/07/25/world/europe/ales-pushkin-dead.html; J Lichtarovič, 'Aleś Puškin: mastak, jaki achviaravaŭ życcio za svaje idei' (*Polskie Radio*, 11 July 2024): www.polskieradio.pl/396/7819/artykul/3402150.

largely used historical symbols and slogans, and amid the Russo-Ukrainian war – reflects the regime's efforts to control the past as a means of misrepresenting the present. By codifying its preferred version of history, the state seeks to eliminate alternative narratives that could threaten its authority, using memory as both a political and legal tool.

IV. LAW AND MEMORY POLITICS IN BELARUS DURING THE RUSSO-UKRAINIAN WAR (2022–24)

A. Mnemonic Constitutionalism Amidst the War

The final timespan under analysis in this chapter begins in February 2022, and marks another evolution in the memory politics of the dictatorial regime in Belarus which has lasted up until the present moment in 2024. Memory policies during this time have been used, in part, to justify the war in Ukraine by largely adopting a Russian colonial perspective on Belarus and the broader history of the region,[94] and opposing national historiography, which is framed as 'nationalist' – that is, purportedly imbued with 'Nazi ideas' and as posing a threat to the ontological security of the Union state of Russia and Belarus,[95] as the Belarusian state TV propaganda claims. During this period, civil society in Belarus ceased to exist, even under the dissident conditions in which it had persisted between 1994 and 2020. Its members were either imprisoned (and often subjected to physical torture),[96] or sought to establish new channels of cultural communication within the growing diaspora of political and economic émigrés, primarily in neighbouring Lithuania and Poland.[97]

A fraudulent constitutional referendum,[98] held immediately after the Russian invasion of Ukraine (which was launched substantially from Belarusian territory),[99] introduced several provisions to the Basic Law,[100] including the following extreme examples of mnemonic constitutionalism:

[94] Ioffe (n 54).

[95] Clingendael Institute, 'Historical and Legal context of the Union State of Russia and Belarus' (*Clingendael Report*, August 2021): www.clingendael.org/pub/2021/an-ever-closer-union/2-historical-and-legal-context/.

[96] Biełsat English, 'Torture Center: Stories from Belarusian Detention Center' (*Youtube*, 21 October 2020): www.youtube.com/watch?v=4AkG3vGUjPo.

[97] McMillin, 'The Recent Belarusian Exodus' (n 50).

[98] 'Belarus: Statement by the High Representative/ Vice-President Josep Borrell on the Constitutional Referendum' (*European External Action Service*, 28 February 2020): www.eeas.europa.eu/eeas/belarus-statement-high-representativevice-president-josep-borrell-constitutional-referendum_en/.

[99] N Reetz, 'Belarus is Complicit in Russia's War of Agression' (*EJIL:Talk!*, 1 March 2022): www.ejiltalk.org/belarus-is-complicit-in-russias-war-of-aggression/.

[100] R Astapenia, 'Belarus' New Dubious Constitution' (*Democracy and Society*, 3 March 2022): www.ips-journal.eu/topics/democracy-and-society/belarus-new-dubious-constitution-5760/; Venice Commission, 'Draft Amendments and Additions to the Constitution of the Republic of Belarus

> [Article 15] The state shall be responsible for the preservation of the historical, cultural and spiritual heritage and the free development of the cultures of all ethnic communities living in the Republic of Belarus. The state ensures the preservation of historical truth and memory of the heroic feat of the Belarusian people during the Great Patriotic War.
>
> [Article 54] Everyone is obliged to protect the historical, cultural, spiritual heritage and other national values. The manifestation of patriotism, the preservation of the historical memory of the heroic past of the Belarusian people are the duty of every citizen of the Republic of Belarus.

These and other 2020 amendments to the Belarusian Constitution have been criticised by the Venice Commission for their incompatibility with rule of law standards.[101] In conjunction with the law on the 'Genocide of the Belarusian People' (2022), the new provisions have laid the groundwork for the mnemonic constitutionalism of the dictatorial regime in Belarus, the latter marked by its distinctive colonial dependence on Russian and Soviet historical myths.[102]

B. The 'Year of Historical Memory' and its Victims

Vladimir Putin infamously justified the Russian invasion of Ukraine through simplistic historical propaganda, at the core of which lies his claim that Ukraine is an 'artificial' and erroneous creation – allegedly established by communists.[103] This narrative aligns with the discourse promoted over the last decade of Putin's presidency and continuously imposed by Russian TV propagandists. They have been seemingly effective in fostering hatred towards Ukrainians while cultivating a delusional belief in Russian superiority,[104] as captured in recent Tweets by former president Dmitry Medvedev.[105] In

Published by the Authorities for Public Discussion' (14 February 2021): https://www.venice.coe.int/webforms/documents/default.aspx?pdffile=CDL-REF(2022)007-e/.

[101] See: European Commission for Democracy Through Law, 'Belarus: Urgent Interim Opinion on the Constitutional Reform' (*Venice Commission*, 5 April 2022): www.venice.coe.int/webforms/documents/?pdf=CDL-AD(2022)008-e.

[102] U Belavusau, 'Historical Imagery and Mnemonic Constitutionalism in Belarus' (2024) 49 *Review of Central and East European Law* 324.

[103] A Smith, 'Putin's "Surreal" Version of Ukrainian History Alarms Experts' (*NBC News* London, 22 February 2022): https://www.nbcnews.com/news/world/putin-russia-ukraine-history-speech-rcna17132; See Putin's speech preceding the invasion here: www.youtube.com/watch?v=_PgG4cfs6Qg. See also, the most recent interview with Vladimir Putin in, Kremlin 'Interview to Tucker Carlson' (*Youtube*, 9 February 2024): www.youtube.com/watch?v=hYfByTcY49k. For the analysis, see DR Marples, 'Vladimir Putin Justifies His Imperial Aims in Tucker Carlson Interview' (*Conversation*, 15 February 2024): https://theconversation.com/vladimir-putin-justifies-his-imperial-aims-in-tucker-carlson-interview-223395.

[104] I Torbakov, 'Examining the Origins of Russians' Superiority Complex vis-à-vis Ukrainians' (*Eurasianet*, 26 May 2020): www.eurasianet.org/perspectives-examining-the-origins-of-russians-superiority-complex-vis-a-vis-ukrainians/.

[105] A Mackinnon, 'The Fall of Dmitry Medvedev' *Foreign Policy* (Washington DC, 23 June 2022): www.foreignpolicy.com/2022/06/23/fall-dmitry-medvedev-russia-war-hawk/.

contrast, until 2020, Łukašenka did not depict Ukraine as an antagonist state, which – ironically – contributed to his notable popularity amongst Ukrainians in the pre-Russo-Ukrainian war era.[106]

On 1 September 2022, the academic year in all Belarusian schools began with an atypical lesson,[107] on 'historic memory',[108] led in Minsk[109] by none other than the country's long-serving President himself, Alaksandr Łukašenka.[110] Earlier, through a decree,[111] Łukašenka's government had proclaimed 2022 the 'Year of Historical Memory' (*hod histaryčnaj pamiaci*).[112] The decree stemmed from Łukašenka's demagogic insistence on controlling the interpretation of certain historical events, symbols and figures – particularly those related to WWII, the 'genocide of the Belarusian people',[113] and the regime's assertions regarding the symbolic and historical affiliations of the country's democratic opposition with 'Nazi collaborationism'.[114]

This first-of-September pedagogical spectacle occurred in the context of Russian military aggression against Ukraine, in which Łukašenka's regime was complicit, having allowed Russian forces to invade Ukrainian territory from Belarus.[115] The usage of domestic territory took place despite the lack of

[106] G Iogge, 'Alyaksandr Lukashenka and the War in Ukraine' (*The Jamestown Foundation*, 28 February 2022): https://jamestown.org/program/alyaksandr-lukashenka-and-the-war-in-ukraine/.

[107] 'Pieršy urok u školach Biełarusi ū dzień viedaū budzie pryśviečany histaryčnaj pamiaci' (*Biełta News*, 22 August 2022): https://blr.belta.by/society/view/pershy-urok-u-shkolah-belarusi-u-dzen-vedau-budze-prysvechany-gistarychnaj-pamjatsi-118924-2022/.

[108] Office of the President of the Republic of Belarus, 'Open Lesson "Historical Memory – The Road to the Future"' (*President.gov.by*, 1 September 2022): www.president.gov.by/en/events/otkrytyy-urok-istoricheskaya-pamyat-doroga-v-budushchee-1662101630/.

[109] 'Historyja ad pieršaj asoby: Łukašenka u Dzień viedaū pravodzić adkryty urok' (*Biełta News*, 22 August 2022): https://blr.belta.by/president/view/gistoryja-ad-pershaj-asoby-lukashenka-u-dzen-vedau-pravodzits-adkryty-urok-119037-2022/.

[110] 'Łukašenka adkazvaje na niazručnyja pytańni školnikaū' (*Biełsat News*, 1 September 2022): www.youtube.com/watch?v=GAQaJEee_r8/.

[111] Office of the President of the Republic of Belarus, 'On Declaring 2022 Year of Historical Memory Decree No 1' (*President.gov.by*, 1 January 2022): https://president.gov.by/en/documents/ukaz-no-1-ot-1-yanvarya-2022-g-1641208594.

[112] Botschaft der Republik Belarus in der Bundesrepublik Deutschland, 'Jahr der historischen Erinnerung' (2022): https://germany.mfa.gov.by/de/bilateral_relations/culture/f81e4a7dccdd58dc.html/. The follow-up year of 2023 was proclaimed to be the 'Year of the Russian Language', emphasising the positive sides of Russification by Łukašenka's administration. It should be noticed, that the tradition to proclaim a year in honour of a certain policy paradigm, including a historical policy, is not limited to authoritarian regimes. Most recently, the period between 1 July 2023 and 1 July 2024, was proclaimed a 'Slavery Memorial Year' by the Dutch Government, see: Government of the Netherlands, 'Slavery Memorial Year 1 July 2023 to 1 July 2024' (*Ministry of Education, Culture and Science*): https://www.government.nl/ministries/ministry-of-education-culture-and-science/events/slavery-memorial-year.

[113] '"On the Genocide of Belarusian People" – Legal Overview of the New Law' (*Human Constanta*, 13 July 2022): https://humanconstanta.org/en/on-the-genocide-of-belarusian-people-legal-overview-of-the-new-law/.

[114] 'Vyjšla kniha pra hienacyd biełaruskaha naroda' (*Naša Niva*, 8 April 2022): www.nashaniva.com/?c=ar&i=287917.

[115] Reetz (n 99).

significant support – unlike in Russia[116] – for the invasion amongst the majority of the Belarusians,[117] their close ethno-linguistic ties with Ukrainians,[118] and a history of overall amical relations between the two nations[119] whose cultural elites have traditionally united against Russian imperialism.[120] Unsurprisingly, Belarusians form a significant faction of the foreign military units fighting on the Ukrainian side,[121] and, despite the intense repression and mass imprisonments within Belarus, there continues to be a partisan movement in support of Ukraine.[122]

The terror inside Belarus culminated in mass protests by its citizens[123] against Łukašenka's impudently falsified election results (in 2020),[124] leading to thousands of political prisoners, widespread torture, and the murder of democratic opponents of the regime.[125] Meanwhile, the President-Elect since 2020, Ms Sviatłana Cichanoŭskaja,[126] who currently represents the country in exile, has spoken explicitly[127] – along with other major Belarusian opposition leaders – in support of Ukraine and against Russia's war.[128] In 2022, she condemned the de facto 'double occupation' of Belarus by both the vassal regime of Łukašenka

[116] P Dickinson, 'More than Three-Quarters of Russians Still Support Putin's Ukraine War' (*Atlantic Council*, 6 June 2022): www.atlanticcouncil.org/blogs/ukrainealert/more-than-three-quarters-of-russians-still-support-putins-ukraine-war/.

[117] A Rudnik, 'Deep Unease in Belarus over Country's Role in Russian Invasion of Ukraine' (*Atlantic Council*, 29 March 2022): www.atlanticcouncil.org/blogs/belarusalert/deep-unease-in-belarus-over-countrys-role-in-russian-invasion-of-ukraine/.

[118] A Kazharski, T Kulakevich and K Lozka, 'Belarus-Ukraine Relations' in S Schäffer (ed), *Ukraine in Central & Eastern Europe: Kyiv's Foreign Affairs and the Relations of the Post-Communist Region* (Ibidem Press, 2023) 45–62. See also: 'Belarus' (*Encyclopedia of Ukraine*, 2005): www.encyclopediaofukraine.com/display.asp?linkpath=pages%5CB%5CE%5CBelarus.html/; A Kotljarchuk and N Zakharov, 'Belarus' Relations with Ukraine and the 2022 Russian Invasion: Historical Ties, Society and Realpolitik' (2022) 17 *Baltic Worlds* 32.

[119] T Zhurzhenko, 'Sisters into Neighbours: Ukrainian-Belarusian Relations after 1991' (2008) 3 *Crossroads Digest* 4.

[120] CARNEGIE: Endowment for international peace, 'Russian Neo-Imperialism and Its Limits' (*Carnegie*, 1 October 2020): https://carnegieendowment.org/2020/10/01/russian-neo-imperialism-and-its-limits-event-7426/.

[121] A Rudnik, 'Belarusian Volunteers See Ukraine War as Stepping Stone to a Free Belarus' (*Atlantic Council*, 11 May 2022): www.atlanticcouncil.org/blogs/belarusalert/belarusian-volunteers-see-ukraine-war-as-stepping-stone-to-a-free-belarus/.

[122] L Kasmach, 'Anti-War Resistance in Belarus: Rail Partisans Slow Russian Troops' *BelarusDigest* (Belarus, 25 April 2022): www.belarusdigest.com/story/anti-war-resistance-in-belarus-rail-partisans-slow-russian-troops/; Rudnik (n 5).

[123] Bekus (n 2).

[124] Belavusau and Steinbelis (n 42).

[125] 'Belarus: UN Report Reveals Extent of Violations in Human Rights Crackdown' (*UN News*, 9 March 2022) https://news.un.org/en/story/2022/03/1113582/; 'Belarus: Events of 2021' (*Human Rights Watch*, 2022): www.hrw.org/world-report/2022/country-chapters/belarus/.

[126] Karliuk and Miadzvetskaya (n 43).

[127] Sviatlana Tsikhanouskaya, 'Sviatlana Tsikhanouskaya's speech at the Kalinouski Forum' (*tsikhanouskaya.org*, 2022): www.tsikhanouskaya.org/en/events/news/da54e5e1f74d83a.html/.

[128] 'Tsikhanouskaya Accuses Lukashenka of "Treason" Over Belarus's Role in Ukraine' (*RadioFreeEurope/ RadioLiberty*, 26 February 2022): www.rferl.org/a/tsikhanouskaya-lukashenka-treason-belarus-ukraine/31725167.html/.

(who actually lost the 2020 elections) and the Russian military, by virtue of their unlawful presence.[129]

In contrast, the new educational policies endorsed by Łukašenka's performative school lesson embraces these changes in legislative memory politics, with further efforts to Russify the educational space, in particular, by discontinuing the usage of the Belarusian Latin alphabet (*łacinka*). The same can be noted about the removal from the school programme (and prohibitions by prosecutors) of the Belarusian classical (including nineteenth- and early-twentieth-century) writers who referred pejoratively to Russians or the Russian occupational forces.[130] Furthermore, efforts are being made to bring changes to legislation regarding tourist guides and interpreters for foreigners during tours, by checking employers for any presence of the 'rehabilitation of Nazism' and 'genocide denial'.[131] More recent explicit attempts to Russify the way history is interpreted in educational institutions include creation of the Joint Russian-Belarusian Commission on History and translation of the history of the 'genocide of the Belarusian people' into the patriotic school upbringing.[132]

Since 2022 was announced as the 'Year of Historical Memory' in Belarus, and 2023 proclaimed the 'Year of the Russian Language', further concerns have been raised in relation to the protection of minorities – especially Lithuanians, Poles, and Ukrainians who are depicted almost exclusively in a negative light by state TV propaganda. Similar concerns deal with the status of the Belarusian language, culture and independent historiography, the safety of historians as well as the broader freedom of academic research in Belarus under the circumstances of the Russo-Ukrainian war. The regime even went as far as demolishing

[129] B Whitmore, 'While the World Watches Ukraine, Putin is Quietly Occupying Belarus' (*Atlantic Council*, 2 February 2022): www.atlanticcouncil.org/blogs/belarusalert/while-the-world-watches-ukraine-putin-is-quietly-occupying-belarus/.

[130] As an example, on 17 August 2023, the prosecutor's office in Minsk declared two poems by Vincent Dunin-Marcinkievič (1808–1884), *The Winds are Floating* and *Conversation of an Elderly Man*, to be 'extremist materials'. These poems are associated with the January 1863 national uprising against the Russian Empire. Additionally, the foreword to the author's collected works, written by literary critic Jazep Januškievič, was similarly classified as extremist. See R Greenall, 'Belarus Declares 19th Century Nationalist Poems "Extremist"' (*BBC News*, 17 August 2023): https://www.bbc.com/news/world-europe-66535462; 'Što adbyvałasia na apošnim pasiedžańni Respublikanskaj rady pa histaryčnaj palitycy – vytrymki z pratakoła' (*Naša Niva*, 29 February 2024): https://nashaniva.com/337460; 'Dva vieršy Dunina-Marcinkieviča prakuratura pryznała ekstremisckimi materyjałami' (*Naša Niva*, 17 August 2023): https://nashaniva.com/324267.

[131] 'Gidov v Belarusi predlagajut proveriat' na prichastnost' k reabilitatsii nazizma' (*Sputnik*, 12 March 2023): https://sputnik.by/20240312/gidov-v-belarusi-planiruyut-proveryat-na-prichastnost-k-reabilitatsii-natsizma-1084415586.html.

[132] 'Biełaruś i Rasija stvaryli kamisuju dla "abarony histaryčnaj praŭdy"' (*Naša Niva*, 26 January 2024): https://nashaniva.com/334930. In relation to the Russian policy towards Belarus, see also Moshes and Nizhnikau (n 61). See also Instruktivno-metodicheskoye Pismo Ministierstva Obrazovaniya Riespubliki Bielarus, 'Ob izuchenii v uchriezhdeniyakh obschego sriedniego obrazovaniya matierialov o gienotsidie bielorusskogo naroda v gody Vielikoj Otiechestrviennoy vojny' (30 August 2024) (Instructive-Methodological Letter of the Ministry of Education of the Republic of Belarus 'On the Study of Materials Regarding the Genocide of the Belarusian People During the Great Patriotic War in General Secondary Education Institutions').

the war graves of Polish soldiers,[133] to give just one example of how the year of 2022 has been unfolding for the 'respect of historical memory'. To date, there is not one single independent TV channel, radio station or newspaper functioning on the territory of Belarus. The state propaganda machine that fully controls the media and press has been emphasising the binary ontology of 'good Russia' versus 'evil Poland and Ukraine' in interpreting the past and the present of Belarus. The truly barbaric aforementioned acts toward Polish burial places have represented just some of the myriad of daily episodes in this memory war of the regime.[134]

C. Memory Wars with Ukraine

The memory wars with Ukraine have intensified too, increasingly resembling Russian 'de-Nazification' propaganda regarding Ukraine. Central to the Belarusian regime's anti-Ukrainian rhetoric is the tragic legacy of Chatyń (in the Anglophone literature, mostly transliterated from Cyrillic *Хатынь* as *Khatyn*) – a Belarusian village, where the entire population was brutally massacred by the Nazis in 1943.[135] This historical event has become a focal propaganda point during the Russo-Ukrainian war, further amplified by the performative and investigatory role of the 2022 law on the 'Genocide of the Belarusian People'.[136]

Chatyń was burned to the ground by members of Schutzmannschaft Battalion 118, a unit composed, amongst others, of Ukrainian collaborators who had been recruited by Nazi forces.[137] This battalion, under German command, was engaged in anti-partisan operations throughout Belarus. On 22 March 1943, 149 inhabitants of this Catholic village, including women and children, were herded into a barn and burned alive. The massacre was part of the Nazis' brutal retaliation strategy aimed at crushing partisan resistance, contributing later to the dominant Soviet narrative of Belarus as a 'partisan republic'.[138] Some historians suggest that amongst the numerous villages in Belarus burned by

[133] 'Poland Says WWII Grave Destroyed by Russian ally Belarus' (*Al Jazeera*, 25 August 2022): https://www.aljazeera.com/news/2022/8/25/poland-says-wwii-grave-is-destroyed-by-russian-ally-belarus/.

[134] See also F Ackermann, T Błaszczak and I Melnikau, 'Memory in Belarusian Policies towards Germany and Poland' (*European Network for Belarus*, June 2023): www.kew.org.pl/wp-content/uploads/2020/12/Memory-in-Belarusian-policies-FINAL.pdf.

[135] Per A Rudling, 'The Khatyn Massacre in Belorussia: A Historical Controversy Revisited' (2012) 26 *Holocaust and Genocide Studies* 29.

[136] See also M Dorman, 'Khatyn and the Myth of Genocide in Lukashenko's Belarus' (*MA Thesis presented at the University of Texas in Austin*, August 2017): https://repositories.lib.utexas.edu/items/b3338016-af8e-4713-b038-a11c04a0f682.

[137] Per A Rudling, 'Terror and Local Collaboration in Occupied Belarus: The case of Schutzmannschaft Battalion 118. Part Two. War Criminality' (2012) 9 *Historical Yearbook* 99.

[138] A Goujon, 'Memorial Narratives of WWII Partisans and Genocide in Belarus' (2010) 24 *East European Politics and Societie*, 6; DR Marples, 'Memory Loss' (2012) 41 *Index on Censorship* 133; S Lewis, 'Overcoming Hegemonic Martyrdom: the Afterline of Khatyn in Belarusian Memory' (2015) 1 *Journal of Soviet and Post-Soviet Politics and Society* 367.

the Nazis, the selection of Chatyń (or, Khatyn) was deliberately exploited by Soviet authorities – with its huge memorial complex[139] – to obscure and divert foreign attention from the Katyń massacre (1940) due to the phonetic similarity between these toponyms.[140] The Katyń massacre refers to the mass execution of Polish officers by the NKVD (Narodnyi Komissariat Vnutriennikh Del – People's Commissariat for Internal Affairs) in a forest in the Smolensk region of Russia.[141]

It is crucial to acknowledge that while some members of Schutzmannschaft 118 were Ukrainian, the unit also included other Soviet citizens who had been coerced into collaboration under the dire conditions of war. Their involvement in the Khatyn massacre was not a product of specific Ukrainian national policy aimed at annihilating Belarusians or any organised effort by Ukrainian forces, but rather the actions of individuals within a Nazi-controlled unit. Despite these historical complexities, both the Soviet Union and, more recently, the Łukašenka regime have emphasised the Ukrainian role in the massacre, often as a means to delegitimise Ukrainian nationalist movements.

In 2021, before the full-scale attack on Ukraine, Putin mentioned Chatyń in the context of the imagined Ukrainian neo-Nazis 'burning people alive in Odesa', in his article 'On the Historical Union of Russians and Ukrainians'.[142] Against the background of the ongoing Russo-Ukrainian war, this narrative has been used to associate Ukraine with Nazism in Belarus too. State propaganda portrays the presence of Ukrainians in Schutzmannschaft 118 as emblematic of Ukraine's alleged historical affinity with fascism – a narrative instrumentalised by Belarusian and Russian governments to undermine Ukraine's current political leadership and justify aggression against the country.[143]

V. CONCLUSIONS

> In my homeland, the entirety of Belarus is in a prison. Journalists, political scientists, trade union leaders are in jail, there are many of my acquaintances and friends among them … The courts work like a conveyor belt, convicts are transported to penal colonies, and new waves of political prisoners take their place.
>
> (Aleś Bialacki, 2022)[144]

[139] G Koshino, 'The Cultural Representation of the Khatyn Massacre in Belarus' (*Hokkaido University*, 2013): https://src-h.slav.hokudai.ac.jp/jcrees/2013Osaka/21Koshino.pdf.

[140] N Davies, *Europe: A History* (Oxford University Press, 1996) 1005.

[141] ibid, 1004–5. See also text to nn 44–45 in Chapter 7 of this volume by Aleksandra Gliszczyńska-Grabias.

[142] Article by V Putin, 'On the Historical Unity of Russians and Ukrainians' (*Website of the President of Russia*, 12 July 2021): www.kremlin.ru/events/president/news/66181.

[143] On this narrative, see G Koshino, 'Ukraine and War in Russian-Language Literature' (2023) 43 *Japanese Slavic and East European Studies* 1 (see, in particular, 4–5).

[144] The Nobel Prize, 'Aleś Bialacki (Ales Bialiatski) Nobel Lecture' (n 1).

One of the key aspects of Belarusian memory laws and policies pertains to their consolidation of Soviet-era narratives that portray Belarus primarily as a victim of external aggression, reinforcing the hagiography of the 'Great Patriotic War' and the 'partisan republic' as defining events in Belarusian history. By legally enshrining this narrative, Łukašenka's regime aims to cultivate loyalty to the state by connecting the legitimacy of the current government to the heroism of wartime resistance (during the 'Great Patriotic War'), in contrast to other ethno-centured narratives about Belarusian history which the regime associates with the democratic opposition. This is a clear continuation of Soviet memory politics, ie, suppressing national movements, but repurposed to suit the needs of Łukašenka's authoritarianism.

The discussion around the memory law of 2022 deepened the divide between the state and opposition movements, many of which advocate a more pluralistic view of Belarusian history. For the democratic opposition, in contrast, the Belarusian identity is tied to the struggle for independence, democratic values, and resistance to Russification. By monopolising historical memory and criminalising alternative interpretations, the regime not only repressed political dissent but also stifled public debate on national identity and historical justice. The passage of the memory law in January 2022 and the enshrining of a 'duty to history' into the Belarusian Constitution in February 2022 coincided with heightened tensions surrounding the Russo-Ukrainian war which started that year. This aspect had significant repercussions for Belarus's geopolitical positioning, especially considering that Łukašenka facilitated Putin's attack on Ukraine through Belarusian territory. In the meantime, Łukašenka's regime increasingly aligned with Russia, using memory politics to justify its domestic and foreign policy decisions. The 'Genocide of the Belarusian People' law is part of this broader strategy, linking Belarusian historical victimhood to contemporary threats posed by Western powers, NATO, and Ukrainian nationalism, thereby drawing parallels between past and present conflicts.

This memory law of 2022 is also emblematic of a broader trend in Belarusian memory politics under Łukašenka, where historical narratives are appropriated to bolster regime legitimacy and traded to Russian elites as a sacrifice of the Belarusian ethnic identity.[145] This shift, which intensified after the 2020 election protests and amid the Russo-Ukrainian war, reflects the regime's efforts to control the past as a means to suppress the uprising against his regime.

Łukašenka's 2022 constitutional reforms, approved in a staged and state-controlled referendum in February of the same year, closely mirror elements of Putin's earlier 2020 constitutional amendments, particularly in relation to emphasising the 'heroism of the Belarusian people' and enshrining a 'constitutional

[145] Kazharski and Lozka (n 61).

duty' to safeguard its memory.[146] Much like Putin's 2020 Constitution and, even earlier, Hungary's 2010 Basic Law under Fidesz,[147] both laden with mnemonic constitutionalism, these Belarusian provisions on historical memory seem designed to obfuscate broader amendments that further erode the remnants of liberal democracy and rule of law.[148]

In contrast to Ukraine's 2015 and 2022 de-communisation laws,[149] Belarusian memory provisions of 2022 highlight a sharp ideological divide. As noted elsewhere, mnemonic constitutionalism[150] – present to some degree in most countries, including those without written constitutions[151] – is not an inherently negative phenomenon.[152] However, in CEE, it has increasingly become a tool of militant memocracy – governance rooted in historical memory – amid the region's democratic decline.[153] Belarus joined this trend, wielding mnemonic constitutionalism and memory laws as weapons, in advance of, and during, the Russo-Ukrainian war. The designation of 2022 as the 'Year of Historical Memory in Belarus' served as an ideological shield to justify the regime's complicity in Putin's invasion of Ukraine. Simultaneously, this Russifying and re-Sovietising mnemonic constitutionalism operated as an ideological sword against Belarusian pro-European, democratic opposition,[154] which overwhelmingly opposes Russia's colonial war.[155]

The tragic reality of the past two years starkly reveals the brutality of these memory politics. In Belarus, one can be arbitrarily arrested for simply speaking Belarusian in public,[156] offering an independent city tour,[157] opening a

[146] U Belavusau, 'Rule of Law and Constitutionalisation of Memory Politics in Hungary and Russia' in M Belov (ed), *Rule of Law in Flux* (Routledge, 2022) 87–107.

[147] G Halmai, 'Rule of Law Backsliding and Memory Politics in Hungary' (2023) 19 *European Constitutional Law Review* 602.

[148] M Bán, 'The Legal Governance of Historical Memory and the Rule of Law' (*PhD Thesis, University of Amsterdam*, 2020): https://pure.uva.nl/ws/files/51201837/Thesis.pdf/. See also Chapter 10 by Marina Bán in the present volume.

[149] L Klymenko, 'Cutting the Umbilical Cord: The Narrative of the National Past and Future in Ukrainian De-communization Policy' in U Belavusau and A Gliszczyńska-Grabias (eds), *Law and Memory: Towards Legal Governance of History* (Cambridge University Press, 2017); 'MCIP updated the list of decisions on relocation or dismantling of monuments in the framework of decommunization and de-russification' (*Ministry of Culture and Information Policy of Ukraine*, 23 June 2022): www.kmu.gov.ua/en/news/mkip-onovilo-spisok-rishen-shchodo-peremishchennya-chi-demontazhu-pamyatnikiv-v-ramkah-dekomunizaciyi-ta-derusifikaciyi/. See also Chapters 5 and 6 by Zhurzhenko and Nekoliak respectively in the present volume.

[150] Belavusau (n 146).

[151] U Belavusau, 'Jewish Past, Mnemonic Constitutionalism and the Politics of Citizenship' (*Verfassungsblog*, 28 July 2024): www.verfassungsblog.de/jewish-past-mnemonic-constitutionalism-and-the-politics-of-citizenship/.

[152] U Belavusau, 'Final Thoughts on Mnemonic Constitutionalism' (*Verfassungsblog*, 15 January 2018): www.verfassungsblog.de/final-thoughts-on-mnemonic-constitutionalism/.

[153] M Mälksoo, 'Militant Memocracy in International Relations: Mnemonical Status Anxiety and Memory Laws in Eastern Europe' (2021) 47 *Review of International Studies* 489.

[154] Dickinson (n 116).

[155] Rudnik (n 5); Mälksoo, 'The Post-Colonial Moment' (n 34).

[156] 'Stała viadoma za što zatrymali krajaznaūcu i žurnalista Ihara Chmaru' (*EuroRadio*, 12 August 2022): https://euroradio.fm/stala-vyadoma-za-shto-zatrymali-krayaznaucu-i-zhurnalista-igara-hmaru.

[157] 'Minskuju ekskursavodku zatrymali za niekarektnyja vykazvańni na adras Łukašenki' (*EuroRadio*, 31 August 2022): https://euroradio.fm/minskuyu-ekskursavodku-zatrymali-za-nekarektnyya-vykazvanni-na-adras-lukashenki.

bookshop with Belarusian literature[158] or sometimes even singing a Ukrainian song in public.[159] Individuals are imprisoned for 'liking' social media posts[160] and face detention, torture,[161] and humiliation[162] for posting photos of the historic white-red-white Belarusian flag.[163] Those who challenge the official historical narrative – for instance, by questioning the legality of Soviet Russia and Germany's 1939 invasion of Poland or expressing scepticism about the term 'genocide of the Belarusian people' – face prison sentences. This is despite the fact that most of the victims of systematic murder in the 1940s were Jewish, the factor that remains rather invisible in the spectrum of Łukašenka's memory policies. In addition, Polish, Lithuanian and Ukrainian identities were put into the box of 'suspicious' and potentially threatening.

Moreover, the regime's brutal crackdown on Belarusian partisans sabotaging railways to hinder Russian military supplies to Ukraine has resulted in severe punishments, with inhumane conditions in prisons and even the threat of execution.[164] All of this reflects the grim reality of a country under de facto Russian occupation, governed by an unelected dictator obsessed with Soviet nostalgia and prone to manipulating the Constitution through fraudulent referenda. Slowly but surely, Belarus is steadily being transformed into a dystopian entity where historical propaganda serves as both armour and weapon, blurring the line between memory laws and memory wars. In this dystopia of Belarusian memory laws and policies, the past is wielded to justify the present, portraying the democratic opposition as Neo-Nazis, marginalising and excluding the Belarusian language and historical symbols, demonising all major national minorities – except Russians – as potential collaborators and traitors, and silencing any future not bound by authoritarian control.

[158] 'Belarusian Publisher, Associate Arrested After Opening New Bookstore' (*RadioFreeEurope/RadioLiberty*, 17 May 2022): www.rferl.org/a/belarus-bookstore-harassment-arrest/31854941.html/.

[159] 'Belarus Young Singer Defies Crackdown' (*EuroradioFM*, 7 August 2022): https://euroradio.fm/en/singer-herasimenka-monitored-law-enforcement.

[160] 'Russian in Belarus Sentenced to 11 Years for Social Media Posts Urging Protests' (*RadioFreeEurope/RadioLiberty*, 27 December 2021): www.rferl.org/a/belarus-russian-citizen-sentenced-protests/31628127.html/; Svaboda, 'Chronika pieraśledu 30 kastryčnika' (*Radyjo Svaboda*, 30 October 2021): www.svaboda.org/a/31537140.html.

[161] 'Ekskluziv DW: Natalja Hershe w Schvejtsarii posle turmy v Belarusi' (*DW*, 26 February 2022): www.youtube.com/watch?v=S_Ln_R6XsVI.

[162] J Drahachrust, 'Chto i navošta prydumaŭ pakajalnyja videa' (*Radyjo Svaboda*, 19 May 2022): https://www.svaboda.org/a/31855304.html.

[163] Tages-Anzeiger, 'Eine Schweizerin in belarussischen Foltergefängnissen' (*Youtube*, 6 December 2021): www.youtube.com/watch?v=cbLfz64M9sk.

[164] S Pirani, 'Belarusian "Railway Partisans" Face Death Penalty' (*International Viewpoint*, 24 July 2022): www.internationalviewpoint.org/spip.php?article7751/; 'Belarusian "Railway Guerrillas" Handed Prison Terms' (*RadioFreeEurope/ RadioLiberty*, 10 August 2022): www.rferl.org/a/belarus-railway-guerrillas-prison-terms-ukraine-war/31982008.html.

9

'Critical Situations' and Mnemonic Legislation: Memory Politics in the Baltic States and Russia's War against Ukraine

DOVILĖ BUDRYTĖ

I. INTRODUCTION

INTERNATIONAL CRISES CAN be conceptualised not only as disruptive events, but as engines of new discourses and identities. As articulated by Dirk Nabers, 'crisis represents a situation in which our everyday beliefs of how the world works are thoroughly disrupted by an event that is out of our control'.[1] Such disruptions challenge our beliefs about the world, our routines, and the ways in which we view the past. Thus, they are likely to exert a significant effect on memory politics and mnemonic policies. At the same time, changes in memory politics and mnemonic policies prompted by international crises may lead to an increase in conflicts over memory which, as Russia's current war against Ukraine demonstrates, are related to actual conflict.

The goal of this chapter is to explore this dynamic relationship between international crises and mnemonic policies, with the latter defined as a set of memory laws and norms regulating public remembrance. Drawing on the growing body of literature in international relations that focuses on the cultural dimensions of international crises, I am interested in analysing the intersection between crises and memory. How do international crises affect mnemonic policies? Are mnemonic policies primarily a result of domestic politics, or do international developments matter? Do all international crises have an impact on mnemonic policies, or are certain international crises more decisive and influential than others?

[1] D Nabers, *A Poststructuralist Discourse Theory of Global Politics* (Palgrave Macmillan, 2015).

To gain insight into these questions, this chapter sets out to analyse changes in the mnemonic policies in the Baltic states that are related to three 'critical situations' (or 'international crises'), namely (1) the disintegration of the Soviet Union, (2) the annexation of Crimea and the proxy war begun by Russia in the Donbas region of Ukraine in 2014 (described in Western media and scholarship as the 'crisis in Ukraine'), and (3) Russia's full-scale invasion of Ukraine in 2022. The disintegration of the Soviet Union introduced new discourses about the illegal annexation of the Baltic states by the Soviet Union during World War II (WWII) and related crimes, including mass deportations, political repression, and resistance to the Soviet regime. (According to official discourse in the USSR, the Baltic states supposedly joined this union 'voluntarily' in 1940.) The 2014 events in Ukraine introduced high levels of insecurity in the Baltic states, making them painfully aware of their 'uncertain sovereignty'[2] and Russia's continued colonial ambitions. This chapter compares these two 'critical situations' with Russia's full-scale invasion of Ukraine in 2022. In doing so, it asks, how is this 'critical situation' similar or different from the other two 'critical situations'? What major developments in memory politics and memory policies are linked to this war?

Section II of the chapter is theoretical, establishing the link between 'critical situations' and memory politics and policies. Section III presents case studies, analysing the three aforementioned 'critical situations' as they relate to the Baltic states. Each case study is structured around the following questions: (1) What was 'critical' about this particular event and why can it be treated as such? (2) Which new memory discourses were created during this 'critical situation'? (3) How were identities reshaped by this 'critical situation'? (4) What new mnemonic policies were created during this 'critical situation'?

II. 'CRITICAL SITUATIONS' AND MEMORY POLITICS AND POLICIES: INSIGHTS FROM INTERNATIONAL RELATIONS

There is no shortage of works exploring crises in international relations.[3] Crises have been conceptualised as sudden events, demanding quick decisions by rational leaders in a very short time, threatening 'vital interests' and raising significant 'uncertainties about war and peace'.[4] This literature, inspired by the 1962 Cuban Missile Crisis and related crises in international politics during the Cold War, focused on the 'successful' management of crises, which implied avoidance of armed conflict. This literature attempted to be relevant to policy,

[2] N Klumbytė, 'Sovereign Uncertainty and the Dangers to Liberalism at the Baltic Frontier' (2019) 78 *Slavic Review* 336.

[3] For a survey on this aspect, see AN Gilbert and PG Lauren, 'Crisis Management: An Assessment and Critique' (1980) 24 *The Journal of Conflict Resolution* 641.

[4] ibid 642.

hoping to offer sound advice to policymakers on how to handle crises and 'manage' conflict. Unsurprisingly, it focused on the actions of powerful states and leaders, largely ignoring the so-called 'peripheral' actors in global politics. International relations specialists, driven by their desire to predict 'successful' crisis management, often simplified complex situations surrounding international crises and ignored the impact of historical context and cultural factors.

The ontological security (OS) paradigm offers a different conceptualisation of crises, instead linking them to identity and memory. Crises, or 'critical situations,' are understood as developments that 'destabilize state identity and its relations with other states'.[5] Such situations are related to anxiety that disrupts predictability and routinised interactions in international relations.[6] Mälksoo's concept of 'mnemonical insecurity' links the study of memory to anxiety, arguing that the securitisation of memory can take place when certain memories are privileged and even protected by law, whilst others are delegitimised.[7] The OS literature has demonstrated that conflicts over historical memory can indeed become new 'crises' in international politics, and can destabilise state identities and make them question their interactions with other states.[8]

The aforementioned literature suggests a different way of thinking about crises in international relations, relating them to identity and memory in international politics. Introducing these concepts into the study of crises means that we need to pay attention not only to the most powerful policymakers, who supposedly have the power to 'manage' crises, but also to groups that find themselves empowered or made visible by crises. For example, this author's investigation of the so-called 2013–14 'crisis in Ukraine', carried out in conjunction with Erica Resende and Didem Buhari Gulmez, in an edited volume, shows that this event empowered various groups, such as Ukrainian women (during the Euromaidan) and the Crimean Tatar diaspora, to articulate their agencies and historical memories during these uncertain times.[9] Paying attention to identity and memory politics demonstrates that 'peripheral' actors and their identities matter in international politics, as their memory politics are intertwined with those of powerful actors. To fully understand complex dynamics in international crises, it is important to identify the ways in which 'peripheral' actors resist strong actors, as well as the ways in which historical memory tends to play a role in legitimising the resistance.

[5] J Subotić, *Yellow Star, Red Star: Holocaust Remembrance after Communism* (Cornell University Press, 2019) 28.

[6] K Gustafsson, 'Routinised Recognition and Anxiety: Understanding Deterioration in the Sino-Japanese Relations' (2016) 42 *Review of International Studies* 613.

[7] M Mälksoo, '"Memory Must Be Defended:" Beyond the Politics of Mnemonical Security' (2015) 46 *Security Dialogue* 221.

[8] Subotić (n 5).

[9] E Resende, D Budrytė and D Buhari-Gulmez (eds), *Crisis and Change in Post-Cold War Global Politics: Ukraine in a Comparative Perspective* (Palgrave Macmillan, 2018).

Despite Baltic states being considered as 'small' states or 'peripheral' actors in international politics, studies of memory politics in the Baltic states suggest that they are inseparable from the memory politics and wars waged by Russia.[10] The study of mnemonic policies in the Baltic states has focused on domestic influences. Acknowledging that memory politics and related mnemonic policies are a result of the interaction between 'big' states (in this case, Russia) and so-called 'peripheral' actors requires international influences on memory politics to be taken seriously. As suggested by Kathrin Bachleitner, international influences may be critical for memory;[11] thus, it is essential to investigate the ways in which international crises have potential to affect memory politics and mnemonic policies.

III. THE FIRST 'CRITICAL SITUATION': THE SOVIET UNION'S DISINTEGRATION AND MAJOR CHANGES IN BALTIC MNEMONIC LANDSCAPE

The disintegration of the Soviet Union coincided with major changes in memory politics in the Baltic states. During the late '80s and early '90s, independence movements started challenging Soviet versions of the past, recalling memories of the independent Baltic states during the Interwar period, and narrating the Soviet occupation as a rupture and even as an ultimate evil. These movements brought to light the secret Molotov-Ribbentrop Pact and made the case that the Baltic states were illegally incorporated into the Soviet Union (despite claims by the USSR, and now Russia, that the Baltic states voluntarily joined). Questioning the legitimacy of the incorporation of the Baltic states has been resisted adamantly by Russia, which has portrayed the USSR as a 'liberator' of Central and Eastern European (CEE) countries, not an 'occupier'. Thus, the narrative created by the Baltic states has presented Russia with a fundamental challenge to the image of 'liberator' it has tried to create internationally.

Questioning Soviet accounts of WWII and the post-war period became part of the agenda pursued by independence movements. For example, in Lithuania, a non-governmental Commission for Research into Stalinist Crimes was created in 1988. Its goal was to record the names of former deportees and political prisoners and restore the historical truth. Similar activities were taking place in Latvia and Estonia, where such commemorative activities became the backbone of emerging memory regimes that focused on suffering (primarily the political repression and deportations under Stalin, which affected most families in

[10] Klumbytė, 'Bipolinio istorinio teisingumo struktūros ir politinė atskirtis' *Sociologija. Mintis ir veiksmas* 2017/2 (41) 137; Budrytė, 'Memory Politics and the Study of Crises in International Relations' (2021) 74 *Journalof International Relations and Development* 980.

[11] K Bachleitner, *Collective Memory in International Relations* (Oxford University Press, 2021).

the Baltic states) and defiance (the anti-Soviet partisan resistance during and after WWII, which was especially fierce in Lithuania and lasted into the 1950s[12]). The focus on suffering and resistance to the Soviet occupation implied that the Baltic societies were eager to fully separate themselves from the Soviet Union and its memory regime, which portrayed the USSR as a 'liberator' from fascism and a force for 'progressive' industrialisation in the Soviet republics. Influential Lithuanian historian and former Defence Minister Arvydas Anušauskas described this mnemonic orientation as 'the politics of a thick line' (*riebaus brūkšnio politika*) – implying a wall of separation between the Soviet past and a new era associated with the fight for independence.[13]

'The politics of a thick line' has been accompanied by numerous mnemonic policies, including renaming streets and other public spaces to get rid of Soviet-era names, issuing declarations condemning Soviet and Nazi occupations, and establishing new days of commemoration to remember the victims of these occupations. Beginning in the 1980s, the three Baltic states held commemorations on 14 June, the day when the Soviet Union began mass deportations in 1941, and 23 August, the day when the Molotov-Ribbentrop Pact was signed in 1939.

The focus was on the evils of the Soviet occupation, these mnemonic policies being pursued during a time of emotional public commemorations involving the return of remains (of deportees) from Siberia and elsewhere back to the Baltic states for reburial. Such events occurred at a time when there was an avalanche of memoirs and testimonies by former deportees and political prisoners about their lives in exile. Organisations of former victims, such as 'Memento' in Estonia or the 'Union of Deportees and Political Prisoners' in Lithuania, became influential political actors, shaping remembrance and influencing the development of mnemonic policies created by government institutions to address the Soviet past.

In addition to these new discourses about mass deportations and political repression under Stalin, other traumas, including the trauma of the Holocaust, became visible as Jewish communities (especially in Lithuania) recovered their voices and made their commemorative ceremonies public. However, these narratives were initially marginalised as the narratives about the illegitimacy of the Soviet occupation became hegemonic in the three Baltic states. Shortly after the restoration of independence for all three states in September 1991, these narratives became institutionalised and routinised. In several instances in Lithuania, the glorification of anti-Soviet partisans, some of whom were involved in

[12] Though partisan movements in the Baltic region were 'wide tents' comprising various groups of people, these people tended to be united by 'patriotism and a desire to restore nationhood': see D Kaszeta, *The Forest Brotherhood: Baltic Resistance against the Nazis and the Soviets* (Hurst and Company, 2023) 235. The movements garnered a lot of support amongst the Baltic populations, revered to this day for their desire to resist the Soviet aggressor.

[13] A Anušauskas, 'Koalicija su KGB' (*Delfi*, 1 October 2012): www.delfi.lt/archive/aanusauskas-koalicija-su-kgb.d?id=59624659.

the Holocaust,[14] was met with resistance from the Jewish community which demanded full condemnation of these partisans. In Latvia and Estonia, the official hegemonic memory narratives condemning the Soviet occupation were resisted by some segments of the local Russian communities.

During the late '80s, however, the memory work completed by popular nationalist movements, whose aim was to restore independence, did not immediately translate into severe ethnic tensions. Initially, there was a lot of cooperation between the popular fronts fighting for independence in the Baltic states and ethnic minorities, as various ethnic groups started to create their own cultural associations, assert their cultural rights and their own narratives about the past of their ethnic group. Opposition to the popular fronts fighting for independence came from Moscow-supported 'international fronts' that attempted to draw support from local Russians in Latvia and Estonia, and local Russians and Poles in Lithuania. Ethnic divisions became more visible in the early '90s, after Lithuania, Latvia and Estonia restored their nation-states, adopted language laws promoting Lithuanian, Latvian and Estonian, and started to institutionalise nation-centred memory regimes (in opposition to Soviet-era narratives about the 'friendship of peoples' in the USSR).[15] As the states re-established their independence, Russia started to be imagined as the clear 'other' and was associated with a colonial past that it refused to condemn. Eventually, strengthening the emerging memory regimes in the Baltic states became associated with distancing themselves from Russia.

In Lithuania, the non-governmental Commission for Research into Stalinist Crimes was succeeded by the Genocide and Resistance Research Centre, a governmental memory institution which became an important actor in the regulation of memory policies. In addition to conducting research into crimes of the occupation regimes (with a focus on Soviet crimes), this institution later became involved in commemorations and practices 'defending memory'. In Latvia, the Centre for the Documentation of the Consequences of Totalitarianism was established in 1992, with its major focus during its initial years being the investigation of crimes against humanity and war crimes committed during Soviet and Nazi occupations.[16] However, later it evolved into a research centre involved in discourse about the legacy of the past.[17] In Estonia, the State Commission for the Examination of Repressive Policies Carried Out During the Occupations (which was created with the participation

[14] Based on the investigation of 1,000 partisan biographies by Dainius Noreika, it is estimated that 5.9% of Lithuanian Anti-Soviet partisans were 'actively associated with aiding the Holocaust', see: Kaszeta (n 12) 236.

[15] D Budrytė, *Taming Nationalism? Political Community Building in the Post-Soviet Baltic States* (Ashgate, 2005).

[16] E Pettai, 'Center for Documentation of the Consequences of Totalitarianism/Totalitārisma seku dokumentēšanas centrs (Latvia)' in L Stan and N Nedelsky (eds), *Encyclopedia of Transitional Justice* vol 3 (Cambridge University Press, 2023) 38.

[17] ibid 41.

of Memento) analysed the repressive policies, crimes of genocide and legacies of the Soviet and Nazi regimes from 1992–2004.[18] In all three states, narratives about the Soviet and Nazi occupations (with a focus on the former) became part of museum exhibitions. (For discussion of the legal dimensions of 'Soviet genocide' discourse in Lithuania, see Sagatienė's contribution in this volume (Chapter fourteen).)

Undoubtedly, the disintegration of the Soviet Union resulted in a major normative change in the Baltic memory landscape. New mnemonic norms were created that condemned the Soviet occupation (with a focus on Stalin's crimes) as the ultimate evil. These new mnemonic norms became a foundation for future memory politics and mnemonic policies that aimed to de-legitimatise and condemn Soviet crimes. This significant 'critical situation' has fundamentally reshaped identities and served as an engine for new powerful and lasting discourses.

IV. THE SECOND 'CRITICAL SITUATION': 2014 RUSSIAN AGGRESSION AGAINST UKRAINE AND RELATED BALTIC MEMORY POLITICS

The 2014 events in Ukraine (the annexation of Crimea and Russia's proxy war in the Donbas region), known as the 'crisis in Ukraine' in the West, had a significant effect on Baltic states and societies. Most importantly, a feeling of 'uncertain sovereignty'[19] was triggered, resulting in people in the Baltic states wondering whether they 'will be next'. Lithuania became the first European country to supply lethal weapons to Ukraine, though all three Baltic states have condemned the invasion.

The aforementioned events have also affected the Baltic mnemonic landscape, including mnemonic legislation. Prior to these events, following the 2008 EU Council Framework Decision on Combating Certain Forms and Expressions of Racism and Xenophobia by Means of Criminal Law,[20] Latvia and Lithuania adopted their own memory laws, prohibiting the denial of genocide. In 2009, Latvia transposed the EU Framework Decision into its criminal law, prescribing punishment for people who commit 'public glorification of genocide, crime against humanity, crime against peace or war crime or public denial or acquittal of committed genocide, crime against humanity, crime against peace or war crime'.[21] Although Soviet crimes were discussed

[18] V Pettai, 'State Commission for the Examination of Repressive Policies Carried out during the Occupations/ Okupatsioonide repressiivpoliitika uurimise riiklik komisjon (Estonia)' in Stan and Nedelsky (n 16) 533.

[19] Klumbytė, 'Sovereign Uncertainty and the Dangers to Liberalism at the Baltic Frontier' (n 2).

[20] The EU, 'Council Framework Decision 2008/913/JHA of 28 November 2008 on combating certain forms and expressions of racism and xenophobia by means of criminal law' (*EUR-Lex*, 28 November 2008): https://eur-lex.europa.eu/legal-content/EN/TXT/?uri=celex%3A32008F0913.

[21] E Pettai, 'Protecting Memory or Criminalizing Dissent: Memory Laws in Lithuania and Latvia' in E Barkan and A Lang (eds), *Memory Laws and Historical Justice: The Politics of Criminalizing the Past* (Palgrave Macmillan, 2022) 184.

during the adoption of this law in the Latvian parliament, the subsequent 2009 law did not explicitly mention such crimes. After heated debate in the parliament, Lithuania adopted a similar memory law in 2010, which specifically mentioned Soviet crimes, making it illegal to 'deny or grossly diminish' the crimes committed by the Soviet and Nazi regimes,[22] though the law revealed a preference for Soviet crimes over Nazi crimes.[23] Following the EU Council Framework Decision, Estonia, unlike Latvia and Lithuania, did not adopt any similar memory laws, although its memory culture was focused on the condemnation of Soviet crimes, with a Museum of Occupations founded in 2003 by former dissidents.[24] Whilst the 2014 events in Ukraine helped strengthen the tendency to focus on the condemnation of Soviet crimes – this tendency already had some level of visibility prior to the adoption of the memory laws in Latvia in 2009 and Lithuania in 2010.

The proxy war that Russia began in the Donbas region and the illegal annexation of Crimea triggered memories in the Baltic states of their annexation in 1940, leading to changes in domestic regulations. Latvia's 2014 memory law was amended to include specific mention of crimes perpetrated by the Soviet Union, an amendment which took place following the ban of Soviet symbols in 2013. (In Lithuania, Soviet and Nazi symbols were banned in 2008). In Lithuania, due to an amendment in 2014 to a Ministry of Culture regulation regarding 'immovable cultural property', local governments were empowered to remove monuments with Nazi and communist symbols as well as 'images of German national socialists or leaders of the Communist Party of the USSR responsible for repression of the Lithuanian population'.[25] In addition, conservative politicians proposed banning the ribbon of St George – a Russian military symbol with black and orange stripes commemorating the veterans of WWII, associated with Russian power and the proxy war that Russia began in the Donbas region.[26] They argued that this symbol should be treated in the same regard as communist or Nazi symbols.

Although in 2016 this proposal did not pass, the events in Ukraine definitely influenced debates about the Soviet past, with Soviet crimes linked to Russia's aggressive behaviour in Ukraine. In Lithuania, the cult of anti-Soviet partisans

[22] ibid 178.

[23] N Koposov, *Memory Laws, Memory Wars: The Politics of the Past in Europe and Russia* (Cambridge University Press, 2017) 174.

[24] V Davoliūtė, 'The Baltic Model of Civic-Patriotic History' (2022) 24 *Journal of Genocide Research* 264, 269.

[25] V Davoliūtė, 'Lithuania's Postcolonial Iconoclasm – Or Politics by Other Means' (*Cultures of History Forum*, 30 September 2023): www.cultures-of-history.uni-jena.de/politics/lithuanias-postcolonial-iconoclasm-or-politics-by-other-means.

[26] ELTA, 'Georgijaus juostelę siūloma priskirti draudžiamai sovietinei simbolikai' (*Delfi.lt*, Lithuania, 29 January 2016): www.delfi.lt/news/daily/lithuania/georgijaus-juostele-siuloma-priskirti-draudziamai-sovietinei-simbolikai-70256610.

who resisted the Soviet occupation became even stronger, with the release of *The Invisible Front*, a film about these fighters. The release of NATO's documentary in 2017, about the Baltic 'forest brothers' (anti-Soviet partisans), distributed via social media, became wildly popular in the Baltic states, linking irregular warfare strategies used by anti-Soviet partisans to preparations for irregular warfare by special forces in the Baltic states.

Russia's aggressive actions against Ukraine in 2014 did not create the 'fighting and suffering' narrative in the Baltic states, but they definitely reinforced it and increased its emotional appeal.[27] The anti-Soviet resistance during and after WWII, which is the backbone of the 'fighting and suffering' memory regimes, formed 'a template through which new potential Russian aggression and resistance to it' became imagined in the Baltic states.[28] The Baltic populations started to prepare for asymmetrical war with Russia and practised 'hybrid resistance', civil disobedience and partisan warfare (as in the past). Historical memory became securitised as 'Russia's deployment of revisionist rhetoric in historical discourse and foreign policy targeted the key vulnerabilities – cultural, social, political and military – of the Baltic states'.[29] (For Russia, those who resisted the Soviet military during and after WWII were deemed to be 'Nazis and their collaborators.') Yet despite increased securitisation of memory, only relatively minor mnemonic legislative changes were implemented in Latvia.

Although the second 'critical situation' (Russia's war against Ukraine in 2014) did not transform the Baltic states into 'militant memocracies' similar to Russia,[30] it became an engine of discourse linking the Soviet past to the present and made ethnic divides visible (especially in Latvia and Estonia). This 'critical situation' had an important impact on identities, as new discourses associated with Russia's aggression presented national majorities as 'endangered' (similarly to how they were endangered, according to the Baltic imagination, when they were part of the Soviet Union) and 'reconstituted as [a] potential victim[s]'.[31] Ultimately, memory politics were inseparable from identity changes. The Victory Day celebrations (9 May), which have been traditionally supported by Russians in the Baltic states, became seen as 'a ritual of threat and disloyalty'[32] because such events became associated with support for Russia's expansionism, which is linked to the celebration of the 'Great Patriotic War'.

[27] Interview with Arvydas Anušauskas, a prominent Lithuanian historian and politician, member of Seimas (parliament) in 2019 (Vilnius, Lithuania, 22 July 2019).

[28] Klumbytė, 'Sovereign Uncertainty and the Dangers to Liberalism at the Baltic Frontier' (n 2) 343.

[29] Davoliūtė, 'Lithuania's Postcolonial Iconoclasm' (n 25) 270.

[30] ibid 274.

[31] Klumbytė, 'Sovereign Uncertainty and the Dangers to Liberalism at the Baltic Frontier' (n 2) 343.

[32] ibid 344.

V. THE THIRD 'CRITICAL SITUATION': RUSSIA'S FULL-SCALE WAR AGAINST UKRAINE AND MNEMONIC CHANGES IN THE BALTIC STATES

A. Feelings of 'Uncertain Sovereignty' and Vicarious Identification with Ukraine

Russia's full-scale invasion of Ukraine, which began suddenly in February 2022, elicited a very strong emotional reaction in the Baltic states. The feeling of 'uncertain sovereignty'[33] felt by people during the previous critical situation became even more acute. Intense insecurity, coupled with the perception of sovereignty as 'recurring and temporary' and as something that could be taken away suddenly,[34] became part of the process through which people in the Baltic states started to identify with Ukraine. The Baltic states started fighting the war at home and abroad, enthusiastically supporting Ukraine in international organisations as well as providing weapons and other types of aid. For example, in 2023, Lithuania donated two million euros for radars in just one hour (with 14 million euros donated in one month).

Russia's war of aggression has become Lithuania's, Latvia's, and Estonia's war.[35] Unlike in other CEE countries, such as Poland and Slovakia (where support for Ukraine has declined due to various domestic influences, including economic competition) support for, and intense emotional identification with, Ukraine has remained strong throughout 2023 and 2024 in the Baltic states. For example, in December 2023, after the US Congress and the EU failed to secure aid for Ukraine, Estonia's (former) Prime Minister Kaja Kallas argued: 'Estonia's long-term military aid to Ukraine will be 0.25% of our GDP over the next four years. Collective commitment of a similar scale could ensure Ukraine's victory over the next 4 years'.[36] When Ukraine's counteroffensive failed in 2023 and Russia regained the initiative in the eastern part of Ukraine in 2024, Ukraine's pain and the fear of war were sentiments felt very strongly in the Baltic states. Describing the situation in Lithuania in early March 2024, leading commentator Deividas Šlekys noted that 'no one seems to question the likelihood that Russia will attack the Baltic states; everyone is trying to guess when this will happen'.[37]

It is possible to argue that support for Ukraine has been more than an expression of sympathy and friendship; the Baltic states have started experiencing

[33] Klumbytė, 'Sovereign Uncertainty and the Dangers to Liberalism at the Baltic Frontier' (n 2).

[34] N Klumbytė, 'Lithuania at the Frontier of the War in Ukraine' (2022) 121 *Current History* 264.

[35] D Budrytė, '"A Decolonizing Moment of Sorts": The Baltic States' Vicarious Identification with Ukraine and Related Domestic and Foreign Policy Developments' (2023) 17 *Central European Journal of International and Security Studies* 82.

[36] K Kallas (*X Post*, 15 December 2023): https://twitter.com/kajakallas/status/1735657607065465046.

[37] D Šlekys, 'Karo lažybos' (*LRT.lt*, Lithuania, 3 March 2024): www.lrt.lt/naujienos/nuomones/3/2213110/deividas-slekys-karo-lazybos.

vicarious identification with Ukraine.[38] As argued by Browning, Joenniemi and Steele, focusing on vicarious identification means detecting instances when 'vicarious experiences that otherwise have been narrated in the third person are actually relayed via first person pronouns'.[39] In the words of the authors,

> vicarious identification may also be evident in how such narratives demonstrate a heightened level of commitment to a specific relationship, establish a sense of historical commonality, blur the distinction between self and other, potentially even appropriating elements of the target's historical experience for oneself, and not least emphasize familial relations.[40]

Baltic leaders in their statements about Ukraine have expressed feelings of 'we-ness' and shared identity, as well as shared history (in the case of Lithuania, the Lithuanian-Polish Commonwealth included Ukraine.) For example, on 14 December 2023, when the EU announced its plans to begin membership talks with Ukraine, Gabrielius Landsbergis, Lithuania's foreign minister and long-time supporter of Ukraine, posted the following on his *X* account, 'Today, as Europe makes [one of] its most important decisions in recent history, I can only say this: *Ya ukrainets*. I am a Ukrainian'.[41]

This sense of 'we-ness' also became embedded in the symbols of state institutions which started displaying the Ukrainian flag next to the national flag, even private businesses began using the Ukrainian flag instead of the Lithuanian, Latvian or Estonian flags. As suggested by Brown and Herring, in addition to serving the function of vicarious identification, the widespread use of Ukrainian flags in the Baltic states also served the function of public pedagogy, which is used to 'develop civic and national identity, promote cohesion and memorialize'.[42]

Memory politics and memorialisation became extremely important as the Baltic states started to develop a collective identity with Ukraine. As recounted by Browning, Joenniemi and Steele, previous experiences of trauma and ontological insecurities form the reasons behind vicarious identification.[43] In the case of the Baltic-Ukrainian relationship, following the outbreak of full-scale war, there was a resurgence of previous experiences of collective trauma which started to play a major role in national consciousness. The experiences of mass deportations and political repression under Stalin, which became the backbone of Baltic memory regimes during the first 'critical situation' in the late '80s and

[38] Budrytė, "A Decolonizing Moment of Sorts" (n 35).

[39] CS Browning, P Joenniemi, and BJ Steele, *Vicarious Identity in International Relations: Self, Security, and Status on the Global Stage* (Oxford University Press, 2021) 81.

[40] ibid 82.

[41] G Landsbergis (*X Post*, 14 December 2023): https://twitter.com/GLandsbergis/status/1735233867093536936.

[42] KD Brown and A Herring, 'The Public Pedagogy of Ukrainian Flag Displays: A View from Lithuania and Estonia' (2023) 4 *The Baltic Worlds* 26, 26.

[43] Browning, Joenniemi, and Steele (n 39) 32.

early '90s, resurfaced in public discourse, and the crimes of Stalin's USSR were linked to Russian crimes perpetrated in Ukraine.

B. Fighting Russia Beyond the Battlefield: Use of the Term 'Genocide'

It is not surprising, therefore, that in 2022, the Baltic states were amongst the first to call Russia's war against Ukraine 'genocide' and to refer to Russia as a 'terrorist state'. The term 'genocide' was used to emphasise the gravity of Russian crimes perpetrated in Ukraine, to make the case internationally that the war is illegitimate, and to argue that Russia should be punished for its actions. Parliaments in the Baltic states voted unanimously in favour of resolutions to call Russia's war against Ukraine 'genocide'.[44] In the words of Eugenijus Gentvilas, a Lithuanian Member of Parliament (MP),

> It is important to acknowledge that the Russian Federation has been demonstrating its desire to eliminate the Ukrainians since the Holodomor in 1932 [the Stalin-orchestrated mass famine in Ukraine]. This desire is clear today, when we witness a systematic annihilation of people and material objects. 181,000 of captured and deported children to the occupying country, approximately one million of deported adults. These are clear characteristics of genocide.

According to Paulius Saudargas, another Lithuanian MP, who introduced the 'genocide' resolution, 'Russia has not changed; in essence since the times of the czar it is an authoritarian state, and Putin is continuing the work of Stalin'.[45]

The anti-Soviet resistance in the Baltic states, which began during the second Soviet occupation in 1944 and continued after WWII, became another important frame of reference. This was particularly the case in Lithuania, where the term 'genocide' is often associated with the repression of anti-Soviet partisans and their families, especially after the ruling of the European Court of Justice in 2018 that the USSR carried out genocide against Lithuanian partisans (see also Sagatienė's contribution to this volume at Chapter fourteen). After the 2014 Russian invasion of Ukraine, the collective memory associated with anti-Soviet partisan resistance became even more pronounced, intersecting with the use of genocide discourse in the context of the ongoing war, as societies in the Baltic states were preparing for irregular warfare in case of Russian invasion. This trend has continued since the third 'critical situation' in 2014.

[44] 'Latvian and Estonian parliaments say Russia committed genocide in Ukraine' (*Reuters*, 21 April 2022): www.reuters.com/world/europe/latvian-estonian-parliaments-say-russia-committed-genocide-ukraine-2022-04-21/.

[45] BNS, 'Lietuvos Seimas rusų veiksmus Ukrainoje pripažino genocidu; Rusiją – teroristine valstybe' (*15 min*, 10 May 2022): www.15min.lt/naujiena/aktualu/lietuva/lietuvos-seimas-rusu-veiksmus-ukrainoje-pripazino-genocidu-rusija-teroristine-valstybe-56-1677498.

C. 'De-sovietisation' in Latvia

The processes of vicarious identification in the Baltic states have included attempts by governments and broader society to completely sever all links with the Soviet past and even Russian culture – a sentiment reflected in the commencement of the movement to get rid of all Soviet-era monuments and other tangible memories. In August 2022, the Monument to the Liberators in Riga – a site of memory associated with glorification of the 'Great Patriotic War' in Soviet Latvia – was demolished. Latvia's parliament voted in favour of this demolition in May 2022, three months after the start of the full-scale war in Ukraine.[46] This mnemonic legislation was followed by the passage of a law requiring all monuments containing symbols associated with the Soviet Union and Nazi Germany to be dismantled by 15 November 2022, with President Levits signing this Bill into law on 22 June 2022.[47]

For years, the monument to the Liberators in Riga served as one of the most important places of memory for Latvia's Russians. Their commemorative ceremonies on 9 May, the Day of Victory of the 'Great Patriotic War' (the name used in the Soviet Union, and presently by Russia, to describe Soviet Union's struggle against Nazi Germany from 1941–45), were held in the vicinity of this monument. These celebrations were linked to Putin's rise in power and pride in Russia's victory during WWII.[48] However, in early 2022, when Russia's full-scale war started, the monument became a symbol of Russian aggression. In April 2022, Sandra Kalniete, a famous politician in Latvia in favour of harsh treatment of the Soviet legacy, argued that the monument should be dismantled, with her tweet garnering enormous political support.[49] Although the 'de-sovietisation' process has not been accompanied by political violence, most of Latvia's Russian-speakers did not support the removal of monuments associated with WWII.[50]

According to a public opinion survey conducted in Latvia, in July 2022, only nine per cent of Russian-speakers supported this mnemonic move, compared with 72 per cent of Latvian-speakers.[51] A report published by the Friedrich-Ebert-Stiftung in 2023 suggested a similar conclusion: among respondents

[46] 'Latvia Demolishes Soviet Memorial in Riga, Latest to Be Dismantled across Eastern Europe' (*RadioFreeEurope/ RadioLiberty*, 25 August 2022): www.rferl.org/a/latvia-demolishes-soviet-memorial-riga-/32004611.html.

[47] T Rostoks and KE Kanasta, 'Foreign and Domestic Policy Implications of Latvia's Reaction to Russia's Aggression against Ukraine' (2023) 9 *Journal on Baltic Security* 5.

[48] M Kaprāns, 'Toppling Monuments: How Russia's War against Ukraine has Changed Latvia's Memory Politics' (*Cultures of History Forum*, 29 November 2022): www.cultures-of-history.uni-jena.de/latvia/toppling-monuments-how-russias-war-against-ukraine-has-changed-latvias-memory-politics.

[49] ibid.

[50] Rostoks and Kanasta (n 47).

[51] LSM.lv, 'Less than half of Russians in Latvia condemn Russia's war in Ukraine: survey' (7 July 2022): https://eng.lsm.lv/article/society/society/less-than-half-of-russians-in-latvia-condemn-russias-war-in-ukraine-survey.a464423/.

who spoke Russian in their families, only five per cent strongly supported this move, compared with 10 per cent who spoke both Latvian and Russian, and 41 per cent who spoke only Latvian in their family.[52] The majority of the younger generation possessed a slightly different – less disapproving – attitude, an exception being the 36 per cent of 18 to 24-year-olds who spoke only Russian at home and who strongly disapproved of the removal of the WWII monuments.[53]

The ideological fragmentation of Latvia's Russians was identified as one of the reasons why they did not engage in widespread resistance to the removal of the monuments, including the monument to the Liberators in Riga, which was so important to many of them.[54] At the same time, it appears that there was little public tolerance for those who argued against the demolition of Soviet-era monuments in Latvia.[55]

D. 'De-sovietisation' in Estonia

Similar processes in memory politics took place in Estonia where Soviet-era monuments were denounced as 'glorifying the Russian occupation' and had to be removed from public spaces[56] (one reason for this denunciation being Russia's tendency to draw parallels between the 'Great Patriotic War' and the current war, for example, the argument about the perceived 'need' for 'denazification' in Ukraine). A law passed in February 2023 by the Estonian parliament empowered local authorities to remove 'inappropriate monuments and symbols'. An additional provision stipulated that publicly displayed statues and monuments could not 'justify' occupation regimes, genocide, or war crimes. The law also attempted to prevent the future construction of 'inappropriate monuments'. Estonia's Justice Minister, Lea Danilson-Jarg, linked the removal of monuments to historical justice, arguing that 'the Bill will finally make it possible to assert the historical truth.[57]

The removal of monuments has been taking place since early 2022. In Narva, a city with a large Russian population, an iconic T-34 tank was removed and brought to the Estonian War Museum.[58] There was some protest against this mnemonic move in early August 2022, prior to its removal, but this

[52] R Krumm, K Šukevičs and T Zarinš, 'Under Pressure: An Analysis of the Russian-Speaking Minority in Latvia' (*Friedrich Ebert Stiftung*, July 2023) https://library.fes.de/pdf-files/bueros/baltikum/20445.pdf.

[53] ibid.

[54] Kaprāns (n 48).

[55] ibid.

[56] BBC, 'Estonia begins removing Soviet-era war monuments' (*BBC News*, 16 August 2022): www.bbc.com/news/world-europe-62562909.

[57] BNS, 'Parliament passes bill on removing Soviet-era monuments' (*Postimees*, 15 February 2023): https://news.postimees.ee/7713628/parliament-passes-bill-on-removing-soviet-era-monuments.

[58] BBC (n 56).

did not prevent the local authorities from proceeding.[59] As the tank was being removed, the process was streamed online, and there was a heavy police presence; however, the removal went smoothly.[60] Public order, historical memory and internal security were identified as the reasons for the removal of the monuments. Reflecting on the memory aspect in particular, Prime Minister Kallas noted that Russia's war had 'opened wounds in our society that these monuments remind us of'.[61]

These events stand in stark contrast to those of 2007, when the Bronze Soldier, a monument to the Soviet 'liberators', was relocated from the centre of Tallinn to a military cemetery. This move caused civil unrest and dissatisfaction among Estonia's Russians. In contrast, reaction to the removal of Soviet-era monuments in 2022 was subdued, with no public expressions of dissatisfaction. It appears that the only vocal resistance to the removal of the monuments came from those who study memory politics. For example, Marek Tamm, a leading cultural historian, argued against decisions made by 'anonymous commissions' in a hasty way. He felt that it was important that future generations should have an understanding of the Soviet past which is in turn connected to the monuments. Tamm described the securitisation of memory associated with the removal of the monuments as an undesirable development.[62]

It appears that the Estonian government attempted to balance the desire to 'de-sovietise' with a pragmatic need to maintain stability in ethnic relations. In January 2024, responding to a question asked by Martin Helme, the leader of EKRE (a right-wing populist party that had previously attempted to obtain the support of Estonia's Russians), Estonia's Prime Minister asserted that there were no plans to remove the notorious Bronze Soldier from the public sphere. She was quoted as saying that Estonia's Russians do not want another wave of tensions that could be exploited by Russia to come and 'free' them.[63]

E. 'De-sovietisation' in Lithuania

Similar developments, in terms of the removal of Soviet-era monuments and debates about their removal, have also occurred in Lithuania. Despite removal gaining support from some politicians and government agencies, it has been

[59] A Chapple, 'Estonia's Contentious Soviet Monuments' (*RadioFreeEurope/ RadioLiberty*, 15 August 2022): www.rferl.org/a/estonia-soviet-monuments-removal/31989524.html.

[60] M Martin, 'The tank is gone but grudge remains' (*Postimees*, 17 August 2022): https://news.postimees.ee/7587147/the-tank-is-gone-but-grudge-remains.

[61] Chapple (n 59).

[62] K Tamelytė, 'Memory politics in Estonia: We shouldn't turn Soviet monuments into a security threat' (*LRT.lt*, Lithuania, 11 December 2022): www.lrt.lt/en/news-in-english/19/1841206/memory-politics-in-estonia-we-shouldn-t-turn-soviet-monuments-into-a-security-threat-interview.

[63] 'Pravitel'stvo Kallas ne planiruyet snos Bronzovogo soldata' (*rus.postimees.ee*, 17 January 2024) https://rus.postimees.ee/7940522/pravitelstvo-kallas-ne-planiruet-snos-bronzovogo-soldata.

resisted by leading memory politics experts (as was the case in Estonia).[64] When the full-scale invasion of Ukraine began, politicians expressed a desire to remove the monuments in one month (before the 9 May celebration); however, leading memory politics experts warned that wartime may be the worst time to remove the monuments because they would endanger societal harmony and possibly promote polarisation. In a public debate, Darius Kuolys, a cultural historian and the first Minister of Culture in independent Lithuania (1990–92), mocked those, such as journalist Andrius Tapinas, who argued for the removal of the monuments (Tapinas being the one who started the movement to remove the monuments): 'The Ukrainians are fighting a mighty foreign military, and we are fighting our war with bones'.[65]

Despite this resistance, the movement to remove Soviet-era monuments, especially those associated with the 'Great Patriotic War', continued. The Department of Cultural Heritage was flooded with requests from local governments to remove monuments associated with the Soviet past. In just one week, in May 2022, the department received applications from 25 out of 60 local governments to remove 65 monuments.[66]

Most of the debates surrounding removal were focused on a monument to Soviet soldiers in a cemetery in Antakalnis, a neighbourhood in Vilnius. The statues were a place of gathering on 9 May for those who were longing for the Soviet past. The decision to remove the monument was even challenged by the United Nations Human Rights Committee (UNHRC), which had received a petition from several people identifying themselves as ethnic Russians asking for protection of the monument for several years until 'investigations' could take place.[67] The Interior Ministry and the municipality reacted to the UNHRC injunction by arguing that they had been 'misled' by the petitioners, and that no desecration of the monument and no reburial of soldiers' remains would take place.[68] The monument was removed in December 2022.

In Lithuania, in addition to the removal of Soviet monuments, another move towards 'de-sovietisation', which is commonly perceived as 'derussification', was made. In December 2022, the Lithuanian parliament passed a law, which came

[64] J Bakaitė, 'Entuziastingai sutikta sovietinės simbolikos iškėlimo idėja sulaukė kritikos: karas – blogiausias laikas paminklams griauti' (*LRT.lt*, Lithuania, 8 April 2022): www.lrt.lt/naujienos/lietuvoje/2/1667529/entuziastingai-sutikta-sovietines-simbolikos-iskelimo-ideja-sulauke-kritikos-karas-blogiausias-laikas-paminklams-griauti.

[65] A Perednis and V Spurytė, 'Dėl sovietinių pamiklų kilusį vajų pavadino gėdingu: pasislėpę už ukrainiečių nugarų, kovojame su kaulais' (*Delfi*, Lithuania, 13 April 2022): www.delfi.lt/news/daily/lithuania/del-sovietiniu-paminklu-kilusi-vaju-pavadino-gedingu-pasislepe-uz-ukrainieciu-nugaru-kovojame-su-kaulais-89961469.

[66] P Tiltas, 'KPD vadovas: išnagrinėta beveik pusė savivaldybių prašymų nukelti sovietinius memorialus' (*Palangos tiltas*, 31 May 2022): www.palangostiltas.lt/kpd+vadovas+isnagrineta+beveik+puse+savivaldybiu+prasymu+nukelti+sovietinius+memorialus,7,2,14203.html.

[67] BNS, 'Vilnius completes removal of soviet sculptures from Antakalnis Cemetery' (*LRT.lt*, Lithuania, 9 December 2022): www.lrt.lt/en/news-in-english/19/1840938/vilnius-completes-removal-of-soviet-sculptures-from-antakalnis-cemetery.

[68] ibid.

into effect in May 2023, that forbade the 'promotion' of authoritarian and totalitarian regimes and their ideologies. Consequently, 'public objects' recognised as promoting such ideologies must be removed from public spaces.[69] According to Bronė Kuzmickienė – an MP from the conservative Homeland Union party who initiated this legislation – it was 'essential' to recognise and remove the remnants of totalitarian regimes because of what was going on in Ukraine. She argued that it was also essential to understand who exactly a 'collaborator' is in the context of the ongoing war.[70] Kuzmickienė's statement suggests that the intent behind this law was primarily to fight the legacy of the Soviet regime, not the Nazi regime – even though the wording of the law suggested that the legacy of both regimes should be confronted.

This was an ambitious law that established 'a system that, if implemented fully, would remove all monuments associated with Soviet or German occupation regimes from public spaces in Lithuania'.[71] However, its implementation was limited, with efforts focused on Soviet-era monuments. Local governments were instructed to come up with a list of objects within their territories that were in violation of the law. These objects could include not only monuments but also streets, buildings, organisations, events, and commemorative dates. The lists were to be submitted to The Genocide and Resistance Research Centre of Lithuania, whose director would then have the power to decide whether or not to remove this object from the public sphere. Local governments were expected to pay for the removal of these objects. A commission consisting of nine individuals, including representatives from universities and the Union of Lithuanian Political Prisoners and Exiles, was created to provide advice and recommendations to assist the aforementioned director.[72] The recommendations of this commission, which became known as a 'decommunisation commission', included changing the names of streets and squares, including those that were named after popular Soviet Lithuanian poets and writers.[73]

In 2022–23, the wave of eliminating Soviet-era monuments and Russian cultural influence received both governmental and popular support in the Baltic states and only relatively weak resistance from some intellectuals. Such support may be interpreted as an expression of vicarious identification with Ukraine – the war against the aggressor being fought at home against symbols of the Soviet Union that are still supported by Russia. This move to get rid of the Soviet past

[69] Teisės aktų registras, 'Lietuvos Respublikos draudimo propaguoti totalitarinius, autoritarinius režimus ir jų ideologijas įstatymas' (*Teisės aktų registras*, 13 December 2022): www.e-tar.lt/portal/lt/legalAct/09a371f081df11ed8df094f359a60216.

[70] J Skėrytė, 'Lietuva uždraudė propaguoti autoritarinius ir totalitarinius režimus' (*LRT.lt*, Lithuania, 13 December 2022): www.lrt.lt/naujienos/lietuvoje/2/1843667/lietuva-uzdraude-propaguoti-totalitarinius-ir-autoritarinius-rezimus.

[71] Davoliūtė, 'Lithuania's Postcolonial Iconoclasm' (n 25).

[72] ibid.

[73] J Skėrytė, 'Desovietizacijos komisija nurodė Vilniuje pervadinti P. Cvirkos aikštę, L. Giros gatvę' (*BNS diena.lt*, Lithuania, 8 January 2024): https://m.diena.lt/naujienos/vilnius/miesto-pulsas/desovietizacijos-komisija-nurode-vilniuje-pervadinti-p-cvirkos-aikste-l-giros-gatve-1155718.

reinforced the established narratives of 'fighting' and 'suffering', and can be interpreted as a continuation of the 'anti-colonial nationalist politics of memory'[74] that intensified in Ukraine and the Baltic states after the 2013–14 events in Ukraine.

F. Tensions in Ethnic Relations

At the same time, the processes associated with vicarious identification with Ukraine may have affected attitudes toward minorities in the Baltic states. Latvia and Estonia are both home to a large ethnic Russian minority, and Lithuania is home to smaller ethnic Polish and Russian minorities. The members of these minority communities have been suspected in the past of having 'dual loyalty' – harbouring some sympathies toward Russia and embracing a more positive view of the Soviet past.[75] Even in Lithuania, which (unlike Latvia and Estonia) granted citizenship to all residents in 1991, the full-scale war in Ukraine changed ethnic relations. According to the results of a public opinion survey conducted by the Diversity Development Group in 2022, 23.1 per cent of respondents would not like to rent housing to ethnic Russians (compared with 10 per cent in 2021), and 13.6 per cent would not like to work with ethnic Russians in the same firm (compared with five per cent in 2021).[76] Moreover, 74.6 per cent of respondents indicated that during the last five years their attitudes toward Russians have deteriorated.[77]

Although it is impossible to generalise about the reaction of Russian-speaking minorities (in the case of all three Baltic states) and Polish minorities (in the case of Lithuania) to the war in Ukraine, it appears that there was a generational difference. In Latvia, the younger generations of ethnic Russians were using social media to express their frustration with older family members who supported Russia's war against Ukraine.[78] Some older Russians held

[74] B Törnquist-Plewa and Y Yurchuk, 'Memory Politics in Contemporary Ukraine: Reflections from the Postcolonial Perspective' (2019) 12(6) *Memory Studies* 699: https://doi.org/10.1177/1750698017727806.

[75] In 2021, 6.53% of Lithuania's population self-identified as ethnic Poles, and 5% as ethnic Russians (Official Statistics Portal n.d.). The ethnic Polish minority has been traditionally more politically active than the ethnic Russian minority. In 2022, 26.3% of Latvia's residents self-identified as Russians (Oficiālās statistikas portāls n.d.). In 2021, 23.67% of Estonia's population self-identified as Russians (Statistics Estonia n.d.).

[76] LSTC etninių tyrimų institutas, 'Lietuvos sociologijos mokslų centro sociologijos instituto etninių tyrimų skyriaus ir VŠĮ 'Diversity Development Group' užsakymu atliktos visuomenės nuostatų apklausos 2021 m. rezultatai' (*LSTC etninių tyrimų institutas*, 2021) www.ces.lt/wp-content/uploads/2010/02/Visuomen%C4%97s-nuostat%C5%B3-apklausos-rezultatai-2021.pdf.; G Blažytė, 'Visuomenės nuostatos etninių ir religinių grupių atžvilgiu: 2022 m' (*LSTC etninių tyrimų institutas*, 2022): www.ces.lt/wp-content/uploads/2023/01/2022-m.-rugsejo-16-27-d.-duomenys.pdf.

[77] Blažytė (n 76).

[78] U Bergmane, 'Latvia's First Response to Russia's War in Ukraine' (*Foreign Policy Research Institute Baltic Bulletin*, 11 March 2022): www.fpri.org/article/2022/03/latvias-first-response-to-russias-war-in-ukraine/.

positive views of the Soviet past associated with Russian hegemony.[79] This often translated into support for Putin's Russia, which was seen as an extension of the USSR. Differences in attitudes regarding the war in Ukraine had introduced tensions and arguments in the families of Estonia's Russians.[80] Most members of the Polish community in Lithuania, despite their preference for Russian news media, supported the Ukrainian cause and had a negative view of Russia.

The war in Ukraine has introduced new insecurities, new vulnerabilities, and even new lines of division within the Baltic societies, demonstrating that vicarious identification is never absolute and that it is a complicated and uneven process. Research conducted by Lithuania's Eastern Europe Studies Centre in 2023 revealed that approximately 20 per cent of respondents to a survey of Lithuanian residents, who belonged to different ethnic groups, expressed a belief that the US and NATO had contributed to the start of the war in Ukraine.[81] (This is one of the Kremlin's propaganda lines.) This finding prompted a discussion about what could be done to subdue such beliefs. These aforementioned newly emerging insecurities, lines of division, and changes in mnemonic policies attest to the power of this 'critical situation' to transform local identities and produce new discourses.

VI. CONCLUSION

The goal of this chapter was to explore the relationship between 'critical situations' (international crises) and mnemonic policies. My hypothesis was that 'critical situations' can have a significant effect on domestic mnemonic policies. My research builds on an emerging body of literature in international relations that treats international crises not only as events that are 'managed' by powerful and strong actors, but as a force that can reshape identities, produce new discourses and change the routines of states and societies. By paying attention to discourses, identities and memory politics, this body of literature tries to decolonise the study of crises, forcing us to pay attention not only to material, but also to non-material factors and the interaction of 'strong' and 'weak' actors.

Having conducted case studies of three 'critical situations' (the disintegration of the Soviet Union, Russia's aggression against Ukraine in 2014 and

[79] A Stewart, 'Ethnic Russians in Latvia divided on the war in Ukraine: "There is a big division"' *Global News* (Canada, 4 March 2022): www.globalnews.ca/news/8657202/ukraine-daugavpils-latvia-generational-divide/.

[80] A Avakova, 'The War in Ukraine is Breaking up Russian Families in Estonia' (*RusPostimees*, Estonia, 16 November 2022): https://news.postimees.ee/7649873/the-war-in-ukraine-is-breaking-up-russian-families-in-estonia.

[81] V Narkūnas and J Bakaitė, 'Kas penktas gyventojas mano, kad Rusija nesukėlė karo: ekspertai sako, kad bausti tokių piliečių neįmanoma' (*LRT.lt*, Lithuania, 20 January 2024): www.lrt.lt/naujienos/lietuvoje/2/2163541/kas-penktas-gyventojas-mano-kad-rusija-nesukele-karo-ekspertai-sako-kad-bausti-tokiu-pilieciu-neimanoma?fbclid=IwAR0XYRG8_KjvrtLNfuQNDPygcABPykjrNMYUeSc5VyYIBmLuExrLMqC788k.

Russia's full-scale war against Ukraine in 2022), it is possible to document the transformative effects of these critical situations on mnemonic politics in the Baltic states and mnemonic policies (especially in the case of Latvia and Lithuania). However, the impact of the three critical situations is not the same. The disintegration of the Soviet Union, which fundamentally transformed memory regimes in the Baltic states and established strong mnemonic norms for the future commemoration and pursuit of memory politics, was the most significant and the most powerful critical situation. During this situation, the Baltic states restored their independence and fundamentally reshaped their identities as they started building their political communities with Russia situated as the 'Other.' The Baltic states started associating the Soviet occupation with the ultimate evil (Lithuania even used the term 'genocide' to refer to it), suffering, and the need to resist it. Their memory regimes were built on the traumas associated with deportations and repression experienced under Stalin and during resistance by anti-Soviet partisans to the Soviet occupation during and after WWII. When Russia started consolidating its memory regime around the 'Great Patriotic War' (which is perceived as the beginning of a new occupation, not liberation, in the Baltic states), it became clear that mnemonic contestation and memory wars between the Baltic states and Russia were inevitable.

Russia's aggression against Ukraine in 2014, and even the full-scale war started by Russia in 2022, built on these established norms and made the memory regimes focusing on 'fighting and suffering' (commemorating anti-Soviet partisans and mourning Soviet deportations) stronger. In a sense, the 2022 'critical situation' was similar to the 2014 'critical situation' – the mnemonic policies and mnemonic norms embraced by the Baltic states were not new, with the recurrent themes of condemning the USSR and linking the crimes of the Soviet Union to the aggressive behaviour of Russia. Memories about the anti-Soviet resistance and suffering under Stalin became lenses through which the Baltic states and societies started viewing Russia's aggression against Ukraine, as the Baltic states were preparing to resist possible Russian aggression in the future. Anyone supporting the memory regime associated with the 'Great Patriotic War' became seen as a source of threat, and this introduced tensions in ethnic relations.

The findings of the case studies suggest that not all 'critical situations' are identical. Some critical situations have a far-reaching, revolutionary effect by establishing new memory regimes and creating the foundation for new mnemonic norms. In her analysis of the developments in Ukraine in 2013–14 and its comparison to the other critical events, such as the disintegration of empires, Erica Resende described events as having a similar impact to a 'wound', and 'there is no healing or overcoming of the wound'.[82] Other critical situations that do not create new memory regimes or create new mnemonic norms

[82] E Resende, 'Crisis and Change in Global Politics: A Dialogue with Deleuze and Badiou's Event to Understand the Crisis in Ukraine' in E Resende, D Budrytė, and D Buhari-Gulmez (n 9).

can be conceptualised as 'scars' – their impact is still felt, and it is felt strongly; however, the impact is not the same as that elicited by a 'wound'.

The case study of the third 'critical situation' (Russia's full-scale war against Ukraine) revealed an important change in Baltic identities. Baltic societies started waging war against Russia vicariously, identifying with Ukraine in a strong emotional way and closely following every move on the front. The pursuit of 'de-sovietisation', by getting rid of Soviet-era monuments, introducing memory legislation (especially in the case of Lithuania) and cleansing themselves of any Russian influence (both perceived and real), has been an expression of this vicarious war. The origins of this development, however, can be traced to 2014 when Russia annexed Crimea and began a proxy war in the Donbas region, or even earlier, to the late '80s and early '90s, when the first moves toward 'de-sovietisation' and the removal of the Soviet-era monuments were made. Unfortunately, the experiences of vicarious identification and related mnemonic policies were accompanied by new lines of division and even ethnic tensions. Their impact is likely to last for years to come.

10

The Transformation of Russia in Hungary's Memory Governance

MARINA BÁN

I. INTRODUCTION

IN THE LAST decade, Hungary's official narratives of its past have been transformed as part of a deliberate systemic alteration of the country's social and political environment in conformity with the reigning government's values. This transformation was initiated from the top down, starting with the adoption of a new constitution and followed by amendments at the statutory and symbolic levels, resulting in complete political control of the nation's perceptions of the historical past and, through that, the entire domestic and international image of the country.[1]

Using the example of Russia's shifting role in this systemic transformation from historical enemy to friend and ally, and finally, oppressor, this chapter examines instrumentalisation of the past in Hungary. It contends that the erratic and radical transformation of Russia's framing illustrates the emergence of a systemic form of control of historical perception by the government. It traces the evolution of the political reality and compares Russia's political representation in Hungary, which varied according to historical context and was often subjected to political manipulation and distortion. However, in contrast to the more fluid and natural perspectives of the nineteenth century, the late twentieth century and the beginning of the twenty-first century, the most recent decade introduced an arbitrary approach, suppressing any reference to the actual historical past and portraying Russia as an eternal friendly partner of Hungary in the political arena. Furthermore, the new political instrumentalisation of Russia's allegedly positive role in the Hungarian system of historical memory directly employs a threatening and quasi-colonial narrative in relation to discourse on the EU, thus, inverting the two narratives, from portraying Russia as the threat and the EU as the friend, to

[1] G Halmai, 'The making of "Illiberal Constitutionalism" With or Without a New Constitution: The Case of Hungary and Poland' in D Landau and H Lerner (eds), *Comparative Constitution Making* (Edward Elgar Publishing, 2019).

the exact opposite, and doing so by relying on nothing else but historical grandstanding, ultimately disregarding historical facts and political realities.

The European and regional context in which the recent Hungarian developments exist involves expansive memory wars between Russia itself and the EU, as well as radically different approaches to shared pasts between several neighbouring Central and Eastern Europe (CEE) countries.[2] The changes in Hungary align with the lack of democratic values and antagonisation of the EU, as seen in Russia under the presidential rule of Vladimir Putin. In practice, this involves heavy use of the narrative of victimhood during WWII and ambiguous evaluation of the post-1945 communist regime.[3] The current framing of the Soviet Union and Russia by the Hungarian government is particularly fascinating as regards this latter issue, as the official historical narratives have to walk a careful line between condemning the communist regime whilst keeping the Soviet legacy (and its use in the current Russian official historical narratives) vague enough as to not jeopardise Hungary's newfound friendship with Russia.

In relation to the general framing of the CEE memory wars, it must be noted that the memory politics of the Putin regime in contemporary Russia emphasises the Soviet Union's contribution to the victory over Nazism in WWII, or the 'Great Patriotic War', as a source of national pride and legitimacy. Consequently, the memory laws enacted by this regime emphasise the atrocities perpetrated by the Nazi occupiers, while minimising or denying the responsibility of the Red Army and the Soviet authorities for war crimes and human rights violations against civilians and prisoners of war in Eastern Europe and elsewhere. Moreover, memory politics under the Putin regime also downplay the repressive and violent nature of the communist system that followed the war, consequently creating tensions and conflicts with the post-communist countries of the CEE region that attempt to confront and condemn their communist past.[4] The current dominant mode of memory politics in Hungary, similarly to Putin's Russia, is one of historical instrumentalisation – which often veers into revisionism, whereby the authorities manipulate and distort the past to fit their current interests and disregard or deny any evidence that challenges the state-sanctioned narrative. Hence, WWII is depicted as an honourable fight, while the violations perpetrated by the Soviet forces are excluded, as they are incompatible with the myth of the Red Army's admirable actions of protecting Russia and reclaiming CEE. Hungary has accepted and all but endorsed this Russian narrative, representing the only nation amongst the CEE region to do so.[5]

[2] This is discussed in great detail in: Nikolay Koposov, *Memory Laws, Memory Wars* (Cambridge University Press, 2017).

[3] N Koposov, 'Holocaust Remembrance, the Cult of the War, and Memory Laws in Putin's Russia' in E Barkan and A Lang (eds), *Memory Laws and Historical Justice: The Politics of Criminalizing the Past* (Palgrave Macmillan, 2022).

[4] ibid 132.

[5] T Drinóczi and A Bień-Kacala, *Illiberal Constitutionalism in Poland and Hungary: The Deterioration of Democracy, Misuse of Human Rights and Abuse of the Rule of Law* (Routledge, 2022).

Therefore, this chapter begins with a much-needed examination of the systemic political manipulation of history in Hungary and its implications for historical scholarship and public memory. Following this, it explores the challenges associated with integrating these historical narratives within broader regional and European historical debates and present memory wars, which Hungary has now involved itself in by reframing, purely on a political basis, its official historical narratives. The chapter then traces the evolution of Russia's role in the Hungarian historical and political reality from the late nineteenth century to the present, across different regimes and contexts. In doing so, it subsequently analyses the political exploitation of the Hungarian-Russian relationship in the historical imagination up until its alignment with the current national vision of the Hungarian government. Finally, the chapter concludes by highlighting the dangers of systemic control and the political instrumentalisation of history, using the Hungarian case as a cautionary tale for the erosion of democracy.

II. THE HUNGARIAN GOVERNMENT'S SYSTEMIC CONTROL OVER HISTORY

Hungary is an exemplary case study for exploring the political implications of legal control over historical memory, as it has witnessed a gradual and systematic reinvention of its past in the last decade. This case is remarkable not only for its exceptionally forceful and organised attempt to subordinate the past to the present, but also for its contrast with Hungary's previous status as a stable CEE democracy with membership in several European supranational organisations, which have often expressed their disapproval of its memory laws and policies.[6] The systemic control of legal governance of historical memory in Hungary has been both a contributing factor, and a conspicuous indicator, of the country's democratic and rule of law regression.

The post-2010 regime has exerted an extraordinary and rapid influence over the interpretation of Hungary's historical past, establishing a legal framework for memory politics that is not only exceptional but which could, regrettably, serve as an effective model for others with similar intentions.[7] The government elected in 2010 secured a supermajority and obtained an unprecedented mandate from the electorate which enabled it to legislate and implement its agenda, without the necessity for consultation or cooperation with other political or civil

[6] eg, Venice Commission, 'Opinion on the Fourth Amendment to the Fundamental Law of Hungary (CDL-AD (2013)012-e)' (*European Commission for Democracy Through Law*, June 2013) https://www.venice.coe.int/webforms/documents/default.aspx?pdffile=cdl-ad(2013)012-e.

[7] M Goldberg, 'Florida Could Start Looking a Lot Like Hungary' *New York Times* (New York, 23 February 2023): https://www.nytimes.com/2023/02/27/opinion/desantis-higher-education-bill.html.

society actors.[8] The systemic appropriation of legal governance of historical memory, along with other policy domains, occurred through the abuse of this mandate.

The Hungarian case provides for a compelling analysis of the ways a government can manipulate and dominate the representation and interpretation of history, in three distinct phases, with each phase corresponding to the repeated re-elections of the post-2010 regime. In the first phase, from 2010 to 2014, the government established the foundations of comprehensive systemic control. With its supermajority, the government swiftly initiated a constitutional change which took effect within a year of Fidesz's second ascent to power.[9] The new Constitution, or 'Fundamental Law', extensively instrumentalised history by incorporating core elements of the government's vision. These elements included the primacy of Christianity in Hungarian culture, the narrative of struggle – victimhood, and the defence of Europe as Hungary's historical mission, with the latter stemming from a nostalgia for the more glorious past (especially the Middle Ages, the Austro-Hungarian era and the Interwar period) and the simultaneous rejection and exoneration of the twentieth-century totalitarian past of Nazism and communism.[10] This constitutional document provided the basis for the implementation of changes in every policy area and they involved an intensified decommunization, often extending to revisionist and politicised domains. This manifested in new memory laws and the reshaping of public spaces, such as, renaming streets and replacing monuments.[11] As the 'Fundamental Law' introduced political use of the past into the Hungarian legal system, it enabled the constitutional court to intervene in this perception of the past and to revive and redefine legal and quasi-legal concepts most arbitrarily.

The government's main tactic for achieving systemic control over history in its second term involved two components. First, the Constitutional Court, now subordinated to the Fidesz government, initiatied a series of cases that linked Hungarian history to national identity and attributed the clash between the EU and the state to historical divergences.[12] The government has devised and employed a strategy in the political and legal spheres to enact policy changes

[8] One of the criticisms of the Fundamental Law was the lack of substantial and meaningful involvement of any public force other than the government. See: GA Tóth, *Constitution for a Disunited Nation: On Hungary's 2011 Fundamental Law* (CEU Press, 2012).

[9] Fidesz had already governed Hungary between 1998 and 2002, led by Viktor Orbán in his first premiership. The policies of this government exhibited several initial signs of its eventual post-2010 illiberal turn. See: A Bozóki, 'Mainstreaming the Far-Right: Cultural Politics in Hungary' (2016) 47 *Revue d'études comparatives Est-Ouest* 87.

[10] M Könczöl and I Kevevári, 'History and Interpretation in the Fundamental Law of Hungary' (2020) 5 *European Papers* 161.

[11] The Hungarian Academy of Sciences provided a list, and a law was subsequently enacted to prohibit naming public places after anybody associated with a totalitarian regime (this is the 2012/CLXVII Act on the prohibition of names related to twentieth-century totalitarian regimes).

[12] See cases from the Hungarian Constitutional Court, such as 22/2016 (XII. 5.) and 32/2021 (XII. 20.).

under the guise of social consent. This strategy involves the following steps: (1) identifying and publicising a problem or conflict, usually with the EU, through official statements; (2) disseminating the government's perspective uncritically through media apparatus established between 2010 and 2014; (3) proposing a legislative or constitutional amendment to implement the policy change, often with symbolic rather than substantive value and without adequate legal analysis and planning; (4) resorting to social consultations or referenda to garner social backing, irrespective of the actual effectiveness of the rhetoric; and (5) inviting the Constitutional Court to endorse the government's position and elaborate its jurisprudence based on historical narratives. The European refugee crisis exemplifies this strategy, whereby the Fidesz government portrayed Hungary as a nation culturally averse to non-European immigrants and used this aversion as a pretext for increasingly hostile measures, including a constitutional amendment.[13]

The final consolidation of systemic control over the historical narrative occurred in the third governmental term (2018–22), building on the foundations laid in the previous two terms and manifesting in three interrelated dimensions. The first is through the Constitutional Court, which expanded its jurisprudence on the connection between Hungarian history, identity, and supranational conflicts, reinforcing the constitutional identity doctrine.[14] The second dimension pertains to government intensification of its hostile and discriminatory rhetoric against various minority groups, invoking historical grievances and myths.[15] Finally, the takeover of every policy domain related to the representation and interpretation of history was completed through the following: transformation of public spaces, such as street names, museums, and monuments; establishment of new research institutions or the elimination and subordination of existing ones; comprehensive reform of history education, including the national curriculum and related materials (including textbooks); and the symbolic renaming of several public institutions to evoke the medieval and imperial eras – including the court system, the administrative system and the relocation of some government offices to the Buda Castle, a historical and cultural landmark.[16] Although

[13] The treatment of the refugee crisis in 2014, began with media presence, followed by two constitutional amendments (Amendments 5 and 6) and Constitutional Court cases (see n 12). See for example: C Cantat and PK Rajaram, 'The Politics of the Refugee Crisis in Hungary: Bordering and Ordering the Nation and Its Others' in C Menjívar, M Ruiz and I Ness (eds), *The Oxford Handbook of Migration Crises* (Oxford University Press, 2019).

[14] The aforementioned 32/2021 case (n 12) is an absolutely excellent example, as it establishes a complete historical overview of the Hungarian past in the service of an ultimate message of the protection of the country's sovereignty (paras [101]–[105]).

[15] eg, the medieval Turkish Wars in particular were used to emphasise the present animosity towards Muslim refugees. P Géza, 'A másfél évszázadnyi török uralom mérlege' (*Múlt-Kor*, 15 September 2001): https://mult-kor.hu/20010915_a_masfel_evszazadnyi_torok_uralom_merlege.

[16] New laws have been adopted on reform of the justice system, the administrative system, and historical education, such as the 2017/I Act on the Court of Administrative Court Procedures and the 2012/XCIII Act on the establishment of 'járás' and the amendments of related laws.

repairs to the castle itself would not constitute illiberal or even political acts in themselves, the nature of the proceedings have been heavily criticised – including, for instance, relocation of the National Library and the National Gallery (formerly housed at Buda) in favour of moving government offices into the castle, regarded as another aspect of aggressively-reinvented memory politics.[17]

The political exploitation of historical memory in Hungary was accomplished in little over 10 years. In this context, any aspect of the country's history has been regarded as a potential political weapon which the government does not hesitate to use. The example of Russia's transforming role in this system shows how the constitutional foundation, and the presentation of the role of Russia in the public debate, are adapted to the convenience of current political leadership.

III. THE HUNGARIAN-RUSSIAN RELATIONSHIP: THE POLITICAL REALITY

The pre-2010 memory politics of Hungary largely reflected the historical reality of Russia's involvement in Hungarian affairs. In contrast, after this period, politics shifted to minimise the economic and political risks posed by Russia to the CEE region, and to emphasise the fictitious colonial domination and exploitation by the EU as the main adversary of the Hungarian nation.[18]

The construction of historical narratives by the Hungarian political elites has always relied on the themes of enemies, oppression, and struggle. The genesis of Hungary's historical memory, in the late eighteenth and early nineteenth centuries, assigned these identities to Austria and the Ottoman Empire, which corresponded with the historical facts relating to Hungary's partition between these two empires and its lack of independence since 1526. Thus, the nationalist aspiration for a sovereign Hungarian state mirrored the political reality.

The late nineteenth century witnessed the emergence of the Austro-Hungarian Empire as a political force in the Balkans, where it contested the pan-Slavist ambitions of the Russian Empire. To understand the contemporary misuse of Russia's role in Hungarian memory politics, it is necessary to explore the historical ties and conflicts between these countries. In the early modern period, Hungary had lost its sovereignty and became a part of the Habsburg and Ottoman Empires, while Russia loomed as another major power on its Eastern frontier.[19] On two occasions, in the late eighteenth and early nineteenth centuries, Russia intervened militarily to assist Austria in suppressing Hungarian nationalist rebellions – namely, the Rakóczi Uprising of 1703–11, and the 1848–49 Revolution and

[17] S Makrai, 'Így zajlott le Budavár kormányzati elfoglalása' (*Magyar Hang*, 18 June 2023): https://hang.hu/belfold/budai-var-kormanyzati-negyed-budavar-elfoglalasa-154891.

[18] K Miklóssy and M Kangaspuro, *Conservatism and Memory Politics in Russia and Eastern Europe* (Routledge, 2022) 123.

[19] ibid 110.

War of Independence. Russia's involvement was especially crucial in the latter conflict, which quelled the Hungarian hopes for independence.[20]

The Austro-Hungarian compromise of 1867 marked a significant shift in the political landscape, as it created a dual monarchy that ostensibly shared equal sovereignty between the two constituent states.[21] Throughout the second half of the nineteenth century, the Russian Empire remained a formidable rival in the region, and a series of conflicts ensued where it aligned with different factions – among them the Crimean War of 1853–56, the Bulgarian Uprising of 1876–78, the Russo-Japanese War of 1904–05, and the Balkan Wars of 1912–13.[22] The Hungarian political elite often expressed opposition to Russian interests, at least verbally if not practically, attempting to thwart Russia's influence in the aftermath of the Bulgarian Uprising and supporting Japan in the Russo-Japanese War. During the initial decades of the twentieth century, and especially after the Bolshevik revolution, the Hungarian ruling classes – like numerous local and Western peers – assimilated the peril of communism and Soviet encroachment under Stalin's leadership.[23]

The outcome of World War I, which saw the defeat of Austria-Hungary and the victory of Russia, had a significant impact on the Russian influence on Hungarian affairs. The communist ideology, which had gained adherents in Hungary before and during the conflict, led to the creation of a Soviet-style regime after disintegration of the empire – the short-lived Hungarian People's Republic (*Tanácsköztársaság*), led by Béla Kun.[24] After its defeat, Hungary experienced political turmoil and violence in the post-war period, and by 1920, power eventually shifted to a monarchist elite, headed by Admiral Miklos Horthy. The leader of the People's Republic fled to the Soviet Union to avoid retribution.[25]

During the Interwar period, Hungary was ruled by a conservative-nationalist regime headed by Horthy that aligned itself increasingly with Nazi Germany, despite its strong antipathy and growing apprehension toward the neighbouring Soviet Union.[26] This regime cemented its alliance with Nazi Germany in the early 1940s and joined the invasion of the Soviet Union in June 1941. The Hungarian forces committed various atrocities in Soviet territory, but by the end of the war, the Hungarian Communist Party gained considerable support within the country, attracting both veterans of the first communist republic and new leaders.[27]

[20] ibid 113.

[21] G Vasin, 'Revolutions of 1848 and 1956: Paradigm of Building the National Identity of Hungarians' (2017) (1) *LIMESplus* 9, 15: https://www.ceeol.com/search/article-detail?id=671562.

[22] P Apor, *Fabricating Authenticity in Soviet Hungary: The Afterlife of the First Hungarian Soviet Republic in the Age of State Socialism* (Anthem Press, 2015) 5–7.

[23] Vasin (n 21) 16.

[24] P Hatos 'Rend és rendetlenség 1918-1919-ben' (2021) 21 *Magyar Rendészet* 169.

[25] ibid.

[26] G Gyáni, *A Nation Divided by History and Memory: Hungary in the Twentieth Century and Beyond* (Routledge, 2021) 45.

[27] A Schwarcz 'Teljes elitváltás Magyarországon a második világháború után' (2009) 18 *Politikatudományi Szemle* 117.

The post-1945 expansion of the Soviet sphere of influence in CEE became a political reality that affected Hungary profoundly. In 1948, the communist party seized power with the backing of Soviet troops that had occupied the country since the end of the war. This marked the beginning of a period of increased Soviet intervention in Hungarian politics, in which the Soviet Union played the role of an ally, an overlord, and a quasi-colonial power.[28] The communist political elite endorsed this situation, but the general public, the political opposition, and the dissident movement increasingly perceived Russia as a detrimental force in the country's affairs. This perception was reinforced by the Soviet military suppression of the anti-communist revolution in 1956.[29] Although some national political leaders requested Soviet intervention, the Soviet tanks became emblems of the regime's violence, creating a distinction between the external and internal sources of oppression. Consequently, the communist system was often seen as an imposition from abroad, with the domestic factors that sustained it receiving less scrutiny.

The negotiations of 1989–90 resulted in dissolution of the communist regime and the establishment of a new democratic regime, which entailed two shifts in the perception of Russia's role in Hungarian memory politics. On the one hand, its role as oppressor was reinforced, as the departure of the last Soviet tank from Hungary in July 1991 symbolised the end of the communist era. The 1956 Revolution, which became a central element of the official Hungarian historical narrative, also accentuated opposition to the Soviet intervention. This was further motivated by the aspiration of the Hungarian political elite to align with Western Europe, especially the EU.[30] On the other hand, Hungarian-Russian relations improved significantly, as Boris Yeltsin apologised in the mid-1990s for the violent suppression of the 1956 revolution.[31] Only one political force, Fidesz, explicitly denounced the Soviet Union as an enemy of Hungary and the source of its woes, while the rest (although conforming to the anti-communist sentiment of the 1990s) refrained from labelling Russia as an oppressor of Hungary.[32]

Hungary's democratic transition raised the issue of confronting its past – not only the preceding communist regime but also other historical events that had been suppressed or distorted by the dictatorship, such as the imperial legacy, the 1920 Treaty of Trianon, the Interwar period, and WWII.[33] In the 1990s, the

[28] Miklóssy and Kangaspuro (n 18) 110.

[29] Apor (n 22) 61.

[30] Gyáni (n 26) 93.

[31] Miklóssy and Kangaspuro (n 18) 115.

[32] G Yankov, 'Can the Memory of a Historical Uprising Reduce Transitional Uncertainty? A Comparative Study of Hungary and the Former Soviet Union' (2008) 16 *Demokratizatsiya: The Journal of Post-Soviet Democratization* 183, 187.

[33] G Gyáni, 'Hungarian Memory of the Holocaust in Hungary' in RL Braham and A Kovács (eds), *The Holocaust in Hungary: Seventy Years Later* (CEU Press, 2016) 226. See also: N Wouters, 'The Use of History in the Field of Transitional Justice: A Critical Introduction' in N Wouters (ed), *Transitional Justice and Memory in Europe (1945–2013)* (Intersentia, 2017) 9.

new democratic regime acknowledged the Holocaust and restored the memory of the 1956 Revolution, but did not address these historical questions in depth. A Committee of Historical Justice, established in 1988, failed to produce any significant results. The first Fidesz government, in power from 1998 to 2002, attempted to revise the official historical narratives but was met with political and public resistance. However, their efforts foreshadowed the changes that would occur after 2010.[34]

Fidesz, upon later regaining power, invoked this historical disengagement as the main justification for a comprehensive systemic change in the official representation and interpretation of Hungary's past. His government argued that the 1989–90 transition was a flawed and incomplete shift to democracy that preserved many elements of the former regime, and that the genuine democratic revolution occurred in 2010, with Fidesz' victory. Therefore, Fidesz has undertaken a 'grand memory project' to enact this true transition.[35]

It can be surmised that until 2010, the role of Russia in Hungarian memory politics was subtly altered to fit the international geopolitical situation, however it always kept its foundational aspects of opposition – ie, Hungary positioning itself as belonging to the West, in contrast to Russia which is interpreted as part of the East.

IV. RUSSIA IN HUNGARIAN MEMORY LAWS AND POLITICS: MANUFACTURED NARRATIVES

In the latter half of the 2010s, Fidesz reversed its stance and cultivated a close relationship with Russia, generating a peculiar inconsistency in Hungarian politics, namely, belonging to the EU and professing democratic ideals, whilst lauding the Russian regime. The government's gestures of friendship to Russia multiplied and became repetitive, and consequently, a distortion of all memory laws and related policies followed in this direction.

Fidesz' new memory politics exhibited a profound double-sidedness in their anti-communist but pro-Russian orientation. Projects such as the Statue Park in Budapest simultaneously 'disavowed and commodified the communist past', while others such as the House of Terror (established during Fidesz's first term of office) emphasised its horrors. The 1956 Revolution remained the cornerstone of the new memory policies as a symbol of national defiance against the Soviets (and other foreign powers in general), but, in conjunction with institutions – such as the House of Terror and the 2013 Memorial to the Victims of Hungary's German Occupation – it also reinforced a 'history of double occupation' and a culture of resistance, subjugation, and victimhood, without

[34] R Uitz, 'The Incomplete Transition in Hungary' in Wouters (n 33) 291.
[35] N Wouters, 'Transitional Justice and Memory Development in Europe' in Wouters (n 33) 384.

substantial engagement and consideration of the historical details.[36] Fidesz' memory politics were driven by a form of 'moral revisionism' that either vindicated Hungary's historical grievances and sufferings or attributed any historical wrongdoing to a coerced compromise. Both of these narratives were used to reframe the role of Russia and the Soviet Union.[37]

A. From Rival to Oppressor to Friend

The following analyses examine the dramatic transformation of the bilateral relations between Hungary and Russia in the 2010s, as well as the implications of this shift for Hungarian memory politics. The current government has adopted a convenient narrative of Russia as a minor historical suppressor of Hungarian uprisings while comparing its relatively minor role in the nineteenth century to the main threat to the Austro-Hungarian Empire coming from the Western powers (specifically Britain and France). Russia's Eastern presence was a constant factor, but not a primary enemy, in the Hungarian national imagination.[38] Thus, this aspect of the past did not require significant revision in the present.

During the initial five decades of the twentieth century, the political influence of Russia diminished considerably in Hungary, obviating the need for significant adjustments. The historical legacy of Hungary's first communist republic is frequently disregarded, as anti-communist endeavours concentrate on the post-1945 era. Consequently, this communist episode of Hungarian history is often overlooked and the Russian impact potentially easily dismissed.

The post-1945 period is the source of the most significant changes in memory policy initiated by the Fidesz government. It has employed three strategies to diminish the evaluation of the Soviet presence and rationalise the Russian alignment to its electorate – whilst some seek to reshape the domestic perception of the communist past, others target the relations with Russia. First, the Hungarian government – after 2010 – completely reinterpreted the legacy of the 1956 Revolution.[39] In the aftermath of the democratic transition in the 1990s, this uprising had become emblematic of Hungarian resistance to Soviet domination and the collapse of communism. The revolution was celebrated as a national holiday and as a glorious example in two ways – showing homage to moderate communist figures, such as Prime Minister Imre Nagy who was executed after the suppression of the revolt, and the commemoration of the often anonymous, mostly young, students and citizens who confronted Soviet tanks on the streets

[36] M Nadkarni, *Remains of Socialism: Memory and Futures of the Past in Postsocialist Hungary* (Cornell University Press, 2020) 117.
[37] M Kopeček (ed), *Past in the Making: Historical Revisionism in Central Europe after 1989* (CEU Press, 2008) 169–76.
[38] Miklóssy and Kangaspuro (n 18) 110.
[39] ibid 114.

of Budapest.[40] The Fidesz government has started to significantly understate the reverence for the moderate communist figures during the revolution and has started to emphasise the anonymous heroes of the uprising.[41] Although this approach might not necessarily be detrimental on the surface, a case could be made that the reassessment of the legacy of 1956 is at least questionable, if not evolving into historical revisionism. Coupled with the reassessment of notable figures of the democratic transition whose achievements have been similarly diminished without much true academic examination, this reinterpretation seems merely political without much historical merit.

The legacy of the 1956 Revolution and its prominent figures has also been subjected to revisionism, especially regarding those who advocated for liberal, pro-European values in their subsequent political careers. A case in point is that of Árpád Göncz, the first president of the democratic Hungarian Republic, who had participated in the 1956 uprising and was later elected as the candidate of the Alliance of Free Democrats (a liberal party) in 1990. He was widely respected for his commitment to democracy, the rule of law, and human rights, as well as his support for European integration. However, his name has been gradually erased from official 1956 commemorations and his image tarnished, as a controversial figure who overreached his presidential duties and power in favour of the liberal party he belonged to before his election. The role of the Soviet Union in crushing the 1956 Revolution has also been downplayed, as the narrative focuses on the Hungarian people's resistance against the domestic communist regime, ignoring Soviet military intervention. The memorial to the Red Army soldiers in Budapest, which is highly controversial among many Hungarians, has been left intact (while other symbols of communism and Soviet influence have been removed from the public space). Furthermore, the government has attempted to distinguish between contemporary Russia and the Soviet Union. Although this distinction is valid, the rhetoric of the Soviet Union as the oppressor has been revived in another context of memory politics – ie, the portrayal of the EU as a looming threat from the West. Since 2017, the government has intensified its anti-EU discourse and propaganda, depicting it as an enemy of Hungarian sovereignty and identity.[42]

As commemoration of the Holocaust became more widespread and emphatic worldwide, Hungary adopted the imperative of 'never forgetting' the genocide but also replicated some of its problematic features, such as exonerating local collaborators and attributing all crimes to the German invaders. The House of Terror Museum epitomises this mode of remembrance.[43]

[40] Yankov (n 32) 187.

[41] The previous iconic figure of the Revolution – communist politician, Imre Nagy – has been increasingly replaced with the myth of the 'Boys of Pest' – often-nameless young boys who fought on the barricades of Budapest against Soviet tanks.

[42] Miklóssy and Kangaspuro (n 18) 123.

[43] M Kovács, 'Global and local Holocaust remembrance' in Braham and Kovács (n 33) 235.

Subsequent endeavours to ameliorate the perception of Russia, unexpectedly, were contingent on the extensive decommunisation initiated after 2010. The Fidesz government – having invoked the notion that the democratic transition was deficient as more reformist communists retained and regained power – proclaimed 2010 as the veritable culmination of the democratic transition and commenced a purge of communist organisations, institutions, toponyms, and monuments.[44]

In addition, the 2022 Russian war of aggression against Ukraine further brought to light the altered role of Russia in the Hungarian political system. Although the Hungarian government joined the initial European condemnation of Russia's conduct, its enthusiasm did not last long and by the first anniversary of the war's commencement, the tone of its resolutions changed considerably.[45] Whilst they advocated for peace, they have contained subtle hints about the overreach of EU action and the misuse of financial support on the part of Ukraine. In addition, the Hungarian government-funded press continues to spread pro-Russian propaganda about the war's causes as well as developments in the country.[46]

B. Flipping the Script: The EU, from Friend to Enemy

With the end of the 2010s approaching, the political alignment of Russia as Hungary's partner and supporter in opposition to the purported colonisation by the EU and the West considerably strengthened.[47] The construction of the EU coloniser narrative can be seen as a response to the shifting position of Russia. Accordingly, Fidesz pursued a cultural conflict to reinterpret Hungary's history by using the concept of 'defensive national identity', meaning that Hungary's conventional and national culture required protection from Western

[44] Prime Minister Orbán has claimed on multiple occasions that Hungary's real democratic transition only began in 2010. See, for example: https://mandiner.hu/belfold/2014/05/orban-2010-ben-valodi-rendszervaltas-tortent (23 May 2014).

[45] The first law on the conflict: 2022. évi XLII. törvény a szomszédos országban fennálló fegyveres konfliktus, illetve humanitárius katasztrófa magyarországi következményeinek elhárításáról és kezeléséről (Act on the military conflict in a neighbouring state and the consequential prevention and management of humanitarian disaster in Hungary).

[46] The commemorative resolution on the first anniversary of the war: 5/2023. (III. 31.) OGY határozat az orosz-ukrán háború egyéves évfordulójáról (Decree on the first anniversary of the Russo-Ukrainian War). Furthermore, the Hungarian government has blocked, on multiple occasions, both the accession attempts of Sweden to NATO, and the initiation of EU accession negotiations with Ukraine. See András Iván, 'Az Egyesült Államok csalódott Orbán Ukrajna-politikája miatt, a svéd NATO-tagság ratifikálását szorgalmazza' (*Telex*, 11 January 2024): https://telex.hu/kulfold/2024/01/11/orban-usa-ukrajna-svedorszag-tamogatas-nato-tagsag.

[47] A Ágh, 'Cultural war and reinventing the past in Poland and Hungary' (2016) 45(1) *Polish Political Science Yearbook* 32, 33.

liberalisation.[48] These efforts were reflected by a growing emphasis on the safeguarding of national sovereignty.

These efforts intensified, especially in 2014–15, amid the European migration crisis. Hungary's xenophobic rejection of any refugees engendered two public political-historical narratives. From the moment of its second ascent to power, Fidesz has invoked the conventional framing of Hungary as the protector of Christian Europe from invasion, stemming from the heritage of medieval conflicts between the Hungarian Kingdom and the Ottoman Empire. Such a narrative has enabled the legitimisation of measures such as erecting barriers, discrimination, and inferior treatment of asylum seekers at the border.

Furthermore, the Hungarian government has adopted a revised understanding of the EU's role in Hungarian history and politics in response to attempts to compel its Member States to share the responsibility of resettling refugees through various measures. While the EU was initially perceived as a Western model, ally, and defender of Hungary upon its accession to Member State status, the Union was subsequently portrayed as a tyrant, an imperial power seeking to colonise (culturally, if not politically) Hungary through imposition of its values and erasure of traditional Hungarian culture. Hence, the government claims to act as the guardian of Hungary's sovereignty and independence by refusing to implement numerous EU directives and initiatives, and passing constitutional amendments to prevent any further infringements. These actions have been backed by an increasing number of judgments from the Constitutional Court, which invoked Hungary's historical legacy to legitimise these governmental actions.

Therefore, Hungarian political discourse in the 2020s has undergone a reversal in terms of the roles and legacies of Russia, the Soviet Union and the EU. This reversal, however, lacks any grounding in political reality, as the source of the challenge to Hungary's sovereignty has not been the West. The recent minimisation of the impact and gravity of the war in Ukraine illustrates this by demonstrating how historical narratives have been entirely subordinated and shaped by political objectives in Hungary.

V. CONCLUSIONS

The political manipulation of Russia's historical legacy in Hungary coincides with a systematic distortion of memory and the strategic use of history for ideological purposes, which has reached an extreme degree of revisionism and propaganda. The role of Russia in this process can serve as an illustrative example of this dynamic. In Hungary, legal frameworks, especially the laws regulating public representation of the past, have become a discretionary instrument in the

[48] ibid 39.

hands of the ruling elite. The official version of history is imposed through state-controlled institutions such as the 'Committee of National Remembrance' and newly-established research centres. The government's narrative focuses on the communist period, but only superficially and selectively. Instead of being critically examined, it is exploited as a convenient scapegoat and distraction from other political agendas.[49]

History has not been immune to pragmatic and political instrumentalisation in Hungary, as successive governments have sought to control narratives of the past. This tendency has been especially pronounced due to the ambivalent relationship that the changing political regime has with historical events. This has been illustrated by the commemoration of several historical events, including the 1956 Revolution, whose legacy is increasingly emptied of its meaning by its symbolic appropriation by both Hungarian democracy and the current regime; and the democratic transition of 1989–90, whose legacy is similarly hollowed out and distorted by its misuse in the present. In this way, historical events and figures acquire an ideological function in each political system.[50]

By contesting liberal democracy, resisting supranational integration, and exploiting media and other instruments of mass persuasion and manipulation, the Hungarian regime can shape and constrain collective memory, especially in the absence of a successful pan-European memory project.[51] While subtle changes in the interpretation of Russia's place in Hungarian memory laws and politics occurred before 2010, in the years following, depending on the European and global political situation, the Hungarian government has risked almost complete political isolation due to its ardent and consistent support of Russia and it policies.[52] As Russia shifts from a perilous neighbour to a model and partner, Hungary becomes vulnerable to adopting its own historical distortions about its memory conflicts with Ukraine (and, to a lesser degree, Poland and the Baltic states) and to acquiring the status of 'collaborator' in Russia's memory war against Europe.

[49] Barkan and Lang (n 3) 251.

[50] Gyáni (n 26) 115.

[51] G Soroka and F Krawatzek, 'Circulation, Conditions, Claims: Examining the Politics of Historical Memory in Eastern Europe' (2022) 20(1) *East European Politics and Societies: and Cultures* 212.

[52] Z Sz Bíró, 'Az orbáni retorika arra épül, hogy Oroszország nem veszíthet' (*444.hu*, 15 January 2024): https://www.youtube.com/watch?v=fcrqozdvHO4.

11

Finnish-Russian Memory Conflicts before and after the Outbreak of Russo-Ukrainian War

TUOMAS FORSBERG

I. INTRODUCTION

RUSSIA'S FULL-SCALE INVASION of Ukraine in February 2022 can be seen as the culmination of a long trend in the history-driven political imagination of Russia's leaders and security elite. Arguably, the war on Ukraine reflects 'retro-politics': Russia's attempt to restore its lost status as a leading global power, rectify perceived past wrongdoings and humiliations, and reinstitute an entire patriotic and conservative historical narrative of the country's past and its place in the world order.[1] Therefore Russia's mnemopolitical challenge does not restrict itself to Ukraine or to domestic politics, it spills over into its attitudes towards its neighbours and interactions in international relations.

The fundamental question underlying all memory conflicts is, to what extent is history an instrument of conflict, or rather the root cause?[2] In Russia's case it is often both, but we cannot presume that Russia's policy is always driven by history or that it will always 'weaponise' history in its relations with other countries.[3] In the post-Cold War era, Russian leaders were willing to mitigate problems pertaining to the past and were able to restore relations with its

[1] See eg T Sherlock, 'Russian politics and the Soviet past: Reassessing Stalin and Stalinism under Vladimir Putin' (2016) 49 *Communist and Post-Communist Studies* 45; F Hill and C Gaddy, 'Putin and the Uses of History' (2012) 117 *The National Interest* 21. For 'retropolitics', see: S Medvedev, *A War Made in Russia* (Polity Press, 2023) 21.

[2] K Bachleitner, 'Diplomacy with Memory: How the Past Is Employed for Future Foreign Policy' (2019) 15 *Foreign Policy Analysis* 492; L Klymenko, 'The International Politics of Memory' in *Oxford Research Encyclopedias* (Oxford University Press, 2022); M Mälksoo, '"Memory must be defended": Beyond the politics of mnemonical security' (2015) 46 *Security Dialogue* 221.

[3] A Shcherbak, 'Russia's "conservative turn" after 2012: evidence from the European Social Survey' (2022) 39 *East European Politics* 194–219.

former enemies, at least partly, by seeking mutually satisfactory evidence-based approaches. However, Russia's so-called 'conservative turn' that became salient when Vladimir Putin assumed his third presidency in 2012, the annexation of Crimea in 2014, and particularly, Russian's invasion of Ukraine in 2022 reopened many historical wounds. Moreover, the confrontation with the West intensified Russia's instrumental use of history in its foreign policy.

This chapter discusses memory conflicts in Russia's relations with Finland. This is an interesting case because in the post-Cold War era, historical memory conflicts in Russo-Finnish bilateral relations were mostly seen as overcome compared to Russia's more contentious relations with the Baltic states and Poland.[4] The lack of mnemonic tensions between the two neighbours was, however, not a result of the past being devoid of sensitive issues; on the contrary, they were largely compartmentalised and avoided at the highest level. As a result, the relations were rather stable and friendly. Finland was a member of the EU, which created its own tensions with Russia, but it had not yet joined NATO. This all changed when Russia started to demand new spheres of influence in Europe and launched its attack on Ukraine in the winter of 2021–22: Russia labelled Finland an unfriendly country, while Finland strongly condemned Russia, participating in the sanctions against it and subsequently joining NATO in 2023.

The main argument of this chapter is that memory conflicts in Russo-Finnish relations have evolved in four stages. The first stage was reconciliation right after the Cold War, when the parties agreed on key historical interpretations. The second stage was compartmentalisation, when historical issues were dealt with by the public and various interest groups mostly in a cooperative spirit, with the past no longer on the political agenda. The third stage was Russia's conservative turn, when Russian interpretations of history began to erode the pre-established agreement, though they did not disturb the fundamentals of the relationship. The fourth stage started with Russia's full-scale war against Ukraine, when the instrumentalisation of history also started to become more pronounced in Russia's relations with Finland. During this stage Finns also adopted more essentialist views of Russia on the basis of its past and reinterpreted the mutual relationship by stressing the permanence of conflict and threat rather than friendship and cooperation. The present tensions in public and collective memory may be followed by a more antagonistic mnemopolitical stage, but so far interpretations of history have *reflected* overall tensions in the relationship rather than *driven* them. However, the revival of national identities and images looking to the past may impede reconciliation even after the Russo-Ukrainian war is over.

[4] See: T Forsberg, 'Overcoming Memory Conflicts: Russia, Finland and the Second World War' in B Törnqvist-Plewa (ed), *Conflicting Memories on Contemporary Europe* (De Gruyter, 2016) 37–64.

II. MEMORY CONFLICTS BETWEEN STATES

Disputes over history are often seen as contributing to unfriendly relations and tensions between nations. Historical problems in international relations most typically derive from wars of aggression, massacres and other war crimes, grave human rights violations, deportations, lost territory or cultural property. Nevertheless, the material losses and their compensation are not necessarily at the heart of memory conflicts; rather, there tends to be some form of factual and normative disagreement over what actually happened or who was responsible for what.[5]

Historical disputes vary in their manifestations and effects.[6] Historical wrongdoings are often seen as traumas that affect the national psyche negatively. This may lead to the avoidance of the source of the trauma and therefore impede cooperation. Historical wrongdoings are also seen as moral questions that may need to be resolved even after a long time has passed.[7] Culpability for past wrongdoings should not be swept away nor past deeds distorted, even when it is no longer possible to convict anyone or compensate the victims. Historical problems can hence burden relations between states because one state wants some kind of justice for perceived historical wrongs. Furthermore, memory conflicts can restrict cooperation and increase conflicts between states because of the way in which they interpret history and deal with their past wrongdoings, with the latter often being seen as a sign of their trustworthiness and intentions.[8] The way history is treated is hence a clue used to judge the propensity of a state to deceive or employ violence in mutual relations, much in the same way as respect for human rights or other principles of democracy are used as signs of the regime's transparency and commitment to shared norms. Moreover, historical problems can affect the present relations negatively because they provide material for identity building and thus possess important elements in 'othering' the other party and making enemy images.[9]

There are also different mechanisms for solving memory conflicts depending on how we see the mutual past influencing the relationship, by hindering cooperation or triggering conflict. Because emotions and rationality play different roles depending on the nature of the historical problem, there is no single route to reconciliation and improved relations. Healing from trauma through mourning

[5] J Jedlicki, 'Historical memory as a source of conflicts in Eastern Europe' (1999) 32 *Communist and Post-Communist Studies* 225.

[6] For this section, see: T Forsberg, 'Overcoming Memory Conflicts' (n 4) and T Forsberg, 'The Philosophy and Practice of Dealing with the Past: Some Conceptual and Normative Issues' in N Biggar (ed), *Burying the Past: Making Peace and Doing Justice After Civil Conflict* (Georgetown University Press, 2001) 57–72.

[7] WJ Booth, 'The Unforgotten: Memories of Justice' (2001) 95 *American Political Science Review* 777.

[8] J Lind, *Sorry States: Apologies in International Politics* (Cornell University Press, 2008).

[9] Y He, *The Search for Reconciliation: Sino-Japanese and German-Polish Relations since World War II* (Cambridge University Press, 2009).

and 'getting even' in moral terms are heavy emotional processes. Settling the issue from the perspective of justice is also a complex issue involving emotions and rational arguments.[10] Judging the other state's interpretations of historical wrongdoings and efforts to show contrition is a cognitive process through which intentions and capabilities to mobilise resources are revealed. Finally, identity formation affects the relationship in a more habitual way in terms of the background thinking that constitutes and shapes the image of the 'other'.

I will return to these four types of historical problems (traumas, concern for historical justice, clues concerning present intentions, and identity formation) causing memory conflicts between states and nations, at the end of this chapter. Let us keep the framework in the background for now, however, and examine the role of problems pertaining to history and the evolution of collective memories in Russo-Finnish relations.

III. PROBLEMS CONCERNING THE PAST IN RUSSO-FINNISH RELATIONS

The historical relationship between Russia and Finland can be interpreted both negatively and positively. There have been enough wars, atrocities, and abuses of power between the two neighbours to give rise to a negative story. However, there have also been long periods of peace and cooperation that can be seen as constitutive of a positive story.

The Finns conceive that they have had a long history of wars with Russia, since they understand the era of Swedish rule as being part of the history of the nation. The Swedish wars against Russia – the Northern War (1701–21), the War of the Hats (1741–43), and the Finnish War (1808–09, which led to Russian occupation of Finland) – are part of the Finnish collective memory. However, the nineteenth-century era of Finland as part of the Russian Empire has much more positive connotations in the public and collective memory, as it enabled the rise of Finnish statehood. Only the period of Russification towards the end of that era has negative associations in the national memory. It is WWII, and the Winter War of 1939–40 in particular, that has been deeply ingrained in the national memory as constituting Soviet aggression towards an innocent victim. Finland was saved from Soviet occupation, but, as a result of the subsequent peace treaty of March 1940, Finland lost the Karelian Isthmus and other territories adjacent to the Russian border, including what was Finland's second largest city, Vyborg. More than 400,000 people lost their homes and were resettled in the remaining Finnish territories. The Winter War was followed by the so-called Continuation War (1941–44) in which Finland joined the German attack against the Soviet Union, initially regained the lost territories, and occupied Eastern Karelia, only to ultimately lose the war.

[10] C Lu, *Justice and Reconciliation in World Politics* (Cambridge University Press, 2017).

The 1940 borders, plus some additional changes, were confirmed in the peace treaties of 1944 and 1947. Thirteen Finnish politicians – among them wartime President, Risto Ryti, but not Marshall Carl Gustaf Mannerheim, who the Soviet leaders trusted as a peacemaker – were deemed responsible for the war in a domestic trial and subsequently convicted. In the Finnish national memory and in its history writing after WWII, the views expressed reflected not only the security threat that the Soviet Union constituted to Finland but also Finland's own culpability and wrongdoings. Despite territorial and human losses, the outcome of the war was seen as a defensive victory given that national independence was preserved.[11]

The Russian view of its historical relationship with Finland is naturally much more benign when it comes to its own role, as for the most part, the past wars with Sweden were not seen as being waged against Finland. Russia regarded itself as a benevolent power towards Finland during the Russian Empire, both in 1917 when Lenin granted Finland its independence, and during the Cold War period. In the Soviet times, WWII was interpreted exclusively through the prism of the 'Great Patriotic War' where Finland's main culpability lay in its stubborn attitude before the war and in joining the German invasion of the Soviet Union in June 1941. The Winter War was mainly disregarded as a minor border war that was strategically necessary for the defence of Leningrad before the 'Great Patriotic War'. The very existence of the secret protocol of the Molotov–Ribbentrop Pact with Nazi Germany, which allocated Finland to the Soviet sphere of interest, was denied. Moreover, in the official Soviet narrative, the Winter War was initiated by Finnish armed forces opening fire across the border on the Karelian Isthmus. The Soviet side thus read history backwards: the fact that Finland allied with Germany in 1941 justified the previous war and the territorial annexations, as anticipatory measures.

After WWII, Finland conducted a policy of friendship in its relations with the Soviet Union. In Finnish foreign policy, this required the avoidance of possible provocative issues and led to a certain self-censorship in public discussion and remembrance known as 'Finlandization'.[12] In particular, the territorial issue and Soviet atrocities against civilians in the war were taboo. The Soviet Union, however, did not insist on any full control of Finnish historiography, school teaching or public discussion. For example, when an attempt was made by some Marxist educational reformers in the 1970s to introduce the Soviet version of

[11] P Torsti, *Suomalaiset ja historia* [*The Finns and History*] (Gaudeamus, 2012). T Tepora, 'Toisen maailmansodan muistokulttuuri – kommunikatiivisesta muistamisesta kulttuuriseen muistiin' ['The Memory Culture of WWII – from Communicative Remembrance to Cultural Memory'] in T Tallberg, A Ojajärvi, and T Laukkanen (eds), *Puolustuskannalla – yhteiskuntatieteellistä ja historiallista tutkimusta maanpuolustuksesta ja asevelvollisuudesta*. Julkaisuja 197 (Nuorisotutkimusverkosto/ Nuorisotutkimusseura, 2017) 127–44.

[12] See: T Forsberg and M Pesu, 'The "Finlandization" of Finland: The Ideal Type, the Historical Model, and the Lessons Learned' (2016) 27 *Diplomacy and Statecraft* 473.

the Winter War in school teaching as the correct interpretation, it was quickly denounced in Finland.[13]

Finland and the Soviet Union were largely able to mitigate the history problems in the Cold War era, though they were not able to solve them. They were only rarely on the political agenda between the states during the Cold War, but there was no real reconciliation based on joint historical memory either. Memories of injustice and suffering had not disappeared with the passage of time, but in spite of this, the neighbours sought to base their mutual relationship on cooperation rather than conflict.

IV. THE RUSSO-FINNISH RECONCILIATION AFTER THE COLD WAR

The Soviet interpretations of WWII only slightly changed in the 1980s following Mikhail Gorbachev's policy of *glasnost* that permitted more press freedom. Some leading Soviet war historians, such as Dmitri Volkogonov, argued that the Winter War was Stalin's fault, but the issue was still sensitive in the eyes of the majority of the old Soviet establishment. In the press, new revisionist interpretations challenging the established narratives of the Winter War emerged only in the autumn of 1989.[14] When Gorbachev visited Finland in October 1989, it was a matter of speculation as to whether he would address the Winter War in his speech. An acknowledgement that the Soviet Union had started the Winter War was dropped at the last minute, and Gorbachev simply referred to the important lessons that both countries had drawn from the tragedy of 1939–44.[15] In December 1989, soon after Gorbachev's visit to Finland, the secret protocol of the Molotov–Ribbentrop pact was condemned by the Soviet Congress.[16]

Although Gorbachev did not acknowledge that the Soviet Union had initiated the Winter War in 1939, Finns were nevertheless pleased that the 50th anniversary of the war could be commemorated in November 1989 without the fear of negative consequences. The state leadership preferred to keep a low profile, but regardless, the political restraints that had hampered public debate about historical interpretations of the war were broken. The Finnish leaders who had been convicted in 1946 as responsible for the war were rehabilitated and regarded as patriotic heroes. Discussion about the lost Karelian and other territories started, but attempts to return the ceded lands did not gain the support

[13] See: 'Pirkkala handout' on Wikipedia, 'Pirkkala handout' (2024): https://en.wikipedia.org/wiki/Pirkkala_handout.

[14] T Vihavainen, *Marssi Helsinkiin – Suomen talvisota neuvostolehdistössä* (Tammi, 1990).

[15] J Blomberg, *Vakauden kaipuu. Kylmän sodan loppu ja Suomi* [*Yearning After Stability: The End of the Cold War and Finland*] (WSOY, 2011).

[16] K Sato, 'Acknowledgement of the Secret Protocol of the German–Soviet Non-aggression Pact and the Declaration of State Sovereignty by the Union Republics of the USSR' (2014) 66 *Europe-Asia Studies* 1146–64.

of leading politicians, who argued that peace treaties could not be renegotiated. Moreover, they believed that the pre-war border, should Karelia be returned, would constitute a constant security problem. Some other former taboo issues were broken too: for example, the war crimes of Soviet partisans against the Finnish civilians in Lapland re-emerged in light of new research.[17] Despite the neo-patriotic wave in historiography, no single perspective dominated but studies containing critical views of the Finnish role in the Continuation War and cooperation with Nazi Germany were also published.

For Finnish politicians, it was more important to safeguard national freedom and to discuss traumatic issues of history domestically than to ask Russia to apologise or show remorse. In practice, Finland tried to facilitate border crossings, create opportunities for evacuees and veterans to visit old home sites or war theatres, and to renovate cemeteries and other cultural monuments. Without making it a big issue, the Finnish government also encouraged joint Finnish-Russian research projects on WWII.

Overall, Russia's politics of history and its policy towards Finland under President Yeltsin was conciliatory. When Yeltsin visited Finland in the summer of 1992, he laid a wreath at the grave of the fallen war heroes in Helsinki and spontaneously declared that he was sorry for the Winter War during his dinner speech. During the visit, the Finnish president, Mauno Koivisto, himself a war veteran, had a chance to explain the Finnish war history and the collective memories to Yeltsin face-to-face. Finland and Russia concluded a treaty on preserving graveyards and war monuments. After the visit, Koivisto felt that most of the pressure of these historical problems had been removed from Russo-Finnish relations. Koivisto was not at all eager to raise any border issues, and he advised Yeltsin to take the Finnish public debate on the lost territories of Karelia 'calmly and in a spirit of friendship'.[18] In May 1994, during then president, Martti Ahtisaari's visit to Russia, Yeltsin publicly admitted that the Winter War had been part of the offensive policy of Stalin's totalitarian regime. In the official dinner speech during the visit, Ahtisaari gave credit to Yeltsin for his 'determination to close the bitter pages once and for all' and reaffirmed that Yeltsin's conciliatory gestures during his 1992 visit to Finland were valued by Finns.[19] Later on, Yeltsin started to be concerned about public discussion regarding the lost territories in Finland and demanded that the Finns stop discussing the issue.

[17] V Erkkilä, *Vaiettu sota. Neuvostoliiton Partisaanien iskut suomalaisiin kyliin* [*The Silenced War: The Attacks of the Soviet Partisans to the Finnish Villages*] (Arator, 1998).

[18] M Koivisto, *Witness to History: The Memoirs of Mauno Koivisto, President of Finland 1982–94* (Hurst & Company, 1997) 250; A Mansala, 'Kaotiska år i Moskva – en tid av ömsesidig anpassning i finsk-ryska relationer 1992–1996' in M Bergquist and AW Johansson (eds), *Säkerhetspolitik och historia. Essäer om stormaktspolitiken och Norden under sjuttio år* (Hjalmarson & Högberg, 2007) 245–62.

[19] M Ahtisaari, 'Speech by Mr Martti Ahtisaari, The President of The Republic of Finland at a State Dinner in Moscow' (*Presidentti.fi*, 18 May 1994): https://www.presidentti.fi/ahtisaari/puheet-1994/p9405.moe.html; see also: T Forsberg, 'Karelia' in T Forsberg (ed), *Contested Territory: Border Disputes at the Edge of the Former Soviet Empire* (Edward Elgar Publishing, 1995) 202–23.

There was no major political debate on the issue, but Ahtisaari, who was born in Vyborg before the war, had stated that the annexation of Karelia by the Soviet Union was seen as a matter of great injustice in Finland. To Yeltsin he affirmed that he was the last man to forbid any discussion of Karelia in Finland.[20]

V. THE COMPARTMENTALISATION OF THE PAST IN RUSSO-FINNISH RELATIONS

President Vladimir Putin continued Yeltsin's conciliatory approach towards a mutual history with Finland. This reflected his general policy at the time of improving Russia's relations with the West. During his visit to Finland in September 2001, he placed a wreath at the cross of the war heroes and visited the grave of the Finnish War Marshall Carl Gustav Mannerheim. This is not as perplexing as it might first seem. Although Mannerheim symbolised the Finnish struggle against the Soviet Union, he was also a former General of the Russian Imperial Army, having participated in the Russo-Japanese war, the First World War and the Russian Civil War – though as a sympathiser with the White Russian counterrevolution against the Bolsheviks. In 2004, when meeting President Tarja Halonen in Moscow, Putin repeated that the Winter War was a mistake by Stalin. However, he also opined that the discussion about Karelia in Finland was detrimental and emphasised that the borders could not be changed because there were too many similar territorial questions elsewhere.[21]

The Karelian question and other problems of the past were not at all central goals for Finnish leaders or diplomats. Instead, they focused on trade, the environment, and developing overall relations between the EU and Russia, for example, by facilitating border crossings.[22] President Halonen contrasted the Finns to the Baltic peoples, whose attitude towards Russia she regarded as reflecting historical trauma.[23] By the same token, it was not seen as controversial that the Finnish leaders participated in the commemorative events of WWII in Moscow. The Karelian question is a good example of how difficult questions in Russo-Finnish relations were handled. Although the issue of lost territories

[20] K Koponen, 'Jeltsin kehotti suomalaisia lopettamaan Karjala-keskustelun. Ahtisaaren mielestä Suomen kansalaisilla on oikeus puhua mistä haluavat' ['Yeltsin urged Finns to end the Karelia debate. Ahtisaari believes that Finnish citizens have the right to talk about what they want'] (*Helsingin Sanomat*, 28 November 1997): https://www.hs.fi/suomi/art-2000003678496.html.

[21] 'Путин встревожен и расстроен' (*Russki Reporter*, 31 January 2011): http://rusrep.ru/article/2011/01/31/putin_fin/.

[22] See: A Mansala, *Kohti Kaaoksen pitkää yötä. Kolme kautta Moskovassa* [*Towards the Long Night of Chaos: Three Terms in Moscow*] (WSOY, 2015) 448. See also: P Sutela, 'Finnish relations with Russia 1991–2001: Better than ever?' (*BOFIT Online* no 11. Bank of Finland, Institute of Economies in Transition, 2001): https://publications.bof.fi/bitstream/handle/10024/44997/101324.pdf?sequence=1&isAllowed=y.

[23] 'Tarja Halonen aiheutti kohun Virossa' ['Tarja Halonen caused a stir in Estonia'] (*YLE*, 10 September 2008): https://yle.fi/a/3-5851625.

was kept alive by civic associations of refugees and a number of politicians and pundits, the issue became politically marginal.[24] Tabloids would occasionally publish headlines on various opinion surveys or proposals to start negotiations over the lost territories with Russia, but none of the leading politicians wanted to officially place the issue on the agenda. The share of Finns who considered it very desirable for the lost territories to be returned shrank to under 10 per cent.[25] Memories of WWII continued to be core material for Finnish identity, but the picture of national history became more multifaceted. The war heroes and their sacrifice as part of the defensive struggle in the war against the Soviet Union were seen as fundamental to the independence and ensuing wellbeing of the nation, but public commemorations of the wars were held without strong enemy images.[26] History did not seem to colour the majority of Finns' views of Russians, and the mutual relationship was largely normalised.[27]

Russia did not want to stir up the history debate either. For example, the meetings of the former Finnish volunteer SS soldiers in Finland who had fought on the Eastern front in 1941–42 never gained negative attention compared to that received by corresponding meetings in the Baltic states. There were attempts – sometimes even with the help of some Finnish pro-Russian intermediates – to reinterpret the history of the Winter War in accordance with the Soviet view, according to which Finland started the war, but they did not get much publicity.[28] Russian history textbooks contended that the Soviet Union started the Winter War.[29] However, they stuck to the interpretation that the war against Finland was merely an unfortunate small conflict before the 'Great Patriotic War'. Admitting the need to adjust the border before the incoming German attack did not change the overall interpretation of Russian heroism in WWII. The fact that the Finns showed armed resistance and were able to defend themselves could rather be used as an argument to mock the Baltic states, which did not.

[24] 'Finland: Soviet Annexation of Karelia Still a Taboo Subject' (*RadioFreeEurope/ RadioLiberty*, 1 July 2003): https://www.rferl.org/a/1103688.html.

[25] R Vainio, 'Yhä harvempi suomalainen mielii Karjalaa takaisin. Karjala-taustaistenkaan enemmistö ei kannata rajan siirtoa' ['Fewer and fewer Finns want Karelia back. Even the majority of those with a Karelian background do not support moving the border'] (*Helsingin Sanomat*, 21 August 2005): https://www.hs.fi/kotimaa/art-2000004331312.html.

[26] H Nyyssönen, 'Remembering the Winter War in Finland' in SM Kvi et al (eds), *Spivpratsia SRSR i Nimetstsini u mihvoennii period ta pid tsas drugoi cvitovoi vijni: pritsini i naclidki* [*Collaboration between the Soviet Union and Germany in the Inter-war Period and During WWII: Causes and Consequences*] (NaUKMA, Agrar Media Group, 2012) 163–79.

[27] T Vihavainen, 'Ryssland i Finlands historia: Några särdrag som påverkar nutiden' (2010) 24 *Nordisk Østforum* 185–97.

[28] V Baryshnikov, *От прохладного мира к зимней войне: восточная политика Финляндии в 1930-е годы.* [*From the Cold World to the Winter War: Finland's Eastern Policy in the 1930s*] (St Petersburg University Press, 1997).

[29] K Kaunismaa, *Punatähdestä kaksoiskotkaan: Neuvostoliiton romahtamisen vaikutus venäläisen keskikoulun historian oppikirjoihin* [*From the Red Star to the Double Eagle. The Impact of the Collapse of the Soviet Union on the Russian Middle School Textbooks*] (University of Turku, 2009).

Hence, the historical political problems related to WWII had become rather marginal issues in Finnish-Russian relations during the 1990s and 2000s, with history only occasionally debated in the media and discussed by historians. Finnish politicians and government officials focused on a forward-looking agenda. Russian leaders did not seem to want to instrumentalise history in Russo-Finnish relations for their own purposes either, as their primary interest was in preventing memory conflicts that could lead to territorial claims or negative attitudes.

VI. RUSSIA'S CONSERVATIVE TURN AND THE SPILL-OVER OF MEMORY CONFLICTS

When Putin reassumed the presidency in 2012 after his four-year term as prime minister, Russian politics took a more conservative turn.[30] This shift, which admittedly had already been the general societal trend, consisted of an emphasis on traditional values, including militaristic patriotism and the Russian Orthodox religion, the growth of authoritarianism, curtailing liberal freedoms, a foreign policy reorientation towards Eurasianism and the non-Western 'rising powers' – the BRICS countries. This change was both supported by, and had huge repercussions for, the Russian politics of history and official remembrance. Whereas President Medvedev (2008–12) had emphasised Russia's modernisation and supported the initiatives of de-Stalinisation (but also set up the short-lived Commission against the Falsification of History), the official history policy started to stress the 1000-year-old statehood of Russia and glorified the heroic achievements of the Soviet Union under Stalin, particularly in WWII.[31]

All of these aspects created challenges for the mutual understanding of history in Russo-Finnish relations. Some conservative narratives returned to old Soviet-era historical interpretations, but some differed in the sense that they questioned the image of Finland's progressive role in the Czarist empire. Conservative mnemopolitical agents would point out that Finland had been an important safe haven for the Bolsheviks and their revolutionary activities, since the Russian secret police could not fully operate in the autonomous Finland. However, the Russian state leadership did not want to accelerate conservative and nationalistic interpretations of history where they concerned Finland, but rather to manage the status quo relationship despite the conservative turn. For

[30] M Kangaspuro, 'Putin's history, politics and conservative turn' in K Miklóssy and M Kangaspuro (eds), *Conservatism and Memory Politics in Russia and Eastern Europe* (Routledge, 2021) 15–24; P Kratochvíl, and G Shakhanova, 'The Patriotic Turn and Re-Building Russia's Historical Memory: Resisting the West, Leading the Post-Soviet East?' (2020) 68 *Problems of Post-Communism* 442–56.

[31] See OY Malinova, 'The Official Historical Narrative as a Part of Identity Policy of the Russian State: From the 1990s to the 2000s' (2016) (6) *Polis* 139–58; F Hill and CG Gaddy, 'Putin and the Uses of History' (*The National Interest*, 4 January 2012): https://nationalinterest.org/article/putin-the-uses-history-6276?nopaging=1.

example, President Vladimir Putin said that the Soviet Union launched the Winter War with Finland in order to 'correct mistakes' that had been made with regard to the borders when Finland gained its independence in 1917.[32] He also noted that

> we have very good relations with Finland today … and this must be done without any kind of confrontation – on the contrary, so that this bloody episode in our shared history will be an example as to why nothing similar should ever be allowed to happen again.

In his long essay on WWII and its outbreak, written in 2020, Putin skipped over Finland. He did not mention the Winter War, nor did he name any of the Finnish leaders on the list of 'traitors and butchers' (containing eg, Bandera, Quisling and Pétain) who collaborated with the Nazis.[33] However, perhaps as a sign of the upcoming changes, the Russian Embassy in South Africa that had an active presence on social media tweeted about the Winter War in 2021, claiming that it was started by Finland in an alliance with Germany.[34]

A salient set of problems in Russo-Finnish relations can be derived from Russian attempts to whitewash the past and block all attempts to rewrite Soviet history by revealing and documenting Stalin-era atrocities. The most prominent case is that of Karelian historian and activist Yury Dmitriyev. Dmitriyev is known for having located and examined secret mass graves at Sandarmokh and Krasnyi Bor in the Republic of Karelia, where thousands of people, including hundreds of Finns, were shot and buried during Stalin's 'Great Terror' in the late 1930s. In 2018, Dmitriyev was charged with making pornographic images of a child in what seemed to be a blatantly politically motivated trial, acquitted but convicted on a related charge of sexual abuse and sentenced to 3½ years; in September 2020, when he had served the original term, the Supreme Court of Karelia significantly increased his prison sentence to 13 years, and in December 2021 the Petrozavodsk City Court in Karelia re-sentenced him, this time to 15 years in a high-security penal colony.[35] Another controversy concerned a memorial plaque that was dedicated to Marshall Mannerheim in St Petersburg. The plaque was first installed by the Russian Military Historical Society in the presence of Sergei Ivanov and Vladimir Medinsky, but it was dismantled and moved to the Museum of the First World War after numerous acts of vandalism by local extremist-nationalist groups.[36] Some Russian military

[32] V Putin, 'Putin: Winter War aimed at correcting border "mistakes"' (*YLE*, 15 March 2013): https://yle.fi/a/3-6539940.

[33] V Putin, 'The Real Lessons of the 75th Anniversary of World War II' (*The National Interest*, 18 June 2020): https://nationalinterest.org/feature/vladimir-putin-real-lessons-75th-anniversary-world-war-ii-162982.

[34] @EmbassyofRussia on Twitter (X, 30 November 2021): https://twitter.com/EmbassyofRussia/status/1465640339113455622.

[35] 'Russian historian who uncovered Stalin's mass graves has sentence increased by a decade' (*YLE*, 30 September 2020): https://yle.fi/a/3-11570901.

[36] 'Controversial St. Petersburg Memorial Removed' *The Moscow Times* (16 October 2016).

history activists even started to spread old Soviet propaganda claims, such as the existence of gas chambers in Finnish-occupied Eastern Karelia and exploding dolls being dropped from aeroplanes to kill Soviet children.[37] In addition, as part of the patriotic education campaign aimed at Russian school children, an NGO, *Otkrytye Vozmozhnosti* (*Open Opportunities*) built a mock concentration camp in Karelia showing the cruel fate of imprisoned Russian children during the Finnish occupation in WWII.[38]

Russian attempts to rewrite history from a nationalist patriotic perspective were also duly noted in Finland, particularly where Russia's relations with Finland were concerned, which created a certain backlash. In particular, the revisionist interpretation of Finland's culpability for the Winter War that started to emerge in speeches, exhibitions, and textbooks irritated Finns.[39] The Finnish Reservists' Association publicly criticised a Russian museum for spreading false information about the Winter War.[40] The Russian annexation of Crimea and the overall trends in Russian politics towards authoritarianism negatively affected Finnish perceptions of Russia as a state, but it did not change the image of Russians as a people or Russian culture much. The debate on the Russian threat was based on views of Russia's behaviour in Chechnya, Georgia, and Ukraine more so than on the distant past, but it was the historical experience of the Winter War, when Finland stood alone, that was a major part of the argument for NATO membership.[41] The discussion about restoring Karelia dissipated as the refugee generation grew older and passed away. For example, the flag-bearer of the Karelian evacuees, the 100-year-old newspaper *Karjala*, went bankrupt in 2022 because the number of subscribers had diminished. A proposal from the youth organisation of the populist Finns party that the ceded Finnish territories should be returned to Finland caused a stir in Russia, although hardly any serious attention was paid to the proposal in Finland.[42] Instead, focus shifted to examination of the question of the fate of the Finns before, during and after Stalin's great terror in Russian Karelia, for

[37] A Paananen, 'Venäjältä uusi hurja sadismiväite suomalaisista: "Räjähteillä täytettyjä leluja pudotettiin lentokoneesta – lapsia kuoli ja vammautui"' ['A new fierce claim about the sadism of Finns from Russia: "Toys filled with explosives were dropped from the plane – children were killed and injured"'] (*Ilta-Sanomat*, 29 May 2020): https://www.is.fi/ulkomaat/art-2000006523491.html.

[38] 'Russia Builds Replica WWII Prison Camp for Kids' (*The Moscow Times*, 13 November 2020) https://www.themoscowtimes.com/2020/11/13/russia-builds-replica-wwii-prison-camp-for-kids-a72035.

[39] A Paananen, 'IS selvitti: Näin Venäjä opettaa talvisodasta – yhdessä kirjassa varsin erikoisia tulkintoja' ['Ilta-Sanomat investigated: This is how Russia teaches about the Winter War'] (*Ilta-Sanomat*, 30 November 2018): https://www.is.fi/ulkomaat/art-2000005917551.html.

[40] 'Finnish Reservists' Association slams false Russian interpretation of Winter War' (*YLE*, 7 December 2019): https://yle.fi/a/3-11107504.

[41] E Nortio, I Jasinskaja-Lahti, M Hämäläinen and J Pakkasvirta, 'Fear of the Russian bear? Negotiating Finnish national identity online' (2022) 28 *Nations and Nationalism* 861.

[42] D Mizin, Неочевидные выборы: как стать истинным финном. Как в Финляндии проходят парламентские выборы (*Gazeta.ru*, 19 April 2019): https://www.gazeta.ru/politics/2019/04/14_a_12301363.shtml?updated.

which a five-year project was initiated by the government.[43] The commemoration of past wars is still important and the few thousand remaining war veterans continue to be highly esteemed in society – perhaps more so than when more of them were alive. However, the undertone of the public memory of the wars has seldom been antagonistic or militaristic. For example, the unveiling ceremony for a new statue on the square in front of the Ministry of Defence did not reflect a Russophobic sentiment; rather, it emphasised national unity and self-sacrifice for the preservation of freedom and independence.[44] Although WWII remains a key part of the Finnish collective memory, forming the theme of many new novels and movies as well as museum exhibitions, more recent events, such as joining the EU, have gained ascendancy.[45]

VII. THE RUSSO-UKRAINIAN WAR AND INSTRUMENTALISATION OF THE PAST

Russia's – and particularly the Kremlin's – interpretations of its and its neighbours' history took a step closer to more nationalistic-patriotic interpretations in the run-up to, and following, the attack on Ukraine.[46] One could argue that the direction was no longer conservative but revisionist: challenging established interpretations in order to justify Russian imperialist tendencies. No longer an occasional commentator on history reflecting moderately on the views of the extreme nationalists, Putin himself started to spearhead nationalistic interpretations of the past.[47]

This change also affected Finland, as Russia labelled it an unfriendly country due to its condemnation of Russia and participation in sanctions. At the same time, Finland commenced the process of joining NATO, which increased Russia's negative propaganda. Subsequently, Russia employed mnemonic instruments as part of its campaign to discredit Finland. The political constraints exercised by the Kremlin so as not to escalate memory conflicts, that still seemed to exist before the war, vanished when Finland had joined the Alliance and assisted Ukraine in its war against Russia.

Russian representatives have tried to create the image that Finns are harbouring territorial claims and planning an annexation of Karelia. Nikolai Patrushev,

[43] 'Finns in Russia 1917–1964' (*The National Archives of Finland*): https://kansallisarkisto.fi/en/finns-in-russia.

[44] 'Finland unveils national memorial to commemorate Winter War' (*YLE*, 30 November 2017): https://yle.fi/a/3-9956974.

[45] E Hakököngäs, A Pirttilä-Backman and M Halme, 'Something Old, Something New: Finnish Living Historical Memory in the 2010s' (2021) 15 *Journal of Pacific Rim Psychology*.

[46] S Gvindadze, 'Explainer: How Russia erases memory of Soviet terror' (*BBC Monitoring*, 13 November 2023).

[47] See: G Bogush, 'Putin's Memory Policies in the Context of Military Aggression in Ukraine', Chapter 3 in this volume.

the Secretary of the Russian Security Council and the man known for being the Kremlin's ideological whisperer of nationalist interpretations of history, most visibly presented such allegations while visiting Petrozadovsk in 2022. Without much evidence to offer, he argued that the West had been supporting separatist movements and terrorist activity in the Republic of Karelia. He drew on historical comparisons from WWII and portrayed Finland as a tool in the West's fight against Russia. He also claimed that Finnish soldiers had shown particular cruelty against Russian prisoners of war in 'concentration camps' in occupied Eastern Karelia.[48] The Presidential Foundation for Cultural Initiatives subsequently launched a project to document Finnish 'Nazism' in Russian Karelia.[49]

Reflecting the new discursive framework, old Soviet interpretations have increasingly emerged in TV programmes and public postings, accusing Finland of cooperating with the Nazis or even being 'in essence the very same as Nazis', having started the Winter War and having collaborated with Nazi Germany already before the war started.[50] According to this view, Russia (the Soviet Union) was too lenient towards Finland after WWII. In school textbooks, Finland's decision to join NATO is represented as a betrayal. On the eve of the 85th anniversary of the outbreak of the Winter War, in November 2024, Sergey Naryshkin, the director of Russia's Foreign Intelligence Service (SVR) and the chair of the Russian Historical Society, participated in a prominent round-table discussion where he claimed that Finns have learnt nothing from the outcome of WWII, and accused the current Finnish leaders of neo-Nazism.[51] At the same time, the Russian media published several articles that blamed Finland for the Winter War.[52] Furthermore, this new Russian narrative contains views that Finland's position as a 'historically neutral' country was based on a deal that it could maintain its independence in 1945 'by promising to remain neutral'.[53] Russians

[48] 'West was pulling Finland into anti-Russian campaign for long time – top security official' (*TASS*, 31 July 2023): https://tass.com/world/1654877.

[49] 'Создание и распространение документального фильма и серии видео-роликов под общим названием: Фашизм по-фински, уроки истории и наши дни' (*The Presidential Foundation for Cultural Initiatives*, 20 February 2024): https://гранты.пфки.рф/public/application/item?id=3e0c3fbb-3743-4db0-a139-3affff2bfae4.

[50] 'Apologists of Russia's War Label Finland Fascist Following its Bid to Join NATO' (*Institute for Strategic Dialogue, Digital Dispatches*): https://www.isdglobal.org/digital_dispatches/apologists-of-russias-war-label-finland-fascist-following-its-bid-to-join-nato/. See also eg: the post of Francis Scarr on a Russian TV show with Alexander Semchenko @francis_scarr on X (Twitter) (*X*, 20 December 2023): https://twitter.com/francis_scarr/status/1737463922372887018?fbclid=IwAR3sCen_0Mn9VWfXvqr2PJ_jVyOszUhBwgbmuTrWhfqrnwo2EoSxkhorgfQ.

[51] 'Russia's SVR chief questions role of NATO membership for Finnish people' (*TASS*, 29 November 2024): https://tass.com/politics/1879601. See also, M. Miagkov, *Чёрная книга. Краткая история шведской и финской русофобии* (Russian Military Historical Society, 2025).

[52] See eg: Уроки «Зимней войны»: русофобия приводит соседей России к потере суверенитета и территорий (*Sobcor*, 28 November 2024): https://sobcor.news/28112024/7583/.

[53] E Mikkonen, 'Katso, millaista propagandaa Venäjä opettaa lukiolaisille historiankirjassa Nato-Suomesta ja Ukrainasta' ['Look what kind of propaganda Russia teaches high school students in a history book about NATO-Finland and Ukraine'] (*YLE*, 1 September 2023): https://yle.fi/a/74-20047953.

also started to celebrate the 'liberation' of Finnish towns that were occupied by the Soviet forces and incorporated into Russia.[54]

The possibility for the Russian domestic public sphere to carry on debate on interpretations of history has been further constrained after Russia invaded Ukraine. For example, a Russian activist was detained after allegedly arguing that the Soviet Union was an ally of Nazi Germany and for referring to a Finnish sniper as a hero of the Winter War. This was seen as a sign that challenging official interpretations of Russian war history and having even nominal connections to Finland may lead to arrest.[55] Moreover, a monument at a Finnish military graveyard on the Karelian Isthmus that was restored by Finnish volunteers in cooperation with the Russian authorities as late as 2019–20 was vandalised and dismantled.[56]

Although territorial claims to its Western neighbours are officially 'out of the question',[57] prominent Russians have started to more openly argue that the imperialist borders of Russia should be restored. These views often question Lenin's decision to grant Finland its independence in 1917. According to Dmitri Medvedev, Lenin, who was a champion of national self-determination, is seen not to have acted in the Russian national interest, having created Finland by mistake.[58] The head of the Russian occupation administration of Zaporizhia (Ukraine), Yevgeny Balitsky, tweeted that Russia's goal is to occupy not only Ukraine, but also the Baltic countries, Poland, and Finland, as these states are 'the historical lands of Russia'.[59]

Putin has not gone as far as Patrushev and other pundits in his essays, speeches, or comments. Nevertheless, he has started to hint that Finland is responsible for some unaccounted-for historical wrongdoings. St Petersburg City Court ruled

[54] 'Russia celebrates "liberation" of annexed Finnish land' (*The Barents Observer*, 8 October 2022): https://www.thebarentsobserver.com/news/russia-celebrates-liberation-of-annexed-finnish-land/224419.

[55] A Paananen, 'Venäläisaktivistit: "Pienikin Suomi-yhteys on vaaraksi" – kommentti talvisodasta vei jo vankilaan ja toi syytteet "natsismin oikeuttamisesta"' ['Russian activists: "Even a tiny connection to Finland is dangerous" – a comment about the Winter War already led to jail and charges of "justifying Nazism"'] (*Ilta-Sanomat*, 25 October 2023): https://www.is.fi/ulkomaat/art-2000009933899.html; see also ургского краеведа арестовали по делу о реабилитации нацизма из-за записей во «ВКонтакте»' (*Mediazona*, 13 October 2023): https://zona.media/news/2023/10/13/spb-delo?utm_source=ground.news&utm_medium=referral.

[56] A Paananen, 'Tältä näyttää Venäjän turmelema Koiviston sankarihauta nyt – Moskova haluaa Suomelta tukun uusia selvityksiä' ['This is how the grave of war heros defaced by Russians looks now'] (*Ilta-Sanomat*, 30 January 2023): https://www.is.fi/ulkomaat/art-2000009347505.html.

[57] 'Russia has no territorial claims to Poland, Latvia or other countries – Putin' (*TASS*, 9 February 2024): https://tass.com/politics/1743923.

[58] D Medvedev, 'Эпоха противостояния' (*Rossiyskaya Gazeta*, 2 July 2023): https://rg.ru/2023/07/02/epoha-protivostoianiia.html.

[59] @den_kazansky on X (Twitter) (*X*, 3 October 2022): https://twitter.com/den_kazansky/status/1709281875934560540?ref_src=twsrc%5Etfw%7Ctwcamp%5Etweetembed%7Ctwterm%5E1709281875934560540%7Ctwgr%5E71eea9a3fa337f450f615af873a4e120aee78c52%7Ctwcon%5Es1_&ref_url=https%3A%2F%2Fwww.mtvuutiset.fi%2Fartikkeli%2Fzaporizhzhjan-miehitysjohtaja-vaatii-venajan-vallattava-asein-myos-baltia-puola-ja-suomi%2F8792222.

that the Siege of Leningrad during WWII constituted a war crime and a genocide against the Russian people in which the Finns also participated.[60] For Putin, the siege is very much part of his family history. At the 80th anniversary of the siege, in January 2023, Putin stated that many European countries participated in it and committed crimes there. He added that 'we have never talked about this before because of a certain tolerance, and so as not to spoil our relations with many countries', as if he was directly hinting at Finland.[61]

In Finland, Russia's war on Ukraine changed the public image of Russia as a state, followed by the image of Russians as a nation, the latter of which had not been negative when the war started. However, and contrary to what some Russians such as Patrushev claim, there was almost no renewed interest in the Karelian question. By contrast, the old adversarial image based on the view of the perpetual threat from the East was revived. In popular books and YouTube lectures, the perception that Russia is untrustworthy, corrupt, alien to Western values, geared towards territorial expansionism, and unchangeable has become widespread.[62] In one survey, 89 per cent of Finns agreed that Russia is an expansionist great power, while only five per cent thought that it was a good neighbour and partner.[63] Remarkably, there has also been a visible shift in interpretations of the Cold War era, as the former policy of friendship with the Soviet Union is now seen as immoral and as no longer benefitting Finland. Incidents related to memory politics also emerged in Finland as the graves of Soviet prisoners of war were sprayed with a pro-Ukrainian slogan in southern Finland.[64] However, the authorities stressed that the agreement on preserving the Russian graveyards in Finland should be honoured.

VIII. CONCLUSIONS: FUTURE MEMORIES OF THE PAST

Finland and Russia share a mutual past that includes a number of sensitive issues, particularly those related to WWII, that are constitutive of the national identity of both countries. After the dissolution of the Soviet Union, these problems were mostly dealt with constructively – although not in accordance with any textbook example of reconciliation, such as establishing shared truths, apologies

[60] 'St Petersburg court finds Finland guilty of "genocide" during 1940s Leningrad siege' (*YLE*, 21 November 2022) https://yle.fi/a/3-12664441.

[61] V Putin, 'Meeting with Great Patriotic War veterans, residents of besieged Leningrad and representatives of patriotic public associations' (*President of Russia*, 18 January 2023): http://en.kremlin.ru/events/president/news/70367.

[62] MJ Kari and A Holmila, *Miksi Venäjä toimii niin kuin se toimii* [*Why Russia acts as it acts*] (*Docendo*, 2023); M Aaltola, *Havahtuminen – Turvallinen Eurooppa* (Tammi, 2023).

[63] 'Suomalaisten enemmistö pitää välttämättömänä, että Ukraina voittaa sodan' ['A majority of Finns sees it as necessary that Ukraine wins the war'] (*EVA*, 18 November 2023): https://www.eva.fi/blog/2023/11/18/suomalaisten-enemmisto-pitaa-valttamattomana-etta-ukraina-voittaa-sodan/.

[64] J Lehtola, 'Neuvostosotilaiden hautapaikalla ilkivaltaa Salossa' ['Vandalism at the grave of Soviet soldiers'] (*YLE*, 14 November 2023): https://yle.fi/a/74-20060269.

and mutual forgiveness, or compensation for the victims – but pragmatically. History problems were mainly taken off the political agenda and consequently, they did not burden the existing relationship between the two countries. Issues related to history were compartmentalised and both nations could preserve their own public and collective memories, which, whilst not identical, did not clash politically.

Russia's conservative turn and its war on Ukraine changed this mnemopolitical status quo, which in hindsight represented perhaps more of a *modus vivendi* than a full historical reconciliation between the two nations. First, Russian patriotic interpretations emphasising the sacredness of the 'Great Patriotic War' have challenged the established equilibrium that both parties were in their own ways culpable, and blaming the other for starting wars or perpetrating atrocities was not a political issue but rather a matter for historians to clear up. The state-led patriotic revision of history in Russia has constrained the public space for open debate and encouraged military historians as well as other pundits to spread propagandistic interpretations and re-established historical enemy images. This spilled over into relations with Finland, although Putin himself still remained rather moderate when it came to views on Russo-Finnish relations. When Russia started its full-scale war on Ukraine in 2022 and Finland chose sides by participating in sanctions against Russia, supporting Ukraine, and joining NATO, this trend continued and as a result, historical arguments were used instrumentally to discredit Finland.

In Finland, changing Russian interpretations of the mutual past have created a backlash effect of sorts, but it has not changed the collective memory greatly. Russia's war on Ukraine opened historical traumas, quite literally, concerning the older generations that either had memories of WWII or whose parents had such memories. Furthermore, the war also revived the old negative image of Russia as a perpetual enemy that is untrustworthy and culturally different, and strengthened patriotic historical memories about the need to defend the fatherland. Russia's unilateral historical interpretations about wars and territorial changes, and Putin's strong identification with Peter the Great and his policy of conquest, have also been seen as additional signs pointing towards Russia possessing offensive intentions towards all its former territories. Russia's new mnemopolitical agenda has also caused moral outrage, viewed as an attempt at historical falsification without any faithfulness to the facts. However, the war did not cause any upsurge in demands concerning the return of lost territories as originally alleged by certain Russian propagandists. The question of restoring justice is more related to Russia's behaviour in Ukraine than it is to Finland's own past experiences with Russia.

Part IV

Shaping European Law and Politics in the Context of Memory Wars

12

German Prototype for Memory Laws and Policies in Europe in the Context of Putin's Instrumentalisation of Denazification

PAULA RHEIN-FISCHER

I. INTRODUCTION

PRESIDENT VLADIMIR PUTIN'S attempt to justify Russia's full-scale war of aggression against Ukraine, waged on 24 February 2022, underscored by the necessary 'denazification of Ukraine' has received many scathing labels, ranging from 'myth',[1] 'grotesque',[2] and 'a code word for … antidemocratic regime change'[3] to a 'cynical abuse of the term genocide, the memory of the Second World War ("WWII") and the Holocaust'.[4]

Scholars have been evidently concerned, and primarily preoccupied, with refuting this claim by mapping out why the Kyiv regime cannot be considered a 'neo-Nazi regime'.[5] This chapter centres around the historical prototype that is instrumentalised by the narrative of 'denazification of Ukraine': to wit, the denazification in post-war Germany and its legal safeguards which aim to prevent repetition of the catastrophe of Nazism and the *Shoah* (Holocaust). These safeguards include provisions that can be conceptualised as 'memory

[1] V Ferraro, 'The Contradictions in Vladimir Putin's "Just War" against Ukraine: The Myths of NATO's Containment, Minority Protection and Denazification' (*SciELO Preprints*, 2023).

[2] T Snyder as cited in J Blake, 'Putin is making the same mistakes that doomed Hitler when he invaded the Soviet Union', *CNN* (2 April 2022): https://edition.cnn.com/2022/04/02/world/putin-invasion-mistakes-hitler-blake-cec/index.html.

[3] R Person and M McFaul, 'What Putin Fears Most' (2022) 33 *Journal of Democracy* 18, 19.

[4] E Finkel and I Tabarovsky, 'Statement on the War in Ukraine by Scholars of Genocide, Nazism and World War II' (*Jewish Journal*, 25 February 2022): https://jewishjournal.com/news/worldwide/345515/statement-on-the-war-in-ukraine-by-scholars-of-genocide-nazism-and-world-war-ii/.

[5] Ferraro, 'Contradictions in Vladimir Putin's "Just War"' (n 1).

laws'; that is, laws which prescribe a specific state-approved interpretation of the past[6] and that are often an expression of the militant democracy concept. The latter, in its most basic form, states that democracies should possess the necessary means to 'defend' themselves against their 'enemies'.[7] Whilst various legal orders embody those safeguards,[8] the German order represents a particularly striking example; hence it is sometimes considered the 'cradle of militant democracy'.[9] This, together with the explicit references by the Russian regime to the German historical precedent, requires zooming in on this precedent and conducting a closer investigation into how it has been instrumentalised by Putin. With this, my overall aim is to examine the extent to which the risk of abuse is inherent in memory policies and laws, as well as to determine which criteria can be deemed suitable to distinguish acceptable from illegitimate memory governance.

Making Putin's claim of denazification the subject of a scholarly investigation runs the risk of lending more seriousness to this idea than it deserves. It should hence be emphasised that, by comparing the claim to 'denazify Ukraine' with the denazification of Germany, I by no means intend to equate Ukrainian actions with German Nazism. On the contrary, this chapter aims to unpack how Putin's speech on denazification instrumentalises and distorts the restoration of German society and its measures to commemorate Nazism, in a way that completely reverses the victim (Ukraine) and the perpetrator (Russia), as well as to explore what further consequences can be drawn from such actions.

The chapter begins by setting out the claim of 'denazification of Ukraine', and the relevant legal measures designed or suitable to implement this goal in the context of Russia's ongoing war against Ukraine (section II). In the next section, I outline the main characteristics of the historical prototype of this narrative, German memory politics and laws on Nazism (section III). On this basis, I identify the relevant factors instrumentalising this prototype in the Russian context (IV). Finally, I use these findings to underpin my main claim that memory policies and laws are inherently prone to abuse, with a sliding scale ranging from legitimate to illegitimate memory laws (V). Section VI concludes.

[6] See: '"Memory Laws" and Freedom of Expression: Thematic Factsheet' (*Council of Europe*, July 2018): https://rm.coe.int/factsheet-on-memory-laws-july2018-docx/16808c1690.

[7] For recent contributions on this concept, see eg: S Tyulkina, *Militant Democracy: Undemocratic political parties and beyond* (Routledge, 2015); PE de Morree, *Rights and Wrongs under the ECHR – The prohibition of abuse of rights in Article 17 of the European Convention on Human Rights* (Cambridge University Press, 2017) 147 ff; A Malkopoulou and A Kirshner (eds), *Militant Democracy and Its Critics: Populism, Parties, Extremism* (Edinburgh University Press, 2019).

[8] See de Morree, *Rights and Wrongs under the ECHR* (n 7), 155 f.

[9] M Thiel, *The 'Militant Democracy' Principle in Modern Democracies* (Ashgate, 2009) 8.

II. THE CLAIM OF 'DENAZIFICATION OF UKRAINE' AND CORRESPONDING LEGAL TOOLS

The claim that Ukraine needs to be 'denazified' is part of a larger rhetorical frame that Egbert Fortuin, referring to frame analysis,[10] has identified as being 'Russophobic Nazi Ukraine government commits genocide on Russians'.[11] This frame is part of the again larger frame 'Any perceived enemy of Russia, including NATO, is … a fascist or Nazi force that aims to destroy Russia and Russian culture'.[12] Of course, these frames had been employed much earlier than the full-scale invasion of Ukraine in February 2022, namely, in post-Soviet Russia and in the Donbas.[13] Between 2003 and 2014, the designation of Putin's opponents as 'fascist' became an integral part of the Russian propaganda machine.[14] However, between 2014 and 2022, the frame of equating Ukrainian state leaders with Nazis developed its full range.[15] A powerful example was Putin's essay of 12 July 2021, 'On the Historical Unity of Russians and Ukrainians', outlining that modern Ukrainian state authorities should be considered 'Nazis' because Ukraine repeatedly voted against UN General Assembly resolutions condemning the glorification of Nazism,[16] its marches in honour of SS war criminals were protected by the authorities, and Nazi collaborator Stephan Bandera was ranked as a national hero.[17] In Russian state-owned media and among Russian politicians, the claim of Nazism was frequently conflated with the argument that Ukraine committed 'genocide' against its Russian-speaking population through its language laws – which limit official use of the Russian language – as well as the fighting in the Donbas.[18] In 2015, the idea was expressed for the first time by Russian-speaking Ukrainian politicians and former pro-Russian Ukrainian government members that modern-day Ukraine needed the same processes

[10] This theory, first put forward by E Goffmann, *Frame Analysis. An Essay on the Organization of Experience* (Harvard University Press, 1974), states that how information is presented ('framed') to an audience, influences the way that information is processed; for an attempt to conceptualise fragmented approaches to framing, see DA Scheufele, 'Framing as a theory of media effects' (1999) 49 *Journal of Communication* 103.

[11] ELJ Fortuin, 'Ukraine commits genocide on Russians': the term "Genocide" in Russian propaganda' (2022) 46 *Russian Linguistics* 313, 315.

[12] ibid 339.

[13] ibid 324; for memory politics in post-Soviet Russia, see A Nekoliak's and P Primbs' Chapter 1 in this volume.

[14] Fortuin, '"Genocide" in Russian Propaganda' (n 11) 324–27.

[15] ibid 330–38.

[16] Submitted annually by Russia, see eg, UN Doc. A/RES/77/204 (2022), A/RES/76/149 (2021) and A/RES/75/169 (2020); the 2022 resolution received less backing than usual.

[17] V Putin, 'On the Historical Unity of Russians and Ukrainians' (*Office of the President of Russia*, 12 July 2021): http://en.kremlin.ru/events/president/news/66181.

[18] See Fortuin, '"Genocide" in Russian Propaganda' (n 11) 313–47, especially 334.

that took place after WWII in Germany, namely, demilitarisation, denazification, decentralisation and democratisation.[19]

Since the launch of the full-scale invasion of Ukraine, the Putin regime has continued to explicitly employ the idea of 'denazification of Ukraine'. In his address of 21 February 2022, Putin repeated that in Ukraine, 'nationalists who have seized power have unleashed a persecution, a real terror campaign against those who opposed their anti-constitutional actions' and that Russia 'know[s] their names and … and will do everything to punish them, find them and bring them to justice'.[20] In his speech of 24 February 2022, he became even more explicit: the invasion's goal was 'to protect people who have been subjected to bullying and genocide by the Kyiv regime for eight years. And for this we will strive for the demilitarisation and denazification of Ukraine'.[21] Two and a half years later, he continues to make claims of 'Neo-nazi dictatorship'.[22]

The idea of 'denazification of Ukraine' must be read in the context of the Russian imagination of WWII and Nazism, which focuses on the heroic role of the Soviet Union as 'the world's saviour from Nazism/fascism'[23] and the undoubtedly horrific Soviet suffering caused by the Nazis, though without regard for its specific targeting of Jews and other victim groups. From this point of view, the collaborations of some Ukrainian nationalists of the time, such as Stephan Bandera and the Organisation of Ukrainian Nationalists, with German Nazis have been primarily considered crimes against the Soviet people.[24] Ukrainian Nationalists are then conflated with the development of a Ukrainian national identity,[25] so that the concept of 'Ukrainian Nazism' can be used to explain why an independent Ukraine should be seen as an attack against the Soviet Union and Russia as its successor state. This is what drove the Putin regime to brand Zelensky, a Jewish president, who lost ancestors during the *Shoah*, as 'neo-Nazi'.[26]

[19] eg, V Konstantinov, head of the State Council of Crimea, RIA Novosti, 5 February 2015; similarly V Zakharchenko, former Ukrainian Minister of Foreign Affairs, RIA Novosti, 3 June 2015, both cited from Fortuin, '"Genocide" in Russian Propaganda' (n 11).

[20] 'Address by the President of the Russian Federation' (*President of Russia: News*, 21 February 2022): http://en.kremlin.ru/events/president/news/67828.

[21] 'Full text: Putin's declaration of war on Ukraine' (*The Spectator*, 24 February 2022): https://www.spectator.co.uk/article/full-text-putin-s-declaration-of-war-on-ukraine/.

[22] 'Putin says Ukraine goals will be achieved as he repeats neo-Nazi claims' (*Aljazeera*, 30 September 2024).

[23] M Mälksoo, 'Militant memocracy in International Relations: Mnemonical status anxiety and memory laws in Eastern Europe' (2021) 48 *Review of International Studies* 489, 498; for details, see ibid 497–99; for details on the complete failure of Russia to reckon with its own crimes, see M Mälksoo, Chapter 15 of this volume.

[24] W Talley, 'Debunking "Denazification"' (*Commission on Security and Cooperation in Europe: US Helsinki Commission*, 21 April 2022): https://www.csce.gov/articles/debunking-denazification/.

[25] ibid.

[26] See: P Cramer, '"Killed in a fire": Zelensky gives new details about his family's Holocaust history' (*Times of Israel*, 23 March 2022): www.timesofisrael.com/killed-in-a-fire-zelensky-gives-new-details-about-his-familys-holocaust-history/.

This is also the light in which Putin's repeated emphasis on the importance of the memory of the 'Great Patriotic War' and the Nuremberg Trials,[27] as well as Russian memory laws prohibiting comparisons between Nazi and Stalinist crimes,[28] must be read. Attempts to qualify Soviet crimes against the Ukrainian people, such as the Holodomor, as genocide are hence considered anti-Russian acts[29] and expressions of 'Nazi ideology'.

There are deeper reasons for the troubles caused by the challenges of the heroic victor-narrative associated with the Soviet Union's role in WWII within Russia. These have been described by Maria Mälksoo as mnemonical status anxiety.[30] Status anxiety arises 'when an actor feels deprived of the status it deems itself to be entitled to, or when an actor is unwilling to cave in to what it sees as inflated status claims of an upstart'.[31] The questioning of the Russian self-image as spotless hero against accounts of Stalinist crimes is particularly painful when it stems from a state like Ukraine, which is in an allegedly subordinated position in the international hierarchy of remembering WWII.[32] The ontological insecurity of Russia is thus what lies at the heart of Putin's current attempt to colonise Ukraine.[33]

In April 2022, Timofej Sergeitsev, who was involved in the election campaigns of former Ukrainian parliamentarian and oligarch Viktor Pinchuk and former Ukrainian president Leonid Kuchma, and who served as an advisor to the former Ukrainian president Viktor Yanukovych, spelled out most explicitly what exactly the Russian political elite imagined they would do with Ukrainian 'Nazis'. He made a distinction between active and passive 'Ukrainian Nazis': On the one hand,

> Nazis who took up arms should be destroyed to the maximum on the battlefield … War criminals and active Nazis should be exemplarily and exponentially punished. There must be a total lustration.

On the other,

> a significant part of the masses, which are passive Nazis, accomplices of Nazism, are also guilty … The just punishment of this part of the population is possible only as bearing the inevitable hardships of a just war against the Nazi system

[27] See eg Putin's address to Participants in the Nuremberg Lessons Forum (20 November 2020): http://www.en.kremlin.ru/events/president/news/64447/print.

[28] See below text to n 50 f.

[29] Fortuin, '"Genocide" in Russian Propaganda (n 11) 336; see also: Putin, 'Historical Unity of Russians and Ukrainians' (n 17).

[30] Mälksoo, 'Militant Memocracy' (n 23).

[31] J Friedrichs, 'An intercultural theory of international relations: how self-worth underlies politics among nations' (2016) 8 *International Theory* 63, 66 (footnotes omitted); TA Onea, 'Between dominance and decline: status anxiety and great power rivalry' (2014) 40 *Review of International Studies* 125–52; Mälksoo, 'Militant Memocracy' (n 23) 493.

[32] Mälksoo, 'Militant Memocracy' (n 23) 499.

[33] For details, see M Mälksoo's Chapter 15 of this volume.

> … Further denazification of this mass of the population consists in re-education, which is achieved by ideological repression (suppression) of Nazi attitudes and strict censorship.[34]

Sergejtsev then outlined the concrete steps to achieve such 'denazification':

- liquidation of armed Nazi formations … as well as the military, information, and educational infrastructure that ensures their activity;
- …
- deployment of the Russian information space;
- withdrawal of educational materials and prohibition of educational programs at all levels containing Nazi ideological guidelines;
- mass investigations to establish personal responsibility for war crimes, crimes against humanity, the spread of Nazi ideology and support for the Nazi regime;
- lustration, publication of the names of accomplices of the Nazi regime, involving them in forced labor to restore the destroyed infrastructure as punishment for Nazi activities (from among those who will not be subject to the death penalty or imprisonment);
- adoption at the local level, under the supervision of Russia, of primary normative acts of denazification 'from below', a ban on all types and forms of the revival of Nazi ideology;
- establishment of memorials, commemorative signs, monuments to the victims of Ukrainian Nazism, perpetuating the memory of the heroes of the struggle against it;
- inclusion of a complex of anti-fascist and denazification norms in the constitutions of the new people's republics;
- creation of permanent denazification bodies for a period of 25 years.[35]

As the reference to 'denazification' suggests, the proposed measures – prohibiting associations and political parties; limiting freedom of expression; banning 'Nazi ideology' including symbols, educational measures, lustration, and criminal justice – were clearly inspired by denazification measures employed in Germany after WWII and partly still in force today under the umbrella concept of militant democracy. This concept, introduced, inter alia, by Karl Loewenstein in 1937, states that democracies should possess the necessary means to 'defend' themselves against their 'enemies'.[36] As will be shown in more detail below, this concept has been completely distorted by its use in the Ukrainian context.

What is particularly worrisome is that many of the suggested measures have not been merely theoretical, as their legal bases would already exist.[37] For

[34] T Sergejtsev, *Ria Novosti*, 3 April 2022, English translation by Ukrainian politician Nataliya Popovychs available at: https://www.facebook.com/1130543768/posts/10226269839988992/.

[35] ibid.

[36] See especially K Loewenstein, 'Democracy and Fundamental Rights I and II' (1937) 31 *The American Political Science Review* 417–32, 638–58; see also above n 7.

[37] The examples here are techniques similar to, though distorting, those of militant democracy; for a more specific analysis of Russian *memory policies* in the war against Ukraine, see G Bogush's contribution in Chapter 3 of this volume.

example, Russian legislation on 'undesirable organisations' offers a rich toolbox for closing down associations considered inopportune.[38] Foreign or international NGOs are held to be 'undesirable' if they threaten the constitutional order, defence capacity or security of Russia (Article 3.1(1) Law no 272-FZ of 28 December 2012). Article 3.1(3) of that law, inter alia, entails a ban on the establishment of subdivisions, the dissemination of information materials, activities of the organisation, and participation in its activities.

Similarly, the 'employment of the Russian information space' appears to mean that Russian restrictions on the freedom of expression and the press would be applied to Ukraine. Fake news legislation,[39] for example, bans the 'public dissemination of knowingly false information about the use of the Armed Forces' of Russia or about the execution of powers by Russian state bodies,[40] and the 'discrediting' of Russian Armed Forces,[41] excluding the designation of the invasion of Ukraine as 'war'.[42] Similarly, legislation on extremism[43] prohibits, inter alia, public appeals to engage in extremist activities,[44] public calls for actions aimed at violating the territorial integrity of Russia,[45] the establishment of an extremist organisation,[46] or the dissemination of extremist material.[47] The long list of 'extremist activities' in Article 1 of the Law on Extremism[48] reflects a broad understanding of extremism.[49]

The envisaged ban of all forms of 'Nazi ideology', including the display and dissemination of Nazi symbols, can also be based on existing legislation. The prohibition of extremist material, highlighting Nazi attributes or symbols,[50] is but one example. The famous ban on 'rehabilitation of Nazism' (Article 354.1 Russian CC) prohibits, inter alia, the denial of facts established by the (Nuremberg) International Military Tribunal, the dissemination of knowingly false information about activities of the USSR during WWII or its veterans, or the expression of disrespect about the days of military glory, memorable dates or symbols of military glory of Russia.[51]

[38] On this legislation as of September 2022, see: A Nußberger, 'Report on Russia's Legal and Administrative Practice in Light of its OSCE Human Dimension Commitments' (OSCE, ODIHR. GAL/58/22/Rev.1, 22 September 2022) 40–43. Legislation included in this chapter refers to the version in force on 2 December 2024.

[39] See in more detail: Nußberger, OSCE Report (n 38) 45–51.

[40] Article 207.3 Russian Criminal Code (Russian CC).

[41] Article 280.3 Russian CC and Article 20.3.3 Code of Administrative Offences (COA).

[42] Nußberger, OSCE Report (n 38) 47.

[43] See ibid 51–59.

[44] Article 280 Russian CC.

[45] Article 280.1 Russian CC and Article 20.3.2 CAO.

[46] Article 282.1 Russian CC.

[47] Article 282.4(1) Russian CC and Article 20.3 CAO.

[48] Federal Law no 114-FZ of 25 July 2002 'On Counteracting Extremist Activity'.

[49] Nußberger, OSCE Report (n 38), 53.

[50] Article 282.4 Russian CC and Article 20.3 CAO, see above n 47.

[51] For details on this provision, see: Nußberger, OSCE Report (n 38) 59–61.

Accordingly, since the envisaged 'denazification measures' can be implemented relatively easily, the crucial question becomes: what distinguishes the denazification measures referred to by Russia from those within the German context? To answer this question and unpack how the concepts of denazification and militant democracy are instrumentalised, it is essential to identify the main characteristics of anti-Nazism measures in the German context.

III. THE FUNDAMENTAL CHARACTERISTICS OF GERMAN MEMORY LAWS ON NAZISM

Most German laws and policies of denazification and militant democracy provisions can be conceptualised as memory laws, or as 'quasi-memory laws',[52] that is, provisions that do not explicitly prescribe a certain narrative of the relevant past event into law, as eg, Holocaust denial bans do, but rather, contain a more implicit mnemonic element. In the German context, quasi-memory laws, aiming to prevent another Nazi dictatorship and protect democracy, implicitly express the mnemonic narrative that Nazism existed, Germany bears full responsibility for it, and that this period is to be assessed as one of the biggest catastrophes in history, which should never be repeated.

Before identifying common features, this section provides a brief overview of German anti-Nazism (quasi) memory laws and policies,[53] with focus placed on those which the Russian regime has called for in the Ukrainian context.

A. Lustration

The mnemonic policy most closely related to the term 'denazification' is lustration, practised after WWII in all four occupation zones. Lustration – the removal of former oppressors (in this case National Socialists) and their supporters from power positions, especially the civil service – was initiated by the Allies in the Spring of 1945 and later handed over to German judiciary panels (*Spruchkammern*). The US differentiated, in terms of legal consequences, between 'major offenders', 'offenders', 'lesser offenders', 'followers', or 'persons exonerated', with those in the former three categories facing removal from their positions or at least limitations in their profession and

[52] This notion has been introduced, inter alia, by U Belavusau, 'Mnemonic Constitutionalism and Rule of Law in Hungary and Russia' (2020) 1 *Interdisciplinary Journal of Populism* 16, 20; see also: U Belavusau, A Gliszczyńska-Grabias and M Mälksoo, 'Memory Laws and Memory Wars in Poland, Russia and Ukraine' (2021) 69 *Jahrbuch des öffentlichen Rechts* 95, 99.

[53] For a more comprehensive analysis, see: P Rhein-Fischer and S Mensing, 'Memory Laws in Germany: How Remembering National Socialism is Governed through Law' (*TOAEPL Occasional Paper* No 14, 2022): https://www.toaep.org/ops-pdf/14-rhein-fischer-mensing/.

financial sanctions.[54] During the early post-war years, the US policy led to the dismissal of large parts of the civil service.[55] The British and French adopted a more pragmatic approach, giving priority to the functioning of administration and the economy.[56] Thus, fewer people became subject to their review.[57] The Soviets, apart from the civil service, also focused on key positions in industry and economics, their aim being not only the removal of Nazis, but 'an antifascist-democratic upheaval',[58] putting in place a new communist elite. From 1947, the Soviets distinguished between actual Nazi activists and formal members of Hitler's National Socialist German Workers' Party (NSDAP)[59] members, who were increasingly rehabilitated.[60] Overall, lustration faced great difficulties given the large part of the population involved in Nazism, and the opposition in German society in view of schematic categorisation and self-victimisation.[61] When the German parliament adopted the 'Denazification Final Act' in 1951, many supporters of Nazism had remained in, or returned to, their positions.[62] Especially few former judges and prosecutors were removed from their posts.[63]

Traces of lustration can still be found in the current legal framework. It is possible to impeach judges who infringe 'the principles of the Basic Law or the constitutional order of a federal State' (Article 98(2), (5) Basic Law), though to date, this provision has never been applied. Civil servants are bound by a 'constitutional loyalty duty' as part of the traditional principles of the civil service (Article 33(5) Basic Law) and as an entry requirement for their position (Article 33(2) Basic Law).[64] Recently, a reform aiming to implement this duty

[54] See: Bundestag Research Service, 'Entnazifizierung' (Wissenschaftliche Dienste, WD 1 3000/072/2011): https://www.bundestag.de/resource/blob/414744/78fc7c8a664a0d7d87621bd9ebc4ed40/wd-1-072-11-pdf-data.pdf, 6; C Rauh-Kühne, 'Die Entnazifizierung und die deutsche Gesellschaft' (1995) *Archiv für Sozialgeschichte* 35, 51.

[55] Rauh-Kühne, 'Entnazifizierung' (n 54) 43.

[56] ibid 39, 44 f; S Romeike, 'Occasional Paper No. 1: Transitional Justice in Germany after 1945 and after 1990' (*International Nuremberg Principles Academy*, 2016): https://www.nurembergacademy.org/fileadmin/publications_images/transitional-justice-in-germany-after-1945-and-after-1990/Transitional_Justice_in_Germany.pdf 25.

[57] Romeike, 'Transitional Justice in Germany' (n 56) 25.

[58] H Weish, 'Antifaschistisch-demokratische Umwälzung und politische Säuberung in der sowjetischen Bestzungszone Deutschlands' in K Henke and H Woller (eds), *Politische Säuberung in Europa. Die Abrechnung mit Faschismus und Kollaboration nach dem Zweiten Weltkrieg* (Deutscher Taschenbuch-Verlag, 1991) 84, 107.

[59] Nationalsozialistische Deutsche Arbeiterpartei.

[60] W Benz, 'Demokratisierung durch Entnazifizierung und Erziehung' (*Bundeszentrale für politische Bildung*, 11 April 2005): https://www.bpb.de/themen/nationalsozialismus-zweiter-weltkrieg/dossier-nationalsozialismus/39605/demokratisierung-durch-entnazifizierung-und-erziehung/.

[61] Romeike, 'Transitional Justice in Germany' (n 56) 23.

[62] See: Rauh-Kühne, 'Entnazifizierung' (n 54) 64, referring to Lutz Nithammer's expression of a 'record of failure'.

[63] See: Rhein-Fischer and Mensing, 'Memory Laws in Germany' (n 53) 81 f.

[64] See also § 60(1) of the Act on Federal State Officials and § 33(1) of the Act on the Status of Länder State Officials.

more effectively in practice and accelerate disciplinary procedures to remove extremist civil servants at the federal level has entered into force.[65]

B. Criminal Prosecution

Another pillar of denazification in Germany was the criminal prosecution of Nazi criminals. The International Military Tribunal, established in Nuremberg by the Allies in 1945, tried those identified as leaders of the 'Third Reich' who had survived the war and not committed suicide. In the Trial of the Major War Criminals, six organisations were charged as criminal organisations, and 24 individuals were accused of crimes against peace, war crimes and crimes against humanity.[66] Three organisations and 19 defendants were convicted, with three defendants acquitted.[67] In 12 subsequent trials before US military courts, another 177 doctors, jurists, industrialists, members of the SS, the police, the military, civil servants and diplomats stood in the dock; 142 were convicted, of whom 24 were sentenced to death; 35 were acquitted.[68]

In West Germany, the Allies also permitted the German judiciary to try Nazi crimes. The proceedings reached a peak in 1948, though only relatively minor crimes such as denunciation of persons persecuted by the Nazis were tried.[69] After the founding of the Federal Republic, the number of proceedings declined rapidly, and during the 1950s, many crimes became time barred. Only the limitation period for murder was prolonged by the Bundestag and later abolished.[70] The *Einsatzgruppen* trial in Ulm in 1958 revealed many details about the *Shoah*, though the defendants were only convicted of *complicity* in murder following the application of a primarily subjective test asking whether they desired the act as an act of their own.[71] In addition, even for complicity, the jurisprudence originally required a specific act of aiding the killing of

[65] 'Gesetz zur Beschleunigung der Disziplinarverfahren in der Bundesverwaltung und zur Änderung weiterer dienstrechtlicher Vorschriften', adopted on 17 November 2023, entered into force on 1 April 2024.

[66] See Article 6 of the London Charter.

[67] Edith Raim, 'Nürnberger Nachfolgeprozesse': https://www.nsdoku.de/lexikon/artikel/nuernberger-nachfolgeprozesse-623; see also Landeszentrale für politische Bildung Baden-Würtemberg, 'Die Nürnberger Prozesse'; Romeike, 'Transitional Justice in Germany' (n 56) 14; for the judgment, see Internationaler Militärgerichtshof, *Das Urteil von Nürnberg. Grundlagen neuen Völkerrechts. Vollständiger Text* (Munich, Nymphenburger Verlagshandlung, 1964).

[68] Landeszentrale für politische Bildung Baden-Würtemberg, 'Die Nürnberger Prozesse': https://www.lpb-bw.de/nuernberger-prozesse.

[69] Romeike, 'Transitional Justice in Germany' (n 56) 15.

[70] Bundeszentrale für politische Bildung, 'Das Ende der „Verjährungsdebatte" – Warum Mord nicht verjährt', 1 July 2019.

[71] See, eg, Federal Court of Justice, Judgment, 19 October 1962, 9 StE 4/62 (1963) *Neue Juristische Wochenschrift* 355; for a critical view see: T Fischer, 'Oskar Gröning und die Beihilfe' (*Zeitonline*, 21 July 2015): https://www.zeit.de/gesellschaft/zeitgeschehen/2015-07/ns-verbrecher-beihilfe-taeter-strafrecht-justiz-fischer-im-recht.

a person, which excluded large parts of the concentration camp personnel. Other landmark proceedings were the Frankfurt Auschwitz trials (1963 to 1965) against Auschwitz personnel of different ranks. However, despite the creation of the Central Office of the State Justice Administration for the Investigation of National Socialist Crimes, in Ludwigsburg in 1958, the shortcomings of the preceding years could not be made up for. Prosecution of Nazi criminals only saw a revival with the Demjanjuk decision of the Regional Court of Munich II in 2011,[72] confirmed by the Federal Court of Justice in 2016,[73] which no longer required a specific act in aid of a person's killing and recognising that service in the concentration camp was itself sufficient to constitute complicity in murder. The last few surviving perpetrators are still being tried before German courts.[74]

In the Soviet zone, criminal trials, largely characterised by arbitrariness and disregard for the rule of law, were held before Soviet Military Tribunals.[75] As of 1947, special criminal courts consisting of judges affiliated with the Socialist Unity Party (Sozialistische Einheitspartei Deutschlands, SED) tried individuals according to the US lustration categories, letting a sense of collective guilt suffice. These trials were also used to remove political opponents and enhance socialist transformation.[76] Prosecution of Nazi criminals reached a peak with the Waldheim Trials in 1950 where several individuals were sentenced to draconian penalties in fast-track procedures.[77] In the 1950s, the number of trials declined again, with the GDR regime using the few criminal trials mainly as propaganda tools to promote the GDR's image as an antifascist state.

C. Re-education

Denazification in Germany also implied rules for (re-)education. The vague principles adopted by the Allied Control Council to democratise the German education system left room for diverging policies. While it was the primary goal

[72] Regional Court of Munich II, Judgment, 12 May 2011, 1 Ks 115 Js 12496/08, (2011) *BeckRS* 139286.

[73] Federal Court of Justice, Order, 20 September 2016, 3 StR 49/16, (2017) *Neue Juristische Wochenschrift* 498, Oskar Gröning.

[74] See, eg, C Richter, 'Die letzten NS-Prozesse in Deutschland, von später Aufarbeitung und schlafender Justiz' (*Deutschlandfunk*, 6 January 2022): www.deutschlandfunk.de/die-letzten-ns-prozesse-in-deutschland-100.html.

[75] M Schmeitzner, 'Unter Ausschluss der Öffentlichkeit? Zur Verfolgung von NS-Verbrechen durch die sowjetische Sonderjustiz' in J Osterloh and C Vollnhals (eds), *NS-Prozesse und deutsche Öffentlichkeit. Besatzungszeit, frühe Bundesrepublik und DDR* (Vandenhoeck & Ruprecht, 2011) 149–66.

[76] Romeike, 'Transitional Justice' (n 56) 20. The SED became the founding and ruling party of the East German DDR (Deutsche Demokratische Republik) from 1949 until 1989.

[77] ibid; for more details, see W Eisert, *Die Waldheimer Prozesse. Der stalinistische Terror 1950. Ein dunkles Kapitel der DDR-Justiz* (Bechtle, 1993).

of the Soviets to reduce bourgeois privilege, the French aimed at putting in place the French school system, fostering social selection and the creation of elites. The British and US initially left school reforms to the Germans, though the US later began to propagate the model of unified schooling for all children regardless of sex, social origin and professional goals.[78]

The prevention of another Nazi regime is also strongly reflected in contemporary school and university curricula. In all 16 federal States, the period of National Socialism is an obligatory subject matter in history classes. In most federal States, students deal twice with this period, usually in year nine or ten and again in year 11 or 12. Many federal States recommend a visit to a memorial site.[79] As far as the study of law in universities is concerned, § 5a(2) of the German Judiciary Act provides that the teaching of compulsory subjects 'also includes a critical analysis of the injustices of the National Socialist regime and of the Communist dictatorship in Germany'.

D. Prohibition of Parties and Associations

Another classic measure of denazification with a strong mnemonic element was the prohibition of Hitler's National Socialist German Worker's Party (NSDAP). The idea of a ban on unconstitutional parties has been reflected in the Federal Republic's Constitution which provides for the ban of parties that 'by reason of their aims or the behaviour of their adherents, seek to undermine or abolish the free democratic basic order' (Article 21(2) Basic Law). Together with the prohibition of associations that are 'directed against the free democratic basic order' (Article 9(2) Basic Law), and the forfeiture of certain basic rights for persons abusing these rights in order to combat the free democratic basic order (Article 18 Basic Law), the prohibition of unconstitutional parties forms the core triad of militant democracy provisions.[80] The prohibition of unconstitutional parties has so far been used only twice, once in 1952 for the Socialist Reich Party (SRP),[81] a successor of the NSDAP, and in 1956 for the Communist Party of Germany (KPD).[82] More recent attempts to prohibit the extremist right-wing National Democratic Party of Germany (NPD) failed twice before the Federal Constitutional Court.[83] The ban on unconstitutional associations has been used much more frequently.[84]

[78] Benz, 'Demokratisierung' (n 60).
[79] For more details, see: Rhein-Fischer and Mensing, 'Memory Laws in Germany' (n 53) 68–70.
[80] ibid 44–48.
[81] Federal Constitutional Court, Judgment, 23 October 1952, 1 BvB 1/51, BVerfGE 2, 23.
[82] Federal Constitutional Court, Judgment, 17 August 1956, 1 BvB 2/51, BVerfGE 5, 85.
[83] Federal Constitutional Court, Order, 18 March 2003, 2 BvB 1, 2, 3/01, BVerfGE 107, 339 and Judgment, 17 January 2017, 2 BvB 1/13, BVerfGE 144, 20.
[84] For more details, see Rhein-Fischer and Mensing, 'Memory Laws in Germany' (n 53) 47 f.

E. Limitations on the Freedom of Expression

Mnemonic policy choices have also resulted in limitations on the freedom of expression. The Criminal Code (German CC) contains four explicit memory laws protecting the memory of Nazi atrocities. The offence of Holocaust denial (§ 130(3) German CC) criminalises the denial, approval or downplaying of an act of genocide committed under the Nazi regime. § 130(4) German CC incriminates the approval, glorification or justification of the tyranny and arbitrary rule of National Socialism, hence also encompassing other acts than genocide under this regime. In 2022, both provisions were supplemented by § 130(5) German CC: this provision criminalises the condoning, denial or gross trivialisation of genocide, crimes against humanity and war crimes directed against national, racial, religious or ethnic groups, against parts of the population or an individual due to membership of such a group, where the statement is likely to incite hatred or violence against these persons and disturb public peace. This provision implemented EU Framework Decision on Racism and Xenophobia (2008)[85] and served to end an infringement procedure by the European Commission against Germany for not fully transposing the Framework Decision.[86] The difference, when compared to § 130(3) and (4) German CC, is that § 130(5) German CC covers not only the denial of Nazi crimes, but also other genocides, crimes against humanity and war crimes. However, it is more restrictive in requiring a likely incitement to hatred or violence against one of the mentioned groups. Before the provision was introduced, such statements were only partly criminalised under the offence of incitement to hatred (*Volksverhetzung* – § 130(1) and (2) German CC).[87] As the legislator did not use the possibility allowed by Article 1(4) of the Framework Decision to make the criminalisation of denial or gross trivialisation dependent on a final court decision regarding the historical crime, the provision has been criticised for being overly broad.[88] A fourth criminal provision, limiting the freedom of speech with an explicit mnemonic reference, is the offence of disseminating propaganda material and the use of symbols of former Nazi organisations (§§ 86(1) No 4, and 86a German CC).

Apart from these explicit memory laws, there are other offences that courts have interpretated in a mnemonically sensitive way that can be used to penalise speech about the German Nazi past. Examples include the aforementioned

[85] Council Framework Decision 2008/913/JHA of 28 November 2008.

[86] 'December infringement package: key decisions' (*European Commission, Press Release*, 2 December 2021); Bundestag Doc. 20/4085, 14 f.

[87] S Bock, 'Die (unterlassene) Reform des Volksverhetzungstatbestands' (2011) 44(2) *Zeitschrift für Rechtspolitik* 46, 47 f; P Rhein-Fischer, 'Demonstrieren für einen Aggressor: Grenzen der Meinungs- und Versammlungsfreiheit' (2023) 78 *JuristenZeitung* 167, 175.

[88] E Hoven, 'Der neue § 130 ist eine Gefahr für die kritische Diskussion' (*Welt*, 26 October 2022): www.welt.de/kultur/plus241798753/Volksverhetzung-Der-neue-130-ist-eine-Gefahr-fuer-die-kritische-Diskussion.html; Rhein-Fischer, 'Demonstrieren für einen Aggressor' (n 87) 175.

offences of incitement to hatred (§ 130(1) and (2)) and insult (§ 185 German CC) that were applied, inter alia, to Holocaust denial before an explicit Holocaust denial ban existed;[89] the offence of disturbance of peace of the deceased (§ 168 German CC), protecting memorial sites for victims of the Nazi regime from desecration and defamatory slogans;[90] the offence of defamation of religious faiths, protecting the Jewish religion from being designated as 'racist'.[91]

Other legal provisions aim to ban or restrict the spreading of Nazi ideology. Apart from the afore-mentioned prohibition on displaying Nazi symbols,[92] for instance, § 3 of the Federal Assembly Act bans uniforms in public or at assemblies. § 15(2) of the Federal Assembly Act allows the restriction or prohibition of assemblies at National Socialist victim memorial sites. The jurisprudence has extended this principle to cover provocative processions organised at memorial days dedicated to the memory of Nazi injustices and the *Shoah*.[93] Authorities can also restrict processions which 'by [their] overall character identify [themselves] with the rites and symbols of the Nazi tyranny and intimidate other citizens by awakening memories about the past totalitarian and inhuman regime'.[94]

F. Fundamental Characteristics

Looking at this compilation, four main common features can be identified. First, almost all memory laws maintained by the German legal order today have a strong link to National Socialism. Three explicit memory laws (the Holocaust denial ban, § 130(3), the ban on glorification of the National Socialist regime, § 130(4), and the prohibition of Nazi symbols, §§ 86 (1) No 4, 86a German CC) explicitly incorporate the memory of the Nazi era or specific crimes of it. The new § 130(5) German CC is the only explicit memory law which also applies to other crimes, even without any link to Germany (with its introduction merely due to pressure from European institutions).[95] This strong focus on

[89] Federal Court of Justice, Order, 28 February 1958, 1 StR 387/57, (1958) *Neue Juristische Wochenschrift*, 599; Federal Constitutional Court, Order, 13 April 1994, BVerfGE 90, 251 f; Federal Court of Justice, Judgment, 12 December 2001, 1 StR 184/00, (2001) *Neue Zeitschrift für Strafrecht* 307.

[90] Bundestag Doc. 13/8587, 25 September 1997, 23.

[91] Higher Regional Court of Berlin, Order, 15 March 2000, (5) 1 Ss 33/98 (19/98), (2014) *BeckRS* 2697, para 37.

[92] See above §§ 86 (1) No 4 and 86a German CC.

[93] Federal Constitutional Court, Order, 23 June 2004, 1 BvQ 19/04, BVerfGE 111, 157; Order, 26 January 2001, 1 BvQ 9/01, (2001) *Neue Juristische Wochenschrift* 1410.

[94] BVerfGE, 111, 157.

[95] However, for (non-criminal) Bundestag resolutions classifying certain historical crimes as 'genocide', see: Resolution of 31 May 2016, Bundestag Doc 18/8613 (Armenian genocide in 1915–16), Resolution of 30 November 2022, Bundestag Doc 20/4681 (*Holodomor* in Ukraine 1932–33) and Resolution of 19 January 2023, Bundestag Doc 20/5228 (genocide against the Yezidi by Islamic State in Iraq and Syria 2014).

National Socialism illustrates the priority that the German legislator assigns to the Nazi regime, as compared to other atrocities in German history such as the SED dictatorship in East Germany, or German colonialism.

Second, although many mnemonic measures have been firmly criticised for not reaching far enough (eg, lustration, criminal prosecution, or re-education) or for exceeding the legislator's competences (eg, denial bans), it is relatively undisputed that the rule-maker's intention was to uphold the truth and tackle 'societal amnesia' and distortion of historical facts. (Although, of course, the relevant laws do not content themselves with protecting facts, but also contain value judgements that may not be universally shared.)

The third fundamental feature is closely linked to the above. Almost all memory laws – putting aside those adopted by the Allies and the general § 130(5) German CC – are self-inculpatory,[96] hence explicitly or implicitly recognising Germany's responsibility for Nazi crimes. The legislating state thus was the very perpetrator of the commemorated crimes.[97]

Finally, most German memory and militant democracy provisions, at least those still in force, contain an element of self-restraint, reflected in their narrow application by courts. This is illustrated by the scarce use of the constitutional provisions on prohibition of political parties and the forfeiture of rights, and the original limitation of criminal denial bans to very few historical crimes. Even their recent extension by § 130(5) German CC remains restrained by the required incitement to hatred or violence.

IV. FACTORS DISTORTING THE GERMAN PROTOTYPE IN THE RUSSO-UKRAINIAN CONTEXT

The Russian regime, when referring to 'denazification' to justify its invasion and when spelling out the envisaged 'denazification measures', transplants the German prototype of denazification into the Ukrainian context but completely distorts its meaning. The present section aims to situate such distortion in a theoretical frame and unpack the factors causing this distortion as well as the goals pursued.[98]

On a theoretical level, distortion of a legal concept represents a form of 'legal transplant' – the transposition of a legal rule or concept from one legal order into

[96] On this notion, see: E Heinze, 'Should Governments Butt out of History?' (*Free Speech Debate*, 12 March 2019): https://freespeechdebate.com/discuss/should-governments-butt-out-of-history/; critically: A De Baets, 'Self-inculpatory laws do not exist' (*Free Speech Debate*, 12 December 2019): https://freespeechdebate.com/2019/12/self-inculpatory-laws-do-not-exist/.

[97] This shared identity exists even legally, as the modern Federal Republic of Germany is considered identical to the German Reich (1871–1945) and not its historical successor state, Federal Constitutional Court, Judgment, 31 July 1973, 2 BvF 1/73, BVerfGE 36, 1.

[98] For the long-time instrumentalisation of the memory of WWII, see also M Mälksoo's Chapter 15 in this volume.

another. Legal transplant literature, of which a rich body has emerged,[99] presently agrees that there are different typologies of this phenomenon, one being concerned with the degree of conformity with the original rule. The scale ranges from 'full convergence' between the original rule and the transposition, through '"fine-tuning" (minimal tweaking of the rule to ensure its "fit") to different modes of transformations and transpositions, from adaptation, through distortion and mutation to downright rejection'.[100] The legal transplant may be designated as distorted in circumstances where the 'transplanted rule loses all material similarity with the original and retains only a surface, textual, similarity'.[101] The goal of distortion is to generate legitimacy for the new rule;[102] by transplanting a rule that served legitimate purposes, legitimacy appears to also attach to the new rule. This operation is based on deception, drawing upon the lack of public knowledge about the context of the original rule and its changed content in the new environment.[103] In this respect, distortion of legal rules and concepts necessarily implies an element of abuse and bad faith. Distortion is also closely related to the recently emerged concept of 'misappropriation'.[104]

On this basis, the relevant question is: what is it precisely that makes measures of 'denazification' applied in the Ukrainian context lose all material similarity with mnemonic denazification measures aimed at eradicating German Nazism? The most striking difference lies in the targeted political current. The German memory laws analysed above aim at actual Nazi ideology – the extremist right-wing ideology pursuing nationalist, antisemitic and racist goals, rejecting democracy, and centring around the idea that an 'Aryan people' must use any means possible to create a 'living space' for itself, while oppressing other, allegedly inferior, people, and aiming to 'free' the world from Judaism.[105] The Russian regime, on the other hand, simply designates political opponents

[99] Fundamental works representing the two opposing camps on the question of the pervasiveness of legal transplants include, A Watson, *Legal Transplants: An Approach to Comparative Law* (Scottish Academic Press, 1974, and 2nd edn University of Georgia Press, 1993); O Kahn-Freund, 'On Uses and Misuses of Comparative Law' (1974) 37 *The Modern Law Review* 1; P Legrand, 'The Impossibility of "Legal Transplants"' (1997) 4 *Maastricht Journal of European and Comparative* Law 111; more recent literature has made "these absolutist visions … [collapse] into a middle ground", see M Cohn, 'Legal Transplant Chronicles: The Evolution of Unreasonableness and Proportionality Review of the Administration in the United Kingdom' (2010) 58 *American Journal of Comparative Law* 583, 587.

[100] Cohn, 'Legal Transplant Chronicles' (n 99) 592.

[101] ibid 593.

[102] See: J Miller, 'A Typology of Legal Transplants: Using Sociology, Legal History and Argentine Examples to Explain the Transplant Process' (2003) 51 *American Journal of Comparative Law* 839, 883.

[103] For examples, see ibid 881; W Osiatynski, 'Paradoxes of constitutional borrowing' (2003) 1 *International Journal of Constitutional Law* 244, 251.

[104] See G de Búrca and K Young, 'The (mis)appropriation of human rights by the new global right: An introduction to the Symposium', (2023) 21 ICON 205–223; see also the symposium organised by J Miklasova, P Rhein-Fischer and C Van de Graaf, 'Misappropriation and Human Rights Implosion', 6–8 November 2023 in Hanover.

[105] K Schubert and M Klein, In Bundeszentrale für politische Bildung (ed), *Das Politiklexikon*, 7th ed. (Dietz, 2020).

as 'Nazis', including the democratically elected Ukrainian government and its supporters.[106] Any criticism of Russia's past, such as the qualification of the *Holodomor* as genocide, is seen as the result of 'Nazi' influences aiming to weaken Russia.[107] The concept of 'Nazism' is thus completely cut off from its historical root and the moral condemnation attached to that term is used to outlaw adherents of a sovereign and independent Ukraine. Unlike the outlined German memory laws, the envisaged goal of Russian measures is not to protect, but to conceal true facts, namely that the Ukrainian government and its supporters, rather than striving for racist goals and conducting genocidal acts against ethnic Russians, aspire to Ukraine's rapprochement with the EU and are fighting for its independence.

A second major difference directly follows from this. While the German memory laws analysed here are self-inculpatory in nature, the Russian narrative of 'denazification of Ukraine' and the suggested post-war measures targeting the very critics of Russia serve to justify a brutal war of aggression and a 'cleansing' of Ukrainian society of Russia's opponents, thus seeking to pretend that Russia is once again a superior and morally flawless victor.

Third, while German anti-Nazism memory laws also follow a political agenda, ie, to prevent another Nazi regime, restore Germany's reputation, assure other states that it has become a peaceful country again, and provide the memory of the victims of this historical era special protection, the political agenda pursued through the proposed Russian measures is very different: They are hardly victim-oriented – the purported 'genocide against Russians in Ukraine' being a mere propaganda tool[108] – with the aim being to secure Russia's hegemonial claims and consolidate a fascist regime in Russia after successful annexation of Ukraine. The alleged 'denazification' does not serve any of the purposes traditionally pursued by memory laws of the German kind, including protecting the memory of the victims or society as a whole, human dignity, public peace or public order.[109]

Finally, while denazification measures in Germany were adopted only after WWII, the narrative of 'denazification of Ukraine' has been used not only in the midst of the ongoing Russo-Ukrainian war, but as a justification for it. In this respect, the Russian measures exceed a pure mnemonic purpose, as they also serve to achieve a military victory and thus actively write history.

[106] Fortuin, '"Genocide" in Russian Propaganda' (n 11) 331 f.

[107] ibid 339.

[108] ibid.

[109] The protected interest is often greatly disputed. For the German Holocaust denial ban, eg, they range from public peace (D Beisel, 'Strafbarkeit der Ausschwitzlüge – Zugleich ein Beitrag zur Auslegung des neuen § 130 StGB' (1995) 15 *Neue Juristische Wochenschrift* 1000), the personal dignity of persons belonging to the victim group (Federal Constitutional Court, Order, 22 June 2006, 2 BvR 1421/05, (2006) *BeckRS*, 24381); the victim's identity and right to historical truth (H Ostendorf, 'Im Streit: Die strafrechtliche Verfolgung der Auschwitzlüge', (1985) 19 *Neue Juristische Wochenschrift* 1062, 1062) to the collective memory of victims and today's society (M Matuschek, *Erinnerungsstrafrecht: Eine Neubegründung des Verbots der Holocaustleugnung auf rechtsvergleichender und sozialphilosophischer Grundlage* (Duncker & Humblot, 2012) 102 ff).

Against this background, the proposed measures of 'denazification of Ukraine' share nothing more with German denazification measures than their name and superficial technical functioning, hence representing a striking example of distortion of foreign legal rules. As Maria Mälksoo accurately puts it in her chapter of this volume, Putin's employing of the term 'denazification' 'is reminiscent of the Humpty Dumpty character in Lewis Carroll's book', boasting that when he uses a word, it means just what he chooses it to mean.[110]

As in other distortion cases, the goal here is to generate legitimacy for the envisaged measures. Although denazification measures were rejected by many in post-war Germany and considered as unjust or insufficient,[111] the general idea behind German denazification today has been met with wide acceptance, both internationally and in Germany. The same is true for persisting memory laws, that, although criticised in their details, reflect a relatively large consensus that the memory of Nazi crimes should be particularly protected in Germany. Therefore, a strong legitimacy attaches to the concept of 'denazification of post-war Germany'. By distorting this concept, Putin's regime seeks to transfer this legitimacy to the measures envisaged for Ukraine. Though foreign governments and populations free from Russian state propaganda may easily recognise this narrative as deception, such propaganda appears to primarily address Russia's own population, serving to increase domestic support for the war and the envisaged post-war measures.

At the same time, by targeting Ukrainian critics of Russia, including those contesting the Russian spotless self-image of a heroic victor of WWII, the denazification narrative reflects mnemonical status anxiety[112] and thus also possesses an international dimension. This narrative further interweaves the self-image regarding WWII with the future memory of the ongoing war against Ukraine, thus seeking to secure Russia a high status in the international hierarchy of remembering this war. Ironically, the tool that Putin's regime uses – blaming Ukrainian leaders and their supporters as Nazis – is precisely what a recent Russian memory law of April 2022 protects its own predecessor against, namely, the leadership and personnel of the USSR.[113]

V. ELEMENTS OF MILITANT MEMOCRACY

The Russian distortion of the German prototype of memory laws raises two more general questions: To what extent is distortion inherent in the categories of memory laws and militant democracy? And are there criteria to identify a

[110] See M Mälksoo's Chapter 15 of this volume. Lewis Carroll, *Through the Looking Glass* (1871).
[111] Romeike 'Transitional Justice' (n 56) 23.
[112] See above nn 30 to 32 and accompanying text.
[113] A Nekoliak and E Klochkova, 'Weaponizing Russia's Memory Law' (*Verfassungsblog*, 11 July 2023): https://verfassungsblog.de/weaponizing-russias-memory-law/.

tipping point where legitimate memory governance turns into illegitimate distortion, or, as Mälksoo has put it, a 'militant memocracy'?[114]

The concept of 'militant memocracy' offers an interesting twist on the concept of militant democracy. Both concepts compromise certain democratic standards for the sake of defending a system's feasibility.[115] However, Mälksoo identifies three major differences. First, unlike militant democracy, militant memocracy is not about defending the liberal core of democracy, but about 'protect[ing] a national historical memory/mnemonic narrative from alternative accounts contesting it'. Second, rather than 'merely compromising with some procedural features of democracy for the sake of thus saving the system from its antithetical contestants', militant memocracy 'can go to great length about restricting liberal rights'. Third, militant memocracy seeks to 'create and control a heroic or victimised fantasy of an entire nation via memory laws designed to discipline and punish anyone endangering such idealised self-image'.[116]

The problem with this distinction is that many characteristics attributed to the militant memocracy concept appear in reality to also attach to militant democracy – at least if memory laws such as Holocaust denial bans are counted in the sphere of militant democracy.[117] For these provisions, while indeed being about defending the liberal core of democracy, can still protect a mnemonic narrative from alternative accounts, namely, the narrative that the Holocaust represented a great historical catastrophe, and possibly even the more controversial interpretation of its historical singularity.[118] Similarly, these laws do more than compromising some procedural features of democracy; rather, they restrict liberal rights such as the freedom of expression considerably. This is precisely why the idea of militant democracy has remained so controversial among scholars.[119] Even the third identified feature of militant memocracy – the idea of self-victimisation – may, to some extent, also be found in certain militant democracy provisions without any negative connotation. For example, an argument could be made that an Israeli Holocaust denial ban can also form part of militant democracy.

[114] Mälksoo, 'Militant Memocracy' (n 23), especially 504–6.

[115] ibid 504.

[116] ibid 505.

[117] For this connection in the case law of the European Court of Human Rights, see P Rhein-Fischer, 'The Legal Value of the Militant Democracy Concept in the ECtHR Case Law on Genocide Denial Bans', in P Czech et al (eds), (2022) *European Yearbook on Human Rights* 483-514.

[118] This long-standing interpretation in Germany has recently been challenged as part of the so-called "second historians' dispute", see S Neimann and M Wieldt, *Historiker streiten. Gewalt und Holocaust – die Debatte* (Propyläen, 2022).

[119] See, eg, Malkopolou and Kirshner (eds), *Militant Democracy and Its Critics* (n 7); D Oberndörfer, 'Germany's "Militant Democracy": An Attempt to Fight Incitement Against Democracy and Freedom of Speech Through Constitutional Provisions: History and Overall Record' in FK Hazan and D Kretzmer (eds), *Freedom of Speech and Incitement against Democracy* (Kluwer Law International, 2000) 235, 242–44; M Steuer, 'Militant Democracy on the Rise: Consequences of Legal Restrictions on Extreme Speech in the Czech Republic, Slovakia and Hungary' (2019) 44 *Review of Central and East European Law* 162, 197 ff.

I therefore argue that militant democracy and militant memocracy are not two clear-cut categories. Rather, they should be conceived as two opposing poles on a sliding scale on which memory laws can be located, while possibly possessing elements of both concepts. There also does not appear to be any 'tipping point' at which a memory law inevitably falls into one category or the other.

More importantly, the distinctive criteria can further be refined. Looking at the Russian distortion of the German prototype of militant democracy, a first crucial feature is that mnemonic militant democracy seeks to protect *true* historical facts, whilst militant memocracy aims to conceal historical truth. However, only *facts* can be qualified as true or false, whereas great parts of mnemonic narratives relate to interpretations and opinions where truth is no useful category. Thus, further criteria are needed, another important one being the image that the memory law draws of the legislating state. While, as illustrated above, not every memory law that attributes responsibility for historical crimes to a third state may be considered 'militantly memocratic', the opposite is correct: the more self-critical and self-inculpatory a memory law is, the more this law leans towards the militant democracy pole. By contrast, laws that are clearly motivated by the idea to present their own nation in a uniquely positive light, attributing to it a heroic role that appears unjustifiable in view of the actual historical circumstances, can be regarded as tending towards the militant memocracy pole. A third indicator appears to be whether the law primarily aims to protect the democratic system against its enemies and victims of historical crimes or whether it pursues other political – eg, imperial – goals, as the Russian measures of 'denazification' do.

VI. CONCLUSION

Overall, as with any legal technique, legitimate memory laws seeking to protect democracy from its enemies appear to incorporate the inherent risk of being abused and completely distorted into a 'militant memocracy'. Though a specific tipping point cannot be identified, criteria indicating whether a law leans more towards militant democracy or militant memocracy do exist. These are: the degree to which they (1) protect or conceal historical truth, (2) are self-inculpatory or attribute an unjustified heroic image to the legislating nation, and (3) seek to protect democracy or pursue other political goals. The Russian example is a particularly clear case of 'memocracy' and distortive legal transplantation, given the extent to which the Russian narrative of 'denazification of Ukraine' perverts the truth, ties in with its self-image of a spotless hero of WWII, and pursues anti-democratic goals of securing the fascist regime in Russia after an annexation of Ukraine. However, other cases may not be as clear, and it is in these grey areas that it is more difficult to assess, for other actors, whether the narrative should be supported or refuted. Against this background, legislators should generally remain cautious when adopting mnemonic militant democracy rules, as they may inadvertently provide the next prototype for distortion.

13

Memory Narratives and Policies in the European Union and the Council of Europe in the Context of Russian Military Aggression from 2014 to 2023

ANNA WÓJCIK

I. INTRODUCTION

THE OCCUPATION AND annexation of Crimea by Russia in 2014, and the ensuing conflict between Russia and Ukraine – which culminated in Russia's full-scale invasion of Ukraine in 2022 – has reshaped the security landscape in Europe and significantly impacted two crucial European transnational organisations, namely, the European Union (EU) and the Council of Europe (CoE). The EU and the CoE considered Russia's actions a violation of international law, and expressed political, military, economic, and humanitarian support for Ukraine, whilst simultaneously emphasising its territorial integrity and sovereignty, and deploring Belarusian involvement.[1] These policies were supported by changes in the official historical narratives of both organisations, which resulted in an important correction of the European memory framework.

Russia attempted to legitimise its aggression through ideological historical narratives and by invoking alleged historical parallels. Ukraine has vehemently rejected such claims and has provided evidence to counter Russian historical propaganda.[2] The leaders and institutions of the EU and CoE have aligned themselves with Ukraine in the realm of historical narrative, actively reshaping the official historical accounts of their organisations in terms of their relationships

[1] See: 'EU response to Russia's war of aggression against Ukraine' (*European Council*) www.consilium.europa.eu/en/policies/eu-response-ukraine-invasion/; 'Russia's war against Ukraine: Follow up' (*Council of Europe*): www.coe.int/en/web/portal/war-in-ukraine/follow-up.

[2] See, eg: U Belavusau, A Gliszczyńska-Grabias, and M Mälksoo, 'Memory Laws and Memory Wars in Poland, Russia, and Ukraine' (2021) 69 *Jahrbuch des Öffentlichen Rechts der Gegenwart* 95.

with Russia and Ukraine. Political leaders, states, and international or transnational organisations who interpret the past in light of present developments and interests, consider historical narratives to be an asset in bilateral and multilateral relations and consequently, part of their diplomatic strategies.[3] In the literature concerning Europeanisation, the role of crises in driving the integration of European states and societies, most notably through the EU and the CoE, is often underscored.[4]

This chapter seeks to answer how the institutions of the EU (that is, the European Parliament (EP) and the European Commission) and the CoE (that is, the Committee of Ministers, the Parliamentary Assembly of the Council of Europe – PACE, and the European Court of Human Rights – ECtHR) have recalibrated official historical narratives regarding Ukraine and Russia from 2014 to December 2023, against the backdrop of Russian military aggression. It explores how the European 'region of memory',[5] a political project created to develop a shared realm of remembrance, has evolved in the past decade and (finally) expanded to include remembrance of Soviet crimes. To achieve these objectives, doctrinal analysis and discourse analysis are performed using official documents from both organisations.

The catastrophe of WWII spurred the project of European integration[6] that included the establishment of the CoE in 1949 and the EU's predecessor, the European Coal and Steel Community (ECSC) in 1951. The European project, essentially a peace and reconciliation project, was aimed at pacifying intra-European relations, primarily through Franco-German cooperation, and further reconciliation and cooperation between other European states. The CoE and the EU have been built around the remembrance of WWII victims, condemnation of the war's atrocities, a pledge to draw lessons from the darkest chapter of recent European history, and to strive for post-war renewal and economic prosperity. Since the late 1970s, Western European democracies, notably Germany, have made commemorating Holocaust victims a central aspect of their historical policy and collective memory.[7] Initially, European integration was built around positive aspects of shared historical heritage. However, in the 1990s and 2000s, the memory of the genocide of European Jews became not only central to the

[3] See, eg: K Bachleitner, 'Memory in International Diplomacy' in M Mälksoo (ed), *Handbook on the Politics of Memory* (Edward Elgar Publishing, 2023) 246–57.

[4] See, eg: S Saurugger, 'Europeanisation in Times of Crisis' (2014) 12 *Political Studies Review* 181.

[5] See especially: S Lewis and J Wawrzyniak, 'Introduction: Regions of Memory in Theory' in S Lewis and others (eds), *Regions of Memory: Transnational Formations* (Springer Nature, 2022) 1–16.

[6] See, eg: PJ Verovšek, *Memory and the future of Europe: Rupture and integration in the wake of total war* (Manchester University Press, 2020).

[7] See, eg: P Rhein-Fischer and S Mensing, *Memory Laws in Germany. How Remembering National Socialism is Governed through Law, a report by the research consortium 'The Challenges of Populist Memory Politics and Militant Memory Laws (Memocracy)'* (Torkel Opsahl Academic Epublisher, 2022) 5.

European memory culture but institutionalised.[8] The EU has gradually built on these initial efforts in order to create a unified project focused on European memory.[9] In the 1990s and 2000s, the European Parliament (EP) passed several resolutions on WWII and the genocide of European Jews. Notably, in 1995, 27 January was deemed to be a European day to commemorate the Holocaust. Later, in 2005, the EP adopted the Resolution on remembrance of the Holocaust, antisemitism and racism.[10] In 2008, the EU encouraged Member States to punish Holocaust denial.[11]

After the fall of the Iron Curtain in 1989, political and legal Europeanisation of formerly communist states from CEE took place. In the 1990s and 2000s, these states were included in the CoE and the EU, the majority acceding through the 2004 EU enlargement round. The new members of European structures were expected to internalise European memory culture, which focused on remembrance of WWII in the context of the Holocaust. After freeing up historical debate in the 1990s, many societies in CEE started to openly discuss the genocide of Jews and the respective involvement of their states and citizens, which often provoked strong domestic and international reactions.[12] In parallel, CEE societies built their militant democracies and mnemonic constitutionalism[13] on the condemnation of fascism and the two totalitarianisms of the twentieth century: Nazism and Soviet Communism. Post-communist states in CEE have challenged the Western European memory canon and appropriated the visual and symbolic means of cosmopolitan memory of the Holocaust to reposition the crimes of communism and equate them with Nazi atrocities.[14] Furthermore, they have demanded the expansion of European remembrance culture and inclusion of their own distinctive historical memories of twentieth-century mass violence, WWII and its consequences, with particular reference to Soviet aggression, occupation, and decades of domination marred by human rights violations.[15] These demands have been met with

[8] See, eg: A Sierp, 'Europeanising memory: the European Union's politics of memory' in Mälksoo (n 3) 81–94.

[9] See, eg: A Sierp, *History, Memory, and Trans-European Identity: Unifying Divisions* (Routledge, 2014).

[10] European Parliament resolution on remembrance of the Holocaust, anti-semitism and racism P6_TA(2005)0018 [2005] OJ C 253E.

[11] Council Framework Decision 2008/913/JHA of 28 November 2008 on combating certain forms and expressions of racism and xenophobia by means of criminal law [2008] OJ L 328/55.

[12] The Polish debate about the pogrom of Jews in the village of Jedwabne in 1941 serves as an example. See, eg: G Zubrzycki, 'Jan Gross's *Neighbors* and Poland's Narrative Shock' (2022) 112 *Jewish Quarterly Review* 234.

[13] See, especially: U Belavusau, 'Mnemonic Constitutionalism and Rule of Law in Hungary and Russia' (2020) 1 *Interdisciplinary Journal of Populism* 16.

[14] See, especially: J Subotić, 'The Appropriation of Holocaust Memory in Post-Communist Eastern Europe' (*Modern Languages Open*, 4 August 2022): https://modernlanguagesopen.org/articles/10.3828/mlo.v0i0.315.

[15] See, especially: M Mälksoo, 'The Memory Politics of Becoming European: The East European Subalterns and the Collective Memory of Europe' (2009) 15 *European Journal of International Relations* 653.

varying degrees of success.[16] The mnemonic region of Europe is at the heart of the global history of reckoning with the violent past.[17] However, despite pressure from CEE countries, the EU and the CoE institutions were hesitant to include the memory of Soviet crimes in the shared European remembrance culture.[18]

This chapter posits that the security and political landscape in Europe which emerged following Russia's annexation of Crimea in 2014 created conditions for integration of the dominant assessment of the Soviet regime in CEE countries into a shared historical narrative of united Europe. The EU and the CoE condemned the current Russian regime's imperialist and expansionist foreign policy as well as its totalitarian turn in domestic policy, both of which are underpinned by historical narratives. In the past, European narratives emphasised historical ties with Russia and portrayed it as both a victim and a victor of WWII, but never the aggressor and oppressor. Recent violations of international law, including the cruel crimes committed by Russia against Ukraine, have incentivised the EU and the CoE to remember historical crimes committed by Russia in its various forms of statehood, including the Soviet crimes against states and peoples that are currently facing territorial demands or other threats from Putin's Russia.

II. THE EUROPEAN UNION

A. The European Parliament

The EP resolutions from 2014 to 2023 reflect a growing recognition of the complexities surrounding EU-Russia relations and a shift in the EP's perception of Ukraine, which was once viewed primarily through the lens of EU foreign policy. The EP's evolving stance towards Russia underscored the EU's commitment to defending its core values and safeguarding the security and stability of its Member States and partners. The EP resolutions address contemporary challenges and weave a historical narrative about Ukraine and Russia.

In 2014, the EP honoured the Maidan Uprising protest victims for standing up for European values. The protests were ignited by the decision of then Ukrainian president, Viktor Yanukovich, to suspend the signing of the

[16] See, eg: M Mälksoo 'Criminalizing Communism: Transnational Mnemopolitics in Europe' (2014) 8 *International Political Sociology* 82; L Neumayer, 'Integrating the Central European Past into a Common Narrative: The Mobilizations Around the 'Crimes of Communism' in the European Parliament' (2015) 23 *Journal of Contemporary European Studies* 344; A Gliszczyńska-Grabias and G Baranowska, 'The European Court of Human Rights on Nazi and Soviet Past in Central and Eastern Europe' (2016) 45 *Polish Political Science Yearbook* 117.

[17] L Neumayer, 'Agents of memory politics' in M Mälksoo (n 3) 116–29.

[18] See, eg: A Gliszczyńska-Grabias, 'Communism Equals or Versus Nazism?: Europe's Unwholesome Legacy in Strasbourg' (2016) 30 *East European Politics and Societies* 74.

Association Agreement with the EU.[19] The EU condemned Russia's aggression against Ukraine's Crimea and its annexation, and responded by imposing its first sanctions against Russia in March 2014. In 2015, the EP refused recognition of, and condemned, the illegal annexation of Crimea. In doing so, it drew a parallel with Russia's prior aggression towards Georgia in 2008, highlighting a pattern of disregard for international law.[20] By 2019, the EP's concerns over Russia's destabilising activities in EU Member States, such as hostile spying, had escalated and the urgency of addressing these security challenges (reminiscent of Cold War-era tactics) was recognised. The EP supported a cautious approach in the EU's Russia policy.[21]

In 2019, on the 80th anniversary of the outbreak of WWII, the EP adopted a Resolution on the importance of European remembrance for the future of Europe.[22] The EP called upon states to raise awareness, conduct moral assessments, and pursue legal inquiries into the crimes of Stalinism and other dictatorships (recital E), and articulated a vision of European memory rooted in acknowledgment of the victims and education about the shared legacy of crimes perpetrated by communist, Nazi, and other dictatorships (recital I). Moreover, the EP recognised remembrance as essential for fostering European unity and resilience against modern external threats (recital I), and denounced historical revisionism and the contemporary glorification of Nazi collaborators within EU Member States (paragraph 7).

In a notable departure from the EU's focus on remembrance culture, the resolution also addressed Russia's current historical narrative. Having acknowledged Russia as being one of the greatest victims of communist totalitarianism (paragraph 15), the EP highlighted the current government's whitewashing of crimes and its glorification of the Soviet regime. The EP underscored the detrimental impact of this distortion of historical facts on Russia's democratic development, framing it as a barrier to progress. In addition, the EP depicted Russian historical narratives as constituting part of an information war aimed at undermining democratic Europe. The EP called on Russian society to come to terms with its tragic past (paragraph 15).

Russian leadership denounced the EP's resolution for attributing the outbreak of WWII to the 1939 Molotov-Ribbentrop pact.[23] Russian officials praised the pact as a Soviet triumph and objected to the equal blame assigned to Hitler and

[19] European Parliament resolution of 27 February 2014 on the situation in Ukraine (2014/2595(RSP)) [2017] OJ C 285.

[20] European Parliament resolution of 11 June 2015 on the strategic military situation in the Black Sea Basin following the illegal annexation of Crimea by Russia (2015/2036(INI)) [2016] OJ C 407.

[21] European Parliament resolution of 12 March 2019 on the state of EU-Russia political relations (2018/2158(INI)) [2021] OJ C 23.

[22] European Parliament resolution of 19 September 2019 on the importance of European remembrance for the future of Europe (2019/2819(RSP)) [2021] OJ C 171.

[23] ibid.

Stalin.[24] Putin made inflammatory remarks accusing Poland of starting the war, triggering condemnation from the Polish government.[25] Russian parliamentarians rebuked Poland, citing Soviet responsibility for defeating fascism.[26] The EU responded to Russia's historical distortion with condemnation. The European Commission intervened, declaring intolerance for historical distortion and framing Russia's actions as disinformation. Vice President of the European Commission, Věra Jourová, emphasised the EU's rejection of false claims and its commitment to fighting disinformation.[27]

From 2020 to 2021, the EP closely monitored developments within Russia and its neighbouring countries. The EP condemned the Russian 'foreign agents' law aimed at civil society organisations,[28] the arrest and poisoning of opposition politician Alexei Navalny[29,30] the military build-up on Ukraine's border, Russian attacks in the Czech Republic,[31] Russia's listing of German civil society organisations as 'undesirable organisations', and the detention of Russian political activists.[32]

In September 2021, the EP adopted recommendations on the direction of EU-Russia political relations,[33] addressing the evolving dynamics and challenges within this relationship. Central to these recommendations were guiding principles designed to inform and shape the EU's approach: deterrence of the Russian security threat; countering its interference in the EU and neighbouring countries in the East; engagement and selective dialogue with Russia's leadership

[24] D Vseviov, 'The echo of the Hitler-Stalin pact, 81 years later' (*Communist Crimes*, 26 August 2020): https://communistcrimes.org/en/echo-hitler-stalin-pact-81-years-later.

[25] Uchwała Sejmu RP z dnia 9 stycznia 2020 r. w sprawie wyrażenia sprzeciwu wobec manipulowania faktami i zakłamywania historii przez polityków Federacji Rosyjskiej w celu dyskredytowania Polski i pogarszania relacji rosyjsko-polskich M.P. 2020 no 34 [PL].

[26] 'Депутаты будут защищать историческую правду на международных площадках (*Подробнее в ПГ*, 14 January 2020): www.pnp.ru/politics/deputaty-budut-zashhishhat-istoricheskuyu-pravdu-na-mezhdunarodnykh-ploshhadkakh.html.

[27] 'EU raps Russia for saying Poland helped start World War Two' (*Reuters*, 15 October 2020): www.reuters.com/article/us-eu-poland-russia/eu-raps-russia-for-saying-poland-helped-start-world-war-two-idUSKBN1ZE2J4/.

[28] European Parliament resolution of 19 December 2019 on the Russian "foreign agents' law (2019/2982(RSP)) [2021] OJ C 255.

[29] European Parliament resolution of 17 September 2020 on the situation in Russia: the poisoning of Alexei Navalny (2020/2777(RSP)) [2021] OJ C 385.

[30] European Parliament resolution of 21 January 2021 on the arrest of Aleksei Navalny (2021/2513(RSP)) [2021] OJ C 456.

[31] European Parliament resolution of 29 April 2021 on Russia, the case of Alexei Navalny, the military build-up on Ukraine's border and Russian attacks in the Czech Republic (2021/2642(RSP)) [2021] OJ C 506.

[32] European Parliament resolution of 10 June 2021 on the listing of German NGOs as 'undesirable organisations' by Russia and the detention of Andrei Pivovarov (2021/2749(RSP)) [2022] OJ C 67.

[33] European Parliament recommendation of 16 September 2021 to the Council, the Commission and the Vice-President of the Commission/ High Representative of the Union for Foreign Affairs and Security Policy on the direction of EU-Russia political relations (2021/2042(INI)) [2022] OJ C 117: https://www.europarl.europa.eu/doceo/document/TA-9-2021-0383_EN.html.

to prepare Russia's transition to democracy; and support of pro-democracy Russian civil society.

In the recommendations, the EP acknowledged historical interdependencies, cultural ties, and substantial economic relations between the EU and Russia, and made a clear distinction between the Russian people and the state before criticising President Vladimir Putin's regime as a 'stagnating authoritarian kleptocracy' (recital B). The EP considered the aggressive and revisionist policies of the Russian authorities as one of the main challenges to the EU's strategic and foreign policy agenda. Moreover, the EP condemned Russia's actions which sought to subordinate territories and destabilise Ukraine, Moldova, Georgia, and Belarus.

Additionally, the EP addressed domestic constitutional developments in Russia. It condemned the 2020 Russian constitutional reforms which expanded presidential powers,[34] whitewashed Soviet history and emphasised Russia as a successor of the Soviet Union. In the recommendations, the EP denounced the introduction of 'the right to intervene internationally' by Russia 'in the defence of Russian compatriots' and prohibited speaking of returning lands claimed by Russia to other countries (recital O). The EP deemed 'President Putin's Russia to be the biggest challenge for European security' (recital AP), criticised his policy of 'Stalinisation of mass consciousness' and repression of independent historians, and called upon Russia to open its archives (paragraph bf). In light of this, the EP called upon the EU to revise its strategy towards Russia and support its pro-democracy civil society. The EP also condemned the use of the 'Russian World' concept as a pretext for interference in other countries or the assassinations of regime opponents and independent journalists. Furthermore, it deplored the erosion of civil liberties in Russia, including imprisonment, killings, and extensive discrimination against the LGBT community.

The EP officially recognised the series of events leading up to Russia's full-scale war against Ukraine in 2022. In November 2021, the EP condemned the Kremlin's use of private military and security companies, acknowledging its continuation of the Soviet Union's historical deployment of proxy forces abroad.[35] In December 2021, the EP expressed concern over the movement of Russian troops near the Ukrainian border, signalling a potential escalation of tensions in the region.[36]

On 24 February 2022, Russia invaded Ukraine. Four days later, Ukraine applied for EU membership. On 1 March 2022, the EP condemned Russian aggression against Ukraine, unequivocally labelling it as an unprovoked and

[34] See, eg: E Teague, 'Russias Constitutional Reforms of 2020' (2020) 5 *Russian Politics* 301.

[35] European Parliament resolution of 25 November 2021 on the human rights violations by private military and security companies, particularly the Wagner Group (2021/2982(RSP)) [2022] OJ C 224.

[36] European Parliament resolution of 16 December 2021 on the situation at the Ukrainian border and in Russian-occupied territories of Ukraine (2021/3010(RSP)) [2022] OJ C 251.

unjustified invasion.[37] Additionally, it condemned Belarusian involvement in the aggression and affirmed its support for the sovereignty and territorial integrity of all Eastern Partnership (EaP) countries.[38]

The EP has remained deeply engaged in addressing the ongoing crisis in Ukraine. Between the onset of the war and December 2023, the EP passed 27 resolutions related to Ukraine. These resolutions addressed various critical aspects of the conflict, such as human rights violations, the fight against impunity for crimes committed in Ukraine, and the call for establishment of a tribunal to address the crime of aggression against Ukraine. Furthermore, the EP actively advocated for the provision of macro-financial assistance to Ukraine and imposition of sanctions against Russia, among other measures aimed at supporting Ukraine and restoring peace and stability in the region. In June 2022, the EP reaffirmed its commitment to the European perspective of Ukraine, the Republic of Moldova, and Georgia by endorsing their candidate status for EU enlargement.[39] This resolution underscored the EP's belief in the European aspirations of these countries and signalled its readiness to advance their integration into the EU.

The EP's support for Ukraine was also expressed in a resolution recognising the historical atrocity against Ukrainians, namely, the Great Famine of 1932–33 (called '*Holodomor*' or 'murder by hunger'), orchestrated by the Soviet Union.[40] The *Holodomor* occurred prior to the adoption of the UN Convention for the Prevention and Punishment of the Crime of Genocide in 1948. However, in 2003, the Ukrainian parliament recognised it as genocide and, in November 2022, called on the world's parliaments to follow this example.[41] While the EP commemorated the *Holodomor* in 2008 as 'an appalling crime against Ukrainian people' and a crime against humanity, it stopped short of officially recognising it as genocide.[42] However, in 2022, the EP denounced the cynical and cruel policy of the Soviet regime as being aimed at suppressing the Ukrainian people and their national identity (recital B) and deemed it genocide. The EP highlighted that the Soviets also used a deliberate starvation policy in Kazakhstan, Belarus, and the North Caucasus. Moreover, the EP drew parallels with the present actions of Putin's Russia in Ukraine (the destruction of energy and agricultural

[37] European Parliament resolution of 1 March 2022 on the Russian aggression against Ukraine (2022/2564(RSP)) [2022] OJ C 125.

[38] The six EaP countries are Armenia, Azerbaijan, Belarus, Georgia, Moldova and Ukraine.

[39] European Parliament resolution of 23 June 2022 on the candidate status of Ukraine, the Republic of Moldova and Georgia (2022/2716(RSP)) [2023] OJ C 32.

[40] European Parliament resolution of 15 December 2022 on 90 years after the Holodomor: recognising the mass killing through starvation as genocide (2022/3001(RSP)) [2023] OJ C 177.

[41] 'The Verkhovna Rada of Ukraine appealed to the parliaments of the countries of the world to recognize the Holodomor as genocide of the Ukrainian people' (*Holodomor Museum*): https://holodomormuseum.org.ua/en/news/the-verkhovna-rada-of-ukraine-appealed-to-the-parliaments-of-the-countries-of-the-world-to-recognize-the-holodomor-as-genocide-of-the-ukrainian-people/.

[42] European Parliament resolution of 23 October 2008 on the commemoration of the Holodomor, the Ukraine artificial famine (1932–1933) [2010] OJ C 15E.

infrastructure, the blocking of Ukrainian grain exports and the theft of millions of tons of grain) and warned that they might lead to large-scale, artificial famine, especially in the Global South (recital B). The EP also shed light on the fact that Soviet crimes have not yet received a precise legal and moral evaluation by the international community. Finally, the EP established a link between the whitewashing and glorification of the totalitarian Soviet regime, the revival of Stalin's cult in Russia, and Russia being a state sponsor of terrorism and a state using terrorist means today.

The EP has not only recognised historical crimes of the Soviet Union against Ukrainians as genocide; it has also condemned Russia's current actions in Ukraine, having drawn comparisons with historical methods of the Soviet Union (deemed to be criminal). In September 2022, the EP elaborated on the strong historical parallels between Russia's actions in Ukraine and Soviet crimes across occupied territories.[43] In particular, it drew attention to the forced mass Soviet deportations and Gulag camps, in an effort to underline the importance of remembrance, historical research, and education about the totalitarian past in strengthening democracies and combatting disinformation.

In November 2022, the EP argued that Russia's war against Ukraine underscored the necessity for a thorough historical and legal evaluation, as well as transparent public debate about the crimes of the Soviet regime.[44] This evaluation was deemed crucial, particularly within Russia itself, as the lack of accountability and justice risked perpetuating the repetition of similar crimes (paragraph 17). Moreover, the EP characterised the repression against civil society in Russia today as 'totalitarian' (recital L). In a resolution from March 2022, addressing foreign influence in Europe, the EP highlighted Russia's resort to historical revisionism, its attempts to rewrite the narrative of Soviet crimes, and its promotion of 'Soviet nostalgia' in CEE societies.[45] All of these were identified as components of a broader disinformation campaign and as foreign interference in democratic processes in Europe. In the September 2022 resolution, the EP called for a free debate on Soviet crimes, particularly within Russia, to promote accountability and historical truth.

To conclude, the EP's changing view on EU-Russia policy, propelled by geopolitical and security developments, and internal developments in Russia in 2014–23, inspired an important change in the EU's culture of remembrance – one which aligns with the EU's long-term emphasis on confronting and remembering historical injustices in order to promote peace, reconciliation, and democracy. The EP denounced Russia's historical narratives glorifying the

[43] European Parliament resolution of 15 September 2022 on human rights violations in the context of the forced deportation of Ukrainian civilians to and the forced adoption of Ukrainian children in Russia (2022/2825(RSP)) [2023] OJ C 125.

[44] European Parliament resolution of 23 November 2022 on recognising the Russian Federation as a state sponsor of terrorism (2022/2896(RSP)) [2023] OJ C 167.

[45] European Parliament resolution of 9 March 2022 on foreign interference in all democratic processes in the European Union, including disinformation (2020/2268(INI)) [2022] OJ C 347.

Soviet Union and other measures used to foster nostalgia for the Soviet empire in Russia's neighbourhood. Regarding Russia's actions in Ukraine, the EP has consistently condemned the invasion and subsequent aggression. Over time, the EP has deepened its critique of Russia's government, drawing parallels between Putin's regime's policies and actions (in Russia and Ukraine) and the historical methods of the Soviet Union, which it has condemned as criminal and totalitarian. The EP has also highlighted the lack of free historical debate in Russia on Soviet crimes as a significant obstacle to democratisation. This observation reflects recognition that open and transparent discussion about historical crimes is essential for fostering democratic principles and accountability within society. To this end, the EP has recognised an atrocious historical crime against Ukraine, the *Holodomor*, as genocide committed against Ukrainians by the Soviet Union. Moreover, the EP has repeatedly and unequivocally denounced historical distortions and examined them as a part of external disinformation campaigns aiming to destabilise the EU through sowing social divisions. Through its resolutions, the EP contributes to shaping a collective memory that acknowledges the Soviet regime's murderous, criminal and totalitarian character while advocating for accountability for Russia's crimes in the present.

B. The European Commission

The annual State of the European Union (SOTEU) addresses by the President of the European Commission serve as a barometer of the evolving dynamics between the EU and Ukraine in the context of Russia's aggression from 2014 to 2023, providing insights into the EU's responses, commitments, and evolving narratives, including historical ones. In the period analysed, there were two Presidents of the European Commission: Jean-Claude Juncker (2015–18) and Ursula von der Leyen (2020–23).

In Juncker's first address in 2015, Ukraine was mentioned cautiously in the context of the migration crisis, with reference made to the European challenge of aiding Ukraine's reforms and prosperity, and recognising Ukraine's EU membership aspirations ('Ukraine's dream is European'[46]). In 2016, Juncker expressed support for Ukraine's territorial integrity, sovereignty, and commitment to the Minsk agreements, which sought to end the Donbas war being fought between armed Russian separatist groups and the Armed Forces of Ukraine.[47] In 2017, he emphasised the importance of the Association Agreement

[46] 'State of the Union 2015 by Jean-Claude Juncker, President of the European Commission' (*European Commission*, 9 September 2015): https://commission.europa.eu/system/files/2015-12/state_of_the_union_2015_en.pdf.

[47] 'State of the Union 2016 by Jean-Claude Juncker, President of the European Commission' (*European Commission*, 14 September 2016): https://op.europa.eu/en/publication-detail/-/publication/c9ff4ff6-9a81-11e6-9bca-01aa75ed71a1.

and the EU's commitment to stability and prosperity in eastern neighbours.[48] In 2018, Ukraine was absent from the SOTEU[49] and accompanying documents listed Ukraine as one of six EaP countries.[50]

The SOTEU addresses reflect not only a shift in focus over time, but also changing geopolitical and security circumstances in Europe. Juncker's speeches primarily addressed Ukraine's integration with the EU and support for its reforms and territorial integrity after the annexation of Crimea. Under von der Leyen, SOTEU speeches reflected the change in EU-Russia policy. In 2020, the President of the European Commission warned advocates for closer ties with Russia that the poisoning of Russian opposition politician Alexei Navalny was not an isolated event.[51] In 2021, Ukraine was once again absent from the annual speech,[52] which showcased how the EU underestimated the threat from Russia. The 2022 SOTEU, delivered after Russia's full-scale invasion of Ukraine, highlighted solidarity with Ukraine amidst the ongoing war, framing it as a battle between autocracy and democracy.[53] Von der Leyen emphasised that Russia wages war not only against Ukraine, but also against the EU's energy security, economy, values, and future.[54] She focused on the plight of civilians and thanked Ukrainians for their courage. She also expressed regret for not listening to earlier warnings about Putin, coming from civil society in Russia, Ukraine, Moldova, Georgia, and EU Member States (Poland, the Baltics, and other states in CEE). Von der Leyen outlined the plan for the adaptation of European societies to the new reality in which Russian missiles threaten the promise of democracy and the rule of law that have underpinned European integration since WWII. The EU roots in the post-war European reconciliation and reconstruction ambitions were also mentioned in 2023 in a speech titled 'Answering the Call of History'.[55] Von der Leyen underscored the EU's historical mission and the need for unity in facing present challenges. Her speech focused on EU resilience in energy and economy, as well as efforts to combat climate change. She

[48] 'State of the Union 2017 by Jean-Claude Juncker, President of the European Commission' (*European Commission*, 13 September 2017): https://commission.europa.eu/system/files/2017-10/state-union-2017-brochure_en.pdf.

[49] 'State of the Union 2018. The Hour of European Sovereignty. Authorised version of the State of the Union Address 2018' (*European Commission*): https://commission.europa.eu/system/files/2018-09/soteu2018-speech_en_0.pdf.

[50] 'State of the Union 2018, by Jean-Claude Juncker, President of the European Commission' (*European Commission*, 12 September 2018): https://commission.europa.eu/system/files/2018-09/soteu2018-brochure_en.pdf, 48.

[51] 'State of the Union Address by President von der Leyen at the European Parliament Plenary' (*European Commission*, 16 September 2020): https://ec.europa.eu/commission/presscorner/detail/ov/SPEECH_20_1655.

[52] '2021 State of the Union Address by President von der Leyen' (*European Commission*, 15 September 2021): https://ec.europa.eu/commission/presscorner/detail/ov/SPEECH_21_4701.

[53] '2022 State of the Union Address by President von der Leyen' (*European Commission*, 14 September 2022): https://ec.europa.eu/commission/presscorner/detail/en/speech_22_5493.

[54] ibid.

[55] '2023 State of the Union Address by President von der Leyen' (*European Commission*, 13 September 2023): https://ec.europa.eu/commission/presscorner/detail/ov/speech_23_4426.

highlighted Russia's use of gas as a weapon and expressed concern for potential repercussions beyond Ukraine. Von der Leyen pledged ongoing EU support for Ukraine, praised increased military aid efforts, and mentioned EU membership prospects for Ukraine, the Western Balkans, and Moldova – stressing the merit-based nature of accession. Concluding, she affirmed that EU enlargement serves as a catalyst for progress.

The speeches by Presidents Juncker and von der Leyen highlighted the EU's solidarity with Ukraine and its condemnation of Russian actions. Von der Leyen has recognised past failures to acknowledge the warnings about Putin's intentions. This indicates a more realistic understanding of Russia's geopolitical ambitions and reflects a reshaping of EU-Russia relations in the past decade. The EU leaders expressed an increased awareness of the function of historical narrative distortion in Russian propaganda and recognised it as an element of a broader disinformation and interference campaign in the EU and EaP. In the course of these speeches, the narrative regarding Russia has shifted, transitioning from a romanticised vision to characterising Putin's regime as the chief security threat to the EU. The speeches after Russia's full-scale invasion of Ukraine emphasised support for Ukraine, European unity, and the need for a unified response to Russian aggression. The EU leadership outlined a historical role for the EU, deeply rooted in the original ambitions of European integration: to assure lasting peace and security in Europe.

III. COUNCIL OF EUROPE

Russia's full-scale war against Ukraine in 2022 profoundly impacted the CoE, leading to significant changes in its composition and response mechanisms. The CoE has strongly condemned Russian aggression against Ukraine, urging immediate withdrawal of forces from Ukrainian territory and expressing full support for the Ukrainian people.

As a consequence of Russia's attack on Ukraine, the composition of the CoE has changed considerably. Russia, a member since 1996, submitted a notice of voluntary withdrawal on 15 March 2022, denouncing the European Convention on Human Rights (ECHR) and requesting membership termination by 31 December 2022. On 16 March 2022, the Committee of Ministers expelled Russia from the CoE due to its aggression against Ukraine.[56] Additionally, all relations with Belarus were suspended, including its participation in meetings and activities.

This crisis prompted the CoE to reassess its role in upholding Europe's architecture and the international rules-based order. The Reykjavik Declaration, issued during the CoE's summit, 'United around our values', underscored the

[56] Resolution CM/Res(2022)2 on the cessation of the membership of the Russian Federation to the Council of Europe (Adopted by the Committee of Ministers on 16 March 2022 at the 1428ter meeting of the Ministers' Deputies).

significance of safeguarding free expression and combatting the manipulation of history.[57] Beyond this, the declaration reinforced the foundations the CoE was built upon in 1949, after the disastrous war, namely, the belief that solid democracies are crucial defences against authoritarianism, totalitarianism, and war. The Declaration warns that democracies in Europe face renewed threats, framing Russia's aggression against Ukraine as an assault on democratic principles.[58]

A. Parliamentary Assembly of the Council of Europe (PACE)

PACE has been actively involved in addressing the situation in Ukraine, passing 18 resolutions from 2014 to February 2023, and 12 resolutions from March 2022 to November 2023. PACE expressed its regret for the dramatic events in Kyiv (Maidan) and reaffirmed its support for Ukraine's independence, sovereignty, and territorial integrity.[59] It suspended certain rights of the Russian delegation after the annexation of Crimea and condemned Russia's actions as breaches of international law.[60] Furthermore, PACE denounced the dire situation of refugees and displaced persons in Ukraine,[61] the situation of missing persons,[62] and abducted or captured Ukraine citizens.[63] In 2016, PACE condemned illegal elections held in occupied Crimea and the incorporation of Ukrainian territory into Russia,[64] and deplored human rights violations committed by Russia.[65] In 2018, PACE highlighted the humanitarian consequences of the war in Ukraine,[66] including violations of Crimean Tatars' rights.[67]

PACE has framed the CoE's response to Russia's war as a means of 'setting the course of European history'.[68] It called Russia's full-scale war against Ukraine an act of great gravity and brutality, leading to the gravest humanitarian

[57] 'Reykjavík Declaration United around our values' (*Council of Europe*, May 2023) 7.

[58] ibid, 9.

[59] PACE, Recent developments in Ukraine: threats to the functioning of democratic institutions. Resolution 1988 (2014).

[60] PACE, Reconsideration on substantive grounds of the previously ratified credentials of the Russian delegation, Resolution 1990 (2014); PACE. Consideration of the annulment of the previously ratified credentials of the delegation of the Russian Federation (follow-up to paragraph 16 of Resolution 2034 (2015)) Resolution 2063 (2015).

[61] PACE, The humanitarian situation of Ukrainian refugees and displaced persons. Resolution 2028 (2015).

[62] PACE, Parliamentary Assembly, Resolution 2067 – Missing persons during the conflict in Ukraine, 25 June 2015. Resolution 2067 (2015).

[63] PACE, The humanitarian concerns with regard to people captured during the war in Ukraine, Resolution 2112 (2016).

[64] PACE, Political consequences of the Russian aggression in Ukraine, Resolution 2132 (2016).

[65] PACE, Legal remedies for human rights violations on the Ukrainian territories outside the control of the Ukrainian authorities. Resolution 2133 (2016).

[66] PACE, Humanitarian consequences of the war in Ukraine. Resolution 2198 (2018).

[67] PACE, Human rights violations committed against Crimean Tatars in Crimea. Resolution 2387 (2021).

[68] PACE, Ensuring a just peace in Ukraine and lasting security in Europe. Resolution 2516 (2023).

crisis in Europe since WWII,[69] provoking immense suffering, destruction and displacement.[70] In response, PACE has demanded accountability for serious violations of international humanitarian law and condemned the official state ideology of the 'Russian world' as a means of justifying aggression and promoting war in the Russian military and society.[71]

PACE called for international accountability for crimes committed by Russia, invited the European Court of Human Rights (ECtHR) to prioritise related cases, and emphasised that there cannot be peace without justice.[72] It has supported the creation of an international compensation mechanism for the war's victims and the establishment of the Special International Tribunal for the Crime of Aggression. In 2023, the CoE established a Register of Damage caused by Russia's aggression against Ukraine during the initial three-year period.[73]

PACE has denounced human rights violations and crimes committed by Russia, including the forcible deportation of Ukrainian children, sexual violence, deprivation of liberty of Ukrainians, the (Russian) passportisation of Ukraine's citizens, enforced disappearances, filtration camps, as well as the weaponisation of energy, economic measures, migration, and environmental issues for the purposes of war. Moreover, PACE recognised the *Holodomor* as genocide and urged CoE parliaments to follow suit. It also compared the present-day actions of Russia to that earlier attempt to wipe out Ukrainian nationhood.[74]

B. European Court of Human Rights

On 28 February 2022, Ukraine invoked Article 15 of the ECHR, allowing derogation from securing certain rights and freedoms under the ECHR.[75] PACE unanimously recommended Russia's expulsion from the CoE on 15 March 2022,[76] prompting Russia's withdrawal from both the CoE and its intention

[69] PACE, Consequences of the Russian Federation's continued aggression against Ukraine: role and response of the Council of Europe. Resolution 2433 (2022).

[70] PACE, Further escalation in the Russian Federation's aggression against Ukraine. Resolution 2463 (2022).

[71] PACE, The Russian Federation's aggression against Ukraine: ensuring accountability for serious violations of international humanitarian law and other international crimes. Resolution 2436 (2022).

[72] PACE, Political consequences of the Russian Federation's war of aggression against Ukraine. Resolution 2506 (2023).

[73] Resolution CM/Res(2023)3 establishing the Enlarged Partial Agreement on the Register of Damage Caused by the Aggression of the Russian Federation against Ukraine (Adopted by the Committee of Ministers on 12 May 2023 at the 1466th meeting of the Ministers' Deputies and amended on 27 September 2023 at the 1476th meeting of the Ministers' Deputies).

[74] PACE, Commemorating the victims of the Great Famine (Holodomor) in the former USSR. Resolution 1723 (2010).

[75] 'Legal analysis of the derogation made by Ukraine under Article 15 of the European Convention of Human Rights and Article 4 of the International Covenant on Civil and Political Rights' (*Council of Europe*, November 2022): https://rm.coe.int/legal-analysis-of-the-derogation-made-by-ukraine-under-article-15-of-t/1680aa8e2c.

[76] PACE, Consequences of the Russian Federation's aggression against Ukraine. Opinion 300 (2022).

to denounce the ECHR. One day later, on 16 March 2022, the Committee of Ministers officially excluded Russia from the CoE.[77] Russia ceased ECHR obligations on 16 September 2022.[78] Despite this, Russia passed a Bill rejecting ECtHR judgments after 15 March 2022.[79] Thousands of applications against Russia await ECtHR review, including Ukraine's application and cases related to Crimea and eastern Ukraine.[80] Communication between Russia and CoE institutions has been at a halt since March 2022. Prior to expulsion, Russia selectively implemented ECtHR judgments and allowed non-compliance with unconstitutional findings.[81] Post-expulsion, the ECtHR continued addressing cases against Russia, acknowledging its occupation of eastern Ukraine. Despite Russia's refusal to engage with CoE, ECtHR judgments remain crucial in documenting the Russo-Ukrainian conflict. For example, the ECtHR classified Russia's rule over Crimea as an occupation.[82] The CoE notes that despite cessation of obligations, Russia still has the duty to cooperate with the ECtHR and, under international law, is obliged to implement all its final judgments and decisions.[83]

IV. CONCLUSIONS

The war waged by Russia against Ukraine has profoundly impacted the EU and the CoE by presenting significant challenges which have required the subsequent adaptation of these organisations in order to address the new security and political reality in Europe. In 2014–23, the EU and CoE expressed support of Ukraine and deplored Russia's actions and rhetoric, by changing the historical narrative related to those states and the CEE region more broadly. The focus of the CoE and the EU leadership on present-day atrocities and crimes against Ukrainians propelled the broadening of a common European remembrance to acknowledge the CEE experience of mass violence perpetrated, or directed, by the Soviet

[77] Resolution CM/Res(2022)2 on the cessation of the membership of the Russian Federation to the Council of Europe (Adopted by the Committee of Ministers on 16 March 2022 at the 1428ter meeting of the Ministers' Deputies).

[78] ECtHR, 'The Russian Federation ceases to be a Party to the European Convention on Human Rights' (Press Release Issued by the Registrar of the Court, ECHR 286 (2022), 16.09.2022).

[79] K Koroteev 'Moving On in Strasbourg: How to Deal with the Russian Retreat from the European Court of Human Rights' (*Verfassungsblog*, 12 December 2022): https://verfassungsblog.de/moving-on-in-strasbourg/.

[80] ECtHR. 'Latest rulings by the European Court set out the procedure for future processing of applications against Russia' (Press Release Issued by the Registrar of the Court, ECHR 036 (2023), 03.02.2023); ECtHR, 'The latest rulings by the European Court set out the procedure for future processing of applications against Russia' (Press Release Issued by the Registrar of the Court, ECHR 036 (2023), 03.02.2023).

[81] A Padskocimaite, 'Execution of the ECTHR's Judgments Against Russia: Some Legal (and Political) Aspects' (*Strasbourg Observers*, 15 May 2023):

https://strasbourgobservers.com/2023/05/15/execution-of-the-ecthrs-judgments-against-russia-some-legal-and-political-aspects/.

[82] *Ukraine and the Netherlands v Russia* App No 8019/16, 43800/14, and 28525/20 (ECtHR, 30 November 2022).

[83] Reykjavik Declaration (n 57).

Union. The EU and the CoE have broadened their efforts in terms of integrating narratives concerning the Soviet Union's role in the twentieth century, particularly prominent in the historical 'bloodlands'[84] of CEE.

Notably, the EU and the CoE acknowledged a historical atrocity by the Soviet Union against Ukrainians, the *Holodomor*, as genocide and have drawn parallels between the Soviet Union's policies and present-day Russia's actions. The EU emphasised the need to comprehensively examine Soviet crimes, advocating for open historical debates, particularly within Russia, and argued that it hinders the country's democratisation.

Furthermore, the EU and the CoE considered Russia's invasion a breach of international law, and in doing so, denounced various human rights violations and crimes committed by Russia. In response to such grave actions, European institutions have called for accountability and for compensation for victims. The EU and the CoE recognised Russia's historical narratives as forming part of the official dangerous ideology espoused by the state and deplored the use of the 'Russian world' concept as a justification for aggression.

The EU and CoE have perceived the Russian threat as a menace to the democratic security of their Member States, with Putin's regime constituting a major security threat. Both organisations harkened back to their origins; they emerged in response to the aftermath of WWII in Europe.

The Russo-Ukrainian conflict also propelled the EU and the CoE to change institutionally. The CoE lost a member, Russia, necessitating institutional and procedural decisions in response to complaints against this state before the ECtHR. Furthermore, the EU has transitioned from viewing Ukraine chiefly through the lens of foreign policy to entertaining the idea of further EU enlargement and launching a debate on necessary institutional reforms of the Union.

The expansion of the European culture of remembrance, including the memory of Soviet crimes, occurred not because of internal efforts by memory entrepreneurs from Member States, or power balances between the Member States, but rather, due to geopolitics and external factors related to security and foreign policy. The memory policy pursued by international organisations such as the CoE, as well as transnational ones like the EU, is functional, and is aimed at achieving goals in the present and future. The correction of the EU's and the CoE's historical narrative about the Soviet regime, including assessments dominant in CEE, serves as a valuable asset in expressing support for and ties with Ukraine and other states in CEE threatened by Russia. The recent changes in European memory politics have strengthened the relationship between the EU and its candidate country, Ukraine, as well as between the CoE and a Member State that has been attacked by a former, now expelled, member. This shift is consistent with the EU's long-term focus on addressing and commemorating historical injustices as a means to foster peace, reconciliation, and democracy.

[84] T Snyder, *Bloodlands. Europe between Hitler and Stalin* (Basic Books, 2010).

14

The Regulation of Historical Memory in the Council of Europe: The European Court of Human Rights before and after 2022

DOVILĖ SAGATIENĖ

I. INTRODUCTION: THE COUNCIL OF EUROPE AND THE GOVERNANCE OF HISTORICAL MEMORY

THE NEED TO legally protect certain historical narratives, foremost the Holocaust, became recognised across democratic societies in the late 1980s – that is, two generations after World War II (WWII).[1] Within the European framework, various institutions of the Council of Europe (CoE, 1949) – including, the Committee of Ministers, the Parliamentary Assembly (PACE[2]), and the European Court of Human Rights (ECtHR or the Court, 1959)[3] – were active in the field of collective European memory, which was shaped primarily by the remembrance of major historical narratives introduced after 1945. In Germany, growing concerns about Holocaust denial inspired the EU to lobby for the drafting of the Framework Decision 2008/913/JHA on Combating Certain Forms and Expressions of Racism and Xenophobia

[1] RA Kahn, *Holocaust Denial and the Law: A Comparative Study* (Palgrave Macmillan, 2004); M Minow, *Breaking the Cycles of Hatred: Memory, Law, and Repair* (Princeton University Press, 2002); LE Fletcher and HM Weinstein, 'Violence and Social Repair: Rethinking the Contribution of Justice to Reconciliation' (2002) 24 *Human Rights Quarterly* 573; N Calhoun, *Dilemmas of Justice in Eastern Europe's Democratic Transitions* (Palgrave Macmillan, 2004).

[2] Parliamentary Assembly of the Council of Europe, for more information, see: 'Parliamentary Assembly' (*Council of Europe*) https://pace.coe.int/en/.

[3] The ECtHR, based in Strasbourg France, is an international court of the CoE, which interprets the 1950 ECHR, and rules on individual or state applications alleging violations of the civil and political rights. All of the CoE's 46-member states are contracting parties to the ECHR. Since 1998, it has sat as a full-time court, and individuals can apply to it directly.

by Means of Criminal Law (FD 2008),[4] adopted by the Council of the European Union,[5] which linked Holocaust denial to hate speech and situated anti-constitutional action as part of secondary EU regulation.[6] Arguably, it was an unusual but necessary measure to combat the spread of radical political beliefs that endangered the liberal democratic order.[7] Although the FD 2008 represents only a very small part of current memory legislation across Europe, it serves as the ultimate example of how law is engaged in protecting certain historical narratives for the sake of peace and stability.

In 2018, the CoE described 'memory laws' as norms that:

> enshrine state-approved interpretations of crucial historical events and promote certain narratives about the past, by banning, for example, the propagation of totalitarian ideologies or criminalizing expressions which deny, grossly minimize, approve or justify acts constituting genocide or crimes against humanity, as defined by international law.[8]

Decades into the development of memory laws, concerns are mounting over their general compatibility with freedom of speech and the rule of law.[9] At the moment, the epicentre of contemporary memory legislation has shifted

[4] 'Framework Decision 2008/913/JHA on Combating Certain Forms and Expressions of Racism and Xenophobia by Means of Criminal Law' (*Council of the European Union*, 28 November 2008) eur-lex.europa.eu/EN/legal-content/summary/framework-decision-on-combating-certain-forms-and-expressions-of-racism-and-xenophobia-by-means-of-criminal-law.html.

[5] The Council of the EU is where national ministers from each EU country meet to negotiate and adopt EU laws. It is different from the CoE, which is an international organisation with the goal of upholding human rights, democracy and the rule of law in Europe, founded in 1949.

[6] Kahn (n 1); JJ Savelsberg and RD King, 'Institutionalizing Collective Memories of Hate: Law and Law Enforcement in Germany and the United States' (2005) 111 *American Journal of Sociology* 579; D Levy and N Sznaider, *The Holocaust and Memory in the Global Age* (Temple University, 2005); see more in Chapter 13 by A Wójcik, 'Memory Narratives and Policies in the EU and the Council of Europe in the Context of Russian Military Aggression from 2014 to 2023', in the present volume.

[7] E Bleich, 'The Rise of Hate Speech and Hate Crime Laws in Liberal Democracies' (2011) 37 *Journal of Ethnic and Migration Studies* 917; RW Smith, 'Legislating against Genocide Denial: Criminalizing Denial or Preventing Free Speech?' (2010) 128 *University of St Thomas Journal of Law & Public Policy* 128, 137.

[8] 'Memory Laws and Freedom of Expression: Thematic factsheet' (*Council of Europe*, July 2018): rm.coe.int/factsheet-on-memory-laws-july2018-docx/16808c1690.

[9] D Grimm, 'The Holocaust Denial Decision of the Federal Constitutional Court of Germany' in I Hare and J Weinstein (eds), *Extreme Speech and Democracy* (Oxford University Press, 2009) 557; for more, see: M Whine, 'Expanding Holocaust Denial and Legislation Against It' in I Hare and J Weinstein, ibid, 538; D Fraser, '"On the Internet, Nobody Knows You're a Nazi": Some Comparative Legal Aspects of Holocaust Denial on the WWW' in Hare and Weinstein, ibid, 513; P Weil, 'The Politics of Memory: Bans and Commemorations' in Hare and Weinstein, ibid, 562; U Belavusau, 'Perinçek v. Switzerland: Between Freedom of Speech and Collective Dignity' (*Verfassungsblog*, 5 November 2015): verfassungsblog.de/perincek-v-switzerland-between-freedom-of-speech-and-collective-dignity/; for more, see: Y-O Jansen, 'Denying Genocide or Denying Free Speech? A Case Study of the Application of Rw'nda's Genocide Denial Laws' (2014) 12 *Northwestern Journal of International Human Rights* 191; A Koltay, 'The Concept of Media Freedom Today: New Media, New Editors and the Traditional Approach of the Law' (2015) 7 *Journal of Media Law* 36.

to Central and Eastern Europe (CEE),[10] where such instruments have become weapons in various 'memory wars', most notably in eastern Europe.[11] Following the spirit of FD 2008, the majority of CEE countries have more or less replicated the formulations suggested therein. However, six EU Member States (Hungary, the Czech Republic, Slovakia, Poland, Lithuania and Latvia) have deviated from this by including communist crimes in their memory regulations and criminalising the denial of past Soviet crimes.[12]

As the potential clash between memory regulations and freedom of speech falls under the case law of the ECtHR based in Strasbourg, this chapter seeks to cover the role of the European Convention on Human Rights (ECHR or European Convention) within the general CoE legal framework on memory legislation, including: a) the major ECtHR case law on protecting historical narratives; b) the challenge of addressing memories regarding Soviet crimes; c) the ECtHR's case law on historical issues emerging from Russia and Ukraine; d) memory laws after 2022, subsequent to the fully-fledged Russian war of aggression against Ukraine. The Russian war has once again presented challenges to the European memory framework, as the official Russian rationale for the full-scale invasion of Ukraine in February 2022 was enshrined in quasi-historical argumentation and drew from 'historical memory'.[13] This chapter aims to address the bigger picture behind ECtHR case law on historical issues by delving into how individual cases have contributed to change in the post-WWII memory framework across Western and Eastern Europe, and thereby facilitating a more inclusive memory model in order to ensure greater geopolitical stability in the future.

II. THE ECHR: FREEDOM OF SPEECH AND THE NASCENT RIGHT TO TRUTH

The substantive role of the ECHR in the field of historical accountability has been primarily shaped through case law related to a core European value – the freedom of expression – and the emerging so-called 'right to truth'.[14] Balancing

[10] U Belavusau and A Gliszczyńska-Grabias, 'The Remarkable Rise of 'Law and Historical Memory' in Europe: Theorizing Trends and Prospects in the Recent Literature' (2020) 47 *Journal of Law and Society* 325.

[11] N Koposov, 'Historians, Memory Laws, and the Politics of the Past' (2020) 5 *European Papers* 107.

[12] E-C Pettai, 'Protecting Memory or Criminalizing Dissent? Memory Laws in Lithuania and Latvia' in E Barkan and A Lang (eds), *Memory Laws and Historical Justice: The Politics of Criminalizing the Past* (Routledge, 2022).

[13] See more in: A Nekoliak, 'Memory laws in Russia and Ukraine' – A study report for the research consortium 'The Challenge of Populist Memory Politics for Europe: Towards Effective Responses to Militant Legislations on the Past (*MEMOCRACY*) (August 2024): https://memocracy.eu/policy-briefs/.

[14] See more: P Naftali, 'The "Right to Truth" in International Law: The "Last Utopia"?' in U Belavusau and A Gliszczyńska-Grabias (eds), *Law and Memory: Towards Legal Governance and History* (Cambridge University Press, 2017) 70; G Baranowska and A Gliszczyńska-Grabias, '"Right

freedom of expression with the prohibition of hate speech, the ECtHR has developed a nuanced approach to the former, delineating between permissible speech and hate speech. In this context, the main discussion pertains to the question of how freedom of expression can be limited without disproportionally hindering discussion about historical events. When dealing with cases concerning incitement to hatred and freedom of expression, the ECtHR uses two approaches for which the ECHR provides: a) exclusion from ECHR free speech protection (under Article 17, prohibition of abuse of rights),[15] where the comments in question amount to hate speech and negate the fundamental values of the ECHR; and b) setting restrictions on protection, as provided for by Article 10, paragraph 2.[16] The latter approach is adopted where the speech in question, although pertaining to the realm of hate speech, is not apt to undermine fundamental ECHR values.[17] However, the well-established case law regarding Articles 10 and 17 is still limited to the more traditional remedies granted by the ECtHR.

The 'right to truth', which emphasises truth and memory policies related to state-sponsored abuse, is still evolving at the European level.[18] On several occasions, the ECtHR has been challenged with requests not only to bring the 'therapeutic benefits of officially acknowledging truth for victims of gross violations' (*Varnava and others v Turke*y [2009], concerning the disappearance of Greek-Cypriots who went missing in the course of the Turkish military operation in Northern Cyprus in 1974),[19] but also 'to reorder an investigation in the operative part of the judgment when the State has repeatedly failed to undertake one'.[20] Moreover, in *Abu Zubaydah v Poland* [2014][21] – involving the alleged

to Truth" and Memory Laws: General Rules and Practical Implications' (2018) 47 *Polish Political Science Yearbook* 97.

[15] Article 17 of the ECHR (Prohibition of abuse of rights) reads as follows: 'Nothing in [the] Convention may be interpreted as implying for any State, group or person any right to engage in any activity or perform any act aimed at the destruction of any of the rights and freedoms set forth herein or at their limitation to a greater extent than is provided for in the Convention'. This provision is aimed at preventing persons from inferring from the ECHR any right to engage in activities or perform acts aimed at the destruction of any of the rights and freedoms set forth in the Convention.

[16] Article 10 of the ECHR (Freedom of expression) reads as follows: '1. Everyone has the right to freedom of expression. This right shall include freedom to hold opinions and to receive and impart information and ideas without interference by public authority and regardless of frontiers. This Article shall not prevent States from requiring the licensing of broadcasting, television or cinema enterprises. 2. The exercise of these freedoms, since it carries with it duties and responsibilities, may be subject to such formalities, conditions, restrictions or penalties as are prescribed by law and are necessary in a democratic society, in the interests of national security, territorial disorder or crime, for the protection of health or morals, for the protection of the reputation or rights of others, for preventing the disclosure of information received in confidence, or for maintaining the authority and impartiality of the judiciary'.

[17] 'Factsheet: Hate Speech' (European Court of Human Rights, November 2023): www.echr.coe.int/documents/fs_hate_speech_eng.pdf.

[18] Naftali (n 14) 71.

[19] *Varnava and others v Turkey* (18 September 2009, ECtHR) App nos 16064/90, 16065/90, 16066/90, 16068/90, 16069/90, 16070/90, 16071/90, 16072/90 and 16073/90.

[20] Naftali (n 14) 78.

[21] *Husayn (Abu Zubaydah) v Poland* (24 July 2014, ECtHR) App no 7511/13.

complicity of Poland in the US Central Intelligence Agency's (CIA) secret detention and rendition of Abu Zubaydah, who was suspected of being a high-ranking member of al-Qaeda – the Court stressed that the right to know the truth may be read as not only pertaining to the parties immediately involved in criminal process, but also as encompassing the legitimate interest of the general public to be informed. Nonetheless, the ECtHR has thus far refused to connect the 'right to truth' with the right to freedom of expression under Article 10. In the case of *El-Masri v Macedonia* [2012] – concerning the unlawful detention, torture, and rendition of a German citizen of Lebanese descent, Khaled El-Masri, by Macedonian authorities in cooperation with the CIA – the Court rejected the applicants' claim that the authorities' refusal to acknowledge and disclose the victim's rendition violated his and the public's 'right to truth' under Article 10.[22]

A. ECtHR Case Law on Protecting Historical Narratives under Articles 10 and 17 ECHR: From the Holocaust to the Armenian Genocide

In several landmark judgments, the ECtHR has navigated the tension between safeguarding the freedom of expression (Article 10) and preventing the abuse of rights, where the comments in question amount to hate speech and negate the fundamental values of the ECHR (Article 17). Existing case law indicates that the negation of the Holocaust is presumed to incite hatred or intolerance, and thus, such denial is never protected under Article 10. This approach, applied not only in denialism cases, but also in early hate speech cases in Strasbourg, was introduced in *Kühnen v Germany* [1988]. Therein, the applicant, Günter Kühnen, a member of a neo-Nazi organisation in Germany, who was convicted under German laws for promoting neo-Nazi ideologies, argued that this conviction violated his right to freedom of expression under Article 10. The European Commission of Human Rights (ECommHR), deciding on admissibility, had to determine whether it should apply a proportionality test pursuant to paragraphs 1 and 2 of Article 10, or bypass the proportionality analysis altogether and instead invoke Article 17.[23] It hence found that publications by the applicant aimed at reinstating the prohibited Nazi Party, which the domestic courts had ruled was likely to revive antisemitic sentiments, clearly contained elements of racial and religious discrimination.[24] Likewise, in *Nix v Germany*

[22] *El-Masri v The Former Yugoslav Republic of Macedonia* (13 December 2012, ECtHR) App no 39630/09.

[23] *Kühnen v Germany* (12 May 1988, ECommHR) App no 12194/86 (admissibility decision).

[24] See more: P Rhein-Fischer and S Mensing, 'Memory laws in Germany: How remembering National Socialism Is Governed through Law' (Policy Brief, 2022) available at: admin.memocracy.eu/wp-content/uploads/2022/11/221109-OPS-14-1-1.pdf.

[2018], the Court accepted the German criminal ban on using Nazi symbols to maintain political peace and prevent the revival of Nazism.[25]

This so-called 'Article 17 ECHR guillotine effect' first emerged in *Lawless v Ireland* [1961], where the ECtHR emphasised how the provision is intended to make it impossible for individuals or groups 'to derive from the Convention a right to engage in any activity or perform any act aimed at destroying any of the rights and freedoms set forth in the Convention'.[26] This was clarified further in *Perinçek v Switzerland* [2015], where the Grand Chamber of ECtHR ruled that the Swiss conviction of the applicant (a Turkish politician) for denying the Armenian genocide violated Article 10, but not Article 17, since there was no 'urgent social need' to protect the legacy of the Armenian genocide (1915–16).[27] In this way, the *Perinçek* case put forward a dual presumption: not only is the close association between Holocaust denial and antisemitism presumed, but so too is it presumed that a 'special moral responsibility' of states that were involved in the Nazis' crimes translates into a pressing social need to enforce a blanket criminal prohibition against Holocaust denial – independent of its tendency to incite hatred or violence.[28]

As noted by Uladzislau Belavusau, the problem is that,

> while acknowledging dignity of the Armenian community under Article 8 of the ECHR, the Court fails to express the necessary outrage about Perinçek's statements … In this judgment, Perinçek … is positioned almost as a partisan of free speech. In combination with an extremely questionable hierarchy between the Holocaust and other genocides, this failure to distance from Perinçek – albeit rightly protecting his freedom of expression – leaves strikingly little to sustain the dignity of the Armenian victims.[29]

Though the Court has seemingly changed its approach to Holocaust denial recently, it still maintains some level of hierarchy between the Holocaust and other crimes. Another ECtHR case regarding the Armenian genocide involved an applicant, a journalist of Armenian origin, who wrote about how Turkish recognition of the Armenian genocide meant so much to Armenians and who was subsequently found guilty by Turkey of denigrating 'Turkishness' (*Dink v Turkey* [2010]). The ECtHR held that the journalist's writings did not constitute hate speech, and thus, Article 10 was found to have been violated by Turkey on account of the conviction regarding denigrating Turkish identity – which in turn had infringed his freedom of expression and made him a target for nationalist extremists.[30]

[25] *Nix v Germany* (13 March 2018, ECtHR) App no 35285/16, 47.
[26] *Lawless v Ireland* (1 July 1961, ECtHR) App no 332/57, 7–8.
[27] *Perincek v Switzerland* (15 October 2015, ECtHR) App no 27510/08.
[28] P Lobba, 'Testing the "Uniqueness": Denial of the Holocaust vs Denial of Other Crimes before the European Court of Human Rights' in Belavusau and Gliszczyńska-Grabias (n 14) 128.
[29] Belavusau, 'Perinçek v. Switzerland: Between Freedom of Speech and Collective Dignity' (n 9).
[30] *Dink v Turkey* (14 September 2010, ECtHR) App nos 2668/07, 6102/08, 30079/08, 7072/09, and 7124/09.

Similarly, in *Vajnai v Hungary* [2008], the ECtHR found that Hungary's conviction of a left-wing politician for publicly displaying a red star does not constitute hate speech, and prosecution for it by national authorities was in breach of Article 10. It was ruled that in matters concerning the use of communist symbols, domestic courts must, in each case, consider all of the relevant circumstances to decide whether the public presentation of a symbol constitutes a form of outlawed promotion of an undemocratic political regime; the courts must be aware of how some symbols carry multiple meanings.[31] The Court held that within this case, the commencement of criminal proceedings for having worn a totalitarian symbol were indeed a violation of Article 10.

Thus, the contrast in ECtHR case law between the legal protection of historical narratives regarding the Holocaust, and other historical crimes – themselves important to other groups of victims – remains. As noted by Aleksandra Gliszczyńska-Grabias,

> the past cases yielded by Nazi history had displayed none of the hesitation, doubts, or straight rights-protective attitudes (resulting in findings that a state breached the relevant Convention rights) that have been shown in the 'post-Communist' cases … This shows that the post-Second World War mood of unwillingness to treat Stalin's crimes on par with those committed by Hitler has a troublingly persistent quality.[32]

These sentiments were once again brought to light with the full-fledged Russian invasion of Ukraine, which reinforced two emerging controversies related to distinct hierarchies: the first concerning the distinction between remembrance of the Holocaust and of other historical events; and the second concerning the contrasting support for stricter legislation against Nazi crimes and symbols compared to Communist ones.

B. The Challenge of Memories Pertaining to Soviet Crimes: ECtHR Case Law from the Baltic States under Article 7 ECHR

The challenge of addressing the memories of Soviet crimes has been well reflected in cases concerning the Baltic region before the ECtHR, whereas Estonia, Latvia and Lithuania have aimed to achieve for the victims of the Soviet regime at least symbolic justice from the USSR successor state – the Russian Federation – for international crimes committed during the two Soviet occupations (1940–41 and 1944–90).[33] With more than 50 years of practice, the ECtHR

[31] *Vajnai v Hungary* (8 October 2008, ECtHR) App no 33629/06.

[32] A Gliszczyńska-Grabias, 'Communism Equals or Versus Nazism?: Europe's Unwholesome Legacy in Strasbourg' (2016) 30 *East European Politics and Societies* 74, 92.

[33] In 1940, the USSR occupied the Baltic states and began violent Sovietisation. However, with aspirations to regain their independence, those states welcomed German forces as liberators in the Baltic capitals in 1941. The Nazi occupation lasted til 1944, when the Baltic states were again occupied by the USSR. Although the Baltic states declared independence in 1990 and the occupation

has dealt with cases related to various international crimes (genocide, crimes against humanity and war crimes) on a number of occasions. Although the ECtHR cannot prosecute individuals for international criminal offences, it may, and does, encounter issues pertaining to core international crimes by virtue of its jurisdiction over the 46 state parties to the ECHR. This occurs mainly in the context of the compatibility of domestic proceedings with Article 7 (principle of legality). It can thus indirectly influence frameworks of historical accountability and memory.[34]

Whilst interpretations of Article 7 in Baltic historical cases have varied, the ECtHR has been confronted with additional legal and political dimensions that transcend those individual cases. Several Estonian cases brought before the ECtHR have addressed the illegal Soviet occupation of the Baltic states and Soviet crimes. In the cases concerning admissibility to the ECtHR of *Penart v Estonia* [2006][35] and *Kolk* and *Kislyiy v Estonia* [2006],[36] three applicants, convicted by the Estonian courts for crimes against humanity in Soviet-occupied Estonia between 1949 and 1954, claimed that their convictions had been based on retroactive application of criminal law and thus violated Article 7. While declaring all three cases inadmissible, as there was no apparent violation of Article 7, the ECtHR also delivered some crucial clarifications about Baltic history: firstly, the Court explicitly recognised that Estonia was illegally occupied by the USSR from 1940 to 1941 and from 1944 to 1991, and, secondly, it affirmed that the same international principles applied to both Communist and Nazi crimes, even though 'the acts committed by V. Penart, A. Kolk and P. Kislyiy were regarded as "lawful" pursuant to Soviet law'.[37] This recognition was essential for opening the door to pursuing accountability not only for Nazi crimes but also for those committed by the USSR, as the latter never had its Nuremberg moment and had never been declared 'criminal'.[38] For the Baltic states, this question has been crucial to national identity-building processes, as the Baltics' claims of state continuity and their right to exist 'contrast with an official historical account that the Russian Federation

nominally ended with the restoration of their independence, it took a few more years for the Soviet army to fully withdraw, with Estonia witnessing the final departure in 1994.

[34] Article 7 of ECHR (No punishment without law): '1. No one shall be held guilty of any criminal offence on account of any act or omission which did not constitute a criminal offence under national or international law at the time when it was committed. Nor shall a heavier penalty be imposed than the one that was applicable at the time the criminal offence was committed. 2. This Article shall not prejudice the trial and punishment of any person for any act or omission which, at the time it was committed, was criminal according to the general principles of law recognised by civilised nations'.

[35] *Penart v Estonia* (, 24 January 2006, ECtHR) App no 14685/04 (admissibility decision).

[36] *Kolk and Kislyiy v Estonia* (, 17 January 2006, ECtHR) App nos 23052/04 and 24018/04 (admissibility decision).

[37] L Mälksoo, 'Kononov v Latvia' (2011) 105 *American Journal of International Law* 101, 107.

[38] S Toymentsev, 'Legal but Criminal: The Failure of the "Russian Nuremberg" and the Paradoxes of Post-Soviet Memory' (2011) 48 *Comparative Literature Studies: Special Issue Trials of Trauma* 296, 297.

supports, among others, through its memory laws: that it acted as a liberator rather than aggressor'.[39]

In pursuance of its mandate, the ECtHR has also grappled with the ongoing denial of Soviet crimes committed during WWII, as has been particularly evident in Latvian cases. The main legal issue presented in *Kononov v Latvia* [2010][40] differed from that of Estonian examples, having focused not on crimes against humanity, but war crimes, which can be committed only during times of war. In this particular case, a former Soviet partisan (Vasily Kononov), who was charged with war crimes for the murder of Latvian civilians in 1944, claimed that Article 7 had been violated by the Latvian courts due to the retroactive application of criminal law. However, in 2010, the Grand Chamber rejected this claim, ruling that the execution of villagers was in violation of international law already established at the time. By doing so, the Court also rejected the assertion that the Nuremberg principles are not universal and should not be applicable with respect to the nationals of the victorious allies, including the USSR, which considered themselves liberators.[41] This case proved to be a crucial milestone in the Baltic states' campaign to expose the atrocities of the Soviet regime and challenge Russia's policy of denying Soviet crimes internationally.[42]

Notably, Lithuanian historical cases have confronted the post-war concept of genocide as defined by the 1948 Convention on the Prevention and Punishment of Genocide (Genocide Convention) by adopting a comprehensive national definition, encompassing social and political groups – and which could enable prosecution for past Soviet crimes in occupied Lithuania.[43] The national criminal legislation on genocide was challenged before the ECtHR in the cases of *Vasiliauskas v Lithuania* [2015][44] and *Drėlingas v Lithuania* [2019],[45] where both convicted applicants (former Soviet officials) claimed that their actions against Lithuanian partisans back in 1953 and 1956 could not have been reasonably foreseeable as genocidal actions.[46] Although in *Vasiliauskas*, the Grand Chamber agreed that the conviction for genocide of political and social groups

[39] See more: A Wójcik, 'European Court of Human Rights, Freedom of Expression and Debating the Past and History' (2019) 17 *Problemy Współczesnego Prawa Międzynarodowego, Europejskiego i Porównawczego (Issues of Contemporary International, European and Comparative Law)* 33.

[40] *Kononov v Latvia* (17 May 2010, ECtHR, Grand Chamber) App no 36376/04.

[41] Mälksoo (n 38) 'Kononov v Latvia' 105.

[42] J Žilinskas, 'Introduction of 'Crime of Denial' in the Lithuanian Criminal Law and First Instances of Its Application' (2012) 19 *Jurisprudencija* 315, 320.

[43] J Žilinskas, 'Broadening the Concept of Genocide in Lithuania's Criminal Law and the Principle of *Nullum Crimen Sine Lege*' (2009) 118 *Jurisprudencija* 333.

[44] *Vasiliauskas v Lithuania* (20 October 2015, Grand Chamber) App no 35343/05.

[45] *Drėlingas v Lithuania* (2019) App no 28859/16.

[46] ECtHR, 'Conviction of an officer in the State security services for genocide was not justified' (*Registrar of the Court: Press release*, 20 October 2015): hudoc.echr.coe.int/app/conversion/pdf/?library=ECHR&id=003-5204869-6446796&filename=Grand%20Chamber%20Judgment%20Vasiliauskas%20v.%20Lithuania%20-%20conviction%20of%20an%20officer-%20in%20the%20State%20security%20services%20for%20genocide%20was%20not%20justified.pdf.

according to Lithuanian post-Soviet legislation had not been foreseeable and violated Article 7, in the *Drėlingas* case, the ECtHR agreed that the systematic killing of Lithuanian partisans was genocide of the Lithuanian nation, as the partisans were recognised as a significant part of the Lithuanian nation.

These rulings by the ECtHR not only recognised that some crimes committed by the USSR could be regarded as genocide; they also created more options for other victims of Soviet crimes to seek justice. More importantly, in these cases the ECtHR, by highlighting the significance of the partisan movement, engaged with an important dimension of Baltic state identity and continuity, particularly given that partisans represented a form of self-defence against occupation, played a crucial role in obstructing Soviet repression, and helped maintain Lithuanian statehood. In the *Drėlingas* case, Lithuanian domestic courts emphasised the importance of Lithuanian partisans as an integral part of the nation as well as the direct link between the concept of genocide and the nation's right to exist.

C. ECtHR Case Law on Historical Issues Stemming from Russia and Ukraine: Potential Violations of Article 10 ECHR?

While the Strasbourg Court has already intervened in cases involving Holocaust denial and some other international crimes, including the Armenian genocide and Soviet crimes in the Baltic states, the historical issues reflected in the memory legislation of Russia and Ukraine have yet to be tested. Despite both countries joining the ECHR in the late 1990s (Ukraine in 1997,[47] and Russia in 1998),[48] there have been no significant ECtHR rulings specifically addressing memory laws in these countries, as, firstly, those memory laws representing the greatest challenge to freedom of speech were adopted quite recently, and it takes significant procedural time to bring them before the ECtHR.[49] Secondly, Russia has not been part of the CoE since September 2022, due to the attack on Ukraine.[50] Thirdly, the prospects for the *implementation* of any potential

[47] M Gnatovskyy and Y Ioffe, 'Twenty Years of the ECHR in Ukraine' (*EJIL:Talk*, 18 September 2017): www.ejiltalk.org/twenty-years-of-the-echr-in-ukraine/.

[48] L Mälksoo, 'Introduction: Russia, Strasbourg, and the Paradox of a Human Rights Backlash' in L Mälksoo and W Benedek (eds), *Russia and the European Court of Human Rights* (Cambridge University Press, 2017).

[49] Russian memory legislation includes: the Rehabilitation of Nazism Law and the Ukrainian Symbols Laws of 2014; the 2022 Administrative Offences Code Amendment; Ukrainian regulations include the 2006 Holodomor Law, 2015 Freedom Fighters Law, and the 2015 Soviet and Nazi Symbols Law.

[50] ECtHR 'The Russian Federation ceases to be a Party to the European Convention on Human Rights' (Press Release, Registrar of the Court, 16 September 2022): hudoc.echr.coe.int/app/conversion/pdf/?library=ECHR&id=003-7435446-10180882&filename=The%20Russian%20Federation%20ceases%20to%20be%20a%20Party%20to%20the%20European%20Convention%20on%20Human%20Rights.pdf; However, under Article 58 of the European Convention, the ECtHR can examine alleged violations of ECHR up to the date of Russia's withdrawal.

ECtHR ruling related to memory laws would be dismal in practice, in Russia and in Ukraine, while the war remains ongoing. Nevertheless, recent memory laws and their compatibility with the ECHR in the context of existing ECtHR case law (mainly regarding Article 10) in both countries remain highly relevant, since memory issues continue to lurk in the background of the Russian war against Ukraine. Challenging memory legislation before the ECtHR after the war would benefit not only the democratisation of Russia, but also the strengthening of human rights in Ukraine.

Russian and Ukrainian memory laws remain polar opposites at the moment, as the regulation of historical issues in Russia mainly targets the legal protection of false Soviet narratives about the Soviet past, whereas Ukraine is attempting to clarify its Soviet past and to crystallise its post-colonial identity in order to claim its right to exist as independent European state.[51] Since Putin's second term, Russia has focused on the 'Great Patriotic War' myth – that Russia supposedly solely liberated Europe – to legitimise itself as a relevant global power.[52] As Nikolay Koposov points out, Putin's 'neo-imperialist ambitions' and historical revisionism after 2004 have increased 'memory conflicts' in the region.[53] Following Russian military involvement in Ukraine and the annexation of Crimea, memory legalisation efforts escalated.[54] In spring 2014, the Russian Duma passed a memory law on the 'Rehabilitation of Nazism and Ukrainian Symbols', which governs historical memory in Putin's Russia.[55] In particular, this statute criminalised the 'denial of facts' about the Red Army's wartime conduct and 'desecration of military glory', which has unique significance in Ukraine's memory wars over the Crimea and Donbas regions.

In 2022, the 'Administrative Offences Code Amendment' prohibited 'any public attempt to equate the aims and actions of the Soviet Union and Nazi Germany during World War II, as well as to deny the decisive role of the Soviet people in the victory over fascism'.[56] This new provision contributed to the development of a narrative of Russian victimhood and fuelled nationalist feelings,

[51] BK Kang, 'Understanding the Ukrainian Conflict from the Perspective of Post-Soviet Decolonization' (2020) 9 *Region* 1.

[52] N Tumarkin, 'The Great Patriotic War as myth and memory' (2003) 11 *European Review* 595; M Mälksoo, 'Militant memocracy in International Relations: Mnemonical status anxiety and memory laws in Eastern Europe' (2021) 47 *Review of International Studies* 489.

[53] N Koposov, *Memory Laws, Memory Wars: The Politics of the Past in Europe and Russia* (Cambridge University Press, 2017) 160.

[54] U Belavusau, A Gliszczyńska-Grabias and M Mälksoo, 'Memory Laws and Memory Wars in Poland, Russia and Ukraine' (2021) 69 *Jahrbuch des öffentlichen Rechts* 95.

[55] State Duma of the Russian Federation, 'Federal law On Amendments to Certain Legislative Acts of the Russian Federation [О внесении изменений в отдельные законодательные акты Российской Федерации]' (Law No 128-FZ, 5 May 2014): publication.pravo.gov.ru/Document/View/0001201405050051.

[56] State Duma of the Russian Federation, 'Federal law on Amendments to the Code of the Russian Federation on Administrative Offences [О внесении изменений в Кодекс Российской Федерации об административных правонарушениях]' (Law No 103-FZ, 16 April 2022): publication.pravo.gov.ru/Document/View/0001202204160015.

making it easier for Putin to frame his aggression against Ukraine. As Francine Hirsch argues, in conjunction with Putin's use of propaganda and disinformation, this legislation has paved the way for his war in Ukraine and highlighted the dangers of manipulating memory as a political instrument.[57]

The main potential conflict with freedom of speech that may arise in the future under Russian legislation stems from provisions criminalising the denial of Soviet past, enacted within the 'Rehabilitation of Nazism Law' of 2014, as the offences envisaged in the second part of the Russian Criminal Code Article 354.1(B) criminalise the 'spreading of knowing falsehoods publicly about the activities of the USSR in World War II'. As stressed by Andrii Nekoliak, this legal construction can hardly be regarded as in accordance with the ECtHR framework on the freedom of expression, as the pursuit of historical truth constitutes an integral part of that freedom.[58] The only special protection in this regard is granted to the crime of Holocaust denial, as it belongs to 'the category of clearly established historical facts whose negation or revision is removed from the protection of Article 10 by Article 17 of the Convention'.[59] Meanwhile the construction of the offence in Article 354.1(B) under Russian law bans negative interpretation of a formerly existing state entity (the Soviet Union) rather than protecting any particular historical narrative. Another potential clash with ECtHR case law on historical issues may be invoked under the legal provision of Article 13.48 of the Administrative Offences Code, which banned comparisons between the actions of the Soviet Union and Nazi Germany during WWII, and punished the denial of the 'decisive role of the Soviet people in the defeat of Nazi Germany and the humanitarian mission of the USSR during the liberation of European countries'. This provision may contradict ECtHR case law, which establishes: a) that free discussion over major historical events and figures should not be restricted, due to the influence of major events and figures on 'the destinies of multitudes of people',[60] and b) the obligation of states to investigate the transgressions and mass repressions committed in the past, which is part of the emerging 'right to truth'.[61]

In contrast to criminally punitive Russian memory regulations, the Ukrainian memory law of 2006 entitled 'Holodomor Law'[62] – which asserts that public

[57] F Hirsch, 'Putin's Memory Laws Set the Stage for His War in Ukraine' (*LawFare*, 28 February 2022): www.lawfareblog.com/putins-memory-laws-set-stage-his-war-ukraine.

[58] *Chauvy and Others v France* (29 June 2004, ECtHR), App no 64915/01; *Ungváry and Irodalom Kft v Hungary* (3 Decembe 2013, ECtHR) App no 64520/10.

[59] ibid 69.

[60] *Dzhugahvili v Russia*, (9 December 2014, ECtHR), App no 41123/10 (admissibility decision), para 32.

[61] *El-Masri v The Former Yugoslav Republic of* Macedonia (13 December 2012, ECtHR) App no 39630/09, para 191.

[62] Verkhovna Rada of Ukraine, 'The Verkhovna Rada of Ukraine appealed to the parliaments of the world to recognize the Holodomor of 1932–33 as genocide of the Ukrainian people' (*Press Service of the Verkhovna Rada of Ukraine*, 16 November 2022): www.rada.gov.ua/en/news/News/top_news/230401.html.

denial of the *Holodomor* (the USSR-orchestrated famine of 1932–33 in Ukraine) is unlawful – may be considered to be in line with existing ECtHR case law on Article 10, as it is declarative in nature and cannot enable initiation of criminal or administrative charges. However, the 2015 'Soviet and Nazi Symbols Law',[63] criminalising the 'production, distribution, and public use of symbols of communist and national socialist (Nazi) totalitarian regimes' and prescribing punishment of up to five years in prison, may contradict ECtHR case law, at least to the extent that the law bans communist symbols, since only the prohibition of Nazi regime symbols has so far been considered automatically legitimate and in full compliance with Article 10.[64]

III. THE COE AND MEMORY LAWS AFTER 2022

The analysis of relevant ECtHR case law on pertinent historical issues indicates that the approach to memory in Europe was slowly shifting before the Russian attack on Ukraine in 2022. However, after 2022, the role of the CoE in harmonising historical narratives became increasingly vital in ensuring stability in the region by including a more comprehensive approach to diverse historical narratives. The activities of the CoE and other related institutions, especially the ECtHR, are indicative of the movement in this direction.

In response to the Russian military aggression, the CoE mobilised to ensure full accountability of the Russian Federation for serious violations of human rights and international law;[65] furthermore, it strongly condemned Russian aggression against Ukraine,[66] and urged cessation of 'the unprecedented crackdown on freedoms of expression, assembly and association in Russia'.[67] The Russian military invasion against Ukraine was also classified as an 'extreme and urgent' example of aggressive and violent nationalism, which must be controlled by increased support for 'basic democratic principles laid out in the European Convention on Human Rights, including freedom of expression, freedom

[63] DR Marples, 'Open Letter from Scholars and Experts on Ukraine Re the So-Called "Anti-Communist Law"' (*Krytyka*, April 2015): krytyka.com/en/articles/open-letter-scholars-and-experts-ukraine-re-so-called-anti-communist-law.

[64] *Vajnai v Hungary* (n 32); *Fratanoló v. Hungary* (2012) App no 29459/10; For detailed analysis see Nekoliak (n 13).

[65] 'Russia's war against Ukraine (*Council of Europe*, 2023) www.coe.int/en/web/portal/war-in-ukraine.

[66] Council of Europe, Statement from Council of Europe Secretary General Marija Pejčinović Burić on the military attack by the Russian Federation on Ukraine' (*Secretary-General, Newsroom*, 24 February 2022): www.coe.int/en/web/portal/-/statement-from-council-of-europe-secretary-general-marija-pejcinovic-buric-on-the-military-attack-by-the-russian-federation-on-ukraine.

[67] Council of Europe, 'Authorities should stop the unprecedented crackdown on freedoms of expression, assembly and association in Russia' (*Commissioner for Human Rights*, 7 March 2022): www.coe.int/en/web/portal/-/authorities-should-stop-the-unprecedented-crackdown-on-freedoms-of-expression-assembly-and-association-in-russia.

of assembly and association'.[68] Moreover, under the Reykjavik Declaration, adopted in 2023 at the CoE summit, the joint responsibility of states in opposing autocratic tendencies, growing threats to human rights, democracy and the rule of law was reaffirmed.[69]

A deeper geopolitical understanding of the nature of the Russia's aggression towards Ukraine may lead to acknowledgment that this war represents the final stage of the decolonisation process of the Soviet empire, rather than a 'local conflict'.[70] Since the 1990s, both countries had centred their memory politics on the remembrance of WWII. However, their memory regulations ended up being governed by different frameworks – in Russia, legislative approaches to the Soviet past reflect a dichotomy between, an authoritarian view that downplays Soviet abuses and promotes a positive image of the regime, and a contrasting democratic view that critically engages with, and condemns, Soviet-era totalitarian practices – revealing how political ideologies shape historical interpretation and memory. Meanwhile Ukrainian legislation concentrates on rebuilding a sovereign Ukrainian identity.[71] It is essential for Ukraine to approach the country's twentieth century totalitarian experience as a single narrative in order to claim the right to exist after the war and to 'begin to make sense to the outside world.'[72]

Even in the aftermath of 2022, the ECtHR's role in human rights development in both Russia and Ukraine, remains solid, and will greatly impact the memory field there after the war. The ECtHR was the first international judicial institution to rule against Russia following its 2022 invasion, ordering 'interim measures' including a halt to attacks on civilians and civilian objects.[73] Although Russia has ceased to participate in the ECHR since 2022, Ukraine remains a Contracting Party and recognises the jurisdiction of the ECtHR as being limited in scope regarding human rights since the start of the war in accordance with Article 15.[74] The ECtHR has also decided to continue considering cases against

[68] Council of Europe, 'Reassembling the building blocks of democracy to respond to violent nationalism' (*European Conference on Democracy and Human Rights, Deputy Secretary General*, 6 May 2022): www.coe.int/en/web/portal/-/reassembling-the-building-blocks-of-democra-1.

[69] Council of Europe, 'Reykjavík Declaration United around our values' (16–17 May 2023): rm.coe.int/4th-summit-of-heads-of-state-and-government-of-the-council-of-europe/1680ab40c1.

[70] BK Kang, 'Understanding the Ukrainian Conflict from the Perspective of Post-Soviet Decolonization' (2020) 9 *Region* 1.

[71] See more: Nekoliak (n 13).

[72] P Dickinson, 'Ukraine's Unique Totalitarian Trauma Offers Key to Historic Healing' (*Atlantic Council*, 9 May 2016): www.atlanticcouncil.org/blogs/ukrainealert/ukraine-s-unique-totalitarian-trauma-offers-key-to-historic-healing/.

[73] J Crawford, 'Ukraine vs Russia: What The European Court Of Human Rights Can (And Can't) Do' (*JusticeInfo*, 7 April 2022): www.justiceinfo.net/en/90187-ukraine-russia-european-court-of-human-rights-can-do.html.

[74] 'Legal analysis of the derogation made by Ukraine under Article 15 of the European Convention of Human Rights and Article 4 of the International Covenant on Civil and Political Rights' (Council of Europe, November 2022): rm.coe.int/legal-analysis-of-the-derogation-made-by-ukraine-under-article-15-of-t/1680aa8e2c.

the Russian Federation, despite its exclusion from the CoE;[75] Russia itself also continues to show interest in proceedings against it, even though it publicly claims otherwise.[76]

As of 2024, Ukraine has two applications pending against Russia before the Grand Chamber. One is in respect of events in Crimea, which encompasses three inter-state applications lodged in 2014, 2015 and 2018.[77] The joined application was declared partly admissible in 2020, and the Court delivered a unanimous Grand Chamber ruling on 25 June 2024 (*Ukraine v Russia (re Crimea)*.[78] This case deals predominantly with the events that took place more than 10 years ago and was concerned, amongst other things, with repressions against Ukrainian and Crimean Tatar political activists and the removal of prisoners to Russia, as well as restrictions on Ukrainian language and culture in Crimea during, and in the aftermath of, the occupation of the peninsula by Russia.[79] The ECtHR not only clarified the story of the campaign of systemic oppression espoused by Russia, that violated almost all substantive rights and freedoms under the ECHR; it also reinforced Ukraine's position and narrative regarding the problem of Crimea, which supports Ukraine's historical claims and counters Russian narratives.

Another case concerns events in eastern Ukraine, including the downing of flight MH17, and Russia's military operations on the territory of Ukraine since 24 February 2022, encompassing four inter-state applications joined in February 2023.[80] It involves over 8,500 individual applications concerning the events in Crimea, eastern Ukraine, and the Sea of Azov.[81] The case also includes 26 states as third parties. The scope of the claims, as well as the number of claimants and complaints, remain unprecedented in the history

[75] 'Date revealed for ECHR hearings on major case regarding occupied Donbas' (*European Pravda*, 8 May 2024): www.eurointegration.com.ua/eng/news/2024/05/8/7185496/.

[76] 'Russia after Expulsion from Council of Europe Continues to Monitor Cases against It at ECHR – Ministry of Justice' (*European Pravda*, 3 August 2023): www.eurointegration.com.ua/eng/news/2023/08/3/7166950/.

[77] ECtHR, 'EC[t]HR puts questions to Russian Government after receiving new inter-State case from Ukraine concerning events in the Sea of Azov' (*Press Release: Registrar of the Court*, 30 November 2018): hudoc.echr.coe.int/eng-press#{%22itemid%22:[%22003-6266330-8160558%22]}.

[78] ECtHR, 'Forthcoming public delivery in Grand Chamber inter-State case Ukraine v. Russia (re Crimea)' (*Press Release: Registrar of the Court*, 18 June 2024): prd-echr.coe.int/web/echr/w/forthcoming-ruling-2.

[79] K Dzehtsiarou, 'Ukraine v Russia (re Crimea): the European Court of Human Rights Goes "All-in"' (*EJIL:Talk*, 27 June 2024): www.ejiltalk.org/ukraine-v-russia-re-crimea-the-european-court-of-human-rights-goes-all-in/.

[80] ECtHR, 'European Court joins inter-State case concerning Russian military operations in Ukraine to inter-State case concerning eastern Ukraine and downing of flight MH17' (*Press Release: Registrar of the Court*, 20 February 2023): hudoc.echr.coe.int/eng-press#{%22itemid%22:[%22003-7575325-10413252%22]}.

[81] See: Z Tropin, 'ECHR ruling confirms Russian invasion of Ukraine began in 2014' (*Atlantic Council*, 14 February 2023): www.atlanticcouncil.org/blogs/ukrainealert/echr-ruling-confirms-russian-invasion-of-ukraine-began-in-2014/.

of the ECtHR's consideration of inter-state cases.[82] The hearings were held on 12 June 2024 (under the title *Ukraine and the Netherlands v Russia*) with judgment due in 2025.[83] The hearing itself, which took more than four hours, raised crucial questions regarding both the interactions of the ECHR with international humanitarian law during armed conflicts and jurisdiction under Article 1 ECHR.[84]

In the wider context, the Ukrainian cases against Russia will definitely address not only narrow legal questions regarding potential ECHR violations, but also complex political questions which are relevant to the memory field in both countries and beyond. As noted by Alla Tymofeyeva, the case of *Ukraine and the Netherlands v Russia* will likely become a milestone in the history of inter-state proceedings, as it concerns many important issues: starting from the intersection between humanitarian law and human rights, going through extraterritoriality in armed conflicts, and ending up with preserving the ECHR's values.[85] For instance, on 25 January 2023, the Court confirmed that the invasion of 24 February 2022 was actually a continuation of the war which had begun eight years earlier in 2014.[86] This decision contributes to reshaping the European memory landscape, as it challenges the Russian state's historical narrative about the nature of the conflict in eastern Ukraine, and emphasises the importance of a unified, accurate representation of events.

IV. CONCLUSIONS

The CoE, together with the ECtHR, has adopted a leading role in the prevention of global circulation of Holocaust denial and has challenged the key historical narratives of the Holocaust in established collective European memory. These institutions became pivotal actors following the EU's eastern enlargement in 2004 by addressing culpability for Soviet crimes in the new EU Member States. Each challenged the post-WWII memory framework by pursuing symbolic justice for victims of the Soviets and accountability for previously forgotten crimes in

[82] 'Russia Wants to Destroy Ukrainians and to Undermine the World Order – Iryna Mudra at the ECHR Hearing on Human Rights Violations by the Russian Federation in the Occupied Territories' (*President of Ukraine Volodymyr Zelenskyy Official Website*, 12 June 2024): www.president.gov.ua/en/news/rosiya-hoche-znishiti-ukrayinciv-ta-pidirvati-svitovij-porya-91473.

[83] Hearing of *Ukraine and the Netherlands v. Russia* (nos. 8019/16, 43800/14 and 28525/20) (*ECtHR*, Grand Chamber Hearing, video recording, 12 June 2024): prd-echr.coe.int/web/echr/w/ukraine-and-the-netherlands-v.-russia-nos.-8019/16-43800/14-and-28525/20-1.

[84] V Botticelli and I Risini, 'Ukraine, the Netherlands and 26 Third States Without Russia Before the ECtHR' (*Verfassungsblog*, 1 July 2024): verfassungsblog.de/ukraine-the-netherlands-and-26-third-states-without-russia-before-the-ecthr/.

[85] A Tymofeyeva, 'A Ray of Light in Dark Times: On the Importance of the Case of Ukraine and the Netherlands v. Russia' (*University of Liverpool, Liverpool Law School, Blog*, 3 June 2024): www.liverpool.ac.uk/law/blog/the-case-of-ukraine-and-the-netherlands-v-russia/.

[86] Tropin (n 82).

the Baltic states. As memory regulation and historical narratives in Europe are deeply intertwined with current geopolitical dynamics, the respective positions of the CoE and ECtHR will continue to be crucial in potential cases on memory issues from Ukraine and Russia after the war – a war which has triggered the revision of European memory landscapes once again, as the ongoing military aggression to some extent originates from the contrasting memory regulations in Russia and Ukraine. The reinforcement of democratic principles and human rights in the region, particularly through the lens of historical justice and 'the right to truth', underscores the ongoing relevance and necessity of these institutions in fostering stability and reconciliation in a post-conflict Europe.

15

The Looking Glass War: Russian Aggression against Ukraine and the Lessons of World War II in International Memory Politics

MARIA MÄLKSOO

I. INTRODUCTION

THE RUSSIAN AGGRESSION against Ukraine serves as a looking glass war in various evocative ways. It holds a mirror up to the identity and mnemonical security-related anguishes in contemporary Russia which constitute a culmination of the Putin-era instrumentalisation, domestic institutionalisation and international peddling of a highly selective and poorly self-reflective 'state story'[1] of World War II (WWII) and the Soviet legacy at large. The war hence enables us to probe the connection between Russia's militant memory politics and its increasingly belligerent and openly revisionist international posturing. The Russo-Ukrainian war has further brought to light distinctly internalised conclusions about WWII in the West and East of Europe, thereby offering a rich canvas to examine the questionable representativeness of some vocal western voices when speaking authoritatively in the name of Europe as a whole.[2] Finally, Russia's attempted recolonisation of Ukraine, embedded in an imperial mindset and memory-political revisionism, is unsettling the traditional place of Eastern Europe in the wider European mindscape and political interactions. The war has exposed distinct visions of Ukraine's, and more generally Eastern Europe's, political agency, along with the persisting rational-emotional

[1] Compare JM Dixon, *Dark Pasts: Changing the State's Story in Turkey and Japan* (Cornell University Press, 2018).

[2] See O Burlyuk and V Musliu, 'The responsibility to remain silent? On the politics of knowledge production, expertise and (self-)reflection in Russia's War against Ukraine' (2023) 26 *Journal of International Relations and Development Special Forum* 605.

hierarchies in international relations as reflected in various political and academic reactions to the 2022 Russian invasion.[3]

But there are deeper allusions to the looking glass metaphor here. For one, 'looking glass war' is a nod to the novel of the same title by the famous British spy writer John le Carré, published in 1965 in response to the public acclaim of his previous novel, 'The Spy Who Came in From the Cold'.[4] In 'The Looking Glass War' sequel, le Carré depicts spy-craft through an unglamourous and resigned lens. Preparing for an assignment in East Germany, a lead character in the book makes a note of how different operating during the Cold War is compared to WWII, quipping: 'But nobody wins this one, do they?'.[5] Since the beginning of Russia's fully-fledged invasion of Ukraine in February 2022, a similar sentiment has also reigned among predominantly Realist International Relations (IR) scholars about Russia's war in Ukraine. For example, the renowned Harvard politics professor Stephen M Walt has predicted a 'grinding and costly stalemate that won't end until the protagonists realize that they cannot achieve all their original goals and will have to accept a less-than-ideal outcome'.[6] Key questions in this context have been: whether or not the war can be militarily won by Ukraine; what the strategic, political and moral dimensions of its desired victory are; and whether Ukraine's victory equals Russia's defeat. For, while Ukraine's victory and, by extension, that of the 'collective West' has been constantly chanted and manifested in the West, the exact parameters and the meaning of the coveted victory have been hardly uniformly understood among Ukraine's supporters. Whereas most Western leaders maintain that they want Ukraine to win, the victory imagined tends to stop short of envisioning a radical defeat of Russia (except for most east European countries who identify emotionally with Ukraine). Particularly in the first months after Russia's fully-fledged invasion, many expressed doubts as to whether Ukraine's victory should entail claiming back the territories Russia had occupied since 2014 (that is, Crimea and Donbas) and suggested that Ukraine's neutrality should be an essential part of a future peace deal.[7] Concerns over saving Putin's face and Russia from humiliation have circulated among the more cautious quarters,[8] along with a certain trepidation regarding the emerging political balance in Europe where the old heavyweights

[3] T Hendl, O Burlyuk, M O'Sullivan and A Arystanbek, '(En)Countering epistemic imperialism: A critique of "Westsplaining" and coloniality in dominant debates on Russia's invasion of Ukraine' (2024) 45 *Contemporary Security Policy* 171.

[4] J le Carré, *The Looking Glass War* (Penguin, 1965).

[5] ibid 203.

[6] SM Walt, 'The Realist Case for a Ukraine Peace Deal' (*Foreign Policy*, 29 March 2022): https://foreignpolicy.com/2022/03/29/realist-case-ukraine-peace-deal/.

[7] See, eg, G Beebe and A Lieven, 'What Can the US Really Do to Protect Civilians in Ukraine?' (*Responsible Statecraft*, 7 April 2022): https://responsiblestatecraft.org/2022/04/07/what-can-the-us-really-do-to-protect-civilians-in-ukraine/.

[8] See G Galindo, 'Macron: Putin shouldn't be humiliated over "historic" mistake' (*Politico*, 4 June 2022): https://www.politico.eu/article/macron-putin-ukraine-invasion-mistake/.

(notably Germany) are required to make more space for the likes of Poland – and the war-seasoned Ukraine itself – after their serious political miscalculation of *Wandel durch Handel* (change through trade) policy vis-à-vis Putin's Russia.[9] In the meantime, Ukraine has insisted on the terms of its victory including a return to the 1991 borders of Ukraine (that is, including Crimea, as well as the Russian-occupied regions in south-eastern Ukraine); reparations from the aggressor in the form of payments for damage caused; aggression and war-crimes tribunals to give the victims of this war a sense of justice, in accordance with the Nuremberg model; the introduction of amendments to international law to prevent similar aggressions in the future; and Ukraine's participation in the architecture of international security.[10]

Secondly, Vladimir Putin's reanimation of the potent tropes of WWII in the run-up to the fully-fledged aggression against Ukraine, and the attempts to mobilise their affective charge for his instrumental aims suggest yet another Looking Glass reference: Lewis Carroll's classic novel, *Through the Looking-Glass, and What Alice Found There*.[11] In this story, the protagonist's climbing through the mirror leads into a world where, just like a reflection, everything is reversed, including logic (eg, to stay put, one needs to run faster; time is running backwards and so forth). Putin's emptying of 'denazification' and 'decommunisation' of any empirically tangible meaning is reminiscent of the Humpty Dumpty character in Carroll's book, who famously maintains:

> 'When I use a word,' Humpty Dumpty said in rather a scornful tone, 'it means just what I choose it to mean – neither more nor less.'
>
> 'The question is,' said Alice, 'whether you can make words mean so many different things.'
>
> 'The question is,' said Humpty Dumpty, 'which is to be master – that's all.'

In a similar vein, as Timothy Snyder has pithily put, Putin's Russia has embodied fascism while claiming to fight it in Ukraine, and Russians have possibly committed

[9] See, eg, J Habermas, 'War and Indignation: The West's Red Line Dilemma' (*Reset Dialogues on Civilizations*, 6 May 2022): https://www.resetdoc.org/story/jurgen-habermas-war-indignation-west-red-line-dilemma/; A Tooze, 'After the Zeitenwende: Jürgen Habermas and Germany's new identity crisis' (*The New Statesman*, 12 May 2022): https://www.newstatesman.com/ideas/2022/05/after-the-zeitenwende-jurgen-habermas-and-germanys-new-identity-crisis; T Snyder, 'Germans have been involved in the war, chiefly on the wrong side' (*Frankfurter Allgemeine Zeitung*, 27 June 2022): https://www.faz.net/aktuell/politik/ausland/juergen-habermas-and-ukraine-germans-have-been-involved-in-the-war-18131718.html; M Schulze Wessel, 'Faschismus? Genozid? Vernichtungskrieg?' (*Frankfurter Algemeine Zeitung*, 25 July 2022): https://zeitgeschichte-online.de/themen/faschismus-genozid-vernichtungskrieg.

[10] O Reznikov, 'I was Ukraine's defence minister. Here's my message for our allies: we must not lose sight of victory' (*The Guardian*, 8 September 2023): https://theguardian.com/commentisfree/2023/sep/08/ukraine-defence-minister-allies-victory-military-oleksii-reznikov. See further: 'What Is Zelenskyy's 10-point Peace Plan' (*The Official Website of Ukraine*, 17 September 2024): https://war.ukraine.ua/faq/zelenskyys-10-point-peace-plan/.

[11] L Carroll, *Through the Looking-Glass, and What Alice Found There* (Hepburn, 1872).

genocide against the Ukrainian nation while claiming to prevent it.[12] Among the numerous mnemonic justifications for war, the Russian president tapped into the tropes of genocide, Nazism and the 'real lessons' of WWII while building the rationale for the full-scale aggression against Ukraine in February 2022.

At a more profound conceptual level, the notion of the looking glass war resonates with the symbolic interactionist idea of a social self: namely, the basic proposition that our formation of a sense of self is based on how we think we appear to others. Social interaction accordingly acts as a looking glass, since presumably one's sense of self and self-esteem are built off others, with identity emerging as an interactional and embodied experience.[13] The Russian, Ukrainian, east and west European identities viewed in the mirror of the Russo-Ukrainian war speak volumes of the affective underpinnings of the respective social selves. These identities are tied to common, yet distinctly interpreted, mnemonical reference points and consequent epistemic habits, the most notable of which will be discussed below.

This chapter reflects on what has been lost and found in the mutual attempts to translate the memories[14] of WWII and its aftermath between the traditional Western and Eastern European quarters against the backdrop of Russia's ongoing war. Translating memories in international politics taps into the broader questions raised by the International Studies research agenda that has sought to conceptualise IR as interlingual relations and zoom in on imperial transitions, cultures of global competition and histories of domination.[15] The discussion will unfold in three parts. I will first contextualise the Russian aggression against the backdrop of its ontological security-seeking, for which the numerous memory laws examined in this volume have served as a symptom and a coping mechanism of sorts (section II). In the ensuing section, the discussion will turn to dominant mnemonical templates that have framed political and academic reactions to the Russo-Ukrainian war in Europe (section III). Finally, the chapter will examine some of the core academic, political and ethical implications of the war (section IV).

[12] T Snyder, 'Ukraine Holds the Future: The War Between Democracy and Nihilism' (*Foreign Affairs*, 6 September 2022): https://www.foreignaffairs.com/ukraine/ukraine-war-democracy-nihilism-timothy-snyder. For a compact discussion of the pertinent Russian manifestations to destroy the Ukrainian nation, see D Azarov, D Koval, G Nuridzhanian and V Venher, 'Understanding Russia's Actions in Ukraine as the Crime of Genocide' (2023) 21 *Journal of International Criminal Justice* 223, 233.

[13] The concept of 'the looking-glass self' is at the heart of Charles H Cooley's symbolic interactionism, tackling the social nature of the self and referring to our concernedness about our own image in the eyes of others. See CH Cooley, *Human Nature and the Social Order* (Charles Scribner's Sons, 1922).

[14] 'Memory' refers here to 'public discourses about the past as wholes or … narratives and images of the past that speak in the name of the collective'. See JK Olick, *The Politics of Regret: On Collective Memory and Historical Responsibility* (Routledge, 2007) 33.

[15] MJ Caraccioli, E Wigen, J Costa Lopez, A Cheney and J Subotić, 'Forum: Interlingual Relations: Approaches, Conflicts, and Lessons in the Translation of Global Politics' (2021) 23 *International Studies Review* 1015, 1016–17.

II. THE ONTOLOGICAL INSECURITY OF GREAT RUSSIA

Russia's attempted recolonisation of Ukraine strongly lends itself to an ontological security-centric[16] interpretation. From this perspective, Russia's disciplining of Ukraine as its 'younger brother' (while simultaneously denying its independent existence as a nation and the legitimacy of its statehood)[17] is not simply the struggle for the Putin regime's survival by dint of the logic that if Ukraine can be a functional democratic state, having overturned a corrupt regime by its Revolution of Dignity in 2013–14, the very same possibility is bound to arise in Russia at some point as well. Putin's ambition 'to take back what is historically ours' by making a historical claim on a sphere of 'privileged interests' in Russia's Eurasian neighbourhood and publicly citing the self-ascribed mission to 'collect Russian lands',[18] is not only reflective of a yearning for a great power status, but importantly, a symptom of struggling with the boundaries of the Russian state 'self'.

Putin's denial of the existence of the Ukrainian state and nation provides a twisted mirror image of Russia's continuing post-imperial soul-searching and the post-Soviet troubles in defining its political, cultural and ethnic boundaries, thereby reflecting its oxymoronic brand of imperial nationalism.[19] It is worth recalling that the historical Russian model of nationhood included today's Russians, Ukrainians and Belarusians along with imperial elites of non-Slavic origins that were Russified in political and cultural terms. Historically, the building of the Russian state has been concomitant with its empire-building.[20] The national identity narrative instrumentalised by Putin relies on the idea of Kyiv

[16] For path-breaking studies on ontological security in IR, see C Kinnvall, 'Globalization and Religious Nationalism: Self, Identity, and the Search for Ontological Security' (2004) 25 *Political Psychology* 741; J Mitzen, 'Ontological Security in World Politics: State Identity and the Security Dilemma' (2006) 12 *European Journal of International Relations* 341; BJ Steele, *Ontological Security in International Relations: Self-Identity and the IR State* (Routledge, 2008).

[17] In one of his most memorable televised 'history lectures' in the run-up to the invasion on 21 February 2022, Putin famously claimed that: 'Modern Ukraine was entirely created by Russia, more precisely, Bolshevik, communist Russia. This process began immediately after the revolution of 1917 … As a result of Bolshevik policy, Soviet Ukraine arose, which even today can with good reason be called "Vladimir Il'ich Lenin's Ukraine." He is its author and architect … And now grateful descendants have demolished monuments to Lenin in Ukraine. This is what they call decommunisation. Do you want decommunisation? Well, that suits us just fine. But it is unnecessary, as they say, to stop halfway. We are ready to show you what real decommunisation means for Ukraine.' See 'Extracts from Putin's speech on Ukraine' (*Reuters*, 21 February 2022): https://www.reuters.com/world/europe/extracts-putins-speech-ukraine-2022-02-21/.

[18] 'Hailing Peter the Great, Putin draws parallel with mission to 'return' Russian lands' (*Reuters*, 9 June 2022): https://www.reuters.com/world/europe/hailing-peter-great-putin-draws-parallel-with-mission-return-russian-lands-2022-06-09/.

[19] E Pain, 'The Imperial syndrome and its influence on Russian nationalism' in P Kolstø and H Blakkisrud (eds), *The New Russian Nationalism: 'Imperialism, Ethnicity and Authoritarianism 2000-2015'* (Edinburgh University Press, 2016).

[20] R Szporluk, 'The Making of Modern Ukraine: The Western Dimension' (2001) 25 *Harvard Ukrainian Studies* 57; S Velychenko, 'The Issue of Russian Colonialism in Ukrainian Thought. Dependency Identity and Development' (2002) 1 *Ab Imperio* 323; M Riabchuk, 'Ukrainians as

(Kiev in the Russian transliteration) as the historical epicentre and cradle of the Russian civilisation (that is, the Kyivan Rus).[21] Accordingly, modern Ukraine is prohibited from politically determining itself as distinct from Russia by default (labelled 'anti-Russian' in the Russian parlance). The war epitomises Russia's wrestling with the perennial question of its boundaries: for what is Russia, if not a leading imperial nation?[22] And what space of existence can accordingly be left for Ukraine and the Ukrainians?

A crucial part of the reason for the current troubles lies in Russia's unprocessed past, Soviet and imperial alike. States and societies can deal with their past more or less reflectively: some are more inclined to think through their darker chapters along with the glorious ones; others are emphatically oriented towards establishing a sense of mnemonical security through making sure that a politically preferred 'state story' publicly sticks at home and abroad.[23] The latter approach seeks to set restraints on the unpleasant and ontologically disturbing interpretations of the past. There is indeed a rich irony in the fact that Russia, which has never conducted anything akin to a systematic state-level coming-to-terms process concerning the communist-era mass repressions and human rights violations after the collapse of the Soviet Union and the end of the Cold War, acts as if it is genuinely entitled to go and try to sort out other states' difficult pasts. Instead of pursuing the politics of accountability towards the perpetrators of the repressions of its antecedent regime, post-Soviet Russia has implemented effective rehabilitation of the Soviet legacy during the long Putin reign, in combination with an increasingly militant stance in contemporary international politics. Digging its heels in and seeking justifications for its great claim to power in the mythologised 'Great Patriotic War' experience[24] has constituted the Russian answer to the challenge of the ontological rupture created by the collapse of the Soviet Union and its effective defeat in the Cold War. Instead of systematic reckoning, an emphatically selective and self-defensive 'state story' of Russia has been advanced with the help of several prescribing and proscribing memory laws. Such laws notably include the 2020 constitutional amendments which prohibit 'diminishing the significance of the heroism of the people in defence of the Fatherland', and

Russia's negative "other": History comes full circle' (2016) 49 *Communist and Post-Communist Studies* 75.

[21] S Plokhy, *The Russo-Ukrainian War: The Return of History* (WW Norton & Co, 2023) 4–11; O Sukhov, 'How Russia steals and rewrites Ukrainian history to justify its claims in Ukraine' (*The Kyiv Independent*, 13 June 2023): https://kyivindependent.com/how-russia-steals-and-rewrites-ukrainian-history-to-justify-its-claims-in-ukraine/.

[22] S Medvedev, *A War Made in Russia*, trans by S Dalziel (Polity, 2023).

[23] M Mälksoo, '"Memory Must Be Defended": Beyond the Politics of Mnemonical Security' (2015) 46 *Security Dialogue* 221; M Mälksoo, 'The Transitional Justice and Foreign Policy Nexus: The Inefficient Causation of State Ontological Security-Seeking' (2019) 21 *International Studies Review* 373.

[24] See Medvedev (n 22); J McGlynn, *Memory Makers: The Politics of the Past in Putin's Russia* (Bloomsbury, 2023).

the 2014 and 2020 amendments to the Russian Criminal Code, criminalising first public dissemination of 'knowingly false information' about the activities of the USSR during WWII and secondly damaging war graves, monuments, memorial plaques, or obelisks that are dedicated to Russia's military glory or the defence of Russia's fatherland and its interests, accordingly.[25] A further law adopted on 16 April 2022 prohibits the public comparison of the 'goals, decisions and actions'[26] of the leadership of the USSR with those of Nazi Germany, alongside the denial of the 'decisive role of the Soviet people in the defeat of Nazi Germany and the humanitarian mission of the USSR during the liberation of European countries'.[27]

Russia's legislation on historical memory has prominently emerged in the form of targeted international dissuasion and disciplinary devices in the still heated contestations over the legitimate remembering and 'rightful' narratives of WWII and the larger Soviet legacy. Whereas the east European states have called for the consideration of the Soviet legacy on par with the Nazi regime, Russia's countering of any attempts to critically probe its role in and after WWII has emerged as the leitmotif of its recent memory laws and policies, with notable self-exculpatory framing.[28] There is a clear link between Russia's militant memory politics, the chronology of adoption of its memory laws, and its increasingly belligerent international disposition in open defiance of international law, particularly in the context of Russia's ongoing aggression against Ukraine.[29] Russian memory laws are designed to reassert the boundaries of the great Russian identity and state – and the fact that Russia's self-ascribed 'memory police' role has an extraterritorial reach speaks volumes here. As Jeffery Olick maintains, the memory-identity nexus manifests itself in the fact that people remember as members of groups, while constituting those groups and their members simultaneously in the act (thus *re-member-ing*).[30] Meanwhile, memory politics at home has distinct international repercussions, as memory laws and policies also signal intentions to other political communities in the international system. The self-exculpatory memory laws of a former imperial power with explicitly declared neo-imperial ambitions consequently have an ominous ring to them for Russia's former imperial subjugates. After all, 'states that deny past violence appear to have hostile intentions and thus appear more threatening; those who admit and

[25] M Mälksoo, 'The Postcolonial Moment in Russia's War Against Ukraine' (2023) 25 *Journal of Genocide Research* 471.

[26] See: 'Federal Law No. 103-FZ dated April 16, 2022 amending the Code of the Russian Federation on Administrative Offences' (11 November 2022): https://balashiha.ru/article/federalnym-zakonom-ot-16-04-2022-no-103-fz-vneseny-izmeneniya-v-kodeks-rossijskoj-federatsii-ob-administrativnyh-pravonarusheniyah-437223.

[27] Article 13.48 of the Administrative Offences Code.

[28] K Gustafsson and M Mälksoo, 'Memory-political Deterrence: Shielding Collective Memory and Ontological Security through Dissuasion' (2024) 64 *International Studies Quarterly* 1.

[29] F Hirsch, 'Putin's Memory Laws Set the Stage for His War in Ukraine' (*Lawfare*, 28 February 2022): https://www.lawfaremedia.org/article/putins-memory-laws-set-stage-his-war-ukraine.

[30] JK Olick, 'Collective Memory: The Two Cultures' (1999) 17 *Sociological Theory* 333, 342.

atone past violence appear benign', as Jennifer Lind maintains in her account of the implications of international apologies for other states' reading of the atoning states' intentions in world politics.[31]

III. EPISTEMIC HABITS IN MAKING SENSE OF THE RUSSO-UKRAINIAN WAR

Russia's ongoing aggression against Ukraine has reanimated a number of epistemic habits in European politics. Such epistemic routines work along certain mnemonical templates, concerning (i) the Holocaust as the equivalent of genocide in German, and more generally in west European, mindscapes; (ii) Nuremberg as a polysemic prototype for a post-war accountability mechanism, and (iii) the politics of appeasement. As an American scholar of memory studies James V Wertsch reminds us, the 'narrative templates' and 'privileged event narratives' that shape national memory not only serve as cognitive instruments that 'grasp … together information about events, actors, settings, and motives into a comprehensible whole', but also entail considerable emotional significance and provide guardians and holders of the respective narratives with 'a kind of moral authority'.[32] In a similar vein, the mnemonical templates guiding various European reactions in the context of the Russo-Ukrainian war do tacit and explicit political work in international debates about ways to handle the aggressor during and after the war. Such templates function as epistemic formations which provide us 'with the possible, with the thinkable, with the constellations of concepts that are in question, what people assume to know about their world and how they disagree over them'.[33] Let us consider them in turn.

A. The Holocaust Template

A disconcerting epistemic habit in European politics that has been made explicit in the context of the Russian aggression is the political and scholarly caution in calling a spade a spade – to wit, the reluctance to openly recognise the genocidal intent[34] behind Russia's case for a fully-fledged war against the Ukrainian

[31] J Lind, 'Apologies in International Politics' (2009) 18 *Security Studies* 517, 521.

[32] JV Wertsch, *How Nations Remember: A Narrative Approach* (Oxford University Press, 2021) 25.

[33] M Somers, 'Where is Sociology After the Historic Turn? Knowledge Cultures, Narrativity, and Historical Epistemologies' in TJ McDonald (ed), *The Historic Turn in the Human Sciences* (University of Michigan Press, 1996) 71.

[34] While notoriously difficult to prove in international law, genocide scholars have argued that genocidal intent is traceable in official or officially-endorsed Russian statements denying the existence

nation. As Vasyl Cherepanyn, Director of the Visual Culture Research Center in Kyiv, has aptly put it:

> Europe still prefers to talk about genocide in terms of history politics, memory culture, and 'coming to terms with the past', often avoiding applying the term to the present for fear of its 'relativization'. This is a typical instance of what in German is called *Schuldabwehr*, the deflection of the guilt. Trauma and fetishized guilt for past atrocities resurfaced when Europe was confronted with the Russian barbarity in Ukraine.[35]

As the mnemonic reflex of west European mindscapes tends to reserve the category of genocide exclusively for the Holocaust, public acknowledgement of the Russian war's aims as genocidal has been piecemeal. As of November 2023, Russia's actions against Ukraine have been recognised as genocide, with varying emphasis, by Ukraine, Estonia, Latvia, Lithuania, Poland, Canada, Ireland and Czechia, alongside the Parliamentary Assembly of the Council of Europe and the European Parliament.[36] The evidence is mounting, including the forcible transfer of Ukrainian children to Russia and their Russification, the mass atrocities against civilians in Bucha, Borodyanka, Irpin and other areas, the destruction of the Ukrainian cultural heritage and the wilful demolition of the living environment in Ukraine.

The labelling of Ukrainians as 'Nazis' by the Russian leadership and the state propaganda machine in turn has sought to function as a mnemonic diffuser or trap in the contested field of meaning-making over the war's rationales. This misnomer[37] has served to reflexively disable Western policy-makers and intellectuals, hindering them from recognising the inversion of the victim and the perpetrator that is really happening in the Russian act of calling Ukrainians 'Nazis'.[38] Since the 'Nazi' label continues to be among the most powerfully charged WWII-situated mnemonic stigmas, it remains a powerful tool in the fight over cognitive control in this conflict.

of the Ukrainian nation, rendering Ukrainians legitimate targets of destruction via the rhetoric of 'denazification', and a genocidal pattern of destruction targeting Ukrainians. See: 'An Independent Legal Analysis of the Russian Federation's Breaches of the Genocide Convention in Ukraine and the Duty to Prevent' (*New Lines Institute for Strategy and Policy & Raoul Wallenberg Centre for Human Rights*, May 2022): https://newlinesinstitute.org/rules-based-international-order/genocide/an-independent-legal-analysis-of-the-russian-federations-breaches-of-the-genocide-convention-in-ukraine-and-the-duty-to-prevent/.

[35] V Cherepanyn, 'Europe after the death of peace of mind' (*Eurozine*, 28 August 2023): https://www.eurozine.com/europe-after-the-death-of-peace-of-mind/.

[36] See: E Whatcott, 'Compilation of Countries' Statements Calling Russian Actions in Ukraine "Genocide"' (*Just Security*, 20 May 2022) https://www.justsecurity.org/81564/compilation-of-countries-statements-calling-russian-actions-in-ukraine-genocide/.

[37] But see also: A Smith, 'Standing ovation for a Ukrainian who fought with the Nazis sparks anger and an apology in Canada' (*NBC News*, 25 September 2023): https://www.nbcnews.com/news/world/canada-speaker-apologizes-ukraine-nazi-veteran-honored-rcna117125.

[38] Compare 'accusation in a mirror', New Lines Institute (n 34).

B. The Nuremberg Template

Comparable caution has surfaced in the discussions over establishing a special international tribunal on the crime of aggression as a key part of ascertaining post-war Russian accountability for the crimes against and in Ukraine. Up until early 2023, advocacy for a special tribunal centred around a handful of Eastern European states in geographical proximity to Ukraine and with prior histories of Russian aggression.[39] The International Centre for the Prosecution of Aggression against Ukraine was established in The Hague in July 2023, but divergences on the institutional model of a future tribunal are yet to be ironed out at the time of the writing. Meanwhile, the support for criminal accountability from non-Western countries has been largely absent, amid fears that a special tribunal would feature as yet another sign of Western dominance and double standards in regard to guaranteeing the same application of the law for everyone.[40]

The Nuremberg template, or the trope of accountability, has distinct meanings for Western and Eastern Europeans, and for Russia, for that matter. It further resonates in a different manner among international legal and IR scholars. In Francine Hirsch's words, Nuremberg has become 'a linchpin of competing national mythologies about World War II and post-war justice', remembered in the US as a triumph of Western leadership and liberal values, while embodying the Soviet victory over German fascism and the emergence of the USSR as a world power for the Soviet Union, and later Russia.[41] From the broader Western perspective, Nuremberg marks the recognition of Nazi criminality and justification of the allied cause in WWII. Meanwhile, Nuremberg stands for the legal and political institutionalisation of the USSR silencing and lying about the Soviet crimes against Eastern European peoples (such as the Katyń massacre of Polish officers and intellectuals). From the east European perspective, the Nuremberg decisions allowed Soviet impunity and bestowed legitimacy on the narrative of the Soviet Union as a 'liberator' from Nazi rule, thereby enabling the obfuscation of the historical fact that WWII began because of Nazi Germany and the Soviet Union's joint attack on Poland and the secretly agreed division of their respective 'spheres of influence' in Eastern Europe.[42] In the context of the Russo-Ukrainian war, 'Nuremberg' has come to mark hope for Ukraine as a

[39] PI Labuda, 'Countering Imperialism in International Law: Examining the Special Tribunal for Aggression Against Ukraine through a Post-Colonial Eastern European Lens' (2023) 49 *Yale Journal of International Law* 271, 276.

[40] ibid 276–77.

[41] F Hirsch, 'Ukraine and Russia Are Both Looking to the Nuremberg Trials – But Finding Different Lessons in the History' (*Time*, 26 May 2022): https://time.com/6181464/ukraine-war-crimes-nuremberg/.

[42] Labuda (n 39).

symbolic shorthand for the aspiration to bring Russia's leaders to justice for waging a war of aggression.[43]

For modern Russia, 'Nuremberg' is the hallmark of their self-exculpatory 'state story' that emerged from the WWII experience). The 'de-Nazification' rallying cries in the context of the aggression towards Ukraine have, inter alia, cited Russia's ambition to 'act as the guardian of the [legacy of the] Nuremberg Trials'.[44] In an ominously entitled piece ('What Russia Should Do with Ukraine') published by the Russian state-owned news agency, *RIA Novosti*, in early April 2022, Russian political consultant Timofey Sergeytsev made the nested arguments that 'a denazified country cannot be sovereign', 'denazification will inevitably also be de-Ukrainization', and 'the denazification of Ukraine is also its inevitable de-Europeanization'.[45] Aptly characterised as 'Russia's genocide handbook',[46] this text makes a blatant case for the destruction of Ukraine as a state along with its national identity. There have been further calls for a 'Nuremberg 2.0' in Russia to try the Ukrainian leadership dubbed as 'neo-Nazi killers',[47] and threats to teach 'a lesson for everyone who has forgotten the lessons of Nuremberg'.[48] Symptomatically, the Russian ban on the 'rehabilitation of Nazism' (that is, Article 354.1 of the Russian Criminal Code) prohibits the denial of facts established by the Nuremberg Tribunal, the dissemination of knowingly false information about activities of the USSR during WWII or its veterans, and the expression of disrespect about the days of military glory, memorable dates or symbols of military glory of Russia.[49] In the Russian 'state story', the Soviet people 'endured the harshest and most atrocious blows by the aggressor',[50] hence Russia's main lesson drawn from Nuremberg is the absolute and incomparable Nazi evil and the righteousness of the Soviet Union and its hard-earned place in the post-war world order.[51] The jurisdictional limitation of the original Nuremberg Tribunal to the crimes of the European Axis powers is

[43] Hirsch, 'Ukraine and Russia Are Both Looking to the Nuremberg Trials' (n 41).

[44] T Sergeytsev, 'Что Россия должна сделать с Украиной' (*RIA Novosti*, 3 April 2022): https://ria.ru/20220403/ukraina-1781469605.html.

[45] ibid.

[46] T Snyder, 'Russia's genocide handbook' (*Thinking about …*, 8 April 2022): https://snyder.substack.com/p/russias-genocide-handbook?s=w.

[47] M Panyukov, 'Andrey Krasov: We will hold Nuremberg 2.0 in Ukraine' (*Soyuznoe Veche*, site of the newspaper of the Parliamentary Assembly of the Union of Belarus and Russia, 10 May 2022): https://www.souzveche.ru/articles/tribune_deputy/63852/?utm_source=yxnews&utm_medium=desktop&utm_referrer=https%253A%252F%252Fyandex.ru%252Fnews%252Fsearch%253Ftext%253D.

[48] 'Head of Crimea: Azovstal criminals should not be exchanged' (*REGNUM News Agency*, 18 May 2022): https://regnum.ru/news/3594053?utm_source=yxnews&utm_medium=desktop&utm_referrer=https://yandex.ru/news/search?text=.

[49] Article 354-1, 'Ugolovnyi Kodeks Rossiyskoy Federatsii' (*Criminal Code of Russian Federation*): http://www.pravo.gov.ru/proxy/ips/?docbody=&link_id=1&nd=102041891.

[50] V Putin, 'Address to Participants in the Nuremberg Lessons Forum' (*President of Russia*, 20 November 2020): http://en.kremlin.ru/events/president/news/64447.

[51] F Hirsch, 'The Soviets at Nuremberg: International Law, Propaganda, and the Making of the Postwar Order' (2008) 113 *The American Historical Review* 701.

accordingly mobilised in the contemporary context to protect a sanitised version of Soviet WWII history, underpinned by the logic that 'the fact that Soviet crimes were not judged at Nuremberg means that they never happened'.[52] Suffering from the Nazi German aggression and crimes is consequently supposed to make any question of the Soviet perpetrator-hood in the context of WWII irrelevant. Further, in today's Russia, it has been deemed illegal – with the Duma's enactment of a provision in April 2022 – to compare 'the goals, decisions and actions of the leadership, command and military personnel of the USSR with the goals, decisions and actions of the leadership, command and military personnel of Nazi Germany and the European Axis countries.'.[53]

The various distinct takes on the legacy of Nuremberg discretely inform visions for the post-war accountability mechanism for Russia. Three institutional design options have been part of the international legal and political discussion: (i) an international tribunal established by a multilateral treaty of state parties (that is, an international regional tribunal); (ii) an international tribunal established with the blessing of the UN General Assembly; and (iii) a 'hybrid' tribunal embedded in Ukraine's domestic criminal jurisdiction and supported by the Council of Europe. A rift runs between the proponents of the 'hybrid'[54] and the 'truly' international (that is, the UN-endorsed) option[55] – a fissure that further resonates with the established divergences between Western and Eastern European mnemonic focal points against the backdrop of WWII

[52] Hirsch, 'Ukraine and Russia Are Both Looking to the Nuremberg Trials' (n 41).

[53] A Nekoliak and E Klochkova, 'Weaponizing Russia's Memory Law: On Russia's Mnemonic Dissidents' (*Verfassungsblog*, 11 July 2023): https://verfassungsblog.de/weaponizing-russias-memory-law/.

[54] See: KJ Heller, 'Options for Prosecuting Russian Aggression Against Ukraine: A Critical Analysis' (2022) 26 *Journal of Genocide Research* 1, 12–15; KJ Heller, 'Creating a Special Tribunal for Aggression Against Ukraine Is a Bad Idea' (*Opinio Juris*, 7 March 2022): http://opiniojuris.org/2022/03/07/creating-a-special-tribunal-for-aggression-against-ukraine-is-a-bad-idea/; A Schüler, 'What can('t) international criminal justice deliver for Ukraine?' (*Verfassungsblog*, 24 February 2023): https://verfassungsblog.de/justice-ukraine/.

[55] See R Tammsaar, 'An International Special Tribunal is the Only Viable Path to a Just and Lasting Peace in Ukraine' (*Just Security*, 9 May 2023): https://www.justsecurity.org/86516/an-international-special-tribunal-is-the-only-viable-path-to-a-just-and-lasting-peace-in-ukraine/; G Grigaitė-Daugirdė, 'The Lithuanian Case for an International Special Tribunal for the Crime of Aggression Against Ukraine' (*Just Security*, 1 June 2023): https://www.justsecurity.org/86766/the-lithuanian-case-for-an-international-special-tribunal-for-the-crime-of-aggression-against-ukraine/; 'Statement: Calling for the Creation of a Special Tribunal for the Punishment of the Crime of Aggression against Ukraine' (4 March 2022): https://gordonandsarahbrown.com/wp-content/uploads/2022/03/Combined-Statement-and-Declaration.pdf; G Brown, 'We owe it to the people of Ukraine to bring Vladimir Putin to trial for war crimes' (*The Guardian*, 24 February 2023): https://www.theguardian.com/world/commentisfree/2023/feb/24/people-ukraine-vladimir-putin-trial-war-crimes; P Sands, 'There can be no impunity for the crime of aggression against Ukraine' (*Financial Times*, 21 February 2023); 'Joint Statement by Albania, Belgium, Costa Rica, Czech Republic, Estonia, Guatemala, Latvia, Liechtenstein, Lithuania, Luxembourg, Marshall Islands, North-Macedonia and Poland on the accountability for the crime of aggression committed on the territory of Ukraine' (*Permanent Mission of Estonia to the UN*, 17 April 2023): https://un.mfa.ee/joint-statement-on-the-accountability-for-the-crime-of-aggression-committed-on-the-territory-of-ukraine/.

and the related sensibilities. With predominantly east European states' backing, Ukraine has proposed a UN General Assembly resolution

> [r]equest[ing] the Secretary-General to negotiate an agreement with the Government of Ukraine to create an independent international tribunal with jurisdiction over crimes of aggression committed against Ukraine and to submit the agreement for the review of the General Assembly.[56]

Some type of a 'hybrid' or 'internationalised' court (eg, a tribunal embedded in Ukraine's domestic criminal jurisdiction, featuring joint Ukrainian and international staff, and supported by the Council of Europe) has meanwhile been supported by Germany, the UK and the USA. The United States announced its withdrawal from the International Centre for the Prosecution of the Crime of Aggression against Ukraine in March 2025. Evidently, what the Ukrainian president fears to be 'a continuation of hybrid peace',[57] works as a pragmatic solution for the advocates of a hybrid tribunal for prosecuting Russia for the crimes committed against Ukraine. From a wider east European perspective, the Nuremberg template is evoked and translated into concrete political proposals for an international tribunal to address the Russian crime of aggression to beat the suspected spirit of appeasement underpinning the hybrid accountability models.

C. The Appeasement Template

The political and strategic debates over the best ways to support the victims, end the war and bring about lasting peace have been, to a large degree, informed by these varying conclusions drawn from WWII and its aftermath in distinct parts of Europe. Different sides in these debates have demonstrated discrete understandings of the manifest and root causes of the current war, reflected in some parties' readiness to accommodate Russia's security concerns regarding NATO's supposed 'encircling' of Russia, and their concomitant dismissiveness of Ukraine's political agency.

For most Eastern European states, the main lesson of WWII has been straightforward: aggression needs to be pushed back, aggressors cannot be appeased for the conflict will thus only be pushed under the carpet for a while, and relative peace achieved only at the direct expense of the frontline states. For several Western European states, the conclusions have been more mixed, hiding behind the convenient, if immoral, shield of the inevitable de facto east European buffer zone, or Russia's sphere of 'legitimate security interests' to keep peace for those in the self-proclaimed 'centre'. While concerns in the west of Europe – notably

[56] Labuda (n 39) 298.

[57] For the 'hybrid court' with some international elements would not be able to prosecute the top leadership for the crime of aggression. 'President: Ukraine stands against hybrid formats of tribunal for Russian crime of aggression' (*President of Ukraine Volodymyr Zelenskyy: Official Website*, 4 May 2023): https://president.gov.ua/en/news/ukrayina-vistupaye-proti-gibridnih-formativ-tribunalu-shodo-82669.

from Germany – have focused on the prospect of nuclear escalation, people and leaders in the east of Europe (broadly speaking) have been more cautious of the price of appeasement as a means of alleviating the perennial escalation fears that have accompanied the decision-making about every new weapon category in this conflict.

The Western dilemma, per Jürgen Habermas's diagnosis from May 2022, has accordingly been 'the range between two evils – a defeat of Ukraine or the escalation of a limited conflict into a third world war'. Since 'nuclear war cannot be fought and cannot be won', as the argument goes, 'global conflagration must be avoided at all costs', Habermas maintains.[58] From the Ukrainian and east European perspective more generally, however, this 'at all costs' has a familiar and sinister ring to it. The cost would quite simply be the existence, freedom, and future of Ukraine. By extension, the already dubious solidity of post-WWII Western moral promises of 'never again' in relation to genocide (qua Holocaust) would further crumble as a result of giving in to Russia's nuclear blackmailing. The Western self-restraint out of fear of escalation also signals, by extension, the sentencing of Eastern Europeans 'back to their cage' – to a space the primary function of which would be to save the world from a 'global conflagration' via Eastern Europeans' effective self-sacrifice, denial and suppression of their own immediate physical and ontological security needs. Habermas admits as much by acknowledging that 'the West … cannot allow itself to be *continually* blackmailed' – and hence simply leaving Ukraine to its fate 'wouldn't just be a scandal from a political-moral perspective, it would also be counter to the West's interests'.[59] Meanwhile, the mantra that 'a war against a nuclear power cannot be won in the traditional sense of the word' persists – which is in itself indicative of a pretty selective memory of some of the defining 'small wars' that were fought against the backdrop of the Cold War (think, for instance, Vietnam).

IV. IMPLICATIONS: ACADEMIC, POLITICAL, ETHICAL

Ingrained epistemic habits, such as the standard scepticism of the IR discipline towards any authoritative insights emanating from non-Western or in-between places like Eastern Europe,[60] can be practically counterproductive. Unquestioned epistemic habits lead to empirical fallacies, ideologically driven theorising, ethical nihilism, and misinformed policy formulation. They

[58] Habermas (n 9).
[59] ibid.
[60] Compare the self-ironic dubbing of 'secondary Europe with secondary colonial difference' by M Vladimirovna Tlostanova, 'The South of the Poor North: Caucasus Subjectivity and the Complex of Secondary "Australism"' (2011) 5 *Global South* 66. For an extended discussion, see: M Mälksoo, 'Uses of "the East" in international studies: provincialising IR from Central and Eastern Europe' (2021) 24 *Journal of International Relations and Development* Special Issue 811.

can paralyse progressive thinking and inhibit the ability to break out from the current political and epistemological standoffs. The Russian war waged on Ukraine has highlighted the frequent empirical flippancy of IR and highlighted the value of knowledge coming from area studies for grasping the nature of the conflict.[61] The IR realists' readings of the war have made it particularly evident that academic discourses are hardly impervious to treacherously habitual ways of thinking either. Just like political discourses, academic truisms must also be ethically interrogated and called out for their dubious presuppositions and methodological misjudgements.

Regardless of the mnemonical multiplicity of the meanings of Nuremberg in contemporary international relations, Russia's ongoing war against Ukraine demands us to think seriously about future ways of co-existing with Russia in international society once the guns have fallen silent. It remains an open question, what really are the prospects for the liberal enterprise of transitional justice to deal with the problem of difference of Russia's scale and size – that is, an authoritarian regime with no clear succession mechanism, no credible democratic leadership alternatives in sight, notably trigger-happy with its nuclear arsenal, and, openly scornful of and confrontational toward liberal values and Western democracy at large? What can be done to advance the dismantling of the Russian imperial mentality, to constructively assist Russian society with unwrapping itself from the experience of having lived in an atmosphere of state-peddled lies and propaganda for generations throughout the past century? This will be the task for at least a generation of scholars and practitioners in their efforts to construct a sustainable post-war security order in Europe. Decolonising Russia's historical memory and the imperial substance of its political sense of 'self' remains a central political imperative for building anything akin to a lasting peace and enabling the peaceful coexistence of Russia with its CEE neighbours in the region.[62] There is a broader question about the limits of tolerance that liberal societies should exercise vis-à-vis openly illiberal memory politics practised by regimes that systematically peddle mnemonical disinformation under the guise of their proclaimed fight against 'historical revisionism'.[63] If a neo-imperial power with an actively revisionist agenda practises memory politics that seeks to securitise desirable and criminalise undesirable perspectives on its past, thereby restricting freedom of speech and freedom of historical research, this is not purely a domestically contained issue. Russia's memory laws and politics have urgent international implications for its former subjugates in

[61] J Dutkiewicz and J Smolenski, 'Epistemic superimposition: the war in Ukraine and the poverty of expertise in international relations theory' (2023) 26 *Journal of International Relations and Development* 619.

[62] See further: C Wittke, 'Peace and Security for Ukraine and Europe are not Created on the Drawing Board of the West' (*Verfassungsblog*, 13 April 2022): https://verfassungsblog.de/peace-and-security-for-ukraine-and-europe-are-not-created-on-the-drawing-board-of-the-west/.

[63] See further: M Mälksoo, 'Illiberal Memory Politics' in M Laruelle (ed), *The Oxford Handbook on Illiberalism* (Oxford University Press, 2023) 415.

the Eastern European space, along with the world beyond, as the war in Ukraine testifies to only too well.[64]

Finally, the Russo-Ukraine war marks the beginning of Eastern Europeans' (states and scholars alike) coming of age in an unprecedented manner against the backdrop of the broader political moment of self-reflection created in Europe by this war. The emboldened east European political and epistemic agency in European politics and the academic study of IR allows them to point with increasing confidence and vocality to the missed opportunity for their Western counterparts to listen to, and indeed trust, their experientially embedded insights on Russia.[65] Vindicated in their sombre assessment of Putin's Russia's accommodation possibilities in the liberal European security order, various east European leaders have begun to vocally claim for themselves the position of 'translator' of Russia to the West – a task traditionally allocated for the inhabitants of various borderlands, both symbolic and material. As Yuri Lotman, the leading semiotician of the Tartu-Moscow school maintains, the 'bilingual and polylingual' boundary of the semiosphere serves as 'a mechanism for translating texts of an alien semiotics into "our" language'. For Lotman, the boundary is the place where what is 'external' is transformed into what is 'internal': 'it is a filtering membrane which so transforms foreign texts that they become part of the semiosphere's internal semiotics while still retaining their own characteristics'.[66] The ways in which this newly claimed role of 'a filtering membrane' would become substantiated politically for Eastern European actors and Europe at large is one of the intriguing open questions emerging from the ashes of the Russo-Ukrainian war. The role of the 'Russia-translator' may remain but a fantasy of borderlands, who naturally would like to claim a role for themselves, even if this role tends to remain limited in the practice of international politics. While there is occasional willingness to listen and compare perceptions on the part of 'the big ones', such as the Germans and the Americans, they are hardly reliant on full 'translations' by east Europeans – particularly where these 'translations' do not temper their open hatred of everything Russian.

V. CONCLUSION

In this chapter, I have highlighted some ways in which Russia's war against Ukraine offers a looking glass for understanding Russia's contemporary search for a meaningful political self-identity, the epistemic habits that have guided the

[64] Gustafsson and Mälksoo (n 28).

[65] See eg: 'Baltic states, Poland, Romania urge EU to counter Russian falsification of history' (*Public broadcasting of Latvia*, 22 July 2022): https://eng.lsm.lv/article/culture/history/baltic-states-poland-romania-urge-eu-to-counter-russian-falsification-of-history.a466447/.

[66] Y Lotman, *Universe of the Mind: A Semiotic Theory of Culture*, trans. A Shukman (IB Tauris, 1990) 136–37.

sense-making attempts and responses to Russia's aggression against Ukraine in various corners of Europe, and the changing positionality of eastern Europe in speaking and practising security in European politics.

The international memory politics on the distinct lessons of WWII in response to the war in Ukraine highlights the continuing gravity of earlier war memories in contemporary Europe, east and west alike. Russia's blunt pursuance of an imperialist vision of the regional security order forces the Western allies to reckon with some very hard questions, such as how to carry on co-existing with Russia after this war, with or without subsequent regime change in Russia, and how to make the security-political edifice of Europe more resilient against the potential of such aggression in the future. The answers to these questions will be, to a degree, decided in the current battlefields of Ukraine. A weighty and less frequently acknowledged part of answering these questions pertains to shaking the epistemic habits which are empirically dubious, morally problematic, and politically counterproductive in relation to the current conflict.

An iconic Polish twentieth-century poet Wisława Szymborska wrote in her 'The End and the Beginning' (2001): 'After every war, someone has to clean up'. Yet, eventually, as she mused on, 'Those who knew what was going on here must make way for those who knew little. And less than little. And finally as little as nothing'. The Russo-Ukrainian war is far from over and the future task of cleaning up remains. It is hard to imagine, though, that forgetting would ever become advisable in relation to the manipulations, lies and atrocities committed on the part of Russia in its war against Ukraine.

Epilogue

The Battle for the Past: War and Memory in the Post-Soviet Space

DAVID R MARPLES

As 2024 approached its end, Europe was once again at war and the post-WWII order had unravelled. Under the extended presidency of Vladimir Putin, now in its fourth term (lasting for six years rather than the original four), Russia has embarked on a war of destruction largely based on memory myths and a sense of self-righteousness, at least in the Kremlin. As hapless hordes advance into Donbas suffering an alarming rate of casualties, the Ukrainian defenders, short of troops and long-range missiles, anxiously implore their American and European allies to assist their resistance. The peaceful independence of Ukraine, which lasted for 23 years, has ended; the state's leaders branded as neo-Nazis, equated with Hitler's occupation regime of 1941–45, and targeted for elimination. It is not a war for a clearly specified goal, other than the removal of a state from the map of Europe, one that conceded its nuclear weapons of the Soviet era 30 years ago.

Russian propaganda has become dominated by historical politics, or the politics of historical memory, and what Uladzislau Belavusau has coined 'mnemomic constitutionalism'. Its reasoning is fallacious but disarmingly simple. Having achieved a victory in a bitter war with Nazism and Fascism, Russia is now intent on ensuring that the spoils are not lost. NATO and the European Union – indeed the whole 'degenerate Western world' – is seeking to drag Ukraine into its own orbit, and away from its mother country, Russia. Poland, the country that according to Putin, started World War II (WWII), threatens to invade Belarus. Russia would thus be further isolated, victimised by the rapacious West.

The problems with this narrative are not diffcult to fathom. Vladimir Putin's grasp of history has never been strong. The most obvious counter is that the war in 1945 was *not* won by Russia, but rather by the people of the Soviet Union and the Western Allies. More than 2.5 million Ukrainians fought in the Red Army. Ukraine and Belarus suffered the main brunt of the Nazi occupation.

Logically, if one is to understand Putin's worldview, which is not consistent and has evolved partly in response to the international situation, the basis of memory politics is the period of Stalin, who transformed a backward rural state into an industrial powerhouse and emerged as the war victor and founder of the new empire, one that stretched all the way to Berlin, superseding the achievements of Tsar Aleksandr I, a key player in the defeat of Napoleon and the Congress of Vienna in 1815. Despite that colossal achievement, it never reached its full potential because the West betrayed its agreement made with Russia at Yalta in 1945 – no distinction is made between Russia and the Soviet Union – starting a Cold War against the former allies and led by the United States.

The formation of new states in 1991 brought the politics of memory to the forefront, as the respective leaders attempted to justify their existence and provided interpretations of the past that sought to legitimise their governments. For Russia, with its imperial past, it was perhaps not difficult, though for several years its first president, Boris N Yeltsin, tried to cooperate with the West and follow its economic guidelines. The low point was his re-election campaign of 1996, when his presidency was revived and renewed with the help of Western political strategists (some of whom had worked on the election campaign of Bill Clinton four years earlier) and in collaboration with oligarchs who had ruthlessly captured and exploited the country's natural resources.

The decline of Russia in the 1990s, the loss of Super Power status, and its financial collapse in 1998, could all be advanced as reasons why a figure like Putin might emerge. But the Putin of 2000 was not the Putin of later years. He was quite willing to cooperate with the United States in combatting terrorism. Further, the formation of historical narratives with the 'Great Patriotic War' at the forefront was not something new. It first emerged in the Soviet Union of the 1960s, on the 20th anniversary of the end of war in Europe. As leaders, both Putin and Belarus's Aliaksandr Lukashenka recognised the importance of the event, and the latter has paid his respects to war veterans on a regular basis.

The turning point for Russia, however, was Ukraine's EuroMaidan protests in 2013–14, known formally as 'The Revolution of Dignity'. The event went through several phases, culminating in the bloody massacre of about 100 protesters in the Maidan by snipers firing from the rooftops. After the pro-Russian president, Viktor Yanukovych, abandoned his ornate residence and fled from Kyiv, Putin made the decision to intervene with the annexation of Crimea, and Moscow-inspired attempts to remove local governments in eastern Ukraine. The attempts largely failed, but succeeded in the cities of Donetsk and Luhansk in the regions collectively known as the Donbas.

Ukraine has long been the *bête noire* of Russians, an entity that cannot be explained by common origins. Nothing really fits. Kyiv was on the map of Europe several centuries before Moscow but was destroyed by the Mongol attack of 1240. The illusion of a common East Slavic fraternity of Russia, Ukraine, and Belarus, which pervaded throughout the Soviet period, evaporated in 2008, when Viktor Yushchenko, Ukraine's third president, also evoked historical memory through the *Holodomor*, opening a museum that portrayed the government in Moscow as 'the other' and 'the perpetrator' of Ukraine's greatest humanitarian tragedy. The acceptance of the term 'genocide' to explain it placed Russia irrevocably as the enemy.

But it was not only the existence of a national Ukrainian state that infuriated Putin; he also sought an adequate retort to the entire Western world that crowed over a Cold War victory and the dissolution of the Soviet state, built into a Super Power under Stalin's authoritarian rule. Externally, he complained of the enlargement of NATO to the Russian border. But privately, his major concern was the loss of empire, gained by the victory over Nazi Germany. The Russian response has undergone several phases: Eurasianism, anti-Westernism, and ultimately a new version of the past based on the 'Great Patriotic War'. Several icons have been dismantled en route, including the founder of the Soviet state, Vladimir Ilyich Lenin, condemned for forming a Ukrainian state in 1922 rather than following Stalin's advice and unifying the republics inside an all-powerful Russia.

Anti-Westernism also provides a loophole for the biggest flaw in the 'Soviet victory over Nazism' narrative, namely, the Molotov-Ribbentrop Pact with Hitler's Germany signed in August 1939. According to Russian historians, and as enunciated by Putin, the West – at this stage the term signifies only Britain and France – had abandoned the USSR, seeking a military confrontation between Nazi Germany and the Soviet Union. The Pact, then, was a temporary measure for survival, until the Soviet military buildup reached full capacity. On the positive side, the Soviet Union was able to free Ukrainian and Belarusian lands 'enslaved' by interwar Poland and reunite them with their own people in Soviet republics, albeit only for 20 months.

Belarus's post-2020 historical revisionism is modelled quite closely on Russia's narratives. As noted, it began in the 1960s and was then advanced by Lukashenka in a quest to base Belarusian identity on wartime victory rather than other events in its history that might seem more obvious, such as the 25 March 1918 Declaration of Independence, or the achievements of the medieval Grand Duchy of Lithuania. The legitimacy of the Lukashenka presidency was seriously questioned in 2020; his regime thus returned to historical memory, with a deeply revised interpretation of the war coupled with the introduction of patriotic education and new textbooks for schools. As in Russia, it is now a criminal offence to question the official interpretation of the war, and to the long-established legends of the partisans has been added a new phenomenon: the 'genocide of the Belarusian people'. The term is particularly offensive to the Jewish population, which suffered approximately one-third of the loss of life inflicted on the territory that made up the Belarusian Soviet Socialist Republic directly before and after WWII.

In some respects, such rewriting of the past can often lead to farce. Investigators in Belarus claim to have found dozens of new gravesites, raising the number of official war deaths from 1.8–2.2 million, to over three million. Moreover, under the supervision of the Belarusian Office of the Prosecutor-General, 400 perpetrators of wartime atrocities were discovered to be alive and Belarus sought their extradition from other European states – particularly Lithuania, with which the government is on particularly bad terms. Supposedly, should these perpetrators be sent to Belarus, one might expect to see trials of people who, logically, would be at least 100 years old.

On the other hand, the 'Great Patriotic War' in Belarus has never been forgotten, and during the 2020 events, protesters made analogies between the German occupiers and the security officials attacking peaceful individuals, as well as the guards in prisons such as the notorious Akrestina. The protesters compared themselves with wartime partisans, and families remembered their ancestors – though by the 2020s, most of those that had participated in the war were deceased grandparents and great grandparents to the new generation.

Though the Minsk regime has seemingly survived the 2020 protests, the war memories are not related to the current intrusion into Ukraine. Some Belarusians, it seems, were partly convinced of the righteousness of the invasion as a means to remove a 'neo-Nazi regime', a result of incessant propaganda and social media campaigns emanating from Moscow. But others were not. The presence of some 500–1,000 fighters in the Kalinouski regiment (a group of Belarusian opposition volunteers) and other units serving in the Ukrainian army is proof of a society deeply divided. Relations between the two states, even at the official level, were cordial until the start of the wider war in February 2022. The regime recognises this fact and declines to cooperate more deeply with Putin by sending the Belarusian army over the border into Ukraine. Such a move might well lead to renewed protests. As it is, the stated goal of the Kalinouski Regiment is to push the Russian army out of Ukraine and then turn on the regime in Minsk and depose Lukashenka.

And yet Belarus is often touted as the chief partner of Russia and subjected to similar sanctions. Some EU states do not discriminate between ethnic Russians and Belarusians as perpetrators of crimes in Ukraine. The truth, however, is that although the Minsk government appears obsessed with the memory of WWII, its memory has not been a sufficient prop to stabilise its legitimacy. Moreover, it retains power only through repressions and crackdowns, backed by the implicit support of the Russian military, while seeking, sometimes desperately, to find means to avoid complete integration into the Russian Federation.

Western analysts often contrast the anomalies of these post-Soviet approaches to the war in Russia and Belarus with those of pro-Western, democratic Ukraine. But while it is correct to say that Ukraine has taken a very different path to its East Slavic neighbours, it would be facile to suggest that its steps are without controversies. We have noted the elevation of the *Holodomor* as the main event of historical memory. Many European countries, as well as the United States and Canada, have accepted that the 1933 famine constituted an act of genocide. Others, including Spain and, expectedly, Russia, reject such a conclusion.

Although Ukraine has dismantled its Communist legacy, replacing it has raised a number of questions. At present, its relations with Poland, formerly its closest ally, are in difficulty because the latter state maintains that Ukraine has never responded satisfactorily to the 1943 Volhynia massacre, when units of the Ukrainian Insurgent Army (UPA) killed tens of thousands of innocent civilians in a bid to carry out ethnic cleansing to ensure that the Polish population was not a factor in the post-war period. The Organisation of Ukrainian Nationalists under Stepan Bandera (OUN-B), a violent far-right political entity, first emerged in 1940 – the original party was founded in 1929 – and sought a 'Ukraine for Ukrainians', assisting Nazi Germany in its initial invasion of the Soviet Union.

Neither of these parties was ever popular throughout Ukraine. They emerged under Polish rule and their leaders either died in battle (eg UPA leader Roman Shukhevych) or fled to Western countries when the war ended. During the first 25 years of Ukraine's independence, far-right parties made little impact politically, even though the Diaspora OUN began to operate in Ukraine and was represented in some political parties, such as 'Svaboda' and ideologically by the 'Right Sector' during the 2013–14 protests. But Russia's 2014 invasion and the wider war after 2022 have brought something of a revival and a new veneration of these groups in Ukraine. Volodymyr Zelenskyy's government has embraced the far-right Azov Division because of its heroic resistance during the Russian attacks on Mariupol. And the parade in Kyiv to commemorate the birthday of Stepan Bandera at the height of the Maidan protests (1 January 2014) is one of the most remembered moments of that long uprising.

The fact is that Ukraine has largely followed decommunisation and the removal of Lenin statues by embracing nationalist myths that evoke the era of the 1930s and involving figures associated with western Ukraine under Polish rule. In this respect, Russian propaganda contains a grain of truth, though it has never been a factor in Ukrainian elections, the make-up of Ukrainian parliaments, or the choices of presidents between 1991 and 2019. But once the nation was in a situation that threatened its future and even its existence, its leaders began to look for examples of 'heroes' who had fought valiantly against overwhelming odds. There is no better example than Roman Shukhevych and his UPA forces in western Ukraine between 1944 and 1950. Yet how does one reconcile such bravery with the same leader's participation in German-run police units in Belarus during the war?

The same questions have plagued the Ukrainian diaspora in Canada for years, fighting off accusations that in raising statues and monuments to Bandera and Shukhevych, they are glorifying Nazism. But these figures have been part of the pantheon of Ukainian heroes in the diaspora since the end of the war. Thus, historical memory can be confusing and hypocritical. My Alberta colleague John-Paul Himka maintains in his most recent book that Ukrainians should acknowledge the crimes of the past, particularly the role of such organisations in the Holocaust. There is little chance of this happening either in the diaspora or in Ukraine.

The current war, however, was not started by Ukraine. It is very much Putin's war, his *Götterdämmerung*. The final war of an era that began with Hitler's invasion of the Soviet Union in 1941, and was followed by the Cold War, and a period when Russia lost its rightful place in the hierarchy of nations. Thus, he needed to rewrite the past to explain the present, a revisionism through new interpretations, social media, and hybrid warfare with the proverbial West, seeking to assert its worldview, as well as political and economic control deep into what was considered the Russian heartland, Ukraine. In his view, repeated as recently as October 2024, Kyiv was subjected to a coup in 2014, neo-Nazis took over the government, and Russia was obligated to push back these dark forces.

This volume has demonstrated the reasoning behind the new war and its deep flaws. It inevitably raises the question, what is to follow? Surely Eastern Europe cannot return to 1991, or Ukraine to its original borders? And what of Russia or *Rossiya* in its imperial form? Will it implode into separate parts and be confined to the Muscovy of the sixteenth century? Or descend into another 'Time of Troubles'? What will happen after Putin dies? His quarter century in office has defined the Russian Federation, a regime that seeks to regain its Great Power status through military conquest, convinced or hoping that the Western response will remain relatively mild. It is a government that lives in the past while distorting that past, using history for political ends rather than explanations of international conflicts. One could even say that it has destroyed history as a discipline and immersed the past in myths and lies in an endless stream of increasingly meaningless narratives.

October 2024

Index

www.ingramcontent.com/pod-product-compliance
Ingram Content Group UK Ltd.
Pitfield, Milton Keynes, MK11 3LW, UK
UKHW020845290926
15470UKWH00004B/1568

9 781509 975303